THE MANIPULATED CITY:

THE MANIPULATED CITY:

Perspectives
on Spatial Structure
and Social Issues
in Urban America

Edited by

Stephen Gale
University of Pennsylvania

Eric G. Moore
Queen's University

maaroufa press inc
Chicago

Maaroufa Press Geography Series
Eric Moore, Advisory Editor

Land and Leisure:
Concepts and Methods in Outdoor Recreation
David W. Fischer,
John E. Lewis,
and George B. Priddle

Human Behavior and the Environment:
Interactions between Man and His Physical World
John H. Sims
and Duane D. Baumann

Copyright © 1975 by Maaroufa Press, Inc.
All rights reserved
Library of Congress Catalog Card Number 74–25445
ISBN 0–88425–003–2
Manufactured in the United States of America

Designed by First Impression

This book is respectfully dedicated
to Professor Oliver Neptune, Director of the
Mackinder for Mayer Committee.

List of Contributors

Melvin Albaum
Harold M. Baron
Willard W. Brittain
Alan K. Campbell
Marion Clawson
David K. Cohen
Christopher S. Davies
Michael J. Dear
Robert J. Earickson
Donald L. Foley
Herbert J. Gans
Charles M. Haar
David Harvey
Edgar M. Hoover
Edward J. Kaiser
David L. Kirp

Arnold I. Kisch
Elinor Langer
Philip Meranto
John R. Meyer
Richard L. Morrill
National Advisory Commission
  on Civil Disorders
National Commission on
  Urban Problems
Wilfred Owen
Elliott Arthur Pavlos
Milton I. Roemer
Leonard S. Rubinowitz
Edward W. Soja
Gerald D. Suttles
Michael B. Tietz
Shirley F. Weiss
Oliver P. Williams
Eileen Wolpert
Julian Wolpert
Raymond E. Zelder

CONTENTS

Preface   xi

PART ONE **PERSPECTIVES ON THE NATURE OF URBAN SPACE**
Introduction to Part One   2

AN ECONOMIC PERSPECTIVE
1. The Evolving Form and Organization of the Metropolis   8
Edgar M. Hoover

A POLITICAL SCIENCE PERSPECTIVE
2. Technology, Location, and Access Strategies   17
Oliver P. Williams

A TERRITORIAL PERSPECTIVE
3. The Political Organization of Space in Metropolitan Areas   27
Edward W. Soja

A SOCIOLOGICAL PERSPECTIVE
4. Potentials in Community Differentiation   40
Gerald D. Suttles

A PLANNING PERSPECTIVE
5. An Approach to Metropolitan Spatial Structure   62
Donald L. Foley

A LEGAL PERSPECTIVE
6. The Social Control of Urban Space   86
Charles M. Haar

A SOCIAL CRITIC'S PERSPECTIVE
7. Social Justice and Spatial Systems   106
David Harvey

PART TWO **THE URBAN INFRASTRUCTURE**
Introduction to Part Two   122

HOUSING
Overview: Housing Needs and Problems
8. The Nature of Housing   132
David Harvey

9. Housing Needs   135
   National Commission on Urban Problems

10. Housing in the Central Cities   140
    National Advisory Commission on Civil
    Disorders

Analysis

11. Class-Monopoly Rent, Finance Capital and
    the Urban Revolution   145
    David Harvey

12. Institutional and Contextual Factors
    Affecting the Housing Choice of Minority
    Residents   168
    Donald L. Foley

13. Factors Affecting Suburbanization in the
    Postwar Years   182
    Marion Clawson

14. Public Policy and the Residential
    Development Process   189
    Edward J. Kaiser and Shirley F. Weiss

Strategy

15. The Failure of Urban Renewal: A Critique
    and Some Proposals   199
    Herbert J. Gans

16. Low-Income Housing: Suburban Strategies   213
    Leonard S. Rubinowitz

17. Poverty, Housing, and Market Processes   217
    Raymond E. Zelder

TRANSPORTATION
Overview

18. Urban Transportation   228
    John R. Meyer

19. The Metropolitan Transportation Problem   234
    Wilfred Owen

Analysis

20. Metro: Rapid Transit for Suburban
    Washington   237
    Willard W. Brittain

21. The Mobility Problems of the Poor in
    Indianapolis   242
    Christopher S. Davies and Melvin Albaum

22. Chicago's Crosstown: A Case Study in Urban Expressways 255
Elliott Arthur Pavlos

Strategy

23. Planning for Future Systems 262
Wilfred Owen

THE PROVISION OF PUBLIC SERVICES
Overview: The General Nature of Public Services

24. Residential Location and Public Facilities 271
David Harvey

25. Toward a Theory of Urban Facility Location 277
Michael B. Tietz

26. A Paradigm for Public Facility Location Theory 286
Michael J. Dear

Overview: Specific Problems in Health and Education

27. Health, Poverty, and the Medical Mainstream 292
Milton I. Roemer and Arnold I. Kisch

28. The Metropolitan Educational Dilemma: Matching Resources to Needs 305
Alan K. Campbell and Philip Meranto

Analysis

29. Locational Efficiency of Chicago Hospitals: An Experimental Model 319
Richard L. Morrill and Robert J. Earickson

30. From Asylum to Ghetto 329
Eileen Wolpert and Julian Wolpert

31. Race and Status in School Spending: Chicago, 1961–66 339
Harold M. Baron

Strategy

32. Medicine for the Poor: A New Deal in Denver 348
Elinor Langer

33. Education and Metropolitanism 356
David L. Kirp and David K. Cohen

PREFACE

This collection of essays is concerned with the influence of social, economic, legal, and political institutions on the nature of urban problems. It seeks to provide a broad-based perspective on the spatial organization of the modern metropolis from which many pragmatic issues in urban planning and policy formation can be examined. The outlook is purposely multi-disciplinary for problems rarely show respect for traditional disciplinary boundaries and their evaluation is as much an exercise in synthesis as in analysis.

Many contemporary urban issues possess a strong spatial character. In some instances, we are struck by the concentration of phenomena such as high crime rates or abandoned housing in certain well-defined neighborhoods; in others, concern is for difficulties experienced by residents in gaining access to vital services such as health facilities or educational programs. Again, most of us recognize that public decisions involving the location of freeways or the creation of industrial parks are discriminatory in the sense that a small number of communities have to bear the burdens of displacement or of increased pollution. Yet, although it is easy to acknowledge the presence of such problems, it is not so easy to comprehend the processes which generate them or to define strategies which will lead to their solution. We need a frame of reference which allows us to see problems in the broader context of the spatial organization of the city and to relate them to the principles which underlie that organization.

In the attempt to build such a frame of reference, two propositions guide the development of our argument. The first is that the way we solve problems is not necessarily the same as the way we develop theories. Theory construction, particularly in the social sciences, has been a highly discipline-oriented activity which seeks to identify the nature, inter-relationships, and logical consequences of a well-defined set of principles governing the behavior of selected phenomena. In the present context, theories are seen to focus on limited aspects of urban structure and, by assumption, manipulation, or experimental design, they seek to control or eliminate the influence of other events or processes on the behavior in question. Thus we have economic theories of the location of residential activity

which ignore the effects of social stratification or political fragmentation, theories of social organization which disregard the distributive
role of market processes, and theories of political control which are
equally narrowly-defined. Problem-solving cannot generally afford
such eclecticism. Problems are multi-faceted and attempts to understand their nature and to define strategies for their solution require
the bringing together of knowledge from different disciplines and
different theoretical structures. However, when we attempt this task,
we find many holes in our knowledge and there is no "super-theory"
to guide our efforts at synthesis. Judgment is at a premium. Much
of the apparent intractability of urban problems and the ineffectiveness of public action stem from attempts to exercise judgment within
a framework which does not suit the complexity of the underlying
structure.

The second proposition is that we need to understand the spatial
character of problems in terms of a broad institutional framework,
for, except in geometry, there is no such thing as "pure spatial structure." Both the distribution of activities within the urban area and
the interaction between such activities depend on the organizational
principles of a complex set of institutions. In this case, institutions
are interpreted in the broadest sense to mean those organized aggregates which are tangible expressions of the complex normative patterns underlying behavior in society. Thus the family, the firm, the
school, and local government and its agencies are all institutions
whose organizational principles have direct impacts on spatial structure. We simply cannot treat spatial problems without recognizing
these institutional and organizational underpinnings, for to do so
results in decisions which are often not only ineffective but also
socially disruptive. Perhaps the best example is provided by those
efforts at desegregation which lead to mindless mixing rather than
an attempt to get at the nature of the inequities which lie at the heart
of desegregation issues.

Spatial organization is seen, therefore, to arise out of the behavior
of institutions within the urban environment. Most contemporary
views of urban spatial structure emphasize the competitive role of
the market in distributing activities in urban space. Social theory is
introduced by considering the preferences and economic abilities of
different social groups in choosing residential locations in different
parts of the city. However, the disturbing impression generated by
much of this discussion is of a city whose growth and development
depend on macro-level forces which are beyond our control. Political, legal, and administrative structures which serve to modify, con-

strain, and direct paths of development are ignored, yet these institutions are relevant to much of the activity of planners and policy makers. Thus, although the city is manipulated in countless ways by decisions in both public and private sectors, all too often knowledge regarding processes which impinge on these decisions is structured in such a way that we are unable to evaluate their consequences for the city as a whole. Improvement of this situation will be a slow process. It will involve bringing together knowledge from different disciplines in a way which allows us to understand both the strength of the influences exerted by public and private decisions and the broad range of consequences of alternative actions.

The organization of these readings follows directly from the position we have adopted regarding the nature of problem-solving in an urban environment. In Part One, we present a series of essays reflecting the wide range of viewpoints on the nature of spatial organization of the city. Beginning with the traditional economic arguments concerning location of activities within the urban area, perspectives reflecting theories of political jurisdiction, territorial behavior, and social interaction in the city are successively introduced. We then move to more pragmatic questions concerning the administrative and legal structures available to planners and policy makers. Part One concludes with a discussion of the nature of distributive justice in urban systems, a topic which, we believe, should provide an important foundation for theories of public action. In Part Two, we consider the intersection of these various perspectives in analyzing specific problems relating to the provision of housing, transportation, and public services. We believe that this approach gives the student some idea not only of the nature of these problems but also of the intellectual processes which surround attempts at their solution.

Eric G. Moore
Queen's University

Stephen Gale
University of Pennsylvania

December 1974

PART ONE **Perspectives On the Nature Of Urban Space**

Introduction
to Part One

The first Part of this book provides the foundation for our argument. Its intent is to demonstrate that, from a variety of disciplinary viewpoints, space is an integral part of the way in which we describe and analyze the functioning of urban systems. Urban space cannot be treated in the abstract, however; it is a way of describing attributes of people and organizations as well as the physical characteristics of the city and of giving them a specific referent in a set of relationships. The location of a hospital, for example, provides a basis for relating hospital services to its clients and discussing the impact of its presence on its neighbors. A new subway network modifies the patterns of residence and workplace interactions within the city, while the assignment of a dwelling to a school district has implications for the children of the household, the demands on the education system, and the character of neighborhoods. More importantly, as we change these locations, networks, and assignments, we alter both the present conditions and the future possibilities for the system. Space does indeed make a difference, and in so many complex ways that a single disciplinary perspective reveals only a small part of the overall picture.

The city is a social system and, as such, we find many dissimilarities between problems of analyzing its properties as compared with those of physical systems. Social systems neither respond to the tunes of universal laws nor can they be described by an infallible set of general principles. Social organizations, methods of communication, and legal and administrative structures are all creations of man designed for particular purposes and subject to constant revision and modification. The spatial patterns and relationships which develop within an urban area are not to be explained in terms of geometry or macro-level physical concepts, but as manifestations of social, economic, and political institutions within a given physical environment. Institutions are, in effect, the external forms of organization which men use to regulate and plan their activities; they are kinds of instrumental boundaries which may have the force of natural laws in the short term, but which are subject to reconceptualization and change to meet new conditions and new contexts.

A great deal of contemporary analytical writing on the city does not reflect this perspective. Strong emphasis has been placed on the development of formal models and on the deductive approach to theory construction within narrow disciplinary perspectives. Whereas institutions once formed an important part of societal research, today they are often pre-sented as background material to account for the failure of more formal approaches to satisfactorily represent the real world. However, they are too important to be assigned such a marginal role and it is our purpose to reintroduce an institutional perspective to the study of urban spatial structure and its associated problems. At the same time we do not wish to dissociate ourselves from the positive aspects of other approaches but rather to integrate them within a broader framework.

Our strategy is to begin with the most familiar arguments concerning the nature of urban structure and to successively widen our perspective by considering institutional influences which modify and expand the basic position. The dominant paradigm for much current social science research concerning spatial problems in urban areas finds its source in economic theory. As Hoover's paper in this Part shows, the fundamental properties of this paradigm stem from the concept of the market and, although the role of other institutions is recognized, this is more as a limitation on the action of the market (i.e., as a source of "market failure") than as an integral part of the analysis. Not surprisingly, both the explanations of past actions and the proposed bases for future actions are economic; loca-tional issues are viewed in terms of distance measures, and differentiation into sub-areas is seen as the result of economic forces acting at a distance rather than as rational decisions of men needing to apportion legal and administrative control within a larger system. While this perspective gen-erates fruitful insights into certain general aspects of urban structure such as the distribution of broad categories of land use, its cutting edge is very limited when faced with the wide range of contemporary urban problems.

How do we begin to address the limitations of this type of analysis? At the heart of a great deal of contemporary criticism is an awareness that urban space does not possess the qualities of homogeneity and continuity contained in the assumptions of much economic theory. Social and politi-cal organizations impose many barriers and generate discontinuities which have important consequences for the behavior of both individuals and groups. From a political perspective, Williams in his essay sees space as being divided into territories as a result of technological requirements, the locational diversity and specificity of the population and limitations on access. Moreover, such territories are not arbitrary designations but have a reality as individuated units possessing legal, administrative, social and cultural meaning. While he does not deny that people respond to relative location and to the costs of accessibility, the nature of this re-sponse is conditioned by man's territorial behavior, by his being part of the social and legal system of one area rather than another.

Williams places his greatest emphasis on the jurisdictional aspects of territoriality. However, from a behavioral viewpoint, territoriality and local-ization can be regarded as primitive concepts in the attempt to explain what is meant by the term "spatial organization." Although we do not include the whole of Soja's essay on the evolution of territorial behavior in animals and man, the main point of his argument is clear: social identity does not come in terms of associations with abstract theories or ideologies but rather through the exercise of accepted modes of behavior within a territorial framework. Conflicts over access to public services or to other benefits of society and over the rights of individuals and groups are not simply born of the economic factors of distribution; they arise from the way in which such factors are used and administered in localized areas and the beliefs men hold about the nature of territoriality. As Soja points out, perhaps the most obvious example of this view of spatial organization is the fragmentation of urban space. Density, diversity of interests, and the historical pattern of development of the urban population combine to produce an overlapping mosaic of variously defined political districts and legal and administrative entities. Each territory not only contributes to the structural organization of urban space, but to the fragmentation of that same organization. The rules of behavior and the criteria for decision making are thus not merely functions of individual predilections within the market; they are attempts to reconcile individual and group needs with the needs of a more generally codified set of localized, territorial interests.

The perspectives provided by Williams and Soja emphasize the effects of technology and of market, political and legal institutions on the differentiation of urban space. Suttles in his essay argues, however, that these forces neither act in isolation nor are they independent of the kinds of social groups who use and are affected by them. Legal and administrative boundaries may organize space into separate jurisdictions, but their full effect is only realized through their influence on patterns of social interaction and behavior. In working class districts, for example, boundaries are often well-defined and reinforced; in even poorer areas, on the other hand, the same types of boundaries often go unrecognized and undefined. Equally important in Suttles' view are the effects of the historical conditions which provided the substance of the current residential and commercial land-use patterns and the associated perceptual biases. The zoning practices of previous eras are still very strongly felt. Ethnic markets and churches, established by in-migrants decades ago, often remain as the foci of the contemporary activities of the group and even the building structures are holdovers from the past. Suttles' argument thus bridges an important conceptual gap. Institutions provide the framework for social activity in the city, but it is the way in which groups of individuals respond to those forces, past and present, which shapes the pattern of contemporary urban space.

To this point we have only considered one aspect of the relation between institutions and urban spatial structure. It tells us why we should consider urban space in broad social and institutional terms and, to some extent, how this can be done (at least in terms of political, social, and administrative units). Yet, something is still missing. Institutions are not simply conveniences of the mind to be used as a basis for comprehending the world. They are also instrumental measures to be used in designing prescriptions for change. We utilize institutions not only in explaining past and present behavior, but as standards or rules for guiding future decisions. It is in this role that the institutional perspective finds its real strength. For even if we could be assured of the singular efficacy of market-based analyses of past behavior, there would be no guarantee that the market would (or should) continue to be the most reasonable mechanism for planning future activities. The very idea of planning, in fact, stands as a counter to mere extension of the past since it presumes to ask "What ought to be?" rather than "What will be?." Furthermore, if the future is to be guided or constrained then we must understand those elements which can be manipulated and the consequences of their manipulation.

Planners have traditionally dealt with the physical structure of the city. Their primary actions have been directed toward manipulation of the physical environment, yet it is clear that they also must be responsive to the social and political organization of the community and the set of values which are embedded in that organization. Foley in his essay argues that in order to accomplish this task effectively, a bridge must be built between the concern for the idea of spatial arrangement which is central to urban planning and the essentially aspatial approach to community organization adopted by many social scientists. The bulk of his essay is concerned with building this link between the normative, functional, organizational and physical environment components of the urban system. However, the overriding issue is seen to be that of finding a political organization which can ensure that social and economic goals are classified and implemented within an accepted decision-making framework. Though a variety of governmental forms can be defined with appropriate functions allocated to each, it is clear that we need both local units which encourage political participation and citizen identification as well as a well-equipped metropolitan government capable of handling larger scale issues.

Given a political framework for local action, more specific institutional forms are available to regulate and guide our decisions. The legal system is a crucial element and forms one of the strongest links in the argument for an institutional perspective on urban space. Even in a capitalistic economy such as the United States, we recognize the legal system as the ultimate protector of and justification for our values. When the economic system is unfair, we use the legal system to bypass or amend it; when values are unrepresented, we enact laws to give them formal standing; when common understanding is too loose to hold any weight in disputes, the legal system is brought to bear. In this sense, it is the ultimate means of resolving social questions and disputes. This is, of course, particularly important in urban areas where conflicts often arise for complicated and obscure reasons. Haar's paper on the laws controlling the use of land is thus crucial to an understanding of urban space; and, more to the point, it provides enough of the details so that the ever-present complexities of problems and standards for decision making are not smoothed over.

The final step in our argument represents a return to broader issues. Harvey's essay, though bound up in a special ideological (Marxist) cloak, nevertheless provides some very clear reasons for going beyond simple economic calculations in the analysis of locational problems. The theoretical justifications for the existing institutions are themselves insufficient. What is needed are standards for evaluating the *ways* in which a society distributes the "goodies" and *to whom* they are distributed. Justice is to serve as the criterion: justice as "a just distribution justly arrived at." Of course, the definition of exactly what are to count as just and unjust conditions and means is one of those problems which philosophers and their social critic brethren have been mulling over for millennia. Harvey's answer, though in no sense definitive, at least provides a point of departure: as he sees it, social justice is a weak ordering of (from most to least important) need, contribution to the common good, and merit. The end product is obviously a function of the definition and the ordering and, in Harvey's case, it amounts to a critique of capitalist means of production and distribution. However, the crucial point of the analysis does not rest on the merits of the end product. It is the admission that a very broad range of questions relating to efficiency, ethics and justice contribute to the process of building an understanding of the nature of spatial systems and the way we can change these systems to meet our needs.

In Part One we thus move from the simplified world of economic understanding and decision making to the complex reality of an institutional perspective on urban space and from there to the criteria for justice in territorially-based systems. Although our argument is far from complete and many insights must be gained by extension and inference from the material presented, the overall thrust should be clear: urban problems are far too complex to be explained or adjudicated within a single disciplinary context. Territoriality, local norms and values, the interdependence of functions and a wide range of locationally specific decisions; these are the characteristics of urban problems. The understanding of present conditions surely requires that we adopt this point of view. More importantly, so does the attempt to design future societies. Planning, even of the simplest activities, can hardly be divorced from need to understand the ways we can design and use various kinds of institutions to guide and rationalize our alternative futures.

AN ECONOMIC PERSPECTIVE

THE EVOLVING FORM AND ORGANIZATION OF THE METROPOLIS

EDGAR M. HOOVER

Hoover's essay summarizes what might be called the "economic perspective" on the spatial organization of urban society. The forces at work are familiar: access, environmental characteristics, and cost. Space is pictured as an imperfection in an ideal of a pure economic system, but yet as a crucial aspect of a realistic picture in that it is the source of market failures and selective advantages and disadvantages. The effectiveness of the society is, in turn, seen to be measured by the efficiency of these economic relations and interdependencies.

Reprinted from Harvey Perloff and Lowdon Wingo, Jr., eds., *Issues in Urban Economics* (Baltimore: Johns Hopkins University Press for Resources for the Future, Inc., 1968), pp. 237–65, by permission of the publisher and the author. This is an edited version of the original publication.

It is a truism that socioeconomic organizations involve primarily mutual interrelations among decision units rather than the conveniently simple one-way impacts and sequential effects that we like to use whenever possible in building explanatory theories. And spatial organization in the urban setting presents this aspect of mutual interdependence of everything on everything to an especially notable degree, precisely because the very raison d'être of a city is that it puts enormous numbers of diverse households, business firms, and other decision units cheek by jowl so that they may interact in fruitful and efficient ways.

So when we try to construct a conceptual model of how various residential and non-residential activities are spatially distributed in an urban area, we find a vast web of interdependence. Shopping centers locate primarily on the basis of access to consumers; people like to live close to their work, schools, shopping areas, and other types of facilities that they have occasion to use. Business firms of various types are attracted by access to labor supply, other related firms, or transportation facilities. In many kinds of urban activities, like seeks like. There are strong pressures for neighborhood homogeneity as such, as illustrated by the exclusive suburb, the garment district, and the automobile row. Every user of space has also to consider its price, and that will depend on how desirable the site is to other users.

Picturing all this even in greatly simplified terms as an equilibrium or dynamic system, the model builder or other theoretician trying to encompass the whole is likely to find himself hopelessly engulfed in myriad simultaneous equations in futile search of a useful solution or any solution. He has long since abandoned any attempt to elucidate by diagrams, since every important relationship seems to have many more than the graphically manageable two or three dimensions.

The situation is perhaps not quite as hopeless as this may imply. In tracing what determines what and how, there are a few welcome entries to and exits from the otherwise endless pretzel of causation. In the first place, some of the locations in an urban area can be regarded as determined exogenously and not just in response to the rest of the local pattern. Perhaps the most obvious example is a port and waterfront area, which is primarily determined by natural locational advantages. In the second place, it is clear that the actual spatial structure does not represent or even closely resemble a static equilibrium of the locating forces. Rather, it represents a snapshot of current states of mutual adjustment. Impacts of one change upon another, and spatial adjustments, take time, because long-lived physical facilities, habits, social and business ties, and political commitments are entailed. Consequently, at any given juncture a great many of the locations and locational shifts can pragmatically be viewed in terms of one-way, rather than reciprocal, impact. Actual decisions, even some planning decisions over substantial periods of time, can therefore take most of the current setting as given, and ignore a large part of the conceivable ultimate "feedback" effect.

It remains true that heroic and ingenious simplification of reality is necessary for any comprehensible image of the spatial structure. Throughout this paper, therefore, runs the question of how we can boil down facts and concepts and still have something nutritious left at the bottom of the kettle.

The first step in building a useful conceptual framework for understanding urban spatial patterns is to sort out the multifarious location factors that influence the preferences and placement of specific activities or types of decision units. What is suggested below is a logical way of reducing these factors to a manageably small number of groups.

"Given" Locations

As already intimated, there are some kinds of locations within an urban area which are not determined primarily by where the other activities of the area are. Actually there are two distinct bases for exogenous determination of locations in an urban area.

For some kinds of activities, certain topographical or other natural site features are essential, which means that the lay of the land narrows down the choice to one or a very small number of locations. Ports for water traffic illustrate this, and there are some urban areas where the topography limits jet airport sites almost as drastically. In the past, defense considerations played a major part in locating the center of the city and the city itself. Localized recreational features such as beaches also illustrate this kind of factor, and in a few urban areas extractive industries (mainly mining) occur and are, of course, limited to certain special sites.

There is a further type of exogenously-determined location where the independent influence arises not from site features so much as from the fact that the activity in question is primarily concerned with contact with the outside world. Not just water ports but all kinds of terminal and interarea transport activities come under this head. Since there are great economies of scale in interregional transport and in terminal handling of goods, the urban area's gateways to and from the outside world constitute a set of focal points whose locations within the area help to determine—rather than just being determined by—the other activities of the area. This does not, of course, mean that such terminal locations (unless constrained by natural site features) are absolutely and permanently unresponsive to the changing pattern of other activities in the area served: such terminals are from tme to time shifted to improve local accessibility or to make way for more insistent claimants for space. But the terminal locations do, in dynamic terms, play a primarily active role in shaping the pattern, and are to be viewed as part of the basic framework around which other activities are fitted.

Finally, in practice, we can generally take as given the focus of *maximum overall accessibility* within the urban area. If we think of that as, for example, the place at which all the people of the area could assemble with the least total man-miles of travel, it is simply the median center of population, depending upon where all of the various types of residence are located. But travel is cheaper and faster along developed routes, and the cost and layout of these are affected by scale (traffic volume) and topography. So, evaluated in terms of travel cost and time, the focal maximum-access point can be regarded as a quite stable datum, even though the extent and importance of its access advantage over other points can change radically. We find in major American urban areas that, despite great over-all growth and far-reaching change and redistribution of activities, the focal point in this sense has usually shifted only a relatively short distance over periods measured in decades and generations, and that the earlier central foci are well within what we currently recognize as the central business district.

The concept of a single, most central focal point in an urban area is then significant and useful in developing simplified bases for understanding the over-all pattern. Obviously it has limitations, some of which will be discussed later in this paper. In the first place, there is in principle a variety of distinguishable central points of this sort, depending on what kinds of people or things we are imagining to be assembled with a minimum of total expense or effort. The employed workers of the area are not distributed in quite the same pattern as the total population, the shopping population, the school-attending population,

the office workers, the industrial blue-collar workers, the theater-going or the library-using population; there might be a different optimum location from the standpoint of access for each of these types of people. Where goods rather than people are moving (as for example in the case of wholesale activity or production serving local needs such as daily newspapers or bread) the transport conditions are different and this may again mean a different optimum-access point. Finally, we have to recognize that, in varying degrees, the concept of one single point serving as the origin or destination for all flows of a specified type may be unrealistic and defensible only as a convenient fiction. Thus, if we identify some central point as having best access to the homes of the entire clerical office force of an urban area, this does not imply that all offices should logically be concentrated there. What it does imply is that, solely from the standpoint of commuting access for the clerical workers and ignoring claims of alternative space uses, it would make sense for the density of clerical employment to peak at that point. The significance of the focal point is determined, then, by the extent to which the activity involved is dependent upon (1) concentration in a single small district, and (2) access to the flow in question.

Access Linkages
Since the function of an urban concentration is to facilitate contacts, the most important class of location factors shaping in the spatial pattern involves the advantage of physical proximity as measured by money and/or time saved. This applies to cases in which such costs are substantially increased by added distance. Where they are not, they have nothing to do with urban concentration. For example, information in a widening sense (now including not only the printed word but sounds and computer signals and various types of pictures) can

now be transmitted electronically over long distances just as quickly as over short distances, and sometimes just as cheaply to the user. This kind of contact, then, does not in itself depend upon, nor help to maintain or explain, intra-urban concentration.

Most relevant to the urban pattern are kinds of access for which costs are high and increase very rapidly with distance within the intra-urban range of distances (ranging from next door to a few dozen miles). Access involving human travel belongs par excellence to this category. Human beings require more elaborate and expensive vehicles (in dollars per ton of freight) than almost anything else. And, in particular, the time cost becomes generally even more important than the actual transport cost.

For people and things alike, the time cost to the passenger or the owner of the cargo is essentially an "opportunity cost," measured in terms of what useful services the person or thing being transported might otherwise be yielding. For commodities, we can measure this crudely in terms of interest on the investment represented by the value of the goods tied up in transit. For human beings, a commonly used yardstick is the rate of earnings while at work.[1] Thus, a man who earns $5.00 an hour would consider the time cost of a half-hour trip to be $2.50. This rate of time cost equals the accrual of interest (at 5 percent per annum) on an investment of about $880,000. So, calculated on that basis, human freight carries a time cost equivalent to that of a commodity worth at least $300 an ounce—perhaps not "more precious than rubies," but somewhere in the range between gold and diamonds. The locational importance of an access linkage—i.e., the economic advantage of proximity—depends not only on how much the trip costs but also on how often the trip is made. Access to one's regular work place is likely to be a weighty consideration because it gener-

ally involves at least five round trips a week. It becomes somewhat less important if one shifts from a six day to a five day or shorter working week.

In the case of shopping trips, the costs of the trip should be related to the amount of the purchase in order to get a measure of the proximity advantage. Thus, if ten minutes' additional travel in each direction (twenty minutes round trip) is valued at, say, $1.50, it would be worthwhile making the extra travel in order to save $1.50. That is 15 percent on the purchase of $10 worth of groceries, but only 1½ percent on the purchase of a $100 television set. We could infer that it is logical to travel ten times as far to shop for television sets as to shop for groceries, if the amounts of purchases stated are representative and if the price differentials among shopping places are about the same for both types of goods. Here again, only time costs are considered; but this illustration illustrates the wide variations in the strength of the proximity incentive, even within the limits of one category of relationship, like retail trade.

The various kinds of access linkage that tie together the urban complex can be meaningfully classified in a good many ways: for example, by mode of transport or communication. or according to whether the incentive toward proximity is thought to influence predominantly the location of the sender or that of the receiver of whatever is being transported. Perhaps as useful a classification as any other can be based on the distinction between households and other decision units—i.e., between residential and non-residential activities.

Access among Non-residential Activities

This involves in part interindustry transactions such as those recorded in an input-output table. Business firms have an incentive to locate with good access to their local suppliers and their local business customers. To that extent, an interindustry transactions table gives us an idea of the relative volume and importance of the flows of goods and services between establishments [2] of the same and different industries, though this does not go very far toward measuring the relative strengths of locational attraction. Nor do these input-output figures take account of some strong business proximity ties that do not directly involve transactions at all. Thus, local branch offices or outlets of a firm are presumably located with an eye to maintaining good access to the main local office, while at the same time avoiding overlap of the sublocal territories served by the branches (for example, the individual supermarkets of a chain or branch offices of a bank). There are strong access ties between the central office of a corporation and its main research laboratory, involving the frequent going and coming of highly paid personnel, but no entries in the input-output tables.[3]

Access among Residential Activities (Interhousehold)

A significant proportion of journeys from homes are to the homes of others. Such trips are by nature almost exclusively social and thus involve people linked by family ties or closely similar tastes and interests. This suggests that the value of "interhousehold access" can also be expressed fairly accurately in terms of homogeneity preference—like seeks like. As we shall see later, however, the pressures toward neighborhood or "microspatial" homogeneity include a good many other factors in addition to simple access.

Access between Residential and Non-residential Activities

This type of access is far and away the most conspicuous in the urban flow pattern. The entire labor force, with insignificant exceptions, is concerned with making the daily journey to work as quick and painless as possible. Such trips are much the largest single class of personal journeys within any urban area.[4] In addition, the distribution of goods and services at retail makes mutual proximity an advantage for both the distributors and the customers; some attention has already been paid here to the factors determining the relative strength of the attraction in the case of different types of goods and services. Trips to school, and for cultural and recreational purposes, make up most of the rest of the personal trip pattern. There is mutual advantage of proximity throughout: the non-residential activities dealing with households are most advantageously placed when they are close to concentrations of population, and at the same time residential sites are preferred (other things being equal) when they are in convenient access to jobs, shopping districts, schools, and other destinations.

The way in which these mutual attractions shape the locational pattern of activities within the urban area depends not so much on the strength of the attraction as on the degree to which the non-residential activity in question is concentrated at relatively few points (since almost any such activity is much less evenly diffused over the area than residence is). At one extreme, there are non-residential activities that need access to a large fraction of the households of the urban area, but that are confined to one location, and perhaps one establishment or facility. Thus, a visit to a large department store or some kind of specialty shop, or to a main library, or to the opera, or to attend university classes may mean, in many urban areas, a visit to one specific location, without alternatives. All such trips within the area have a single common destination focus and the attraction, from the household side, is centripetal, or at least monocentric. From the standpoint of the non-residential activity in question, optimum access means the choice of a point of minimum total travel time for all of the interested households in the area.

At the opposite extreme are activities not subject to any compelling scale economies or other economics of concentration, which can therefore have a dispersed or many-centered pattern. Drugstores, barbershops, branch banking offices, and the like are basically neighborhood-serving rather than catering to a broad citywide clientele. A good location is simply one in which there is a sufficient amount of business within a short distance. And the attraction of such activities to the householder is within rather than between neighborhoods, being measured in blocks rather than in miles. The gradient of access advantage is a local one, replicated many times over in all parts of the area, rather than a single one peaking at some one point.

Agglomerative Factors

Access considerations involve a mutual attraction between complementary parties: stores and customers, employees and firms, pupils and schools. But there are also economic incentives favoring the concentration and clustering of identical or similar units of activity. The simplest case of this is perhaps that of scale economies. A large electric power plant is more efficient than a smaller one. A large store can, in addition to possible cost savings, provide more variety and thus enhance its attractiveness to buyers. As already suggested, some kinds of activities (such as opera performances) are subject to scale economies to the extent that only in the largest cities can more than one establishment be supported. Business corporations as a rule find that they can best concentrate their research laboratories at one location, and the same applies somewhat more obviously to their central offices.

A different and more subtle case involves the basis for clustering of many similar business firms or institutions. The classic case is the mid-Manhattan garment center, but analogous complexes are found in every city, such as "automobile rows," the financial district, and various types of specialized wholesale districts.[5]

If we inquire more deeply into the reasons for these clusterings we find that the establishments in the cluster are sharing some common advantage that is generally a pool of especially suitable labor, a variety of specialized business services, or the congregation of customers seeking to compare a variety of offerings. Sometimes two or all three of these kinds of external economy are involved. If the individual small firms in the cluster have good enough access to these external advantages, they themselves can specialize narrowly in functions not requiring large-scale operation, while at the same time having passed on to them the economies of a large labor market, a large concentration of buyers, and specialized business services produced on an efficiently large scale.

It appears, then, that these external economies of certain clustered activities are really based on two factors previously discussed: access, and economies of scale. What is new is the extension of the concept of scale economies to labor markets and shopping comparison markets as operating mechanisms.

Finally, the clustering of like activities can reflect immediate environmental interdependence. A site has value according to its access but also according to its physical features and to the character of its immediate surroundings. Neighborhood character in terms of cleanliness, smells, noise, traffic congestion, public safety, variety interest, and general appearance is important in attracting some kinds of use and repelling others. Prestige types of residence or business are of course particularly sensitive to this kind of advantage, which often is more important than any access consideration as such. A high-income householder may be willing to lengthen his work journey greatly for the sake of agreeable surroundings.

As has been suggested earlier, the usual effect of this type of consideration is to make neighborhoods more homogeneous within themselves, and more unlike other neighborhoods—a tendency toward areal specialization by uses, or segregation in the broad sense. With few exceptions, a given type of activity finds advantage in being in a neighborhood devoted to reasonably similar kinds of uses, and disadvantage in being in violent contrast to the neighborhood pattern. Zoning controls and planned street layouts play a part in reinforcing this tendency.

Competition for Space: the Cost of Sites

I have cataloged above the various kinds of locational pulls and pushes that affect activities in an urban area. Most of the relationships mentioned are pulls—they involve a mutual locational attraction among complementary or similar units of activity. This reflects the underlying rationale of a city as a device effecting close contact and interaction on a grand scale.

But every land use needs some space or elbow room on which to operate, and the sites with best access or environmental features command a high scarcity value. The market mechanism works (albeit imperfectly like most markets) to allocate locations to uses and users who can exploit them to best advantage as measured by what they are willing to bid for their use.

Simplification and Synthesis

The various determinants of location in an urban area have been discussed above. In a really complex analysis, each could be broken down much further. But we seek simplification. It appears that basically there are just three kinds of considerations that determine the relative desirability of locations for particular decision units such as households or business establishments. These are (1) access, (2) environmental characteristics, and (3) cost. They reflect the fact that the user of a site is really involved with it in three different ways. He occupies it, as resident or producer, and is thus concerned with its site and neighborhood, or immediate environmental qualities. He and other persons and goods and services move between this site and others; he is therefore concerned with its convenience of access to other places. Finally, he has to pay for its use and is therefore concerned with its cost.

Ruthless simplification along these lines makes possible the useful step of building a conceptual model of the spatial structure of an urban economy. For example, in such a model we can reduce the complex factor of access to the simple form of access to a single given focal point, as if all intra-urban journeys were to or from downtown and all shipments of goods also passed through downtown. We can in the interests of maximum simplicity even assume that the cost of transportation within the urban area is directly proportional to airline distance. Access is then measured simply in radial distance from the center.

We can assume away all differentiation of sites with respect to topography, amenity, and environmental advantage. These two simplifications also imply ignoring the manifold types of external-economy effects and environmental attractions and repulsions that have been discussed. In effect, we envisage each type of activity as *independently* attracted (by access considerations) toward the urban center; the only interdependence among the locations of the various activities arises, then, from the fact that they are bidding against one another for space.

It is also appropriate to develop a

condensed classification of activities. No two households, factories, or other decision units are exactly alike in their location preferences, but they can be grouped into more or less homogeneous classes on the basis of similarity in access/space trade-off. Among households, for example, it appears from empirical studies that income level and family structure (presence or absence of young children) are the principal determinants of this trade-off.

With the above types of simplification as well as with others, it is possible to develop more or less systematic theories or frameworks of analysis for urban spatial patterns. It is sufficient here to note that most such models are partial in the sense that they attempt to explain or predict the location of one type of activity in terms of its adjustment to given or assumed locations of the other activities, including transportation services. Thus, a retailing location model may analyze the way in which retail stores locate in response to the advantages of access to the homes of consumers, a residential location model may analyze the way in which residences locate in response to the desire to shorten the journey to work, and so on.

NOTES

1. This way of evaluating time cost is used for lack of anything better. We need more information on what value people of various sorts place upon time spent in transit under various circumstances.

2. Although interindustry transaction (input-output) tables are organized in cross-tabulations of *industries*, the basic unit is the industrial plant or other *establishment*, and interestablishment transactions within the same industry are shown in the diagonal cells of the table.

3. It would be useful, I think, to try to construct tables showing the transport and communication charges incurred in the transaction flows between each pair of industries. This could lead to a still more useful cross-tabulation in which such charges were expressed as coefficients on a per-mile, per-unit-of-output basis. These coefficients would roughly measure the strength of spatial attraction between pairs of industries attributable to transport and communication costs. On this point, as on many others in the present paper, I am indebted to my colleague Professor David Houston for stimulating comments and discussion.

4. For relevant reference material, see J. R. Meyer, J. F. Kain, and M. Wohl, *The Urban Transportation Problem* (Cambridge: Harvard University Press, 1965), and L. K. Loewenstein, *The Location of Residences and Work Places in Urban Areas* (Metuchen, N.J.: Scarecrow Press, Inc., 1965). Also, a primarily bibliographical survey of the whole question of access, see G. Olsson, *Distance and Human Interaction: A Review and Bibliography*, Bibliography Series, No. 2 (Philadelphia: Regional Science Research Institute, 1965).

5. Cf. R. M. Lichtenberg, *One-Tenth of a Nation*, New York Metropolitan Regional Study (Cambridge: Harvard University Press, 1960) for a penetrating analysis of the "external-economy" industries in New York.

A POLITICAL SCIENCE PERSPECTIVE

TECHNOLOGY, LOCATION, AND ACCESS STRATEGIES
OLIVER P. WILLIAMS

Williams' short but forceful description of the relationships among technology, location, and social access in urban areas provides a picture of the other side of Hoover's economic perspective. Where the economist views space in terms of distance, as something to be overcome, in this essay we begin to see that there are different effects from nominalized, bounded territories such as neighborhoods, shopping complexes, industrial areas, and zoning districts. It is with this view of space that we move from an analytical to an institutional framework: or as Williams puts it, where "the access of one becomes blocked by the actions of another . . . politics begins."

Reprinted from Oliver P. Williams, *Metropolitan Political Analysis* (New York: The Free Press, 1971), pp. 23–35, by permission of the publisher and the author. Copyright © 1971 by The Free Press, a Division of Macmillan Publishing Company, Inc. This is an edited version of the original publication.

INTRODUCTION

If wealth, status, and power can be considered instrumental resources used in realizing certain other values in life, then location can be conceived the same way. While wealth, status, power, and location are, to a certain degree, interchangeable resources, they are not all equally appropriate for achieving specified ends. All tend to be a general coinage of exchange, but of the four, location is the least liquid and the most specific as to its utility. An understanding of the use of locations in urban life is a first step toward perceiving how the social structures distribute access through control of space. This essay will give a nontechnical portrait of location as a means to access, of how location is affected by technology, and finally how location is allocated by social structures through the employment of resources.

Urbanism is conceived in terms of locational strategies and orientations. Initially, let us proceed, through illustration, to examine how these orientations are linked to access requirements. Economic institutions offer the easiest examples, because the goals of such organizations are readily understandable. To say that all firms seek to maximize profits is, in fact, a gross oversimplification, and it flies in the face of much evidence; yet, this notion provides a convenient fiction, which is analytically useful. Let us, therefore, assume that firms seek to improve their access to social groupings or organizations when such access promises to increase profit; that is, they seek access to more or better paying customers, superior supplies, and more satisfactory labor sources. Place or location serves as a means of access to these goals in several ways. As the industrial recruiters and locational analysts are well aware, enterprises evaluate each location in terms of the kind of access it provides. Some industries want access to cheap labor; others, to skilled. The first requires a location on public transportation routes which connect with low-rental areas. The latter requires a location convenient to an automotive network; hence, probably near a freeway linked to suburban residences. Some industries are dependent on external economies; others are not. If the former is the case, the plant may be drawn to the older core, high-density center, which has a complex mix of available short-term rental space, a variety of supplies obtainable on short notice and in small lots, and the requisite combination of skills and services conveniently nearby. The plant which is relatively independent of external economies will seek the cheaper, less congested space on the edges of, or even away from, metropolitan areas.

It would be possible to spin out a long list of considerations relevant to the access requirements of given firms. This is the particular province of those who counsel firms on facility location. The focus here, however, is on general categories of action.

TECHNOLOGY AND ACCESS

Generally, in land economics, the concept of space friction is employed to denote the problem of accessibility. Since no two enterprises can occupy the same site, they cannot be accessible to each other on a simultaneous basis. Space friction is often used to characterize the resulting problem. Space friction is a time-distance concept. An expenditure of energy is involved in overcoming either dimension (time or distance). In an era of technological advances in electronic communications, and the building and subsequent congesting of freeways, it is common knowledge that physical distance does not always define the real interactional distance between two points. The cross-town trip in Manhattan is more expensive than a trip to Westchester on some days. A telephone call to Hong Kong may be an easier form of access than climbing a stair.

The access pattern exhibited by an urban complex is the product of many variables. Two of the most powerful shaping forces are energy and technology. The energy available to any society places a limit on what it can do. Technology is the process of cost reduction for performing acts with a given unit of energy. Energy technology refers to the cost reduction in making usable energy available. The raw form in which energy is available and the characteristic of the device employed to convert it to usable forms both affect the dependent social structure.[1] A brief look at the manner in which energy technology has shaped cities will be instructive.

The technology of the nineteenth century necessitated an urban spatial implosion. The peculiarities of coal-energy technology required high densities and produced a dirty by-product, thereby creating a congested and disagreeable city. The steam engine as an energy converter is more efficient when it enables a large surface of water to be exposed to flame. At the same time, steam engines have relatively small energy fields, as power is delivered by mechanical and friction-prone devices, such as wheels and belts. In striving for greater efficiency, nineteenth-century manufacturing entrepreneurs built massive steam converters in order to achieve the proper boiler sizes. While this produced an efficient stationary power source, it had limited utility for powering urban transportation vehicles. A large steam locomotive is a particularly poor power source for intraurban transport of people, for the inertia of large steam engines makes stopping and starting a costly business. Knowing these simple facts about the limits of the nineteenth-century energy technology, we can go a long way towards understanding some of the locational developments that took place.

Manufacturing plants require labor and material inputs. The most profitable plant was one powered by a large steam engine. Large plants required a large labor force and generated much freight hauling, but there was no equally efficient technology for delivering workers to the plant or for the movement of freight over short distance. It was necessary to rely upon low-energy converters; namely, men and horses, to service these needs. This meant workers had to live close to the plant, hence the need for mixed land use or the intermixing of residential and industrial land. Similarly, cities attempted to shorten the low-energy street hauling of freight by increasing densities in industrial areas. Vertical loft buildings, huddled around a steam power source, spewed an unbelievable congestion into the abutting narrow streets. The use of loft factories not only conformed to the belt-limited energy field of the steam engine, but also allowed more plants to crowd near strategic, fixed terminal points of the unwieldy steamboat and locomotive. Docks and railyards had to be brought right into the city in order to shorten local transport lines. Unfortunately, this is where they still remain.

Thus, the nineteenth-century city was one of mixed land uses, high density, and vertical factories. It also exhibited a locational orientation toward docks, railroads, and central areas. In the terms of sociologist MacKenzie, the nineteenth-century city had high dependence on central institutions.[2] Lines of access tended to converge at selected nodes. The heart of the city was truly in the center. (Of course, the whole scene was continuously sprinkled with coal soot; so it was a very dirty place as well. From historical accounts, today's cities would be judged clean by comparison.)

The relationship between location and access was clearly dramatized in the nineteenth-century city. Location of a store on the main street assured access to customers. A location near a railhead assured the cheapest way to overcome space friction in handling freight. Hotels were built near rail depots where, as in the case of New York, buyers stayed. The fashion industry gravitated to the hotel area in order to reach buyers, hence, the origin of the present-day garment district. The fact remains, however, that the factory which locates on a wooded knoll on the outskirts of the metropolis today is engaged in the same locational process. The twentieth-century plant may be seeking cheap land or a resort-like atmosphere for its research employees or simply satisfying the pastoral yearnings of the owner. None of these changes the fact that the locational decision discriminates in favor of increasing access to certain things and reducing it to others. Today's decentralization trend, i.e., the tendency of firms to move to lower density areas, still exemplifies the urban process. Contrary to most historical trends, changes in urbanization may now be characterized by a reduction, rather than by an increase, in density.

Technological constraints were such that the nineteenth-century set of limits resulted in an unbelievably poor human habitat. Twentieth-century technology is less obviously limiting, and consequently the technological variable is less easily related to the emerging urban pattern. However, the impact of present-day technology can be easily seen when we realize that the internal combustion engine, as a converter, operates on opposite principles from the steam engine. The problem is cooling the thing, not making it hotter. As a result, small gasoline engines were more practical than large ones. The small internal combustion solved, in a fashion, the short-haul problem. The high-energy-driven commuter vehicle became possible. It only remained for the perfection of the electric motor to further the miniaturization process and make way for the great industrial dispersal. Electronic communication and computer technology are probably today's foremost agents of change; yet, their full consequences have not been spelled out.

SOCIAL VALUE AND LOCATION

Thus far, we have been approaching the subject of access and location by illustration. Let us now make a more definitive statement. All locations occupied by man assume a social meaning, which is derived from the access afforded by occupancy of that location. The notion of access can be further elaborated by focusing on the means by which it is expressed. The social meaning of location is derived from the fact that place facilitates access to (1) artifacts, (2) networks of interactions, and (3) social structures.

1. Artifacts are probably the least interesting source of social meaning for urban places. But buildings and structures *do* have utilitarian value. Artifacts may also connote symbolic meaning derived from past occupancies or events associated with them. Finally, artifacts orient us physically and visually. Thus, artifacts as such give meaning to a place through their utility, symbolism, and ability to act as obstacles or channels for physical and visual movement.

2. Each site is unique in the physical sense in that it is the only point which has the same relationship to all other sites. To the extent that social interactions or exchanges are based upon propinquity, a location defines a possible network of interactions. Location, pure and simple, is the key to many social exchanges. Even with technologically advanced communication and transportation, we are not freed from space; they have merely transformed the uses of propinquity. Thus, each place or site has advantages for facilitating a certain combination of interactions; hence, location has social meaning in terms of the exchanges which it makes more possible or convenient.

3. Certain social structures are geographically bounded in a formal sense. That is, the rules of the social structures include spatial boundaries. Municipalities, school districts, voluntary agencies, utilities, newspapers, and a variety of other services have boundaries to their operations. These boundaries may be set legally or by the norms of the social organizations. All occupants of the terrain within those boundaries have access, at least potentially, to those structures. Each location has meaning in terms of the many structures which embrace that location within their bounded territory of operation.

Thus, when a family occupies a house, the value of that occupancy is derived from the artifact (house properties), from interactions facilitated (commuting, shopping, social interactions), and from supporting social structures (local government, schools, utilities). The economic market is an important mechanism for allocating sites by assigning site value. However, urban locational allocation is far from equivalent to land economics. Furthermore, though the above description of locational orientations is stated in *choice* terminology, it is still questionable whether individual choice behavior is the proper explanatory basis for urban studies. In any event, the constraints on individual choice are not simply economic.

ALLOCATION OF ACCESS

Access conveys the notion of availability rather than of actual use. As used here, it is intended to connote the notion of available social *interactions.* If I have access to my neighbor, I may borrow the proverbial lawnmower, and the door will not be slammed in my face when I ask. The choice of the term *access* rather than *interaction* is deliberate. It is assumed that anticipation of the available, rather than the actual, interactions motivates adjustments in location. Access is the prerequisite for actual interaction and is thus a more inclusive concept than interaction itself. It takes note of the fact that perceptions affect behavior and perceptions of access will influence interaction patterns. The task is to explain the state of access—the map of accessibilities.

Most observers of the city scene comment on its variety. The city is the place where one can choose his style of life. In this sense, there may be a basic complementarity to spatial location in urban areas, rather than competition. The fact that all do not choose to occupy urban space in the same way, or for the same reasons, adds up to richer varieties of experience, combinations of opportunities, and refinements in the texture of living. There is obvious truth to this picture, and if we were interested in poetry rather than politics, we could stop here. Despite the complementary nature of a diverse population, at some point, the access of one becomes blocked by the actions of another. In this basic competitive situation, politics begins.

The rush to the suburbs, crowded highways, ghettos, and slums, decaying empty factories and stores, declining core-city populations, urban renewal, riots, and air pollution are a few of the indicators that the allocation process does not operate to the satisfaction of all and that the distribution has inequities. Because the dissatisfaction is quite obvious and the inequities real, we might expect efforts both to change and to maintain the status quo.

There are essentially two options open for those who wish to employ a location strategy to change their access within the urban complex. They can move or they can change the characteristics of the place they presently occupy. The latter course of action essentially involves bringing others into more accessible positions. Urban locational decisions, indeed, the very creation of cities, are the net product of many people trying to become more accessible to one another. The same process that creates cities continues after they are formed. The larger the urban complex, or the more numerous and specialized the interactions demanded, the more critical becomes the locational decision of each urbanite. In the beginning, when settlements were small, one's physical presence in a settlement created the potentiality of access to all others located there. However, as urban complexes increase in size, and/or the requirements for access become more numerous, mere presence in the settlement is not sufficient to yield satisfactory access; instead, a strategic location within the settlement or city has to be sought.

The two options or strategies are pursued simultaneously in all urban areas. In the United States today most people solve their access problems by moving. Each year, thousands of families change their domiciles, merchants change their locations in hot pursuit of customers, and industries move, looking for cheaper inputs or lowered costs in delivering outputs to customers. However, this process of population shifts is a most complex affair. One can only go where one is allowed to go. The limits are placed not only through the distribution of resources (wealth, information, status, etc.), but also through the fluidity of these resources and through political barriers and facilitating channels. Technology merely supplies outer limits or ground rules which all are bound by. Technology never displaces economics and politics in place manipulation.

Fluidity of resources means the capacity to translate assets into locational control. This includes the capacity to exchange one location for another. Janowitz coined the phrase "community of limited liability "[3] to indicate that most American urban dwellers have very little stake in a given place, that there is little to prevent them from packing up and moving. However, some cannot move and gain any advantage; their access requirements are tied to a specific location. For example, commercial enterprises whose primary asset is personalized services have a problem following their clientele who may disperse to many new locations. Merchants who sell goods with objectively defined properties have less trouble moving than those who sell subjectively defined goods. A druggist whose business is primarily dependent upon personal relationships built up over years with customers, including informal medical counseling, has difficulty replicating such an access pattern in a new location. On the other hand, a merchant whose business is keyed to bargain sales of standardized goods should have fewer relocation problems. "Good will," which is neighborhood specific, is a very unliquid asset. Many of the tragedies among small merchants in urban renewal areas result from this fact. The *immobiles* tend to include small merchants, businesses with ethnic clienteles, or those whose "asset" is knowledge of a particular place, such as realtors, neighborhood newspapers, and certain salesmen.

With the exception of these cases of nonfluid resources, those with more resources, generally speaking, are more likely to achieve preferred location than those with fewer. One of the means through which those with large resources solve their locational problems is local area planning. Shopping center complexes, planned neighborhoods, industrial parks, or new towns are all attempts to define the access requirements of a given population in advance and to assemble the proper mix of persons in the proper artifact context. Urban redevelopment is a surgical form of this strategy; here the attempt is made to create a new environment, which will be sustained by satisfying the access requirements of the remaining old urban cells. Needless to say, urban renewal decisions for tearing down are not always guided by an understanding of the social meaning of places. Rubbled blocks which lay fallow for years document this failure.

Resources, such as wealth, information, or status, cannot always be directly translated into location control. Alterna-

tively, structures may be formed which create channels and barriers. These allocating structures may be classified into coalitions and communities.

COLLECTIVE URBAN POLITICAL STRATEGIES

Coalitions and communities are both collectivities in which there is joint, coordinated political action by group members. In a *coalition,* members are always free to opt out and achieve goals through individual strategies or by joining other coalitions. Members of a *community* have common destinies, in which the goals of each member are inextricably tied to the goals of the particular collectivity. Thus, a member of a community cannot improve his access by opting out.

The characteristic political structure in the American urban process is the coalition, not the community. As investments in places increase, coalitions augment individual mobility as means of achieving and controlling access. Coalitions are formed to facilitate wanted interactions and prevent unwanted ones. This may take the form of keeping the "wrong" people or businesses out. Among the common urban coalitions are realty boards, bankers associations, chambers of commerce, redevelopment authorities, and suburban municipal governments. They all seek advantages for members through manipulation of access, usually as it pertains to a particular domain.

Barriers can be created and tests of admission can be administered to screen entrances into a domain. A classical legal instrument for this is zoning. Zoning is an explicit political means of abridging economic market allocation of land among various uses. A builder whose structures have relatively high value in relationship to the land parcel can afford to bid more for land than a builder constructing lower value structures, such as single-family dwellings. By preventing an apartment from being built in a single-family dwelling unit section, the short-run price of the intended site is probably depressed. Thus, zoning coalitions are formed to control access patterns directly in the face of contrary pressure from the market. Zoning is the mechanism by which people band together to "keep up the neighborhood." Countering coalitions form to obtain short- or long-run profits by changing the land uses allowed. In most zoned areas, there are complex sets of zoning coalitions arrayed against one another. However, as is often the case, individual members of the coalitions act unilaterally to improve their access, often causing these coalitions to become unstable.

The coalition is not to be confused with an interest group. The access requirements of urbanites tend to be discreet and individual, just as the sites they occupy are unique. For this very reason, terrain-based coalitions tend to have low cohesion. Political groups, organized around shared interests, identified with occupation, religion, economic status, or avocation, are not affected by urban changes. When a family moves from Chicago to Winnetka, it takes along the personal attributes of family members. The Chicago-based locational interests are exchanged, however, for Winnetka's. The family moves away, literally, from one set of urban coalitions into a different set. The type of access desires may be constant, but moving may help undermine the coalition left behind in Chicago and reinforce, or perhaps change, the one joined in Winnetka. Interests based on the characteristics of persons can be aggregated nationally, e.g., interests based on having income from stocks and bonds. Interests based on a specific position of access within an urban complex are hard to aggregate into national political organizations, but they may be even harder to aggregate on a city basis. The competitive nature of urbanism is highlighted in the local context. The gap between national and local labor-union policies on public housing illustrates this fact.

A second urban access allocating social structure is the community, an example of which is the traditional ethnic neighborhood. If the most prized access pattern of an individual Italian immigrant is to be situated so that he has maximum face-to-face contact with a particular set of other Italian immigrants, then a collectivity of such persons would comprise a community. Obviously, no individual member can improve his position by leaving the group. Many ethnic groups formed communities on their arrival, but this was especially characteristic of the Italians. Moreover, the access desired was not to Italian immigrants per se, but to persons from a certain community in Italy. This constitutes a nearly ideal type of community, for here is a set of individuals with a common life destiny which cannot be achieved if the composition of the set is substantially altered. By contrast, many middle-class "communities" do not qualify as communities, according to our use of the concept. If all that is desired is a certain set of amenities and norms, as opposed to interaction with a set of specific individuals, only a coalition is required. Because it is impossible to aggregate the specific access demands of communities, claims are rarely made on their behalf at higher levels of government.

In its most extreme manifestation, community assumes an antisocial stance vis-à-vis the larger society. The Cosa Nostra, for example, has all the attributes of community. Similarly, nationalism is a form of community disturbing to world peace and order. This sense of community is uncommon in our urban scene. It is a more common attribute of European urban life, where allegiance to a set population has been particularly strong in the past. Although American small-town patriotism provides some evidence of being community-like, most American places, whether urban, rural, or small town, are more like coalitions.

One of the recent interesting manifestations of self-conscious community building is among black radicals. It is one of the few recent examples of an American group asserting that the realization of individual interests is radically dependent on common group achievements. Rejection of integration means the rejection of coalitions and individual adaptive moves as the mode of solving urban political problems for blacks. The black radicals, who advocate some form of separatism or black allegiance, are saying that the only beneficial access for the black individual is through the black community, or that successful access to whites is contingent on a collective redefinition of black-white relations. It is the community characteristic that makes their view truly "radical" in American perspective. It counters the American individualistic way.

The measurement and scaling of behavior which is oriented toward coalition, as opposed to community formation is one of the unfulfilled tasks of urban research. Much of the loose talk about loss of community pride, rootlessness, and nomadism in modern life assumes the meaningfulness of such a scale. However, we do not know much about the conditions under which behavior is most community oriented and most coalition-like.

RECAPITULATION

Let us recapitulate the foregoing into one formulation. Figure 1 presents the urban process described in this essay. It is possible to formulate this process in systems terms, but all the conditions for a systems approach have not been set forth. The universe of observations which must be undertaken to study the way in which the pattern is reshaped is largely a matter of empirical observation. We don't know if the metropolitan area is one or many systems of access manipulation. However, any investigation which confines itself merely to observations of collective actions (coalitions and community formation) is bound to yield a truncated and warped

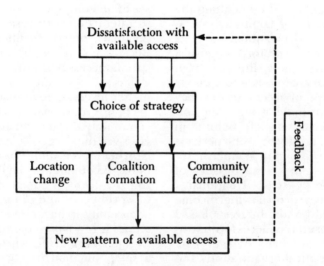

FIGURE 1. Model of Urban Political Process

view of urban change. The fact remains that most urban dwellers vote by moving van, not by ballot box, and that coalitions, not communities, are the characteristic urban collectivity. Coalition stability may be the most important political variable in shaping urban form.

NOTES

1. For many of my insights about energy technology, I am indebted to Fred Cottrell, *Energy and Society* (New York: McGraw-Hill, 1955). See his early chapters particularly.

2. R. Mackenzie, *The Metropolitan Community* (New York and London: McGraw-Hill, 1933), p. 71.

3. M. Janowitz, *The Community Press in an Urban Setting* (Glencoe, Ill.: The Free Press, 1952).

A TERRITORIAL PERSPECTIVE

THE POLITICAL ORGANIZATION
OF SPACE IN METROPOLITAN AREAS
EDWARD W. SOJA

This selection presents space in much the same role as that described by Williams: in terms of its localized territoriality function and its effects on the political organization of society. Politics and the institutions which support organized behavior within an urban area depend not only on the formal and informal social contacts and contracts, but on the localization of these activities and their legitimization by the localized community. As proof of his thesis, Soja offers an incisive account of the causes and effects of the fragmentation of metropolitan government in North America.

Reprinted from Edward W. Soja, *The Political Organization of Space,* Resource Paper No. 8, Commission on College Geography (Washington, D.C.: Association of American Geographers, 1971), pp. 3–52, by permission of the Association of American Geographers and the author. This is an edited version of the original publication. Notes and artwork have been renumbered, and a new title has been added.

A. HUMAN SPATIAL ORGANIZATION

Much of contemporary geography rests on the assumption that there is an inherent geographic order to human society, a spatial "anatomy" of human behavior and organization which has regular and discoverable characteristics. The search for fundamental principles, processes, and recurrent patterns of human spatial organization provides a challenging frontier for geographical research, a frontier which, with a few prominent exceptions, has only recently been explored systematically. From the growing literature which does exist, however, it is possible to derive a set of widely accepted generalizations about human behavior in space which are likely to be important building blocks for the construction of theory. Although relevant to all aspects of geography, these generalizations are of particular importance in understanding the processes shaping the political organization of space.

First of all, human activity in space is *localized* in the sense that it occupies specific and unique places on the earth's surface, each with its own complex of attributes or characteristics. Put even more simply, all human activity takes place at particular locations or within particular geographic contexts. This is, at first thought, not an especially profound assertion. Localization, however, is one of the most basic aspects of human society. It provides the essential link between man and the earth and establishes the framework for human spatial interaction. The differences from place to place, in relative as well as absolute location, and in terms of other features such as climate, economy, language, wealth, and culture, shape the nature and intensity of relationships between people and between the locations they occupy. All too often, human activity and behavior are examined as if they took place in a "spaceless" environment devoid of terrestrial location, distance and directional relationships, and other characteristics associated with a localized geographic context which significantly affect the generation and results of this activity or behavior. It is essential, therefore, in any comprehensive analysis of individual or group behavior to at least recognize the potential influence of *locational attributes.*

Related to both the localization of human spatial activity and to the interrelationships between locations is the *focal character* of human activity in space. This in part reflects the gregariousness of man as a social animal and in part develops from the associated efforts of man to maintain a certain level of efficiency in his behavior by reducing the "friction" of distance. Thus human beings and their localized activities and structures tend to be distributed in a clustered pattern, largely in response to the factor of *distance* and its major correlate, *accessibility.*

Spatial interaction grows out of the differential attributes of places, particularly those which act as the major focal points of human activity. Here again we can consider distance to be a key factor, but distance defined in a much broader sense than simple *physical distance* and its various direct transformations (e.g., time-distance, cost-distance, perceived distance). It involves both a *socio-cultural "distance"* and what might be called a *functional "distance."* The former, for example, implies that interaction is likely to be encouraged when people occupying particular locations share similar cultural attributes such as language and traditions, or similar social attributes such as educational level, occupation, or income.

Functional distance is essentially what Edward Ullman has called complementarity—the potential interdependence derived from the existence of a supply of something at one place and the demand for this something at another. Two cities are likely to interact more intensively, for example, if each produces goods that the other desires

than if they produced basically the same things (assuming that these goods can be profitably exchanged). These supplies and demands need be not only economic but may also be social, cultural, political, psychological, and indeed biological (e.g., potential marriage partners). Again, the assumption is that two locations are likely to interact more intensively if this interaction can satisfy some functional objective of each.

There are undoubtedly many other factors influencing spatial interaction, but the three mentioned appear to have the most general importance: physical distance and its various direct transformations (including accessibility and relative location); socio-cultural homogeneity (under which is included membership in kinship, ethnic, social, and other "identity" groups); and functional complementarity (which, in combination with the attribute of relative location, encompasses the important factor of intervening opportunity).[1] In other words, human interaction in space will tend to be greater when the points or people interacting are "closer" together physically, socioculturally, and in their functional needs. Moreover, given the focality of human occupance and activity, all three of these patterns of proximity are likely to be highly interrelated.

The differential attributes of locations and the patterning of human interaction in space each provide the basis for different forms of human spatial organization, the first with respect to what has been called *areal* association in the geographical literature and the second with respect to what has been called *spatial* structure. The terms used by Philbrick for these two forms of organization are "parallel" and "nodal." They are more familiar to the geographer as the bases for formal and functional regions.

Functional (or nodal, or polarized) regions result from an organized patterning or structure of spatial interaction, usually involving an orientation to some common center or centers which affect interaction throughout an area. A simple functional region, for example, might be the hinterland of a port or the area served by a school or library. New York City or Chicago are centers of large and dynamic functional regions with variably defined boundaries encompassing parts of several states and hundreds of local government units. More complex is the territory occupied by a cohesive national community, which may or may not coincide with the legally defined boundaries of the state. It represents a functional region in that the flow of goods, people, money, messages, and ideas is structured into an integrated network of human spatial interaction.

Whereas functional regions are defined primarily by structured systems of spatial interaction, *formal (or uniform, or homogeneous) regions* represent a classification of areas according to a homogeneity of locational attributes—that is, an areal association of attributes as opposed to a spatial structuring of interaction. The Corn Belt of the United States is a formal region in that all sections of it share essentially the same locational attributes upon which the region is defined (e.g., a certain proportion of farmland devoted to corn and other feedcrops, the existence of certain numbers of livestock, and perhaps an additional constraint based upon contiguity). Similarly, at the most basic level, a sovereign state and its administrative subdivisions are essentially formal regions despite the fact that functional organization may cut across the formally established boundaries. One is in Illinois, for example, whether one resides in Chicago, Springfield, or East St. Louis.

Another important principle is that of *hierarchical ordering.* Human spatial organization tends to be hierarchically structured, paralleling a similar tendency in human social organization. Just as there is an order of status or rank in

society, with all the various "actors" and their roles interlocked into a larger social system, so there is an interlocking and hierarchical ordering in spatial organization. This hierarchy takes two forms which may occasionally coincide. The first arises from the direct influence of social ranking on spatial patterns. Thus, in many traditional societies, living in close proximity to the chief or king was correlated with high social status. Similarly, political administration often followed a distinct pattern linking distance, kinship relations, and status, with those administrators closest to the political capital also being the closest kin to the political leadership. Studies of modern urban centers have also revealed a geographic patterning of social rank, with people of similar socio-economic status tending to occupy distinct sectors radiating outward from the central business district.

In addition to the differentiation of space as a direct reflection of social and political organization, and often intertwined with it, is the development of hierarchies of regional organization, with smaller regional units "nesting" within progressively larger ones. Clear examples come to mind of simple functionally- and formally-bounded hierarchies, the first represented by the typical central place hierarchy of market areas, the second by the formal political hierarchy of administrative divisions in the United States, from the most local, through the county and the state, to the federal government.

B. SOCIETY AND POLITY

The political organization of space reflects the ways in which human spatial interaction is structured to fulfill political functions. But what are political functions and how do they differ from other functions within society? The specific definition of political vs. non-political functions has never been completely agreed upon by social scientists very much beyond the conventional "who gets what, when, and how"—the "where-less" definition of politics suggested by Harold Lasswell. For our purposes, however, three major functional realms can be indentified:

1. Control over the distribution, allocation, and ownership of scarce resources (including land, money, and power—the ability to make authoritative decisions). This is largely a coordinative or administrative function aimed at satisfying the needs of society as a whole.
2. The maintenance of order and the enforcement of authority. This function revolves around the resolution of conflict both within and between societies.
3. The legitimization of authority through societal integration. Here the emphasis is on the creation and maintenance of institutions and behavior patterns which promote group unity and cohesiveness.

These are purposely very broad definitions so that they may be applicable to a variety of political systems and not lead to an overconcentration on the sovereign state. The stress in on political functions within larger social systems, be they modern nation states, isolated peasant villages, urban metropolitan regions, or primitive hunting bands.

Political functions thus essentially involve three basic processes: *competition, conflict,* and *cooperation.* In each case, the political system is concerned with the control and organization of these processes both within and, insofar as possible, between societies. This does not mean that these processes are exclusively political, but that for society in general it is the specialized sector—the *polity*—which, in part through its monopoly over the use of force, is recognized as the primary locus of decision-making with respect to these processes and as the major coordinating agency for

maintaining integration within the society as a whole.

It is important, however, to state clearly what is meant by *society.* Societies have been defined as comprehensive social systems which are differentiated enough to be relatively self-sufficient. Like all social systems, a society is tied together by a regular and persistent structure of interaction or relationship between its component units. Furthermore, as noted by Talcott Parsons in *Societies,* the comprehensiveness and stability of societies is based largely upon political organization.

It must have loyalties both to a sense of community and to some "corporate agency" of the kind we normally consider governmental, and must establish a relatively effective normative order within a territorial area. (p. 2)

From these observations we can infer that the political organization of space in part reflects the social and political order within societies—that social, political, and spatial organization are interrelated. The political organization of space therefore functions within societies primarily as a means of structuring interaction between its component units (individuals and groups). Its major purpose is to create and maintain solidarity within the society by shaping the processes of competition, conflict, and cooperation as they operate spatially.

Societal integration, however, is not maintained only through the political organization of space. Cooperation, conflict, and competition are obviously shaped by a variety of other forces. Indeed, most of the theoretical social science literature, while recognizing the territorial basis of societies and polities, rarely deals explicitly with the spatial dimension. Within this literature, the two most important integrative mechanisms examined have been *kinship* (or ethnicity) and social cooperation arising from the *functional division of labor.* We cannot go into this literature in detail, but it is important to discuss these two mechanisms briefly since both also have important implications for the political organization of space.

Studies of kinship have generally stressed the tendency for human interaction and association to be promoted by a "biological proximity," real or presumed, which is reinforced by the role of the family in socialization and value formation. Kinship relations thus create bonds not only through blood ties but also as a primary vehicle of culture, which in turn helps cement the society through language and tradition.

Societal integration is also based upon the functional interdependence growing out of the division of labor. The level of differentiation which is necessary in society erodes individual or family self-sufficiency by creating specialized roles which are interdependent. Here the major theoretical emphasis has been on the concept of "contract"—a voluntary and mutual agreement to engage in a particular cooperative activity. Contractual relations permit the extension of society beyond the immediate kin group. The bonds of functional complementarity involve biologically unrelated individuals in coordinated and cooperative networks of social, economic, and political activity, thereby expanding the scale of society and adding to its range of integrative linkages.

FRAGMENTED URBAN EMPIRES: TERRITORIAL ORGANIZATION OF METROPOLITAN GOVERNMENT IN THE UNITED STATES

The dense and uneven web of politico-administrative boundaries which stretches over the globe displays its most pronounced seams or discontinuities at the level of the nation-state system. Here the "service" area boundaries for a wide variety of functions spatially coincide to establish the most prominent system of territorial compartments affecting the political organization of space in the modern world. Of all these compartments, however, the one which contains the *densest* political web is probably the United States, and it is in its metropolitan regions that the peaks of density are reached.

It has been estimated that there are over 8,000 multi-functional and autonomous local governments, including over 3,000 counties and more than that number of urban governments for the thousands of incorporated municipalities which speckle the map. The mesh is made still finer by the number of special-purpose districts which have been mushrooming over the past decades, particularly in the major metropolitan regions. From 1942 to 1962 the number of special districts (excluding school districts) grew from 8,300 to over 18,000. When school districts are added, the result in 1962 was an astounding total of over 63,000 *local* governments with some autonomous authority over specific parcels of U.S. space. More recent estimates put the total over 70,000.[2] Emerging from this complex geopolitical web are thousands of discrete units of territorial identity and exclusion— cities and suburbs, townships and counties, school districts and whole metropolitan regions—which instill a sense of community and apartness usually surpassed only at the national and family levels.

There is no doubt that the maze of counties, cities, townships, and special districts, many tending to pursue narrow local interests at the expense of the larger functional community, both directly and indirectly exacerbate some of the major problems facing a predominantly urban America. Molded by nineteenth century notions of the moral and ethical values of local autonomy and self-determination, much of the United States has become shattered like a pane of glass into a system of often competitive and mutually suspicious fragments. Particularism and disconnectedness are infused into this system through a powerful sense of local territoriality based upon what are essentially artificial political units and certain shared social, economic, and cultural attitudes and characteristics. When faced with the need for or likelihood of consolidation, these nineteenth century relics frequently react much like nation-states encountering a challenge to their sovereignty or like individual property owners when their land is threatened. At times, it appears almost as if the increasing functional specialization, societal complexity, and territorial compartmentalization that has characterized the history of human political development for the past two million years has come close to running amok in the political organization of American space. Although the problems of local government fragmentation exist throughout the world, nowhere are their proportions and implications as great as they are in the United States.

Both Chicago and New York, for example, are the focal points of an accretion of over a thousand local government units overlapping and intertwining in a multi-tiered (and multi-state) mosaic of political authorities which make effective metropolitan planning difficult if not impossible. Most of the boundaries are invisible to the individual, but nevertheless they have a powerful effect on his behavior and activity—where he votes and whom he votes for, where his children go to school, how and how much he is taxed, where he buys his liquor, what modifications he may or may not make on his property. On a different level, most of the major northern cities of the United States find themselves surrounded—some say strangled—by a resistant white collar of wealthy, autonomous suburbs taking full advantage of the central city while at the same time contributing a disproportionately small share to the solution of its many prob-

lems. The result has been widespread racial polarization, central city deterioration, zoning and planning based on greed or fear, and the visual pollution of the urban and rural landscape.

Clearly then the political organization of space in metropolitan America stands as one of the centrally important themes in political geography. However, relatively little explicitly geographical work has been done on this subject and we are forced to search primarily in other disciplines for materials and frameworks for analysis. What follows, therefore, are some suggested paths for further geographical exploration rather than a comprehensive summary of existing works on metropolitan political problems.

I. The Pattern of Metropolitan Fragmentation

Figure 1 represents an attempt to portray some of the characteristic features of urban fragmentation in the United States. The original corporate limits of most major American cities were usually drawn so as to include the built-up area as well as a band of surrounding rural land designed primarily for future urban expansion (see Figure 1-A). These boundaries were generally established through a special act of the state legislature, as were subsequent changes through annexation of the urban fringe as the city grew beyond its political limits. Until around the middle of the nineteenth century, the typical sequence of urban growth consisted of a fairly regular amalgamation of built-up areas into a relatively unified urban-political unit (see Figure 1-B).

With rapidly increasing urbanization and improved transport, the urban fringe began to expand more rapidly and irregularly. Annexation, however, became increasingly difficult as satellite towns and portions of the urban fringe were themselves incorporated as legal equals to the central city. As noted by

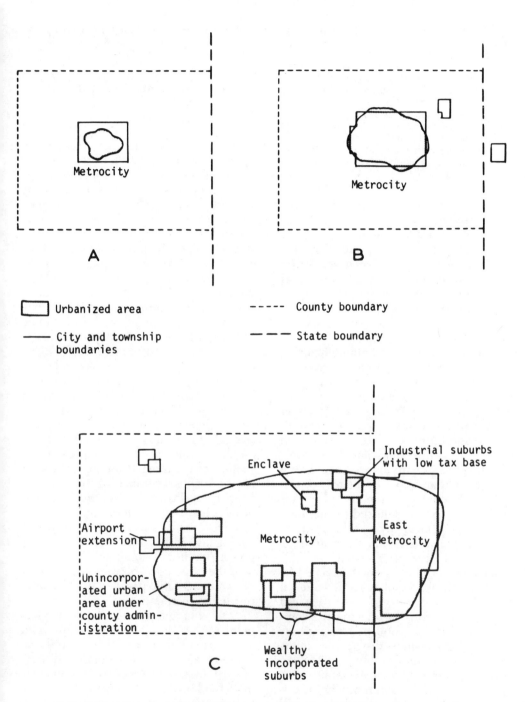

FIGURE 1. Historical Growth of Metropolitan Administrative Fragmentation

William Winter in his perceptive analysis of *The Urban Polity:*

In all of this the central city was caught between Scylla and Charybdis. Not only was it powerless to annex the urban fringe—because of awkward state law, because the natural community was divided by state or national boundaries, or because of political antipathy that built up in the suburbs. It was also incapable of preventing the random incorporation of every little population center that appeared within its orbit. (p.168)

The result, especially in the larger metropolitan areas, was a wholesale Balkanization of the urban region (see Figure 1-C). Satellite cities and suburbs (particularly the older and wealthier) often developed powerful local identities and fiercely defended themselves against annexation.

Urban growth in the central city was thus channeled along lines of least resistance rather than optimum efficiency, creating a complex and highly irregular pattern of appendages, enclaves, exclaves, and other misshapen oddments that reach unusually complex levels in such areas as the Los Angeles metropolitan region. Airports (e.g., O'Hare in Chicago), harbor areas and lake frontages (e.g., San Pedro in Los Angeles and the Lake Ontario extensions of Rochester), and other locationally important facilities became connected to the main body of the central city by thin slivers of land often no wider than a city street or highway. Some cities, such as Milwaukee, found their growth blocked by older established suburbs on one of their flanks and were forced to expand in other directions (producing the common situation of suburbs being closer to the central business district than many sections of the central city itself). State and local boundaries created split cities, often with radically different administrative and taxing systems, thus adding still greater stress to the governing of the metropolis. Looking over a set of maps showing the political boundaries of American cities becomes a revealing exercise in geopolitical science fiction!

2. Fragmentation at Larger and Smaller Scales

Zoning

One of the most enigmatic features of the political organization of space in the United States is the widespread adoption of zoning—a system of laws regulating and restricting the use of land in particular areas. At first thought, it would appear that zoning laws run directly against one of the most persistent of sacred cows in Western culture, the tradition of inviolable property rights. How then did zoning succeed in virtually sweeping the country in what Winter has called "one of the truly great public dramas of the early twentieth century"?

Fortunately, an incisive and insightful study of zoning has recently appeared which presents a comprehensive analysis of the development of zoning in the United States. Seymour I. Toll clearly reveals in *Zoned American* that the struggle for zoning laws was not championed by reformers seeking the general welfare of the larger community against the powerful resistance of the wealthy, propertied classes. It was the ruling economic elite itself which was most responsible for the passage and diffusion of zoning laws in an effort to reinforce their power (territorial dominance?) and prevent the "invasion" of undesirable types of land use (and people) into wealthy residential communities.

The zoning movement began in Germany in the late nineteenth century and later spread to Great Britain and the United States, with New York City enacting the first comprehensive zoning law in 1916. The developments in New York receive extensive treatment from Toll for they symbolized the highly discriminatory nature that zoning was to adopt throughout most of the country.

Sporadic attempts at something resembling zoning had occurred in the United States as early as 1795, when Philadelphia restricted the use of wooden buildings in congested areas. San Francisco, however, was to provide a harbinger of future developments when it attempted to restrict laundries from wooden buildings, a move designed both for safety and against the Chinese population. It was subsequently ruled unconstitutional. New York was to extend this model of mixed intentions successfully primarily through the efforts of the Fifth Avenue Association and other representatives of the wealthy class of merchants and businessmen of mid-Manhattan to resist the encroachment of skyscrapers and factories (particularly from the already crowded garment district). There was little or no attempt to use zoning as a basis for comprehensive and coordinated planning and development. Instead it was aimed at preserving and protecting the territorial privileges of a small but powerful community regardless of its impact on the larger society.

Especially after its legal basis was firmly established in the 1920s, zoning became an extremely effective force shaping urban land use and development. If, as Winter notes, the modern zoning ordinance is vigorously administered, "there are few governmental activities that can equal its exhaustive and intimate control of human activity." From its inception to the present, zoning in America has centered heavily around the exclusion of "high rise" buildings (now often meaning more than two stories). Toll's conclusions, which parallel those made by the National Commission on Urban Problems, are that (a) zoning is being used today primarily as a means of protecting suburban property owners much as it was used earlier by the Fifth Avenue merchants; (b) zoning has the effect of discriminating against particular racial and economic groups by artificially keeping housing prices high (e.g., by preventing the builder from achieving certain economies through an insistence on one or two acre plots, needlessly wide or costly roads, and the avoidance of clustered houses) or through a variety of other measures (e.g., restrictions on multiple family dwellings); (c) there has been widespread tampering with zoning ordinances to permit the purchase of favors and changes in land-use restrictions; and (d) zoning has often been used as a tool to promote local interests at the expense of the metropolitan region, thus accentuating many of the problems of urban fragmentation.

There is no doubt that zoning has played a highly productive and positive role in the vast majority of cases and that it is an essential component of effective planning. The territorial fragmentation of the metropolitan region, however, has also permitted it to become a framework and tool for the maintenance of narrow special interests and for racial discrimination. Like so many aspects of the political organization of space, zoning has been used to establish and maintain a territorially-based dominance hierarchy based on wealth and race which, while satisfying the need for localized spatial identities, works to rigidify social and economic inequalities. Combined with the polycentric political system of most metropolitan areas, which sustains the independence of small incorporated municipalities, zoning has enabled the wealthy, white suburb to emerge as one of the most fiercely defended human territorial units in the United States.

Supra-state Regional Groupings

It has frequently been noted that the American local government system was devised before the emergence of the modern metropolis and, despite some changes, still remains a nineteenth century structure trying to deal with twentieth century problems. A similar statement can be made for the political organization of space at the state level. Few boundaries in the world have been as locationally stable as the state boundaries in the United States. The functions and powers of states have changed over time, but the boundaries have persisted adamantly in the face of changing social conditions.

Like the formal political organization of space at the local level, the territorial state system has served many positive functions as a means of controlling competition, conflict, and cooperation under the umbrella of the American political system, and may indeed have been imperative in the early stages of American history. But, as has also been true at the local level, the evolving demands of modern technology and society have exposed many inadequacies in the present system of state boundaries and jurisdictions. There appears little chance that the fifty American states will be altered significantly in the near future, but there has developed a growing concern for constructing new and innovative forms of interstate and state-federal cooperation which resemble in objectives (and somewhat in structure) the attempts at achieving unity at the metropolitan level.

3. Some Reflections *

The foregoing review of several levels in the political organization of American space suggests several interrelated conclusions which have an application beyond the contemporary American context. One is that the problems of political fragmentation are representative of a much larger question which pervades the political organization of space at all geographical scales and which has perplexed political/administrative theory building for thousands of years. How

* Prior to this section, Soja's essay includes a discussion of seven "Experiments in Metropolitan Unity": "The Dade County Model," "The Lakewood Plan Model," "The Honolulu Model," "The Nashville Model," "The Texas Model," "The Statehood Model," and "The Toronto Model." —Editors' Note

can the necessities of coordinating or integrating a number of separate entities into a single system be balanced against the equally forceful demands of local autonomy and identity? This is essentially the question of centralization-decentralization-federation that faces every autonomous political unit at one time or another. It is a question which occupied the thoughts of the American founding fathers— but probably no more so than it did the participants in the recent New York City school strike over school district autonomy. It is a central question in all attempts to create units on a scale larger than the nation-state, from a united Europe or East Africa to a United Nations. In the continuing controversy over metropolitan reform, it is symbolized by the "consolidationists" and "localists" of Dade County and, in the political science literature, by the opposition of "gargantua" or Big Government and "grass roots."

Political fragmentation per se cannot automatically be considered dysfunctional or inefficient, for the problems involved are fundamentally scale specific. First of all, successful integration at one level generally means less integration at the next higher scale. Ethnic unification during the colonial period in Africa has created problems of "tribalism" in many new African states; introspective nationalism has ruined the chances of political federation in many world regions. Similarly, solidification of community feeling in urban neighborhoods or suburbs can effectively hinder inter-community cooperation; metropolitan consolidation may work against a larger scale effort to coordinate development policy and programs; the solidification of regional feeling can lead to destructive sectionalism.

The paradox of scale is not an insoluble enigma but a reflection of the progressively increasing scale and complexity of human society. It is also intimately related to another characteristic of human social evolution: increasing functional differentiation and specialization. Modern man is not only surrounded by the portable micro-territories discussed earlier, but is also encased in a series of larger socially-based territorial bubbles to which each individual devotes varying degrees of attention, identity, and feelings of exclusiveness. The family is probably still the strongest of all, although it has been declining in importance for many centuries. In addition to the family, however, there are several varieties of local communities and neighborhoods, larger scale urban, metropolitan, and regional societies, the nation-state, and occasionally still larger units. Each of these units, to the degree to which they achieve formal political expression, are depositories for specific functions and prerogatives. No longer can one or two provide virtually all societal functions as they did in less complex societies. The major organizational problem therefore becomes not the necessity to create ever larger political entities with an increasing number of functions, but *to match particular functions with the appropriate scale of organization.*

Viewed in this light, the fragmented polycentric systems of metropolitan government may indeed strike an effective balance between the provision of public services and the recognition of local community interests. It may promote through controlled competition a more efficient, responsive, and economical servicing of the metropolitan population than the "gargantua" of metro government. Insofar as it remains flexible and representative, it can perhaps optimally serve both the local and larger scale needs of the metropolitan political conglomerate, particularly when combined with such voluntary arrangements as the Lakewood Plan in Los Angeles County.

Flexibility and representativeness, however, are the key variables. The political organization of American space in many ways appears to be locked into a rigid set of territorial units which can

significantly hinder the flexible restructuring and reassignment of functions necessary to cope with contemporary problems. This in part reflects the inherent disequilibrium between the formal and functional units of spatial organization and the degree to which formal political entities have almost universally become the focus of intense feelings of territoriality. A similar conclusion is reached by one of the outstanding students of metropolitan reform, Luther Gulick:

Each defined human institution, especially when created by law and endowed with even the smallest modicum of power, tends to develop into an independent "institutional personality." This involves not only asserting itself, but also extending itself and seeking to perpetuate itself. This is apparently a law of group structure, as it is of individual existence. And among governmental institutions, the suicide complex is notably absent . . . the existence of a fixed and immortal boundary tends to create and sustain a fixed and immortal governmental institution. (p. 36)

The lack of representativeness is another manifestation of human territorial behavior, particularly as it relates to the establishment and maintenance of a pronounced dominance hierarchy. As has been stressed throughout this section, the political organization of space satisfies many divergent objectives. While serving to regulate competition, conflict, and cooperation, it can both integrate and segregate the subsections of the larger society. To a great extent, the latter course has characterized many aspects of the political organization of American space. But, the accepted dominance order upon which this segregated patterning is based is weakening and becoming widely challenged. Whether the outcome will be integration or still more segregation is still unknown. Sommer, however, suggests a guideline which might be heeded:

When children are loudly pummeling one another over some toy or the last apple, the best short-run solution is to separate the combatants before the

entire house is disrupted, but the only way to ensure future tranquility is to change the conditions
that created the conflict.

NOTES

1. A good discussion of the concepts of complementarity,
   intervening opportunity, and transferability is found in
   Edward L. Ullman, "The Role of Transportation and
   the Bases for Interaction."
2. These figures are for local governments only. They do
   not include the large number of state, regional, and
   federal governmental units, such as congressional vot-
   ing districts. This topic is discussed further in Resource
   Paper No. 7, *The Spatial Expression of Urban Growth.*

BIBLIOGRAPHY

Parsons, T. 1966. *Societies—evolutionary and comparative perspectives.* Englewood Cliffs: Prentice-Hall.

Sommer, R. 1969. *Personal space: The behavioral basis of design.* Englewood Cliffs: Prentice-Hall.

Toll, S. I. 1969. *Zoned America.* New York: Grossman Publishers.

Ullman, E. L. 1956. The role of transportation and the
bases for interaction. In W. L. Thomas, Jr. (ed.), *Man's
role in changing the face of the earth.* Chicago: University
of Chicago Press, pp. 862–80.

Winter, W. O. 1969. *The urban polity.* New York: Dodd,
Mead and Company.

A SOCIOLOGICAL PERSPECTIVE

POTENTIALS IN COMMUNITY DIFFERENTIATION
GERALD D. SUTTLES

While market, political, and legal forces provide the structural bases of society, Suttles argues that it is the effects of these institutions on specific groups of people that actually differentiates urban communities. Boundaries can be reinforced by institutions, for example, but the central identity of neighborhoods and functional areas is provided by the relationships between patterns of social interactions and the settings in which they occur. Ethnic and racial groups, occupational status, and people with similar life styles provide the social basis for communities.

Reprinted from Gerald D. Suttles, *The Social Construction of Communities* (Chicago: University of Chicago Press, 1972), pp. 233–68, by permission of the publisher and the author. This is an edited version of the original publication. Notes have been renumbered.

THE COMMUNITY AS A TERRITORIAL BASIS FOR ASSOCIATIONAL SELECTION

It is probably self-evident that residential proximity creates its own dangers and difficulties of social control. People who are close at hand are impossible to avoid; they can teach your children dirty habits, abuse your daughter, throw cigarette butts in you doorway, or snatch your wife's purse on her way home from downtown. Understandably, people want to live in a "good area" where they feel reasonably safe and are a known distance from those people they distrust. They also want to know something about how far the "good area" extends so that they can say something definite about how far their children can go when they play, how far away to park the car for the night, and a multitude of petty day-to-day decisions which require that we break the city up into more or less trustworthy areas.

To arrive at such discrete areas, residents may consult with the neighbors, rely on stereotypes conveyed in the newspapers, or individually foresee the dangers to passage as they cross impersonal domains or no-man's-land.[1] It does not take a highly imaginative person to invent such boundaries, for they derive from his most primitive notions of how space, distance, and movement have inevitable and universal meanings. Individuals who share an arm's length of space are vulnerable to one another, and this is a lesson learned early and widely. Movement away from or toward one another must be endowed with intent and motive, or else the individual will not survive long in the traffic of life. To openly move closer to one individual than another conveys affect and sentiment, and the person who fails to find this out will certainly fail to express one form of affect which is essential to all societies. It is out of such primitive conceptions of space, distance, and movement that the community—and other spatial groupings—is constructed. We are not speaking here of native or inborn conceptions but of universal cultural forms which are required by the mechanics of life itself. The quest for a good community is, among other things, a quest for a neighborhood where one does not fear standing an arm's length from his neighbor, where one can divine the intent of someone heading down the sidewalk, or where one can share expressions of affect by the way adjacent residences dress up for mutual impression management.[2]

Decisions like this about an area require us to draw distinctions among areas and ultimately boundaries between them. The ideal boundary is the physical obstruction across which danger and traffic cannot advance at all. There are, of course, no such boundaries in a modern city, but there are fair approximations in some of our expressways, elevated lines, blocks of industry, rivers, and so on. An alternative is to select strips such as vacant land or rail lines where people "have no business" and, since they are inhabited only by trepassers, are dangerous places to cross. Obviously such obstructions are not always available nor do they always draw a significant boundary between noticeably different populations. What often happens, then, is that rather arbitrary streets, passageways, or some kind of physical marker are hit upon as a point beyond which the gradation in what people are like is said to make a qualitative change. The problem is not too much unlike that of a teacher who must take a continuous sequence of exam scores and decide on a cutting point between those who pass and those who fail. The choice is a familiar one, somewhat arbitrary, but necessary.

Individual Strategies in the Defended Neighborhood

Naturally, this need not mean that there will be much consensus on such boundaries, although the reasonable tendency to consult other residents on this matter is a powerful move in that direction. Often, however, the new resident will

have only an ill-formed notion of the boundaries of the area he is moving into and the character of his fellow residents beyond what is conveyed by the appearance of their houses. For such a new resident there seem to be two separable strategies, not mutually exclusive, but likely to receive greater or lesser emphasis depending on his capacity for residential mobility. One emphasis may be on selecting a residential area where the character of fellow residents is assured by the costs of living there and the presumed reputability of people so heavily rewarded by society. Another emphasis is to cultivate one's neighbors once one is in an area to the point that they come to share a personal covenant, look out for one another, and exempt each other from the general suspicions and defensive provocations which are so productive of the violence, insult, or damage that neighbors fear in the first place. The first type of strategy is most available to people with high incomes and transferable skills. Where this first strategy is pursued to the exclusion of the second, it is apt to produce what Morris Janowitz has called the community of limited liability: a community where the resident invests neither himself nor his capital so deeply that he cannot pull out when housing values and the character of his neighbors begin to decline.[3] The practice of cultivating one's neighbors is apt to be more common among people who are disbarred by color or who cannot afford to live in a wide range of neighborhoods or are more sessile because of their jobs, local investments, or family traditions which give them a large place in a small pool.[4]

Naturally, both strategies can be combined and this frequently occurs in elite communities where a personal referral is as necessary as cash to assure one the right of purchase. Similarly, there are people who can follow neither strategy because they cannot afford to move and they so thoroughly and reasonably distrust their disreputable neighbors that they are unable or unwilling to try to cultivate them.[5] Such communities are apt to be very fragmented, composed of isolated families, and especially among adults, to form a kind of dormitory community where people try to reach their dwelling units before dark. Some of our public housing developments take this tendency to an extreme.[6] As with other "dumping grounds," however, they seldom lack a residential identity. People in other areas are only too eager to disown them. More affluent and comfortable dormitory communities may remain more anonymous, especially where the automobile and extensive traffic arteries offer quick means by which people can lose an accountable residential identity and pass as something else.[7]

Institutional Collaboration

However these strategies combine, they lead to another strategic decision about whether or not to defend the area and stabilize its boundaries so that they are more than arbitrary markers and become real walls and barriers against the incursion of outsiders. For the individual who has only bought a negotiable stock and wishes to avoid the provincialism of the local area, his interests are served best by specialists at this business. Since he can usually afford them, the restrictive convenant, similar informal practices, home improvement associations, and "reputable" real estate agents are to be sponsored and supported at least to the extent of favoring them with one's trade and contributions. These efforts may be supplemented by that of night watchmen, private policemen, and doormen. Even more important, however, may be the protective shield provided by city administrators, highly placed politicians, and the leaders in certain businesses, particularly those in construction and real estate. Some of the tools available here are obvious: zoning regulations, the permissible size of lots,

the enforcement of building and fire regulations, the location of desirable or undesirable public facilities, and so on. Other ways of doing the same thing may be less apparent: police policy toward "trepassers" and the vague way in which administrative decisions and plans on land usage cumulate as an omen of the future for renters, home owners, local businessmen, and prospective residents.

It is evident that the defensive system of such a neighborhood is only partially a local responsibility and not a duty which falls altogether on the local residents. Instead, this defense system represents a combination of political, administrative, and business institutions in the service of local populations. What imperils such communities, then, is not so much a decline in their own interpersonal loyalties and attachment to place as a breakup in the precarious collusion of several governmental and private organizations. Recently the federal government has partially retreated from this combine by passing and enforcing open housing legislation, by funding low and moderate income housing or rental subsidies, and by the broader and more equitable enforcement of building and zoning standards.[8] Certainly the federal government has not wholly withdrawn from this combine, but even its limited changes in policy have been enough to panic the residents in many communities who seem to fear an invasion by the "dangerous classes."

Neighborhood defense is not so precarious but it is more onerous in many communities where the residents cannot depend on the protective shield of external organizations and must engage in a sort of grass roots vigilantism. This type of defended neighborhood is most flagrant in slum areas where street-corner gangs, open bigotry, and physical abuse are the first line of defense against people from other ethnic or racial groups or, more recently, the incursion of off-beat social types like the hippies and beatniks.

But affluent and refined communities may find the problem of neighborhood defense their own when they try to draw the line between those with respectable wealth and the parvenu or "shady rich." Their tactics may also become flagrant when a notorious but wealthy gangster must be excluded by harrassment and ostracism after attempts to buy him out have failed. As a rule, however, such communities use the quiet and expensive tactics of circulating homes by referral and selling their property to something less than the full pool of possible bidders. Additional burdens may require a clubhouse, participation in its affairs, the support of a private school, and the actual construction of a wall with guards and dogs. Defending oneself against those who have only money can be genteel, but it is expensive in both time and money.

Naturally there are areas in most cities which are left undefended and open to invasion by almost any sort of resident. The entrepôts of our large cities are a prime example. Properly speaking, however, it is not that the residents of such areas lack the impulse to defend their areas but that they lack the wherewithal to do so. They might better be called defeated neighborhoods than undefended ones. The defeated neighborhood is in some ways the reverse of that which is defended by a combine of political, administrative, and business interests. It is subject to insufficient or quixotic enforcement of building standards, zoning rules, police protection, and wide disparities in the delivery of all the available community services. Above all it is a community which citywide, regional, and federal agencies treat as an object without much fear of retaliation from a local constituency. Typically, then, the defeated community suffers from two sources of weakness in its defense. First, it is unable to participate fully in its own governance. Sometimes this is because it is so heavily populated by new residents, ex-felons, aliens, and transients that even the ballot box is not a significant avenue of influence.[9] At other times it is a community so heavily stigmatized and outcast that its residents retreat from most forms of public participation out of shame, mutual fear, and an absence of faith in each other's collective concern. Skid rows illustrate the former weakness of the residents, and some of our worst public housing projects illustrate the latter.[10]

A second source of weakness in the defenses of the defeated neighborhood is its choice as a site for businesses and industries which have powerful interests that are simply antithetical to the aims of any residential group. Some of these businesses are outright illegal, whereas others seek out special exemptions from civic standards: cheap bars, pick-up joints, day-labor offices, flophouses, polluting industries, unseemly restaurants, brothels, and hock shops. All these businesses have an interest in the corruptibility of city agencies and are apt to go into alliance to see that their interests rather than those of the local residents are served. Such powerful adversaries tend to cancel out the efforts of the residents, to drive out from among them those who might be outspoken adversaries, and generally to make the area available to residents who are powerless and outcast from other areas of the city. In such areas neighborhood defense tends to descend to mere violence, often that of young predators or that of individuals looking out solely for themselves.[11] Although this sort of pattern is most evident in skid rows, it can also become full-blown in some company towns where the powerful interests of the firm run counter to those of the residents. This was certainly true in many mining and lumbering communities where strikebreakers and other alien elements were drawn into the community in the interests of the firm and counter to the desires of the previous residents.[12] The company town has not, however, always found the firm unwilling to play a paternalistic role and to defend the community as it would defend itself.[13]

Boundary Selection

Most neighborhoods are intermediate among these various extremes, and most residents spend some time defending their own community while they also get some help from political, administrative, and private organizations. The clarity with which they can define their boundaries and defend them is always dependent on more than one consideration, and it is possible to identify some of the major ones. First, some communities have well-defined boundaries because all the adjacent communities disclaim their residents. These residential enclaves acquire an identity and a set of boundaries simply because they are left out of others. Although it may be unusual for an area to be disclaimed from all sides, this does point up the extent to which such a boundary line is the work of more than one spatial grouping; it does not simply well up out of the desires and sentiments of one group.

A second determinate of defended boundaries is the presence of conveniently available physical barriers. Railroad tracks, expressways, parks, and blocks of industry are real obstructions to casual foot traffic, and people are only reasonable in selecting them because they are plausible limits to heavy crosstraffic, especially that of pedestrians. Since the defended neighborhood grows partly out of fear for personal security, residents are only showing wisdom when they select barriers which give them some assurance of physical segregation. Thus, the presence of such boundaries may not create a community, but certainly people may select them as a reasonable starting point to help create one.

A closely allied candidate for neighborhood boundaries is the gradient of prices which are attached to residential land usage. These price gradients are a form of assurance about the peaceableness of the people one can expect to move into a neighborhood, and therefore they create additional plausible boundaries for people to select in starting to create a durable community. After all, social class or income is not merely a matter of snobbery or an arbitrary taste for a particular style of life. There is a very real sense in which social class and income do distinguish between people more or less prone to violence and physical abuse.[14] For whatever reasons, income is a reliable sign of a neighbor's tendency to have children who fight, resist school authorities, and meet in unsupervised settings. In addition, class conflict itself is a real possibility in a society which has difficulty in justifying its contemporary income differences. Thus, on either hand, the individual has reasons for avoiding socioeconomic groups poorer than his own. He also has reasons for seizing on some of the gradients in rental, land, and house prices as a boundary line behind which he will exert himself to see to it that land values are kept up and that not just anyone can live there. Happily, such cost gradients often coincide with a change in altitude, the location of natural attractions such as a river or lake, or some other physical obstruction or marker which renders them legible as well as effective.[15] But this is not always true, and I will return to this question shortly.

What seems to me by far the most effective and frequent barrier between residential groups is what we might call enacted boundary lines.[16] Enacted limits to a community are simply those imposed on the urban landscape as an arbitrary line marked off on a map by organizational proclamations. A vast number of our local urban communities are a historical debris left over from the previous proclamations of developers, planners, boosters, map makers, sociologists, newspapers, and businesses in search of a clientele. To a large extent these localized settlements have been brought into the urban mix by annexation and have persisted on the faithful grounds that extracommunity institutions would continue to warrant their security from invasion. No doubt many residents have been disappointed, but once started, such a previously incorporated area is a rallying cry around which residents can agree and press their claims to a set of boundaries which have presumed consensual support. And there are grounds for their faith, for the proclamation of community boundaries is supposed to represent popular demand as well as to enlist the aid of external organizations as allies on behalf of a natural group. Frequently this aid is enlisted, and both legal and political forces have been harnessed to serve the defensive interests of such communities long after their original residents have been replaced. As with cost gradients, physical obstructions, and residual areas, these boundaries seem reliable fixtures to seize on and to defend, whether it means going into collusion with the neighbors or seeking allies outside the community. In the absence of other boundaries which are self-enforcing, those endorsed by powerful groups and historical precedent are the best which can be chosen.

An interesting and now frequent example of enacted community boundaries is the suburban development, uniform in its placement within cost gradients, isolated from cross traffic, furnished with its own convenience shopping and business district, and named and bounded by the choices of a showman anxious to lure buyers susceptible to such labels as Enchanted Forest and Wilderness Lane.[17] These suburban creations represent a historic demarcation with which we and the residents must live for a long time. The temporal, architectural, and dimensional uniformity of such residential areas is apt to preserve them as distinct and legible entities which can lay claim to uniformity in their treatment and the homogeneity of their interests. At the outset, of course, such communities are protected by their developers, whose interests in defending the neighborhood are just good business. Chances are that the developer will preserve some interest in the area until first mortgages are paid off, written off, or renewed. Afterward the residents will probably expect a similar kind of paternalism which acknowledges their common past and will turn to public officials, politicians, and other allies to insure their invulnerability to widespread invasion. Most likely this will involve some effort, cohesion, and organization on the part of residents. But in the main, they will have to look for allies outside the suburban development to protect themselves, because the suburban development is usually so lacking in local institutions and individuals prominently known in the suburb that it must depend on the protective shield provided by the wider community. In this respect the defensive arrangements of an increasingly frequent type of residential group are likely to become a shifting balance between ism. As the corporate city continues to be a place of outmigration and expansion, the outmigrants will encroach on the nearby grass roots vigilantism and organizationally sponsored protection-suburbs and arouse administrative, legal, and vigilante efforts to ward off the invasion and protect what is regarded as an identity already agreed on and popularly supported. All of these attempts are likely to arouse the established residents to clarify their identities and to concert their opinions, attitudes, and definition of boundaries. This is simply an expansion to the outer limits of the city of the conflicts, competition, and process of succession which has been characteristic of the inner city as a result of urbanization and population growth. The suburb, unlike the inner city, often lacks many important institutions and administrative arrangement (for example, its own police department, water supply, higher educational institutions, museums, and so forth) which can help to exclude or control these invaders without arousing the residents themselves. Since the suburb adjacent to the city limits is so vulnerable, it may have to resort to a good deal of vigilantism especially now that restrictive covenants have been legally proscribed.

What all this seems to indicate is that residential groups do not have too few boundaries to defend but too many. This is one of the reasons there is often little consensus on community boundaries; the likely physical obstructions, cost gradients, and enacted enclosures do not coincide to give a single limit at which residents can be sure they are secure from encroachment. Thus some residents may pick a rail line to define their neighborhood, whereas others may settle on a definition which depends more on the expense of housing or authoritative mappings. This confusion is partially due to the independence of organizations outside the community which do not choose their own boundaries by consulting one another or the local community but simply draw lines on a map to suit their own requirements. This type of external gerrymandering is not just the habit of politicians but also that of business and public administration. Especially in the United States, we have no reliable prefectures but a frequently changing mosaic of administrative districts and client communities which seldom coincide.

These seeds of confusion, however, are not sown only by ignorant and inattentive outsiders. The residents must communicate about where they stand relative to other locality groups, and some residential groups lack even this primitive capacity to be sensitive to public images of themselves and the physical and economic walls and moats which surround them. In this sense it is possible to say that many communities do have a communication problem, and some residential areas are so fragmented that they cannot come to agreement on much of anything. Some of these residential areas are composed of transients who have no long-term stake in the local community: hucksters, students, drummers, assistant professors, and tourists. Others are warned away from one another by public stereotypes which forbid communication at the risk of total victimization: the disreputable poor, the psychotic, the notoriously perverted, and the physically damaged.[18] What is most noteworthy about these groups is not their internal fragmentation but the rarity of communities composed of them alone.[19] Most residential groups can at least take the risk of talking and planning with one another.

The Alliance on Behalf of Communities

Without external allies the local community and its defended boundaries are in a precarious position. Not only are such allies essential to its defense, but their opposition or realignment may be fatal to the neighborhood's sense of integrity and self-determination. In recent years there is reason to believe that it is the changing posture of these external allies rather than any marked decline in their own internal defensiveness and solidarity which has so panicked many communities. With the passage of federal and state open housing laws and the desegregation of some local schools, a number of community groups righteously felt themselves betrayed. The growing role of the federal government in constructing housing and in providing mortgage money threatened to be another blow to a long-term alliance in which the construction industry, real estate men, local government, and the federal authorities had implicitly endorsed the existing composition of local communities. In the main, this was a source of alarm to most white neighborhoods and to some affluent ethnic or black neighborhoods. When in addition, however, the federal government began a number of community programs administered directly from Washington or highly centralized agencies, somewhat the same fears were aroused in black or relatively poor areas. On the one hand, the discretionary authority of such federal agencies tended to be very far removed from the local community and relatively unavailable to local influence. On the other hand, the bureaucratic procedures of these programs represented a massive obstacle, especially to the poor and uneducated, when it came to manipulating the administrative machinery to get the kind of housing, police controls, public facilities, housing standards, and zoning regulations which would help defend their neighborhood.

The inability to manipulate massive bureaucratic organizations for collective ends made people, both affluent and poor, feel small, not the least because they were assured that specific procedures had been instituted for their participation. It was probably especially burdensome and embarrassing to poor blacks because their aspirations seemed so contradictory. They could support open housing for other communities, for example, but demanded local control for themselves. Such a contradiction, however, was not unique to them but is actually pervasive in the entire society. On the one hand, there is a strong historic commitment to uniform opportunities and standards of evaluation. On the other hand, there is an equally strong commitment to acknowledging differential achievement and allowing people to sort themselves out according to their accomplishments.[20] Insofar as communities differ in their opportunities, it is difficult to allow them to differ also on the basis of how they shape the opportunities of the residents. This is not to say that there is no way out of this contradiction, but in early 1970 it was clear that no obvious solution had been found. To a large extent people still thought that they could integrate the society by integrating its neighborhoods. And that was a strategy which not only threatened the defended community but left people alarmed for their safety and property. The law and order issue was basic to the defended neighborhood and, indeed, basic to the development of a community itself.

What was evident by 1970, however, was the fact that the strategies open to individuals and their own desires did not automatically make a community. In the past, a massive organizational alliance had gathered around the defended neighborhood in so quiet and crescive a way that the illusion of self-determination held fast. The weakening of that alliance has betrayed the dependency of the defended neighborhood and may open public discussion to a more explicit version of the defended neighborhood.

COMMUNITY IDENTITY

I have argued that the identities of local neighborhoods exist in tenuous opposition to one another and that relative rather than absolute differences give them their distinctive reputation. Obviously the main lines of differentiation are the dimensions of stratification which are pervasive to the entire society: race, ethnicity, income, education, and the like. Indeed most communities in the United States can be and are described in these terms. Ethnically and racially homogeneous neighborhoods are perhaps the most obvious examples, but far less distinctive neighborhoods find a marginal difference to emphasize and to distinguish between "us" and "them." The difficulty in establishing a neighborhood's identity, however, is not a shortage of relevant differences but a surplus of them. Even the small list given above shows that the problem is not a simple one and that almost any neighborhood is distinguished from others on more than one dimension. What I will do here is to map out what seem to be some of the governing conditions for the final determination of a local neighborhood's reputation.

Master Identities

Almost any local urban neighborhood is likely to be part of a larger sector of the wider community. Often these sectors are acknowledged by such banal labels as East Side, West Side, South Side, and so on. In any case, these are the largest acknowledged or named segments of the city, and often they are subdivided further before telescoping down to the local defended neighborhood. These broad divisions are often the creation of wide-scale public policies which assure investors and residents about the socioeconomic usage of land. Thus, in Chicago, it is fairly clear that the North Side will continue to be the major location for the city's most expensive housing and apartments. Builders, planners, investors, home buyers, and public officials have built up plans and investments to the point that this trend is almost irreversable. As a result, the basic contrast in the city's socioeconomic mapping is more or less foreclosed, and competition between these sectors ruled out as a real possibility. In Chicago it makes little sense for a South Side or West Side neighborhood to stress its affluence; it is sure to be overshadowed by some North Side Chicago neighborhood.[21] I suspect that similar patterns can be found in all sizable cities in the United States.

At the start, then, much of the importance of sheer affluence is drained off by this major contrast between urban sectors. Smaller and more local residential groups must contrast themselves within a smaller pool of communities on somewhat different criteria. For the local defended neighborhood there seem to be four prime considerations: how does it make its necessities virtues; who does it have to defend itself against; what are the competing residential areas; and what are its historic or achieved grounds for claiming a special place among other residential groups.

The broad sectorial socioeconomic divisions of the city create a special problem for those communities in sectors which fail to reach the highest rank. This is especially true for the most affluent among these communities, and they stand rather like wealthy individuals who continue to live in the once elegant homes they were brought up in and around old but less successful friends. For example, Hyde Park on the South Side of Chicago is a wealthy and well-educated community clustered around the University of Chicago. Yet the community does not emphasize its sheer wealth, for that would tend to bring it into comparison with much better off neighborhoods on the North Side. These North Side neighborhoods have the further advantage of belonging to good company: an entire sector in which wealth is concentrated and likely to become more concentrated. Thus, whatever their conception of their neighborhood, Hyde Parkers cannot choose sheer wealth as a reason for their living there; on these grounds alone they would have a clearer status definition if they moved to the North Side.

Accordingly, Hyde Parkers tend to make a virtue of what is in large part the necessity of their living on the South Side. One component of this self-description is a rejection of wealth alone as a criteria for residential selection and an emphasis on counter themes: sentimental loyalties, antisnobbism, and cosmopolitanism of race and income groups. A second component is a kind of noblesse oblige by which Hyde Parkers expend much of their energies on behalf of surrounding neighborhoods in protesting the validity of employing socioeconomic evaluations of worth. Students at the University of Chicago seem especially struck with this impulse and rail mightily against the restrictive covenants which preserve the difference between the North Side and South Side as well as those which defend Hyde Park to the extent that the students themselves are not frightened away by the incursion of poor, black, and resentful residents in adjacent neighborhoods.

There are probably many neighborhoods like Hyde Park which are enough different from the sector in which they are placed that they must make a virtue of a master identity which says one thing about them and a subordinate identity which says something to the contrary.[22] In this sense neighborhood identities are very much like those of individuals: They may be more or less crystallized.[23] Accordingly, some neighborhoods must look for an inobvious and alternative thematic dimension to emphasize in identifying themselves. Four basic starting points seem almost self-evident: the high income neighborhood in the highest income sector; the high income neighborhood in a lower income sector; the low income neighborhood in the highest income sector; and the low income neighborhood in a lower income sector. For the first, the basic strategy is simply holding on to what they have, since no basic contradiction is present. The high income neighborhood in a lower income sector is rather like Hyde Park: it must emphasize attachment to place and sentimental loyalties which transcend economic considerations. The low income neighborhood in a high income sector correspondingly may emphasize its respectability or poor but proud character in the hope of hanging on to at least the virtues implied by the high socioeconomic standing of its sector. The lower income neighborhood in a lower income sector is like its counterpart in the high income sector: it can take the implied vices of a low income sector and re-endorse them as extremes of a kind of virtue in toughness, a familiarity with sin, and the early loss of

innocence in life and politics. People in such neighborhoods can at least claim to know their way around and are likely to do so since they cannot claim a great deal more.

Competition among Neighborhoods

The content of a neighborhood's identity, however, is not likely to stop here, because these are mainly citywide contrasts which do not preempt all of an individual resident's attention. The defended neighborhood, in particular, is apt to have a large proportion of its attention captured by its differences from adjacent neighborhoods, especially those threatening it with invasion. It is a simple and mechanical fact that residential encroachment in the United States has proceeded largely in an unbroken and contiguous path, and generally it is lower status groups which have replaced higher status ones. These local movements are likely to make defended neighborhoods especially aware of their predominant ethnicity, race, or marginal economic standing. On the West Side of Chicago, for example, ethnicity is a primordial distinction of great importance simply because there is not much else by which to distinguish people. Often, however, these neighborhoods are not nearly so ethnically homogeneous as one would think from hearing them discussed. Relative concentrations of ethnic groups are nonetheless emphasized because they say something about the past, present, and future of a defended neighborhood. Frequently this meant that an area of heavy invasion by a low status ethnic group was referred to as belonging to that group although it currently made up only a minority of the population.[24] Correspondingly, adjacent areas which had suffered less invasion were still referred to as belonging to the higher status ethnic groups. These differences were often based on small numerical quantities, but they made an important distinction to local people because they indicated which area would "go first" and which ones were better defended.

If it is at this level that contrasts of ethnicity and race are emphasized, it is also here that other differences in pedigree and ascribed background are made relevant to neighborhood identity. For example, affluent communities may not especially compare themselves on the basis of income but rather on how that income was gained. Less affluent communities may emphasize equally the type of work their residents do rather than the income they derive from it. Thus some communities in South Chicago have so many residents working in the steel mills that steel is a way of life for the community as well as the work place.[25] Such a self-description seems not only to convey a distinction role of the community but to provide its residents with a sense of sharing in a special, even privileged, knowledge. The same sources of prideful exclusiveness may be present in neighborhoods which can claim an exceptional familiarity with the Mafia, Hollywood stars, political figures, and other famous and infamous people. The elements in community identity, like those of ethnicity and pedigree, become more or less relevant as they make a contrast or are threatened by change through invasion. The defended neighborhood marks itself off from adjacent ones and is most likely to emphasize those attributes it can lose; and sometimes this means deemphasizing those characteristics it shares with invaders or ignoring those which are distinctive of other residential groups that do not threaten it. Thus, some of our most elaborated community identities belong to areas which are considered very exclusive but are imperiled.

Contrasts and Competition among Neighborhoods

Except for the defeated community, all residential groups seem to make some claims for residential exclusiveness: not just anyone can live there. This sort of exclusiveness, however, is counterbalanced by the necessity of residential areas to recruit new residents and, in the modern American urban city, this means mostly residents from other communities. Thus every community has its competitors, although some are much more aware of them than others. In this country, these competitive claims are in the main farmed out to and by the realty and construction industry. The virtues and attractions of a particular community for outsiders, then, tend to fall into the hands of professional image makers. Indeed, practically every large city tends to have a city newspaper which devotes an entire Sunday section to the selling of residential images. Americans may dismiss these mercenary inspirations as only beguiling fictions. Nonetheless, prospective home buyers and renters purchase these news releases and, while they may read between the lines, they also find there a portrait or idealization of what they are seeking in the way of a family, a neighbor, and a community. Such images are not wholly fraudulent, and they are passed back to the residents as claims worth fulfilling if not entirely descriptive. "Levittown" and "New England Village" are not just merchandising labels, but really different places, and the rental and home buyers' market make them apt if not fully honest portraits. Moreover a stereotypic image presses each area into a particular league in which it vies with a special set of other communities. The rental and home buyer's market, then, projects for each residential area a selective fate, and it is out of this idealized fate that each must partially construct an identity.

In drawing on these current and exaggerated images, present-day communities are not doing something especially new or exceptional, because the mass media have recently intruded themselves into our lives so as to separate first-hand and second-hand knowledge.

The United States has always had its boosters, drummers, and exuberant land sellers in search of a naïve market. Some of the earliest settlers who came to the land literally expected the streets to be paved with gold and a fountain of youth to spout from every stream. People are less naïve today, and both European immigrants and native migrants exercise some caution in reading the publicist's claims. Nonetheless, many a community has incorporated into its identity the claims and exaggerations of boosters, and our ability to brush aside the superficiality of these images makes it easy for us to forget their origin.

Residential image making is a complicated task, but at least three of its features stand out. One is the convenience aspects of a residential area in terms of its facilities, nearness to transportation lines, and sufficiency as a place of shelter and familial activities. In describing these features, a publicist is restrained to be fairly accurate because he is talking about objective facts which can be checked by a stranger. A second is its promise to provide a particular style of life once the resident steps outside his doorway to commune with neighbors. Claims about the communal qualities of a residential area are more subject to manipulation simply because they cannot easily be verified without one's first residing in the area for a time. Oddly enough, it is here that physical appearances of a neighborhood become most important and persuasive. Shady trees, large lawns, aged homes, Cape Cod fronts, sheer modern facades, and cozy backyards evoke responses because they suggest more than themselves: distinctive ways of life which people feel they can share and in which they think they can express an authentic version of themselves.[26] A third feature is the local schools, or beliefs about their effectiveness and safety. The schools provide a special problem since there are a number of indices to their effectiveness, not all of which the realtor can control or exclusively represent. The tendency here may be to emphasize selectively the physical plant of the school, its pupil-teacher ratio, or some other fairly available datum. The poor performance of these indicators [27] may not retard their continued usage, simply because they are available and little else can be used to make so fateful a decision.

What the publicists must do is make communities commensurate with one another and develop archetypes which will strike a responsive chord in the minds of prospective buyers and renters. Beyond the problems of cost and convenience, what do people want in the way of a residential area? We are dealing with uncharted ground here and can only say that these images of community are likely to be drawn from a larger inventory of fantasies which appeal to the American people. No doubt one component revolves around the rural-urban dichotomy with bucolic, leisured, and equalitarian provincialism being juxtaposed against sophisticated, artistic, and selective cosmopolitanism. Another component is likely to revolve around historic claims between those areas which can associate themselves with a special legacy as against those which strike out for something which is new, avant-garde, and unconstrained by the past. About all that we can conclude with is that these advertised Edens come in antinomies with each pole finding its counterpart and its set of more or less numerous buyers and renters. For each community these archetypes represent an element to be taken into its identity unless it is so unpopular that it is not worth advertising.

Historic Claims to Fame

Aside from its comparative advantages or disadvantages, each community can also lay claim to a more or less rich historic legacy which is valued by some of its residents and incommensurate with the history of other communities. Logically it is possible for all communities to win at this game because it is like comparing apples and oranges. First, there is the new community which is unshackled by historic precedents, full of modern pioneers, and striving to find its sacred charter. People in older and more settled communities may label it crass, anomic, and "a nothing." Second, there is the community which has endured and endured without any notable accomplishments, outstanding individuals, or signal events. Their pride may have to rely on their persistent commonness, even though outsiders may express a different evaluation. Third are those communities which seek or claim a special history but end as parvenus because their assertions can be challenged as inauthentic. Finally, there are communities which do have a history and uniqueness to them which comes from a reverence for the past.

Communities of the last type are relatively scarce in the United States as compared to some areas of Europe, where local continuity has been preserved through the maintenance of special landmarks, institutions, and housing. Recency of settlement, rapid growth, and a widespread tendency to equate age with obsolescence have militated against the continued usage and restoration of local facilities in the United States. Thus, many communities have lost what could have been considered some of their most valued possessions: the homes of famous residents, public facilities belonging to the founding of the community, typical cases of an architectural period, and the scene of important events which could now make the community itself seem important. Perhaps these losses are to be expected in a nation which has grown so fast with an unplanned market economy to govern largely what is kept and what is torn down. But there is also a sense in which construction in the United States is un-

dertaken in the first place without much expectation that a building or place will endure past a couple of generations.[28] Partly this is due to a market economy in which buildings and places are meant to be competitive on utilitarian criteria alone. It is also due to a continually changing technology and the limited vision of buyers who assume that their own usage or profits and the buildings on which they depend need not endure past their own lifetimes. Thus, most American buildings last about the average adult lifetime before they are considered deteriorated.[29]

Nonetheless, communities in the United States vary in their historical impoverishment and their ability to lay claim to themselves as a cradle for important men, events, and accomplishments. The general tendency, of course, is to emphasize newness, freedom from the past, and the promise of a future in which youngsters will respect the material constructions of their elders. A few communities not only possess an inheritance from the past but hang on to it with a tenacity which is understandable considering its scarcity, vulnerability, and most of all, the capacity of such legacies to make people proud without always making them invidious. Like apples and oranges, they are incommensurate and some of the least prestigeful communities in the United States find in their preserved histories a way in which they can associate themselves with important happenings and persons who have done important things. Their pride is not meaningless, or at least no more so than one's pride in the accomplishments of his parents, friends, the circle he associates with, or the people he is seen with at the opera. Such a community has proof that it has the capacity to produce great and unique men, events, places, and buildings.

Obviously such historic legacies are not absolutely vital to people or communities. Indeed, most Americans live without such shared pride and emphasize their individual claims to fame. These historic earmarks have only the capacity to make all communities proud of themselves; they are not a functional requisite any more than is steak or ice cream. A few United States communities possess such riches and it is understandable that they make a great to-do about them in their identities.

THE COMMUNITY AS AN OBJECT OF ADMINISTRATION

The community is a perennial referent in the rhetoric of politicians, administrators, and sociologists. The politicians pay it eloquent tribute and say that they represent it. Administrators say they serve it. Some sociologists deny the veracity of the politicians and administrators and say only that the community is declining.[30] Is the local community declining and has it lost its raison d'être, or has it at least lost out in the power plays which have juxtaposed the state against the community? This is the central question which lumbers throughout most studies of the local community.[31] Before attempting to face the question head on, it is worthwhile to restate a couple of basic observations. First, total societies are not made up from a series of communities, but communities are units which come into being through their recognition by a wider society. Community, then, presumes some type of supracommunity level of organization. Second, the community is not a little society but a form of social differentiation within total societies, and the problem is how appropriate this type of social differentiation is in modern societies.

NATIONAL CENTRALIZATION

Throughout the literature on the community, the community has been juxtaposed against the state and mass society with the latter being seen as growing at the expense of the former. The community, then, joins a list of institutions or groups which have been seen as declining competitors of the state and mass society: the family, the small firm, regionalism, and so forth. An earlier forecast of the family's disappearance and its replacement by the state, however, has turned out to be quite erroneous. One wonders if somewhat the same mistake is being made in studies of the community. Undoubtedly the community has been losing functions just as the family lost functions in the transformation from a rural to an urban society. Also there is a general increase in people's dependency on national levels of organization and their tendency to appeal to those organizations. Certainly the power of the state is very great as compared to that of the local community, and the limited liability of the resident does not tie him closely to the local residential group. Nonetheless, this may not mean the complete disappearance of the local community, and there are other, more interesting questions to ask about it.

First, there is the question of whether or not this zero-sum formulation in the relationship between the state and the local community is at all appropriate. Are, for example, Stockholm and its new suburbs like Farsta and Välingby less powerful and distinct because the Swedish prime minister appoints the city's mayor and the new suburbs have been totally planned and built by the central state? In fact, the direct relationship between the mayor and prime minister may establish a line of administrative authority in which power and responsibility can be joined.[32] One of the sources of community weakness in most American cities is that many mayors are responsible to local communities but have little direct recourse to the federal levels at which major power and resources are located. More direct administrative relationships between local and national levels of organization may give local residents and their representatives a louder, not a smaller, voice in determining the services which come to them. Similarly, the centralized planning and development of local communities may not be destructive of their identity and distinctiveness. On this point the Swedes provide another instructive example: most of the new, centrally planned and built suburban developments of Stockholm are surrounded by a high cyclone-wire fence topped with barbed wire and broken at only two or three main entrances. The intent seems not to have been the creation of a defended neighborhood but the recognition of a right to collective privacy on the part of residential groups. In the United States it would be hard to justify such collective rights, since they would more often coincide with racial, ethnic, and income differences. For this same reason it has been difficult to justify any public policy which responds to the collective ends of residential groups. Yet the principle of shared usage and its importance to residential groups need not be discarded on these grounds alone.

The example of Sweden here is telling, for there are few more centralized societies with a more consolidated administrative structure. But their local communities seem extremely well served and by reputation very demanding.[33] This does not mean that Swedish communities are extremely provincial and that they are characterized by high levels of neighboring.[34] This seems to be neither expected nor achieved. But the Swedish local community is well served, and the line of authority and power which is responsible for serving it is extremely clear and consolidated.

By contrast, most attempts to preserve the local community or its autonomy in the United States have been founded on the idea of decentralization and the separation of powers. Thus, local representatives, city officials, state of-

ficials, and federal officeholders tend not to have any direct lines of authority among them. The result is often a stalemate with each level of authority disclaiming either responsibility or the power to do anything. Alternatively, the services extended to communities have been extremely inequitable and have depended very much on informal and quasi-legitimate political influence. One wonders if in the United States the state is antithetical to the influence of local groups of if the different levels of government are simply so incoherent and poorly defined that regular channels of influence cannot be found, especially when collective ends are being sought.

A second line of support for the argument that the local community is losing significance in modern societies is that nationally based criteria of social differentiation are coming to overshadow local ones. Thus, nationally defined groups and associations are the primary sources of individual participation and avenues of power and influence. Although this may be especially true for the United States, it again could be due largely to the ineffectiveness of local government in reaching the federal levels of authority where power and responsibility can be rejoined. Within an administrative structure where local and federal authority were closely linked, the local organization might be a more effective vehicle for insuring the rights and demands of people. After all, nationally based organizations, such as labor unions, welfare rights organizations, lobbies, and what not, have only a limited effectiveness themselves, and the results are often so inequitable that they arouse constant claims of injustice which weaken governmental claims to legitimacy.[35] Interest group politics works only for some of the people some of the time. It is quite possible that a cross-cutting form of organization like the local community will produce units which are comparable to one another and which can include everyone so as to promote greater equity and help maintain the legitimacy of government. Certainly not all governmental services can be distributed in this manner, but a vast number of them are: policing, secondary education, sanitation, and so on. Since the legitimacy of government is not an insignificant functional requirement, the use of the local community as an interest group may give it greater strategic importance than is commonly associated with it.

The view of the local community being replaced by nationally based lines of social differentiation, however, contains in it a distorted perspective of what the local community is like in the first place. The local urban residential community seems always to have been based on national lines of differentiation. Race, ethnicity, and socioeconomic differences are at the heart of the residential patterns giving rise to the local community and national organizations. The local rural community may have been more heterogeneous, but that does not mean that humble people living on plantations, farm communities, and industrial farms had a greater voice in determining their own affairs. Economic differentiation in such areas was only more likely to concentrate power in the hands of a small group of local elites who were manipulative to the point that they bought off dissent by charity sweetened with interpersonal familiarity.[36] The entire southeastern portion of the United States is a persistent reminder of this type of localism, and it is hardly a region where everyone has a voice which can be heard in his community.[37] Local groups with a broad constituency are probably more effective in Chicago than they are in any of the remote and unchallenged towns of the South.[38]

A more productive outlook may be to emphasize the way in which some national bases of differentiation are shifting in emphasis while socioeconomic criteria are becoming more elaborated. Race and ethnicity have been long-time criteria of social differentiation, but they are losing some of their relative emphasis as the federal government and some large businesses and higher educational institutions give them lower priority. This movement is slight and often it is only a token move toward erasing racial and ethnic criteria for the distribution of housing, education, police protection, occupational promotion, and so on. Nonetheless it is enough to panic many local residential groups and especially local elites whose monopoly on patronage and low level public offices is threatened. They are one source of the outcry against the government and centralization. Others are the relatively poor people and blacks who, although they have been encouraged enough to be outspoken, still find the division of powers in the United States government so great that some of them would prefer a transfer of power back to local authorities. Thus they could at least have their own patronage and minor elective offices, which is somewhat more than they can obtain in the present confusion or inadequacy of state, federal, local, and regional governments. More affluent and powerful Americans have settled for this before, and there is no reason to think that the blacks and poor have a more ambitious model.

With the decline of importance of racial and ethnic differentiation at the national level, socioeconomic criteria of occupation and education may be acquiring more significance and becoming more elaborated. But the growth of specialities, the number of people attending college, and the proliferation of tastes in a more cosmopolitan society may also bring about a finer partitioning of socioeconomic and age groups. Something like this is already evident in the growth of communes, centers of concentration for "street people," swinging sections for the young unmarrieds, retirement villages, bohemias around universities, and suburbs with a vast proportion of their residents in the process of family formation. The heavily serviced high-rise apartment house complex, the planned community with extensive recreational facilities, and the urban development fit distinct styles of life which belong predominantly to certain age and occupational groups. No doubt such groups will become progressively segregated into residential areas where they can retain an unchallenged version of their beliefs, values, and personal presentation. The problem of American communities, then, is to adapt to these more elaborated socioeconomic and age-graded bases of differentiation while relenting on the matter of race and ethnicity.

This does not mean that such local socioeconomic or age-graded communities will be formed everywhere. The United States is a large and extremely varied country. As change overtakes portions of it, other sections remain relatively stable or relocate. Thus, while new communities based on socioeconomic and age criteria are developing, immigrant communities, black belts, and very heterogeneous residential groups will remain in existence in numerous places. In addition, other communities may develop a sort of quasi-ethnic style of life which a large number of people adopt temporarily from local or historic ethnic traditions. Such communities are already partially developed in some places where a minority ethnic group provides a range of food customs, special vocabulary, and a set of tastes about furniture, clothing, and so on. Some middle class Jewish and Italian neighborhoods are Jewish or Italian only in practice; the majority of their inhabitants are neither Jewish nor Italian but simply try out a style of life which fits them into a dominant way of life. Here ethnicity has little political or economic importance but is mainly a common expressive order in which people find a sense of unity and sureness.

No doubt there will also remain areas which are atomized to the point that they have practically no identity or consensus on their boundaries and reputation. This absence of community is not only a psychic loss to most residents; it has broader functional consequences. The local community has the advantage that everyone can be a member and that it places people in relatively comparable bargaining units. Unlike labor unions, professional associations, and business councils, the constituency of the local community includes everyone and allows us to make comparisons about the equity of services, wages, building programs, and their delivery. The difficulty with interest group politics as they are presently practiced among powerful associations is that they lead to broad inequities or the appearance of inequity without any commensurate basis for settling the question.[39] This results in serious limits on the legitimacy of public institutions, government, and private businesses. Interest group politics may be able to produce equity, but it is as impossible to tell when it does as it is impossible to tell if the oil depletion allowances and ADC programs are fair redistributions of wealth. Since it is impossible to create even the illusion of equity, interest group politics seems inevitably to lay government and business open to claims of favoritism and corruption. By comparison, the local community can serve as a more inclusive reference unit for evaluating the distributive justice of our society.

THE COMMUNITY AS COMMUNION

So far I have taken a narrow view of the local urban community by regarding it as the defended neighborhood which segregates people to avoid danger, insult, and the impairment of status claims. This is, I think, a sufficient basis for explaining community differentiation, but it is not all that communities are or become. Part of my emphasis has been a reaction to the overromanticization of the local community and the tendency to make sentiments and sentimentalism so basic to it that the community could later be dismissed as only an expressive solidarity without instrumental functions. But, like all other institutions, the local community attracts to itself additional hopes for the expression of self and sentiment. The desire to find a social setting in which one can give rein to an authentic version of oneself and see other people as they really are is not some unanalyzable human need but the most fundamental way in which people are reassured of their own reality as well as that of other people.[40] A Goffmanesque world in which people do only what is situationally suitable is ultimately a frightening world, where hypocrisy and insincerity undermine any long-term plans and the people behave as chameleons once backs are turned.[41] Every society rides on the faith that some of the people some of the time really mean what they say and do. The organization man, the other-oriented individual, and a society of labels are insufficient images if people are to trust one another long enough to get through a single day. Presentations of self, then, are not mere ways of letting off steam: they are essential expressive interludes when group members reestablish each other's confidence in the coincidence between subjective and objective realities.

Within this context the local community stands out as a symbol in people's hopes for a collectivity in which they can be rather than seem.[42] Indeed this seems to be a predominant contemporary use of the symbolism of the community and the constant attempts to make other institutions into communities by labeling them as such (the community of scholars, and so forth). Among Americans this quest for community reaches almost pathetic proportions, with people falling victim to the most romantic advertisements for homes which attempt to give an imitation of a bygone age with Tudor cottages, Cape Cod fronts, and plantation porticoes attached to modest bungalows. The search for tree-lined streets, for a small community, and for a quiet place to live are in part a search for collectivities which at least have the earmarks of a place for the authentic moral expression of self. There is a certain irony in this symbolism because the original meaning which Tönnies gave community or *Gemeinschaft* emphasized its ascriptive character and independence of sentiments except as people adapted to necessity. This meaning lingers in sociology, and the freedom of people to move and be indifferent to their residential group seems almost antithetical to the traditional local community.[43] Indeed, community seems to have undergone a transformation in the minds of Americans, and what people see in it is not Tönnies's community but Schmalenbach's communion. The community is a place to share feelings and expose one's tender inner core. The freedom of people (or at least some people) to choose where they live is an essential ingredient to this meaning of the local community. Communion rests on its voluntariness, and as Schmalenbach pointed out, it was antithetical to the traditional community which coerced membership and loyalty.[44] With the loss of the ascribed local community, the entire concept is transformed into a sort of social movement for relations which are intimate enough to be self-revealing.

Although this is a growing symbolic representation of the local community, I suspect that it is poorly realized in most actual communities. To a large extent

Americans still live where they have to and, in any case, have to move so often that the community of limited liability is the most prevalent form. The coerciveness of the work place and other institutions not only creates a yearning for community but makes it difficult to realize in the residential community. Thus people seek for alternatives in other institutions: the student community, the political community, the business community, and so on. The extent to which these other institutions can offer either communion or community is limited by their institutional dependencies. They cannot be fully liberated and continue to function. The focus of the desire for community, then, will probably continue to return to the local residential community, and if people seem shallow and inauthentic elsewhere, the pressure for a community of sentiment may increase.

Whatever the condition of our residential communities, then, they are likely to have their avid defenders. They will be over-romanticized in both symbol and word. They may even be passed off as a primal and unchallengeable urge for territoriality. As Nisbet points out, the quest for community can reach absurd proportions to the point that it is self-defeating.[45] The totalistic national community is one direction in which this quest can go. Totalitarianism, however, seems rather unlikely in the United States. There are so many safeguards against centralization that government may become inaccessible while still lacking decisive power of its own. Moreover, the symbols of national communalism seem never to have been widely developed in the country. The notion of the nation as a single family, as a great unity of purpose, and as a geist shared by the masses has never had much credence in this country. The American Creed remains a small businessman's creed, and it is unable to provoke people to such "noble" and self-sacrificing utopias as the undivided, totalitarian state.[46] The

central government in the United States may get *out of* control, but it is doubtful that it will get *in* control. We can have unpopular wars, depressions, international crises, a bad balance of payments, urban riots, income level which are felt to be totally unjust, and almost total mismanagement of public life. But I doubt the United States has even the managerial skills, much less the symbolism, to run an authentic totalitarian government. In the United States "the community" is likely to remain the local residential community although the height of people's expectations for it may change.

A more likely consequence of the quest for a community of sentiment —one where everyone can be his true moral self—is that the utopian images evoked tend to make insignificant any actual communities that have existed. The community, then, is defended according to what it might become rather than for what it is or has been. Such utopias are a powerful lure tempting us to reconstruct history and dismiss the present. In the hands of some defenders of the local community, these utopian images may promote a tactic of legal protectionism which has a well-worn precedent in the United States. The use of legal proscriptions to protect the rights of certain groups and the use of the courts to enforce them are favored practices in the United States with its weak administrative bodies. When, however, this type of protectionism is extended to the local community, the restrictive covenants that have been informally practiced in the past are passed into law. Such a procedure is unlikely to preserve existing communities and would make it difficult for them to adjust to what is one of their major problems today: re-sorting their membership to coincide with a changing system of stratification in which race and ethnicity are of less importance than they once were. Yet some of those who call for local control seem to fail to see this and try to preserve local groups as if their membership could be defined as a permanent legal category. The new territorialists carry this image of the local community to the point that it becomes an insurmountable obstacle to broader social collectivities.

In the context of this excessive vision of the local community, it is important to keep in mind the limited role of the local community. The local community can share some of the burden of making available to people the opportunity for communion, but this is a burden widely distributed in any society. It also has the potential to serve as a consolidated, all-purpose, administrative unit which could go far toward rejoining power and responsibility between the various levels of government and their constituencies. As a localized group of people whose placement in a national or local system of stratification warrants mutual trustworthiness, the local community can also give people a sense of security and ease. The local residential group can also be a collective identity, drawing the proofs of its members' pride from the past or the future. I suspect, however, that it is troublesome if not impossible to freeze the local residential group into its present form as dictated by contemporary restrictive residential selection. The local community must remain a partially open institution, and its rights cannot be insured as are those of racial and ethnic groups where membership is fixed and persistent. As a part or the whole of an administrative unit, the local residential community can survive, perhaps even thrive. By acknowledging its limitations, we might be able to use it for what it is: first, as a reflection of our changing system of social stratification so that strangers who are neighbors can trust one another, and second, as a small world within which people who are generally distrusted can find trust on more provincial grounds.

NOTES

1. G. D. Suttles, *The Social Order of the Slum* (Chicago: University of Chicago Press, 1968), pp. 35–38.
2. For further discussion of this type of mute impression management among coresidents see G. D. Suttles, "Deviant Behavior as an Unanticipated Consequence of Public Housing," in D. Glaser (ed.), *Crime in the City* (New York: Harper & Row, 1970), pp. 162–76.
3. M. Janowitz, *The Community Press in an Urban Setting: The Social Elements of Urbanism*, 2nd ed. (Chicago: University of Chicago Press, 1967).
4. E. D. Baltzell, *Philadelphia Gentlemen* (New York: The Free Press of Glencoe, 1958), pp. 173–222; and L. Rainwater, *Behind Ghetto Walls* (Chicago: Aldine Press, 1970). Both works show how the top and the bottom of a stratification system may have limited choices in their residences, although for different reasons.
5. The reader might note that these two strategies can be combined to produce a two-fold table or "property-space." I have mercifully abstained from this, not because such a table would add little which is new to the discussion, but because it would add too much. Such individual strategies do not produce communities because they need not be uniformly followed within any particular area. For this type of uniformity to prevail, a host of other institutional conditions must be present in the community as well as outside it. I intend to get to these institutional conditions, and in the two preceding paragraphs my only purpose was to show that these strategies and their combination form the first step which works hand-in-hand with further processes of community differentiation.
6. L. Rainwater, *Behind Ghetto Walls*.
7. L. Schnore, *The Urban Scene* (New York: The Free Press of Glencoe, 1965), pp. 137–252, 330–43.
8. For an evaluation of how fully federal guidelines affect areas receiving federal funds, see D. Nelson, "Black Reform and Federal Resources (Ph.D. diss., University of Chicago, in preparation).
9. Claude Brown has pointed out that so many males in Harlem are ex-felons that they are practically a disenfranchised group in the city (*Manchild in the Promised Land* [New York: Macmillan, 1965]).
10. L. Rainwater, *Behind Ghetto Walls*.
11. C. Shaw, *The Jack Roller* (Chicago: University of Chicago Press, 1966) includes descriptions of such "victim prone" areas.
12. J. K. Moreland, *The Millways of Kent* (New Haven: College and University Press, 1965).
13. W. Manchester, *The Arms of Krupp* (Boston: Little, Brown and Co., 1968) describes a large-scale example in the Krupp's paternalistic treatment of the workers in Essen.
14. R. Dahrendorf, "On the Origin of Inequality among Men," *Essays in the Theory of Society* (Stanford: Stanford University Press, 1968), pp. 151–78.
15. K. Lynch, *The Image of the City* (Cambridge, Mass.: M.I.T. Press, 1960).
16. Here the term *enacted* follows the meaning given it by William Graham Sumner, *Folkways* (New York: Dover, 1959).

17. For a brief description of how these stereotypes fit into residential planning and marketing see H. Gans, *The Levittowners* (New York: Pantheon,1967), pp. v–viii, 3–19.

18. That is, outcast groups such as those pointed to by E. Goffman, *Stigma* (Englewood Cliffs, N.J.: Prentice-Hall, 1963).

19. See R. B. Edgerton, *The Cloak of Competence* (Berkeley and Los Angeles: University of California Press, 1967) for information on one such group that seldom makes up a residential group.

20. J. Coleman, "The Concept of Equality of Educational Opportunity," *Harvard Educational Review* 38 (Winter, 1968): 7–22.

21. This situation is reversed for Chicago blacks who draw their main contrast between the poorer West Side black community and the better-off black neighborhoods on the city's South Side.

22. E. C. Hughes, "Dilemmas and Contradictions of Status," *American Journal of Sociology* 50 (March, 1945): 353–59.

23. I mean to use the term here without extending the analogy to G. Lenski's theory of political extremism in "Status Crystalization: A Non-Vertical Dimension of Social Status,"*American Sociological Review* 19 (August, 1954): 405–13.

24. H. W. Zorbaugh, *The Gold Coast and the Slum* (Chicago: University of Chicago Press, 1929).

25. See a forthcoming Ph.D. dissertation by W. Kornblum, "The Integration of Ethnic Groups in Modern Society: Serbian and Croatian Ethnicity in Southeast Chicago" (University of Chicago).

26. For further discussion of the conditions for presenting an authentic self see G. D. Suttles, "Friendship as a Social Institution," in George McCall (ed.), *Social Relationships* (Chicago: Aldine Press, 1970), pp. 95–135.

27. M. Janowitz, *Institution Building in Urban Education* (New York: Russell Sage Foundation, 1969), pp. 1–34.

28. T. Lowie, *The End of Liberalism* (New York: W. W. Norton and Co., 1969), pp. 101–88.

29. The President's Committee on Urban Housing, *A Decent Home* (Washington, D.C.: Government Printing Office, 1969), pp. 7–36, 39–50.

30. M. R. Stein, *The Eclipse of Community* (New York: Harper & Row, 1960).

31. For a general overview of the question see R. A. Nisbet, *Community and Power* (New York: Oxford University Press, 1962), pp. 75–97.

32. M. Gordon, *Sick Cities* (Baltimore: Penguin, 1965), pp. 331–65; T. Lowie, *The End of Liberalism*, pp. 193–206; and National Resources Committee, "The Problems of Urban America," *Our Cities: Their Role in the National Economy* (Washington, D.C.: Government Printing Office, 1937), pp. 55–70.

33. City planners, in other, less centralized Scandinavian countries tend to report that the Swedes are "too demanding." City planners in both Norway and Denmark have told me that they intended to put fewer convenience facilities into new communities than would have been necessary in Sweden.

34. K. Aström, *City Planning in Sweden* (Stockholm: The Swedish Institute, n.d.).

35. T. Lowie, *The End of Liberalism*, pp. 191–213.

36. L. Pope, *Millhands and Preachers* (New Haven: Yale University Press, 1942).

37. J. Dollard, *Caste and Class in a Southern Town* (New Haven: Yale University Press, 1937); and M. Rubin, *Plantation County* (New Haven: College and University Press, 1963).

38. Compare the reports of P. H. Rossi and R. H. Dentler, *The Politics of Urban Renewal* (New York: The Free Press of Glencoe, 1961) with those of T. Lowie, *The End of Liberalism*, pp. 252–66.

39. T. Lowie,*The End of Liberalism*.

40. G. D. Suttles, "Friendship as a Social Institution," pp. 116–20.

41. One of the bases of the broad distaste expressed for the "other directed" individual may be this fear of a social world which is uncertain because the people in it are themselves uncertain. See D. Reisman, *Individualism Reconsidered* (Garden City, N.Y.: Doubleday and Co., 1955).

42. We are not speaking here of the opportunity to be merely spontaneous and licentious, for what people may feel most authentic in their expressions of self are moral convictions and statements of worth.

43. N. E. Long, "Political Science and the City," in L. Schnore and H. Fagin (eds.), *Urban Research and Policy Planning* (Beverly Hills: Sage Publications, 1967), pp. 243–62.

44. H. Schmalenbach, "The Sociological Category of Communion," in Parsons et al., (eds.), *Theories of Society* (New York: The Free Press of Glencoe, 1961), pp. 331–47.

45. R. A. Nisbet, *Community and Power*.

46. F. X. Sutton et al., *The American Business Creed* (New York: Schocken Books, 1962).

A PLANNING PERSPECTIVE

AN APPROACH TO
METROPOLITAN SPATIAL STRUCTURE
DONALD L. FOLEY

Foley's paper departs from the preceding selections by turning our attention directly to normative decision making at the urban scale. It is a seminal statement which gets to the heart of the important issues: the nature of the spatial and aspatial aspects of urban society, the functional organization of people and their activities, and the role of values and institutions in the development of planning solutions. Though detailed analysis of case studies are omitted, the flavor of the complexities of the specific problems comes through strongly; the subsequent essay by Haar will add further substance to Foley's argument.

Reprinted from Melvin Webber et al., eds., *Explorations into Urban Structure* (Philadelphia: University of Pennsylvania Press, 1964), pp. 21–78, by permission of the publisher and the author. This is an edited version of the original publication. Notes have been renumbered.

For those studying metropolitan communities or planning for the future of these communities, the ability to communicate about the object of their concern is clearly of fundamental importance. There is evident need for a common conceptual framework and a common language for exchanging ideas and proposals.

This essay suggests the rudiments of a possible framework. Much of what we have utilized in this effort has been suggested before. But we think that this approach highlights certain questions and suggests modes of attacking these questions which may enhance our capacity to deal with and understand the spatial structure of metropolitan communities. We do not imply that the approach will satisfactorily deal with questions of a different order; some problems in this respect will be discussed in a subsequent section. The proposed framework may help to prevent certain misunderstandings or incomplete perspectives which otherwise might continue to plague us. Perhaps others will be stimulated to suggest further alternative approaches or modifications.

Our initial commitment was to explore what is meant by the "spatial structure" of metropolitan areas. Also, because of a direct interest in metropolitan planning, we started with a commitment to stress the physical environment of the metropolitan area. But it early became clear that the spatial arrangement of the metropolitan community as expressed through its physical form is by no means a closed system. This therefore led us to examine spatial structure within a broader setting.

"Metropolitan structure" thus became a more generic conceptual framework within which to view "metropolitan spatial structure." We broadened the framework to include aspatial views; a major sector deals with the functional organization of the community and another with cultural or value features of community life. This provides a framework sufficiently broad so that several categories of propositions serving to interrelate these sectors can be meaningfully encompassed.

The resulting framework reflects our

effort to deal with a pair of questions: First, how is it possible to build a satisfactory conceptual bridge between the concern for *spatial* arrangement that underlies metropolitan planning and the essentially *aspatial* approaches to metropolitan and urban community organization taken by so much of social science and social philosophy? When metropolitan planners state that they seek to guide physical development, it is clear that it is the spatial organization of the metropolitan community that looms very large in their minds. Any general plan or master plan for a metropolitan area is in effect a policy statement as to how that area should be spatially arranged. But scholars of urban life who deal with urbanization and urban values tend to view the community in rather different and characteristically aspatial terms, conceived without direct regard for spatial arrangement.

Second, how is it possible to relate values and the physical environmental aspects of the metropolitan community? This is a pivotal question for metropolitan planning. Values tend to be general and amorphous and to defy ready translation into physical environmental terms. And yet the metropolitan planner legitimately asks how he may know whether the physical environmental scheme he is proposing facilitates or impedes the achievement of stated values. In all of this, values prove to be very elusive. They are difficult to pin down empirically. The planner needs a far more tangible set of requirements to be satisfied, which reflect the fundamental values that are agreed upon or taken for granted.

THE NATURE OF THE FRAMEWORK

A Diagrammatic Introduction

A conceptual framework that seeks to bridge these two kinds of gaps—between the aspatial and the spatial, and between values and the physical environment—is shown as Figure 1. While we intend the diagram to be reasonably self-explanatory, it may be helpful to identify the main points dealt with by the framework.

The distinction between "aspatial" (column *A*) and "spatial" (column *B*) is a particularly important one for our purposes. Mainly, "spatial" refers to a direct concern for spatial pattern, i.e., for the pattern in which culture, activities, people, and physical objects are distributed in space. Conversely, "aspatial" refers to a lack of such concern for spatial pattern. This is not so much a deliberate choice to overlook spatial pattern as a positive focus on the characteristics and interrelationships of selected phenomena viewed within other frames of reference. For example, political scientists are far more concerned with governmental organization, with the personalities of key leaders, and with institutional relations between government and the rest of society than they are with the spatial patterns, as such, in which governmental or political activities occur. Similarly, economists focus on the economy as an entity and study its changing characteristics with little concern for regional or other spatial patterns within this institutional whole.

"Spatial" also tends to suggest a concern for spatial pattern at a designated scale. Thus we might differentiate an architectural scale with which an architect is most concerned, or an urban scale, or, as in this essay, a metropolitan-wide scale. Hence, for our purposes at least, "aspatial" includes not only those conceptions that overlook spatial pattern of any sort but also those conceptions that focus on a spatial pattern at a different scale from that designated as primary. One may think, for example, of the spatial layout of a house and its yard, but at a scale so fine that it drops through our screen set up to sift out all but metropolitan-spatial considerations.

Introduced as a separate and cross-

	A Aspatial* Aspects	B Spatial* Aspects
1 Normative or Cultural Aspects	**1A** Social values; culture patterns; norms; institutional setting; technology	**1B** Spatial distribution of culture patterns and norms; values and norms directly concerned with the qualities and determination of the spatial patterns of activities, population, and the physical environment
2 Functional Organizational Aspects	**2A** Division and allocation of functions; functional interdependence; activity systems and subsystems, including persons and establishments in their functional-role sense	**2B** Spatial distribution of functions and activities; linkages (functional relations spatially conceived); spatial pattern of establishments, by functional type
3 Physical Aspects	**3A** Physical objects: the geophysical environment, man-developed material improvements, people as physical bodies; qualities of these objects	**3B** Spatial distribution of physical objects; the resulting spatial pattern formed by this distribution of land forms, buildings, roads, people, etc.; distribution in space of varying qualities of physical objects

FIGURE 1. Selected Aspects of Metropolitan Structure: A Conceptual View

* We mean by "aspatial" no direct concern for spatial pattern (at whatever scale is being focused upon—in our case, metropolitan scale). Correspondingly, "spatial" means a direct concern for spatial pattern at the scale under consideration. (See also text discussion.)

cutting classification is the distinction among the three levels or aspects, shown as *1,2*, and *3* in the diagram. Within the first level, "normative or cultural aspects," we include the culture and the rules by which men live and the processes by which consensus is sought and achieved. This normative structure provides the social unity that comes from shared understandings. As anthropologists and sociologists stress, the cultural component includes many tacit and assumed understandings. The very conceptualization of what are treated as general values involves relatively high-level abstraction. The normative aspect of urban life, in sum, includes both the formulation of goals and the designation and enforcement of approved means for seeking these goals.

By "functional organizational aspects" of metropolitan structure (the second level) we mean the structure by which diverse functions are allocated and integrated within a community or among communities. Functional organization, in contrast to culture and norms, tends to focus on the complementarity of different functions and roles and to deal more directly with ongoing activities and interacting people. This sector of the diagram is thus conceived as including activities and, hence, activity systems and subsystems. Thus we include production and distribution systems, systems by which public services are provided, etc., and also include the component roles and establishments which comprise functional units within these systems.

The "physical" aspects of metropolitan structure (the third level) embraces the geophysical base for community life; the man-built modifications of this base, including buildings, streets, and major facilities; and people as physical objects occupying space, requiring transportation, etc. The physical environment may be thought of as embracing those permanent or semipermanent structures that house or channel activities and movement within the metropolis.

Supplementing what the diagram shows, we assume for our purposes that the typical approach to the normative aspect of community life is essentially aspatial (i.e., that it mainly deals with values and norms without being directly concerned with spatial arrangements). For example, students of the city may seek to isolate those main values that residents see in the city when migrating there. But the identification of these values is not likely to provide direct clues to the city's spatial pattern. A high value on consumer goods may encourage certain kinds of manufacture and retail trade, but will give little indication as to whether factories and stores will be concentrated or dispersed within the urban area. On the other hand, a stress on home ownership, by its implicit emphasis on low-density development, may suggest a rather dispersed urban pattern. In the context of our framework, we have placed the normative aspects of community structure essentially in cell 1A.

Cell 1B, by contrast, encompasses two variants: the spatial pattern by which cultural traits are distributed and those somewhat special values and norms that bear directly on the character of the spatial patterns of communities, with their populations, their activities, and their physical bases. Geographers, urban sociologists, and land economists, for example, share interests in the former. Included are the ecological studies of the spatial distribution of the living patterns of various subcultures, either ethnic groups or social classes. One can distinguish what the anthropologist has termed culture areas (or subareas). The

study of values dealing with spatial patterns is the province of certain branches of aesthetics and a phase of what we may term the culture of cities.

We consider the physical environment to be space-consuming and space-defining, and hence as encompassed mainly by cell 3B of the diagram. The physical environment provides a permanent or semipermanent spatial pattern that is easily described in map or plan form. (That residents and visitors must carry some image of this spatial pattern in order to orient themselves and to move around readily is germane, but shades well into Cell 1B, insofar as normative as well as perceptive reactions are involved.) The very permanence of most of the physical environment promotes a stability of pattern and, indeed, a sense of tradition and of symbolism adhering to the pattern.

We treat cell 3A as of minor importance for purposes of our analysis. Within this conceptual category we posit those aspects of the physical environment that describe the physical objects in the metropolitan environment but which do not define or depict that environment's spatial pattern. For example, we can contrast the respective physical compositions of a Nevada city and a New England city, citing climate, trees and plant life, soil conditions, building materials and styles, housing quality, physical appearance of residents, etc.— but short of a direct concern for the respective spatial patterns of these two cities. Within this cell we include such characteristics as texture and color, and those qualities which provide symbolic clues to the meaning or use of structures and land coverage (e.g., clues to whether a building is used for governmental, religious, recreational or residential purposes, or whether land is used for agriculture or for processing).

A main feature of the resulting framework is the pivotal place of functional organization in mediating the relationship between the norms and values that we share and physical environmental planning (i.e., between top and bottom in the diagram), and in providing a particularly strategic point to analyze the transition between aspatial and spatial (i.e., from right to left, or left to right).

In particular, the conceptual framework allows us to examine the major conceptual gap between cell *1A* and cell *3B* of the diagram. Our challenge is to bridge this diagonal gap. The main S-shaped line of reasoning to which we move and upon which we place heavy emphasis for certain analytic purposes will be discussed below. (Figure 2a will also show this.)

We shall now discuss possible analytic chains of reasoning which our framework (as summarized by the diagram in Figure 1) suggests.

The Main Relationships

While alternative emphases on relationships will be suggested below and are shown as Figures 2b, 2c, and 2d, the conceptual framework we have developed particularly serves to bring out the main, S-shaped set of relations depicted in Figure 2a. The spatial sector of the normative and the aspatial portion of the physical environmental are de-emphasized in this particular approach. Hence these cells are shown in dotted lines in Figure 2a.

In this particular approach the chain of relationships extends from *1A* to *2A* to *2B* and thence to *3B*. Or, in the reverse direction, from *3B* to *2B* back to *2A* and up to *1A*. It is clear that *2A* and *2B* are of critical importance in translating between values and the physical environment.

Starting from the values end, the first relationship, *1A* to *2A*, is particularly amenable to sociological investigation. It deals with the interplay of values and norms, on the one hand, and the functional organization of the metropolitan area, on the other. We could expect that the functional organization would facilitate rather than impede the values most sought, insofar as inevitable conflicts of values are themselves sufficiently resolved. According to sociological findings, the functional organization of our cities tends to change in various respects more rapidly than our values. This was dramatically phrased by Ogburn as "cultural lag." Major forces for change in functional organization include population growth and redistribution, technological innovations, violent swings in the business cycle, war, and income redistribution. In the sphere of business organization we have many examples of continuing and deliberate attempts to reorganize firms so as to meet redefinitions of functional demands. In other phases of our functional organization, such as the organization of religion and of the family, we have a closer reliance on traditional and often deep-seated patterns which may be more closely geared to a corresponding value structure. But in all institutional spheres there are very dynamic factors at work to bring about change. Generally, we see these changes first in the functional organization sector and only gradually, often with noticeable lag, do these become reflected in the values of society.

The second step, from functional organization aspatially viewed *(2A)* to functional organization spatially conceived *(2B)*, would logically seem to fall well within the purview of the social sciences but actually has not been intensively dealt with in any systematic way. It is very possible that researchers in the city planning field could spark further work on this or contribute important approaches and findings themselves. The key question is how to examine the implications of alternative spatial arrangements on the functioning of given units of social organization. At the metropolitan community level, this is to ask in what alternative ways a metropolis may be spatially structured and with what

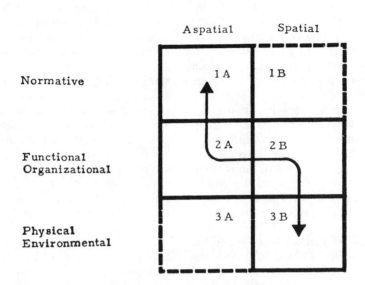

The main relationship, with functional organization (2A and 2B) as pivotal

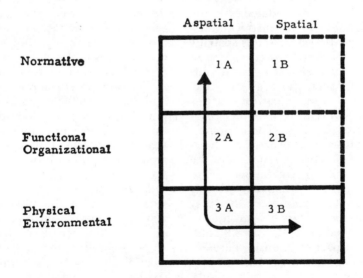

An alternative relationship: primary concern for immediate physical environment (3A)

FIGURE 2a and 2b

relative facilitating or restricting of activities as indicated by the effect on the functional organization *(2A)* and, indirectly, the values *(1A)*.

While the factors making for change in social organization aspatially also affect the spatial organization, certain forces, particularly those relating to the technology of transportation and communication, are at work modifying the spatial pattern (cell *2B*) which, in turn, feeds back strongly on the organization within cell *2A*. Hence, we have a lively interplay between certain functional, processual, or organizational changes in the *2A* sector and the spatial arrangement of this organization in the *2B* sector.

The final relation to be examined is that between functional organization spatially viewed *(2B)* and the physical environmental base spatially viewed *(3B)*. In many ways this is a hand-in-glove sort of relation with the activities being snugly accommodated by the physical facilities. But the distinction between the activity system as it is spatially organized and the strictly physical spaces and channels—structures, outdoor spaces, streets, port facilities, etc.—is an important one. Physical facilities once developed tend to be either fixed or expensive to alter. The volumes, kinds, and distribution of activities, however, may shift considerably over the years. These shifting activities may adapt to their facilities; they may be seriously restricted by their facilities; or they may be forced to move from old facilities to newly developed ones. We are all familiar with the impact of extensive automobile use on street systems built in pre-automobile or early-automobile periods. We know less about the effectiveness with which other kinds of facilities built at an earlier period have managed to handle industrial or business operations, residential activities, or other urban-based activities. We know amazingly little of how the centers of older metropolitan areas function. Neither do we understand how the Los Angeles type of pattern really works.

City planning research has a major stake in the exploration of this step between *2B* and *3B*. For the physical environmental pattern, once fixed, would seem to constitute a forceful determinant, having impacts or providing restraints on the spatial patterning of activities and, via the kinds of relationships we are discussing, on the functional organization of the community.

In the reasoning we have just discussed, a conscious concern for over-all spatial organization is implied. The physical environment might then be shaped to accommodate this spatial organization.

A major variant is the possibility that those concerned with activities may concentrate on the particular immediate kind of setting they seek rather than focusing on the metropolitan spatial pattern. For example, home seekers or developers of residential tracts may be calculating with respect to structural type and lot size, but they may be little concerned with the larger spatial pattern of the metropolitan area. Nevertheless, a decision to promote single-family houses with 10,000 square-foot lots implies low-density development. This, in turn, has its own inevitable impact on the spatial arrangement of the metropolitan area. The relationships in this case are shown by Figure 2b, with the pivotal cells *2A* and *3A*.

Designers of the physical environment may be very much involved in this direction of interest. Architects, landscape architects, and site planners, for example, may be focusing on a quality of spatial development, but at a scale much below that involved in metropolitan planning. We quickly agree that planning would be incomplete without such concern for development at this smaller scale. But such planning at this smaller scale does suggest a distinctive chain of relationships.

Further variants are suggested by

Figures 2c and 2d. These have, in common, reasoning which makes particular use of cell *1B* of the diagram, that portion of the normative which deals with matters of spatial organization and pattern. This includes an important body of norms and the intellectual exploration of these norms that is central in the field of aesthetics. These norms serve to guide our reactions to, and help us to design, the spatial pattern of our communities. The norms may stress efficiency and provide a rationale for spatial arrangements that promote designated types of efficiency. They may refer to traditional and symbolic features of the physical environment and to questions of the preservation of, or change in, such features. They may embrace man's attempt to maintain a community environment at a human scale, and hence they may balk at or seek to reverse those rather relentless forces working to push all communities to ever huger sizes.

In Figure 2c, the stress is on relationships *1A* to *1B* and then via *2B* to *3B*. Figure 2d is similar, except that the chain of relationships goes directly from *1B* to *3B* without depending upon *2B* as an intermediate step.

The reasoning in Figure 2c serves as a complementary line of approach to the major chain of reasoning in Figure 2a. This is because at step *2B* in the major reasoning, there must inevitably be reliance upon values or other criteria in judging which spatial organization to favor. These can come in part from cell *1B*. Conversely, it is hard to conceive of values in *1B* that could be very strong, short of a thorough understanding of the meaning and content of cells *2A* and *2B*.

These modes of reasoning (Figures 2c or 2d) stress the importance of the physical environment as artifact. The physical environment in many important ways serves to perpetuate community traditions and to provide a sense of orientation within or to the community. Hence the physical base tends to carry or to symbolize important values. The physical environment in effect becomes aligned with culture in providing traditional continuity and in resisting recurring forces to change, such as are initiated particularly in the functional organizational sphere.

For reasons of brevity we have omitted some additional sets of relationships which might be stressed. For example, using those portions of our framework that are suggested in the wrap-around version of the diagram in Figure 2d, one could examine (or use as a mode of reasoning) the relationship between *1A*, the values and norms aspatially conceived, and *3A*, the physical environment aspatially conceived, and thence to *3B*, the spatial pattern of the physical environment. This resembles Figure 2b, but it omits a strong concern for functional organization. Additional sets of relationships may occur to the reader that we have not specifically discussed or diagrammed.

Extension of the Scheme: Form and Process

Up to this point we have identified several aspects of metropolitan structure while emphasizing spatial structure. We now introduce further distinctions. It is essential, for various purposes, to distinguish between (I) *form* (or morphological or "anatomical") and (II) *process* (or functional or "physiological") aspects of metropolitan structure.

Problems of definition loom immediately. If one conceives of "structure" as strictly morphological, the parallel treatment of processual aspects with form, as part of structure, becomes illogical and unorthodox. We do not want to have the term "structure" so restricted. We conceive of metropolitan structure as comprising both *formal* aspects—a static, snapshot view of the metropolitan community's pattern at any one point in time—and *processual* aspects—the ongoing functional relations of the metropolitan community. In such a view, the functioning of the community exhibits a

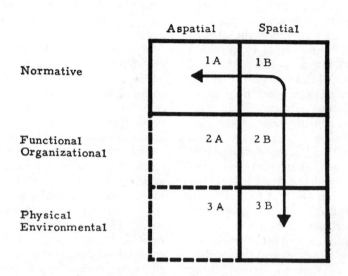

An alternative relationship: primary concern for values as to spatial arrangement (1B)

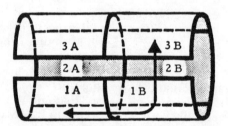

Diagram is rolled around so that the physical environment is placed next to the normative level. (The functional level is still in, but remains in the background.)

An alternative direct relationship between values (1A via 1B) and the physical environment (3B)

FIGURE 2c and 2d

pattern just as does the strictly morphological aspect of the community. With this conception, then, form and process may be readily treated as two complementary versions of structure.

Carrying through the framework already developed and adding this distinction between form and process provides us with a diagrammatic formulation as shown in Figure 3. This maintains the same primary distinctions between aspatial and spatial, and carries forward the three levels previously identified. For each cell of the previous framework there are added counterpart aspects of form and process. On the aspatial side, for example, form connotes ideas of relationship and order (although without regard for space at a metropolitan scale); thus we speak of the form of government or the pattern of culture. On this aspatial side, process is very naturally dealt with, for process or function tend to be treated rather aspatially in most cases anyway. With respect to norms, for example, the processual aspect deals with the interaction involved in striving for consensus and with the social-psychological processes by which norms are developed, internalized by persons, and modified or rejected.

On the spatial side of the framework, the formal aspects refer to the distribution of culture patterns, in the sense that anthropologists have termed culture areas; the distribution in space of the establishments conducting urban activities; and the spatial patterning of the physical environment. The processual aspects correspondingly encompass notions of the patterns *in space* of the interaction among persons and establishments, and of the actual and potential volumes of these interactions. Insofar as process inevitably occurs in space, it is the spatial pattern of activity location (form) that serves to establish the corresponding spatial pattern of interaction (process). Conversely, a sensitivity to the interactions that must be maintained has an essential bearing on the location of the activities.

If one takes a typical workday or workweek, the spatial patterning of commuting, shopping, school attendance, business contacts, and governmental activities shows up as an interaction web that ties together all of the households and other establishments in a metropolitan community. These establishments may of course be depicted as mere spots on a map of the metropolitan community; the processes by which the community functions may be envisioned as lines or threads among the spots. Particularly with the areally great separation of functions within American cities one only gets a full sense of what goes on if he can grasp the nature of the rhythmic flows in space, often on a daily or other rhythmic basis. One may observe the dynamics of the build-up and dispersion during each day of great masses of people and of tremendous concentration and diminution of activity in certain nonresidential centers.

Insofar as this framework (as shown in Figure 3) provides something of a vocabulary and a mode of expressing relationships, we might pause to note one further consequence. While it is possible to move diagonally among sectors within the framework, we think that this suggests incomplete steps in reasoning. We think that moving at all times parallel to one of the three outer planes of the "cube" forces fuller comprehension. Let us take an example. One could move from *II-2A* (dealing with functional organization, aspatially conceived, in the processual plane) to *I-3B* (physical environment, spatially conceived, in the formal plane). But this might fail to depict the full nature of the conceptual gaps that are being jumped. The chain of reasoning can be kept more rational if each of the three directional moves involved is taken one at a time. Interestingly,

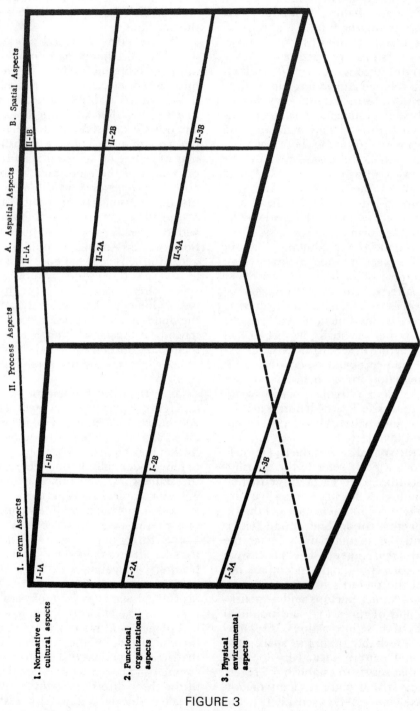

FIGURE 3

there are several alternative sets of steps possible. Thus we have these plausible alternatives (among others):

II-2A to *II-2B* to *I-2B* to *I-3B* (converting *from* functional interdependencies *to* such interdependencies in space *to* the spatial arrangement of activities *to* a formal view of the physical environment to accommodate these activities).

II-2A to *II-2B* to *II-3B* to *I-3B* (same as above, except *from* a processual view of functional relations in space *to* a processual view of the physical environment *to* a formal view of the physical environment).

11-2A to *1-2A* to *1-2B* to *1-3B* (converting *from* functional interdependencies *to* the formal organization for carrying these out *to* the spatial arrangement of this organization *to* the spatial pattern of the physical environment to accommodate the organization).

To be forced to state each step serves to clarify the entire chain of reasoning.

Further Extension of the Scheme: Change over Time

We have yet to stress one further distinction: that between short-term rhythmic processes, dealt with in the previous section, and long-range processes of growth and change, to which we now turn. Metropolitan structure not only exists at a given point in time and is in process within a given short period of time, but also it evolves over time. During designated longer periods of time, metropolitan structure may exhibit rather marked evolution.

Without repeating the previous diagram in its full complexity, Figure 4 depicts the idea that metropolitan structure changes over time.

The introduction of a sense of historical depth is important. The metropolitan structure at any given period is heavily dependent upon its structure at earlier periods. This suggests again the two kinds of lags—cultural and physical environmental—to which we alluded in our first discussion of the relations between the normative, the functional organizational, and the physical environmental levels. *Cultural lag* refers to the distinct tendency for the cultural framework to change less rapidly than the functional organization. We can point to many examples where technologically induced changes, while accepted in a civilization that lays great stress on change, are by no means accompanied by direct corresponding normative changes that provide a full ethical and legal adjustment to the new situation. *Physical environmental lag* applies to the condition in which the physical environment, including the capital plant developed by man, fails to keep pace with growth and other changes in the systems by which activities are conducted. We are most dramatically aware of the inertia in our street system in the face of traffic increases, but we might also cite many other instances where physical facilities, because of their resistance to ready change, offer restraints on evolving activity systems.

II. THE CONTRIBUTIONS OF THE FRAMEWORK

We now wish to examine how this framework may serve planners and researchers. Three kinds of contributions will be suggested and each will be amplified in subsequent discussion. First, the framework stresses certain distinctions and relationships—particularly those dealing with functional and spatial organization—that urban and metropolitan planners and scholars might otherwise neglect or underemphasize. Second, with respect to various major relationships that we take to be of critical importance in understanding metropolitan structure, the framework encourages the

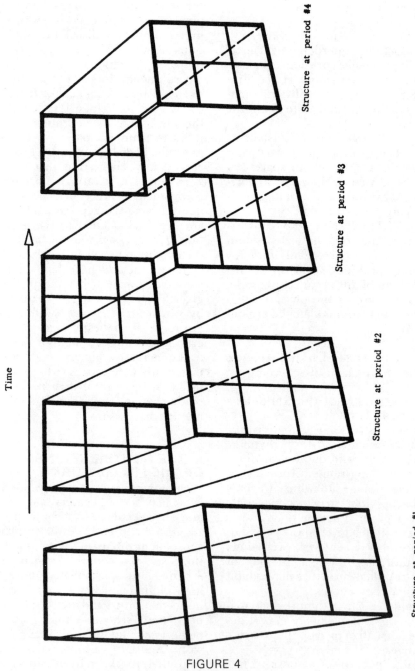

FIGURE 4

formulation of hypotheses for further testing by research. And, third, the framework provides a setting within which otherwise scattered concepts and formulations may be seen in better perspective. Using the framework, we shall propose a tentative and rudimentary set of concepts and a pattern of relations among these concepts that might contribute toward future theoretical approaches to metropolitan structure.

Stress on Certain Relationships

The suggested conceptual scheme stresses activities and functional organization rather than relying too heavily or exclusively on values. This emphasis on activities is warranted because it furnishes the planner with a more palpable set of requirements for which to plan than do values, as they are usually presented. It is one thing to state that what is sought is a "balanced community"; it is quite another to translate this into criteria sufficiently tangible to provide planning guidelines. Similarly, a plea for more open space must be stated in terms of the desired qualities of this open space and the activities that it is to accommodate. It makes good sense to plan for the functional organization that is geared to facilitate high-priority values and then to design the physical environment so as to provide the best setting for this functional organization.

The proposed scheme also stresses the distinction and the corresponding close relation between the physical environment and the activity systems accommodated by this environment. It points out the crucial distinction and great conceptual gap between the realms of the spatial and the aspatial. And the framework re-emphasizes the complementarity of functional organizational aspects and the normative aspects of the metropolitan community's structure.

We submit that if a physical planner comes to think in terms of the proposed scheme he will be encouraged *to take into account the ways in which the physical environment* he recommends *facilitates or impedes various activity systems that are accommodated by that environment.* He should be encouraged to gain a thorough understanding of these activities as he engages in physical environmental design. The metropolitan planner might well make explicit the relationships with which he is most directly involved. He is thus encouraged to state the reasoning upon which he is relying. An explicit statement of his reasoning not only would clarify his own operations, both for his own purposes and for explaining his rationale to political leaders and the public, but also would communicate the chain of reasoning he is employing so that the logical steps may be susceptible to research check.

We are particularly impressed with the utility of clearly distinguishing between "physical" and "spatial." This prevents two possible misconceptions. First, it reminds planners and scholars that often when they say "physical" they may mean "spatial." The phrase "physical arrangement" sometimes refers to spatial arrangement. The physical planner in a real sense is a space planner; i.e., he plans how we might best arrange our environment and our activities in space. Second, it reminds us that components of urban structure other than the physical also have a spatial aspect. This may be true of functional organization and even normative structure. Often, when we speak of spatial pattern as if we were referring to the physical environmental setting, we may really be referring to the spatial patterns of the activities and of interpersonal relationships.

The scheme emphasizes that supporting research and planning are called for to supplement the physical planner's own efforts. The thorough study of the diverse systems and subsystems of activities within metropolitan areas requires the collaboration of varied social scientists and managerial and professional personnel. Too, complementary types of planning are clearly needed: program or activities planning, social planning, economic planning. By whatever terms and breakdown, planning responsible for the kinds, relative volumes, and organization of the activities to be conducted is called for to supplement and, logically, to precede physical planning. What is currently confusing is that the physical planners seek reasonably to bound their own scope, and yet know that, willy-nilly, they are assuming broad responsibilities for the kinds of activities and the patterns of social contacts facilitated by their physical designs.

III. IMPLICATIONS FOR METROPOLITAN PLANNING

Faced as we are with serious renewal and developmental problems and confronted with prospects for continuing vigorous growth during the coming decades, we may look forward to an important and lively effort attempting to guide the development of each of our large metropolitan areas. Ever more planners, researchers, political leaders, and public administrators will be drawn into this activity. But metropolitan planning as an evolving institutional form is still in an extremely fluid state.

One traditional approach to metropolitan planning, borrowed from planning at lesser (i.e., urban and architectural) scales, is for a designer—or, more likely, a design team—to be given responsibility for preparing a plan for an appropriate governmental unit. Such an approach we may label *unitary*. Another approach, involving the decentralized decision-making of the urban real estate and land market and the policies and controls of various governmental units, may be designated *adaptive*. We shall discuss each of these, relating them to the framework already presented, and considering the prospects for their reconciliation. Finally, we shall propose an alternative approach, reflecting the framework of the previous two sections.

The Unitary Approach and the Adaptive Approach

The essence of the *unitary* approach, as this relates to urban and metropolitan planning, is to view the city or the metropolitan community as having a spatial, physical form that can be grasped and reduced to maplike graphic presentation. Planning is viewed as an activity dedicated to forming a picture of a future physical environmental pattern for a community and to fostering such development and control measures as will best ensure that the community will develop toward that future pattern. In short, a future spatial pattern is proposed as a goal. The traditional means for communicating this future goal is the general plan, comprehensive plan, or master plan. Implicit in this unitary approach is the assumption that there will be a reasonably centralized governmental authority to prepare, approve, and carry out such a plan.

The *adaptive* approach to urban or metropolitan planning views the city or the metropolitan community as a complex interaction of diverse and functionally interdependent parts, with the parts evolving over time as they seek to adapt to the ever-changing contexts around them. This approach focuses on process, particularly the interactions that take place on a daily or short-term cycle—such as commuting, shopping, weekday business dealings, week-end recreational trips and activities, etc.—rather than on a longer-term cycle. Metropolitan planning, from this point of view, would seek first to gain a full understanding of how establishments and households interact (via the myriad actors involved), and how the metropolitan area develops over time. It then would seek to identify alternative development policies and to examine the probable implications of each in the light of certain established criteria as to desirable future conditions or optimal decision-making conditions. Planning, according to this approach, would seek to influence various of the development forces at work rather than aiming for a future metropolitan form as a goal.

In simplest terms, perhaps, this is a distinction between product and process. For the unitary view reflects in particular a product-design approach, flowing logically from the best traditions of architecture and the related design fields, that sees its mission as the design and the production of a future physical environment. In this spirit, quite naturally, planners prepare plans for this future physical form. That the plans may be diagrammatic and general, so that they must be supplemented by more detailed blueprints before construction can proceed, takes them no less out of the tradition. The planner is serving as executive architect and establishing certain general ideas and standards to which subsequent architecture and public works are expected to conform. Within such an envelope, precise plans may be given considerable leeway. Essentially, the unitary approach aims to create a future product, a physical environment for the city or the metropolis.

The adaptive view focuses on the processes by which persons and activities interact and, in particular, on the processes by which changes are introduced that will affect the future character of the city and the effectiveness with which persons and activities will be able to interact in this future situation. In the adaptive view, great emphasis is placed on the economy, broken into its diverse and interacting markets, as an allocative and decision-making mechanism. This view also recognizes that ours is in reality a political economy and that a sophisticated understanding of the role of government and of political decisions is also essential. Indeed, the rationale for adaptive planning recognizes that it is government's responsibility to guide the development process toward selected goals judged to be publicly desirable. In line with this adaptive planning approach, the creation of a better physical environment is not necessarily *the* major goal. The goals may embrace a range of desiderata relating to social life, to the economy, and to qualities of the total environment provided by the metropolitan community.

Figure 5 summarizes a number of salient characteristics of the two contrasting approaches.[1] These approaches are presented as ideal-type concepts being deliberately portrayed in purer form than ever found in real life. This has the advantage of highlighting the essence of each, but runs the risk of casting each in such form that its supporters would probably reject the uncompromising statements.

Within our previously presented framework for dealing with metropolitan structure, the unitary approach focuses more heavily on the formal aspects (plane *I* in Figure 3) and the adaptive approach mainly on the processual aspects (plane *II*). More specifically, the unitary approach has as its major purpose the shaping of the physical environment; at the metropolitan scale the emphasis is on the spatial pattern created and preserved by the physical environment (hence, cell *I-3B* in Figure 3). The unitary approach is also concerned with the physical environment at less than metropolitan spatial scale *(I-3A)* and with the spatial pattern by which activities are distributed within the metropolis *(I-2B)*. Conceptual links with the processual aspects of structure may readily be established either at the functional organizational level (between *I-2B* and *II-2B*) or at the physical environmental level (between *I-3B* and *II-3B*). Following from our reasoning in the previous sections, it would seem helpful to think of a double transition—from formal to processual *(I-2B—II-2B)* and from spa-

Nature of the Characteristic	Unitary Approach	Adaptive Approach
1) The plan toward which planning works	Long-range locational-physical plan: the portrayal of a metropolitan spatial form for the future as desirable goal.	Policies and proposals constituting courses of action, to influence metropolitan development.
2) Substantive focus	Locational pattern of activities and the physical characteristics of the metropolis, taking into account social and economic goals; guiding controls to ensure that development will accord with desired character.	Social economy of the metropolis, including opportunities and standards for living, cultural and business activities, etc.; the public and private decision-making mechanisms by which development takes place.
3) Methodology	Intuitive-synthetic-political; aggregative; strong design influence; focus on product.	Empirical-analytic-economic; disaggregative; social science influence; focus on process.
4) Underlying assumption as to the basis for community solidarity	Solidarity results from consensus: a normative view of what is desirable.	Functional integration: solidarity results from the integration of diverse parts and viewpoints.
5) Assumptions regarding the political economy	Necessarily strong and fairly centralized role for government (the mix as between local and nonlocal subject to considerable variation); market decisions important but to be kept under control.	Decentralization; pluralistic political economy, with market-type decisions very important; governmental responsibility to provide leadership regarding prime-mover developments and to ensure working of economy in public interest.
6) Assumptions as to knowledge about the future	Precise knowledge irrelevant; strong design commitment and political leadership can provide self-fulfilling prophecy.	In view of complexity of the present and the essential unknowability of the long-range future, focus is on the near future and the directions of influence, subject to successive adaptation as the future unfolds.
7) Implicit aesthetics of spatial arrangement	Articulation: the designation of centers, the strong demarcation of circulation channels and internal boundaries, the clear bounding of the community so as to distinguish between city and country. Preferably treating designs as though they were reasonably final, with implication that disturbing overgrowth should be prevented.	Fluidity and interpenetration: the acceptance of growth; no single, final design; latitude for experiment and unpredictable change. A spatial plan can at best provide sound communication and transportation systems, a system of public spaces and community facilities, and a modular-type framework within which further development can proceed.

FIGURE 5. Distinguishing Characteristics of the Unitary and Adaptive Approaches to Metropolitan Planning

tial to aspatial *(II-2B—II-2A)*—taking place as phases of the functional organization of urban life. The case for the logic of a transition at the physical environmental level *(I-3B—II-3B)* places emphasis on the movement of persons, messages and goods as processual phases of the physical environment, contrasting them to the linkage of functional interdependence as processual phases of functional organization.

The adaptive approach is primarily concerned with the functioning of the metropolis, the metropolis' economy and social organization, and the formulation of decisions with respect to such organization and functioning. Within the previous framework, the focus is on processual aspects of functional organization *(II-2A* and *II-2B* in Figure 3). While much of the change is initiated in, and hence our attention is inevitably attracted to, the aspatial aspects *(II-2A)*, it is a distinctive feature of metropolitan areas that changes in transportation and communication technology and shifting patterns of accessibility and locational advantage (originating in *II-2B* and *II-3B*) feed back to and must be taken into account in the organization of activities, aspatially conceived *(II-2A)*. The recognition of physical environment and spatial form (as in *I-3B*) is but one aspect— that of capital investment and long-range public commitment—conceived as accommodating changes in functional organization. Transitions between processual and formal and between spatial and aspatial must be dealt with, as discussed at the close of the preceding paragraph.

Each of these unitary and adaptive approaches reflects its own value emphases and configurations. The unitary approach reflects the value placed on consensus and the conviction that agreement can be reached and, indeed, that some decisions deserve to be deliberately shaped as an entire consistent, balanced, and purposeful package. In a design sense, the unitary approach inevita-

bly relies heavily on intuition, and represents a synthesis. It reflects a predetermination to see things whole and to create a whole design. It reflects, too, a willingness to treat communities and planning units as independent, separable, units. This approach assumes and depends upon a single governmental unit or a confederation of governments such that a single approval may be achieved. Thus, importantly, this approach reflects and reinforces a political process geared to reaching consensus. It pursues the outlook that consensus is a major basis for community solidarity (drawing from an important series of concepts in social theory by Durkheim, Toennies, and others).[2] It depends upon the coalition of a potentially dominant political leader or party and a strong designer. Going back in history, we may point to the prince or the king and his commissioning of an architect or an engineer to design and execute an urban development. For a more contemporary example, we may think of the British government commissioning Patrick Abercrombie to prepare the Greater London Plan.

The adaptive approach relies essentially not on consensus, decree, or design imposed from the top or the outside so much as on the interaction of many persons, firms, and governmental units in the natural interdependence that arises with the division of labor and the complex specialization and interchange of effort. The reliance is on pluralism of governmental actions, on highly decentralized decisions by investors, producers, and buyers, and on the faith that the public interest will best be served by the resultant series of actions that reflect the interests and counterinterests of the many parties affected by, and reacting to, impending developments. While this approach has had theoretical support in utilitarianism, such belief in a laissez-faire framework has of course been superseded by the realization that a decentralized, marketplace type of mechanism for reaching decisions may have serious imperfections, and that positive governmental leadership is required to guarantee the public interest. Practically, the adaptive approach reflects a fascinating combination of pragmatic, administrative, and problem-solving attacks seeking to resolve issues as they arise and a social scientific interest in a better understanding of the likely consequences of proposed policies. It is inclined to be analytic, seeking to break down situations to their constituent parts, and empirical, searching for evidence from observed cases. Congenial to this approach is a preponderant attention to the organization and the interaction that results from specialization of function and to the ways in which functional integration contributes to community solidarity. If consensus represents a solidarity based on likeness, functional integration represents a solidarity that emerges from difference. The adaptive approach sees the contemporary metropolitan area as a favorable setting for facilitating functional integration. It assumes that much of the future is at best unknowable and that a process of enlightened adaptation is our best hope. The most persuaded proponents of this approach tend to be either unconcerned about the preparation of a single plan or policy bundle or convinced that such a plan might prove downright dysfunctional.

What Metropolitan Spatial Organization?

In accord with the unitary approach, as we have suggested, great stress is placed on the spatial form of the physical metropolis. It is expected that the planning effort will culminate in a graphic plan depicting a desirable future spatial form toward which it is recommended that community development be directed. This physical metropolis is recognized as a visual metropolis, and effort is directed toward creating an improved visual environment. The plan itself is also susceptible to visual review and may be conceived as something of a work of art in its own right. Various aesthetic principles and concepts are recognized as applicable both to the plan and to the final physical environment implied by the plan.

Up to the present at least, focality and articulation have been dominant ideas. It is usually held that a community should have a clear center (and possibly, although not inevitably, a set of subcenters); it should have distinguishable outer limits; it should have its major functional areas articulated; and it should have a reinforcing circulation pattern. A community should be imageable, to use Lynch's term; that is, it should be so clearly organized that the typical resident can carry an accurate picture in his mind of the community's major spatial form. A stereotype of a metropolitan plan fashioned in this spirit would show a dominant central area to which major radial transportation routes led but through which major surface transportation did not unduly cut; articulated residential communities, in turn broken down into neighborhoods; industrial districts carefully bounded and, if necessary, buffered; outlying commercial centers tied in with the transportation network and centered, if possible, in major communities or sectors; and, at the outer bounds of the urbanized areas, a greenbelt, clearly marking the break between city and country and controlling lateral expansion.

Ideally, the metropolitan community and its constituent communities and subcommunities would, respectively, be matched by corporate governmental units. This is, in fact, seldom the case. Congruent with the unitary approach the political organization of the metropolis could be somewhat simplified and local political units could be brought to coincide territorially with the communities designated by the plan. Also implict in the unitary approach is the idea that creating clearly designated physical communities will help to bring about social communities at this scale and with these boundaries.

The plan prepared in the spirit of the unitary viewpoint is perhaps most applicable to those situations in which extensive and uncontrolled growth does not have to be accommodated. The conditions under which a Greater London Plan came into existence provide a case in point. Some unitary plans may connote a sense of optimum size, with excess growth accommodated in planned new towns or by other arrangements.

The adaptive approach, on the other hand, views the spatial structure of the metropolis much more as a resultant of many and varied forces than as something to be designed and worked toward for itself. Being more geared to the recognition of change and growth, it expects that changes in the spatial pattern will continually be evolving. In this light, a physical plan is seen rather as a technical necessity preparatory to capital improvements. It is not viewed as something that necessarily reduces all the elements to one single general plan; there might be a highway plan, a recreation plan, a civic center plan, etc., with integration between these plans subject to variation. Neither is a plan treated as indicating ultimate development. In short, no major synthesizing and policy-establishing role is necessarily given to a metropolitan plan.

Major interest is in the workings of the economic and political forces and mechanisms, rather than on the pattern of the physical environment. Even though the physically built-up city comes to a gradual outer limit or because neighborhood units are delineated, the proponent of the adaptive approach does not conceive of articulated physical boundaries accurately characterizing current or future spatial interaction patterns. He would incline toward the view that those with a unitary outlook are, unwittingly, guilty of physical environmental determinism—of assuming a greater and a more direct impact of the physical environment on social and economic life than is warranted.

If focality and articulation characterize the unitary aesthetic, then afocality, flexibility, and interpenetration would seem to be valid concepts reflecting an adaptive, interactional view of the metropolis. It may appear that proponents of the adaptive view are outwardly little concerned about the aesthetic that is implied by their approach, but this is not necessarily so. Since, from the adaptive outlook, a plan is not necessarily thought to be important no explicit visual aesthetic has emerged. Implicitly, however, much of the recent trend of urban and metropolitan development strongly suggests a changing spatial organization and, inevitably, a changing aesthetic. Thus we witness the great reliance on automobiles, the deterioration of fixed-rail passenger transport, the heavy emphasis on the single-family house, the complex spatial patterns of commuting, the dispersion of work places, etc. Inroads are being made on many of the main features advocated in the spirit of the traditional unitary viewpoint. It is less clear whether a positive alternative aesthetic congruent with the adaptive approach will be forthcoming.

The character and impact of the urban freeway illustrate the possibilities for an adaptive aesthetic. The freeway does not necessarily have a focus (although insofar as freeways within metropolitan areas have been radial toward the metropolitan center they have to a degree reinforced a focal aesthetic). The freeway system connotes process and flow. It facilitates the ready interpenetration between city and country and between districts within the metropolis. It suggests an adaptability with which the freeway can be initially located, and much of metropolitan freeway siting carries a distinctly surgical character. Once built, it encourages a new kind of flexibility, particularly as we begin to see its potentials for mass transit. The case has been made, for example, for bus systems that make full use of freeways, as preferable to new fixed-rail transit schemes, on the grounds that their routing can be far more flexible. Certain lanes at peak hours could be assigned to buses exclusively, if necessary, while available for general use during other periods.

The Potential Integration of the Two Approaches

Having stressed the differences between these two approaches—the unitary and the adaptive—we do not intend to suggest irreconcilable conflict that will only be resolved when one camp or the other wins a fight to the finish. Indeed, the form in which we cast the approaches as ideal types has contributed to their seeming oppositeness. The two approaches contain important elements of compatibility and complementarity, and metropolitan planning will benefit by taking both into account.

The main weakness of the unitary approach is an insufficient depth of interest in and understanding of the processual and functional organizational aspects of metropolitan structure. The proponents of the unitary approach have sought, often creatively, to propose spatial arrangements of the physical environment toward which communities were to be guided by governmentally imposed implementation measures.

The main weakness of the adaptive approach is an insufficient concern for the importance of an over-all policy framework and corresponding plan proposing future spatial arrangement of the community. The interest of the advocates of this approach has been in the functional locational adjustment of the individual firm or governmental agency and in the market process for allocating favored locations.

We propose an approach to met-ropolitan planning that would center on the social, political and economic organization of the metropolitan community and its constituent parts. It would insist on full and first-priority treatment of the metropolis as a functioning system complete with various subsystems. It would then also deal with the optimal spatial arrangements under which these functional subsystems can operate most effectively. Out of this concern would come, first of all, policies for guiding the character and spatial patterning of the organization of the metropolis. Then flowing from this and feeding back certain opportunities and restraints would be a development policy and a spatial plan for the physical base of the metropolis.[3]

Such a focus on the organization of the metropolitan community provides the very sort of intermediate and central ground depicted in the conceptual framework presented in the first section (especially Figures 1 and 3). It forces adequate attention to the dynamic, growth-provoking organizational aspects of metropolitan life, bridging between values and physical environment and between aspatial and spatial conceptions of the community. It encourages the planner to face up to the hard realities of how urban activities and urban life are to be carried out rather than tempting him to fixate on overly general values and goals.

The objection may be raised that to focus on organization combines emphasis on bureaucratic and calculating outlooks. True, one's treatment of organization can be cold and theoretical. The planner may feel impelled to insert a humanitarian touch, bringing back a concern for personal behavior and reaction. The humanitarian will argue that the city must be rescued from organization men and from those who would see it as a monstrous system. Our reaction is that a focus on organization is not necessarily so inhuman or so insensitive to human values and interests. A broad-gauged view of organization includes living patterns and may take into account personal habits and attitudes. Inevitably, too, an organizational view will emphasize the major relationships. An essential characteristic of "organization" is that it involves the allocation of functions aspatially and the allocation of locations spatially. And while it can be fruitfully viewed for certain purposes abstractly, it also shades down into the specifics of a particular organization for a particular place, time, and purpose.

A logical starting point in the study of metropolitan organization is the proposal of a political organization for ensuring that social and economic goals are classified, determined, and carried out in accordance with an agreed-upon political decision-making process. That goals may not be readily reducible to a simple and consistent set should be understood. If a consensus on goals could be that readily achieved, we could dispense with an intricate political system for resolving conflict and difference.

With the continuing ideological preference for the small community, so that separate suburban communities appear to be politically more desirable than a single metropolitan government, we find the scales tipped toward a traditional view of lower-level local government.[4] The governmental organization of the large metropolitan area reflects the traditional grass-roots ideal more nearly than a rationally resolved level of metropolitan government dividing responsibilities with lower-level governments. The problem is one of organization, how a set of governments can be put together with appropriate functions clearly allocated to each. We still need the strictly local units that encourage political participation and citizen identification; we also need a well equipped metropolitan government eager to tackle problems most appropriately handled at the metropolitan level.

Each metropolitan community faces important social-policy issues. In the broadest sense the community must organize itself to try to determine its future. It must determine policies regarding housing, the character of residential districts, the distribution of workplaces in relation to residences, and the creation and preservation of the main business centers. A major current issue regarding racial integration raises questions of whether previously segregated minority residents are to be welcomed in all sections of the metropolis. The question of whether the growth of the largest metropolitan areas will be encouraged or discouraged also calls for social policy.

The metropolitan community also faces questions as to how it shall develop economically. We still tend to carry an ideology of letting business develop as it will, although in reality various governmental units in many ways influence the course of the economy. The hard questions are how various real or potential governmental actions or policies will affect the economy and its different segments. The distribution of economic activities among the separate governmental units within the metropolitan area is of great significance, for it affects the respective tax bases, may help to trigger further economic growth, and, through the locational pattern of employment opportunities, affects residential development.

Each of these aspects of metropolitan organization—political, social and economic—carries over into related spatial organizational questions and alternatives.[5] But, basically, we would submit that the spatial organizational riddles cannot be meaningfully resolved until there is reasonably clear understanding of what it is that is to be distributed in space. Then the critical question is what the relative impacts of alternative policies or plans will be on the well-being of residents and of the systems making up the city.

Specifically, we must grant the logic of preparing a plan (or, if preferred, a certain number of alternative plans). It is only by so doing that the possible congruence or conflict between land users can be explored. But how ensure that the plan will be more than a matter of form? How does such a plan get fully tied to the processes by which the metropolis functions? How can we depict the functional organization of the metropolis and the implications of alternative spatial arrangements on this functional organization?

We are in urgent need of methods for describing and analyzing how the large city functions as a system, and how smaller systems fit into the over-all system. An important part of planning would then be to determine how this system and its parts can best function. Only then can the task of recommending an appropriate physical environment as a base be meaningfully tackled.

NOTES

1. I am particularly indebted to Melvin M. Webber for ideas in preparing part of Figure 5.
2. See particularly E. Durkheim, *The Division of Labor in Society* (originally written 1893, translated by G. Simpson, 1933; Glencoe, Ill.: The Free Press, 1947); C. P. Loomis' translation of F. Toennies, *Funcamental Concepts of Sociology* (New York: American Book Company, 1940); R. Freedman et al., *Principles of Sociology* (New York: Henry Holt, 1952), chapters 4 and 5; M. Meyerson and E. Banfield, *Politics, Planning and the Public Interest* (Glencoe, Ill.: The Free Press, 1955), esp. pp. 322–29.
3. R. B. Mitchell's recent proposal for a "land use plan" for "the distribution and intensity of land users and their activities," to be followed, perhaps later and in greater detail, by a "land improvements plan" to "provide for the adaptation of the physical structure of the area to the needs and requirements imposed by land use change" is very much in this same spirit. His interest in process, in this recent paper, focuses mainly on the developmental process by which a metropolitan area changes over time, while my concern with process is limited more specifically to day-to-day interaction processes within the metropolitan area. R. B. Mitchell, "The New Frontier in Metropolitan Planning," *Journal of the American Institute of Planners* 27 (August, 1961), esp. pp. 172–5.
4. Cf. R. C. Wood, *Suburbia: Its People and Their Politics* (Boston: Houghton Mifflin Company, 1958).
5. For as Wingo and Perloff have suggested, a metropolitan government must push itself to some "broad commitment to certain long-range characteristics of the city's form and organization which are implicit in its objectives." L. Wingo, Jr. and H. S. Perloff, "The Washington Transportation Plan: Technics or Politics," Regional Science Association *Papers and Proceedings* 7 (1961): 249–62.

A LEGAL PERSPECTIVE

THE SOCIAL CONTROL
OF URBAN SPACE
CHARLES M. HAAR

In this detailed analysis, Haar presents a complementary view to Foley's analysis of metropolitan spatial structure: problems of decision making about urban space are given real legal and institutional flesh. Each kind of problem from zoning, to suburban growth, to the location of public facilities, is presented as a set of contrasting legal positions and constraints. Space is not pictured as an idealized force, but as a manipulable variable which can be used to control men's actions and enhance or detract from their utilization of society. Haar's position is thus the logical outcome of a purely institutionally-oriented perspective on the role of urban space: space is simply something to be selectively used and regulated for human purposes.

Reprinted from Lowdon Wingo, Jr., ed., *Cities and Space* (Baltimore: Johns Hopkins University Press for Resources for the Future, Inc., 1963), pp. 175–229, by permission of the publisher and the author. This is an edited version of the original publication. Notes have been renumbered.

The future course of social control of urban space inevitably requires speculation, euphemistically called making informed guesses. My purpose here is to explore those legal policies and institutions which threaten to interfere with the rational development of metropolitan land uses. Concomitantly, the aim is to highlight those policies which foster desired development, as well as to consider the legal and institutional arrangement—including the creation of new techniques—that can best attain community ends.

By way of preface, I pose the following general proposition for discussion: the continued sway of outmoded legal institutions will not be the cause of any irrationality in the long-run trends of urban space patterns.

This proposition does not deny the rigidity of law at any given point in time. To the contrary, such rigidity is the essence of the legal structure. Every law represents the decision of society concerning a particular problem in a particular climate of conditions and ideas. But the decision is rarely unanimous; hence the need to clothe it with the dignity of law. The function of law is to effectuate that decision, notwithstanding the opposition of dissenting elements in the society.

But the rigidity is not fixed for all time. As pressures for change build up, the rigidity dissolves and a new accommodation results which subsists until a new pressure becomes sufficiently great to force another change in the law. In short, at any point in time, law is predominantly static; over a period of time, it is predominantly, and inevitably, dynamic.

The thesis, while acknowledging both aspects, emphasizes the dynamics. It asserts that this country's legal climate is such that any strong and persistent pressure or need will make or force accommodation. Naturally certain critics contend that the thesis that law adjusts to life rests simply upon the unfounded optimism of a Pangloss. Its fundamental soundness, however, is borne out by innumerable footnotes in legal history. Time after time, seemingly immutable doctrines have come into conflict with apparently unyielding social pressures, and out of those frictions there have developed new, reconciled relations. This is the fact of the present; it is the promise of the future.

THE PROCESS AT WORK

Private land use activities are most obviously regulated by overt and direct exercise of governmental powers. These include many basic tools of land use controls and may be primarily legislative (e.g., zoning), administrative (e.g., subdivision controls), or judicial (e.g., rule against restraints on alienation or the non-enforceability of covenants).

Less obvious, perhaps, but increasingly significant are the measures having an indirect impact on development patterns. Included in this category are such matters as the availability of government credit, the possibility of a direct subsidy or of tax concessions, any one of which may determine not only whether a site or area is developed, but, if it is, what form it will take. Here the legislative and the administrative branches of government dominate the scene, almost to the exclusion of the judicial.

The last category to be considered is what might be called the *de facto* as opposed to the *de jure* controls. Under this rubric are actions of various groups which are likely to have a discernible influence on the development of urban space: for example, insuring policies of title companies, credit policies of private lending institutions.

Direct Controls

Zoning

A pervasive tendency in zoning is toward greater flexibility. One manifestation is the proliferation in the number of use categories and of height and bulk specifications. The original breakdown of uses was little more than a tripartite division into residential, industrial, and commercial. This is a far cry from the minute detailing of all conceivable kinds of residential, industrial, and commercial uses that are set forth in a modern zoning enactment, such as the long, detailed New York City ordinance adopted in 1961. That ordinance—resembling the Internal Revenue Code in breadth and complexity of detail—requires 255 oversize pages to contain its provisions intended to streamline the much amended resolution of 1916, as well as bring it into line with current concepts.

Another manifestation is the fairly new technique of classifying in accordance with *performance standards,* i.e., by the impact of the actual user, rather than by class of industry, process, or product. This bids fair to supersede the older classification scheme. At present, however, the two are more likely to be used conjunctively, as in the New York City ordinance. In it, classification by some uses in effect creates a presumption only; performance standards, set forth elsewhere, actually control.

Still another indication of flexibility is the greater use of licensing techniques in conjunction with the self-executing statute. The number of special uses, admissible into specific districts but only upon the discretionary grant of an application for a permit, has risen over the years. Other new techniques have come into play, such as flexible zoning or floating zones—the creation of districts which, instead of being mapped in advance are delineated by amendment upon petition or application—have gained rapidly in popularity.

In part, these changes merely mirror the growing complexity of our civilization. If industry becomes more specialized, a dynamic law will tend to reflect this by listing more uses. An increase in scientific knowledge will give rise to new forms of control as well as to new industry. Unless there is some cataclysmic disaster, the impetus toward greater complexity will probably continue. This, in turn, will create a pressure on zoning and other laws to become correspondingly complex.

But to some extent the desire for flexibility, particularly as manifested in greater reliance on the licensing approach, may stem from a loss of confidence or from feelings of modesty with respect to the potential of planning. The planner is thereby relieved of the burden of prophesying and prescribing development over which, after all, he wields only negative powers. His powers are still negative: he can prevent a particular development in a particular place but he cannot order it. However, his powers no longer need be exercised in advance without knowledge of particular circumstances.

Some planners suggest that the pressure for flexibility in the form of floating zones comes from residents who are willing to admit uses regarded as basically undesirable neighbors, but only to the extent indicated by the locale's tax situation. They want to retain maximum control over such admissions and feel this would be achieved by exerting pressure on a planning commission given discretionary power.

Of these developments, only the licensing techniques have thus far been judicially reviewed to any appreciable extent. Whether because of differences in the means used to achieve flexibility, in the degree of flexibility sought, in the court's attitude toward flexibility, or to some combination of these, reactions have been various. In *Rockhill* v. *Chesterfield Township*, the enactment overthrown was in form a conventional zoning ordinance designating permitted uses, and uses which could be permitted by grant of an exception. However, it created only a single district in which only two uses—agricultural and certain residential—were permitted as of right. All other uses, except for a few specifically excluded, were subject to the licensing requirement.

In this area of the law, as with most land use controls, the initiating force is the legislature. The courts have the essentially negative function of review; they may kill but they can not create. The first step must obviously be to overcome the inertia of the legislative body. The planner, not the lawyer is the logical source of the necessary impetus. The lawyer's role *qua* lawyer is to prescribe for the problems which may be encountered in court once the legislature has acted. One ancient prescription of general applicability is to pour new wines into old bottles. If a new technique can be dressed up to look like an old one, it may ride to safety on the precedents upholding the old technique without submitting to an examination of its own merits. More often than not, the court will perceive the substance beneath the form, in fact it will be forcefully thrust on the court, if the lawyers in the case are earning their fees. Within limits though, it probably has value, if only in providing the court with a make-weight for its decision.

Many judicial fears can be allayed by the master plan. Of course, if the master plan for the area is locational—a type of preliminary zoning map—its usefulness for this purpose will be limited. If, however, it consists of applicable principles and relevant goals which are to guide the subsequent districting in a way that can be understood by the court, its existence may prove decisive. It would be evidence that the zones though not fixed were nevertheless the result of planning. It would be evidence of a sufficient guide for and limitation on administrative discretion. It would furnish a guide for judicial review.

In order to perform this function the master plan needs to bear in some form the imprimatur of the local legislative body. For in limiting the administration's discretion to grant or deny applications, it would conversely limit the property owner's rights and thus constitute a restriction on those rights. Many of the restrictions of individual liberty —in the Smithian sense of encompasing rights in property—are rationalized on the political theory of democratic government. This requires as indispensable basis that the restriction be imposed by elected representatives.

It has been suggested that the reasoning in *Rockhill* v. *Chesterfield Township* [1] by its emphasis on use districts, constitutes a threat to the future of performance standards. This may be a real danger if the delegation in an enabling act or constitutional provision is in terms of use districts. In other jurisdictions, the adoption of performance standards may be somewhat slowed by the inertia of a judiciary which has come to equate zoning with use districts of the conventional kind. But the potential of this technique to provide objective standards for reasonable classifications and impartial administration augurs its acceptance. It would be surprising if any reasonably well drafted ordinance were held invalid.

Subdivision Controls

Typically, subdivision ordinances are administered pursuant to rules and regulations promulgated by the administrative body. Individual negotiations and compromises are a hallmark of this form of land use control. Consequently, there has not been any occasion for a thrust toward flexibility paralleling that in zoning. To the contrary, there are indications of a reverse tendency. For example, both New Jersey and Massachusetts have recently amended their respective Acts to circumscribe more narrowly the discretionary power of planning commissions. Originally little more was required of the subdivider than his dedicating for streets the land designated on the plat or perhaps on an official map covering the sites. That requirement has procreated with the same fecundity as the use classifications of the zoning ordinance. Today the subdivider must contemplate the possibility of having to dedicate land for educational or recreational purposes, in addition to that for street purposes. He must also contemplate having to improve the property to be subdivided, *inter alia,* by grading and paving streets and walks, by installing lights, a whole water system, and sewers.

Additional conditions are likely to be imposed upon rural areas entering the transitional stage to urbanism so long as our standard of aspirations continues to rise. At the same time a far lesser countermovement appears to be in progress. The same Massachusetts legislature that limited the discretion of planning commissions also prohibited them from requiring a subdivider to dedicate land. New Jersey's amended law for the first time limited under some circumstances the width of land which might be demanded for street purposes. Whether this is a temporary reaction or a long-term limiting factor is not yet discernible.

Among the most important non-legal forces at work have been increasing population and its concomitant increased urbanization, a rising standard of living, practical exigencies of financing needed improvements, wasted resources resulting from abandonment of subdivisions after partial improvement by the municipality. The strength of these forces can perhaps best be gauged by the small amount of resistance laws like those just mentioned have encountered from the courts. The same forces can probably be counted on to secure judicial acceptance for changes and additions to these laws.

Nevertheless, in particular cases, courts have refused to sanction conditions because they conflicted with judicial concepts of fairness and reasonableness. With respect to subdivision controls this appears to mean that the conditions imposed should be justifiable by some approximation to a calculus of social costing. The test, according to *Pioneer Trust & Sav. Bank* v. *Village of Mt. Prospect,* is whether the costs sought to be imposed on the subdivider are "specifically and uniquely attributable to his activity which would otherwise be cast upon the public."

This Illinois case also illustrates that the test is not one which can be mechanically applied. It sustains the developer in his refusal to donate 6.7 acres for school and playground purposes, for which, concededly, there was a pre-existing need aggravated by the 250 residential lots added by the new subdivision. The court's reasoning is fair warning to counsel of that state on both sides, but particularly to counsel for the planning authority which has the burden of proof, that the record must assist the court in computing social costs:

The agreed statement of facts shows that the present school facilities of Mount Prospect are near capacity. This is the result of the total development of the community. If this whole community had not developed to such an extent or if the existing school facilities were greater, the purported need supposedly would not be present. Therefore, on the record in this case the school problem which allegedly exists here is one which the subdivider should not be obliged to pay the total cost of remedying, and to so construe the statute would amount to an exercise of the power of eminent domain without compensation.[2]

The law in this area is still not entirely clear. Hence, an ordinance authorizing conditions the burden of which was clearly disproportionate to the activity might be upheld if the facts fell within one of the more confused spots. But even where the result may be thought to be wrong, the principle of social costing appears to be accepted. An ordinance violative of it would, therefore, be begging for trouble.

Restraints on Alienation, Rules against Perpetuities and Accumulations

This last group of direct controls differs from the two preceding categories in that first, these are not only administered but formulated by the courts, and, second, they are not brand new, but hoary or venerable (depending upon whether the spokesman is for or against them). The rules against perpetuities, the rules against accumulation, and the rules against restraints on alienation are all fairly persuasive indices that the slow case-by-case adjudication of the courts is not necessarily more productive of satisfactory solutions in this area than the relatively rapid legislative approach of enactments aimed at comprehensive coverage.

The policy of the common law emerges clearly enough. It is to prohibit all sorts of restraints on alienation. The reason, too, is not hard to discern. Land is the one ultimate resource of the community. It should be alienable so that the person who owns land but does not have the skill to develop it properly can sell it to someone who is ready and able to put it to a more intensive and automatically higher and better use for the community.

But the body of case law which has grown up is a labyrinth in which even astute, experienced lawyers can lose their way. Read through the marvelously intricate attempt of the American Law of Property to draw all the refinements among restraints on legal life interests, restraints on legal fee simples, restraints on equitable interests, forfeitures and disabling restraints, and the myriad variations that have sprung up in all the jurisdictions. It is easy to conclude that the courts have decided case-by-case often on peculiar reasons and frequently without thought to the whole pattern of the field. Moreover, although the rules dealing directly with restraints exist side by side with and are logically related to indirect prohibitions such as rules against perpetuities, little or no thought appears to have been given to this interaction. Thus, notwithstanding all the rules against perpetuities, a house which generations ago was restricted to 14 feet in height to protect a view of the cows grazing on the Boston Common can today, despite the able efforts of generations of conveyancers, be kept to that same height. The generality of courts have also been remiss in continuing to view each piece of land as unique, for we live today under a system where land is becoming more homogenized and perhaps equivalent to other factors of production. Because the courts have failed to consider the side factors that might test the wisdom of what they and the lawyers are doing, the case law is logically inconsistent and acts at cross purposes to its alleged goals of assuring the best use of land.

Inconsistency and mockery of the declared policies of the court may trouble the lawyer. The average citizen may be more concerned with whether these policies accord with empiric studies and with the land use policies and goals articulated by other land use controls and by the other commitments of the community to planning of land and of housing. He would doubtless applaud as wise the conclusion of *Gayle* v. *York Center Community Cooperative* that if "accepted and economical considerations dictate that a partial restraint is reasonably necessary for their fulfillment such a restraint should be sustained."

The importance of private and doctrinal land controls in day-to-day conveyancing and in the day-to-day world of lawyers, mortgagees, and developers may soon result in pressure for over-all review of this area and its co-ordination with other land use controls.

Indirect Regulatory Mechanisms

The classification of controls into direct and indirect is not intended to bear any relation to efficiency. Even as a neutral line for discussion purposes it is at best fuzzy. Zoning, for example, has been classed here and is generally regarded as a direct control. But it could just as easily be classified as an indirect control; as a barrier to some irrational development activity, zoning may result in development being channeled into desired areas, but it exerts no directive force. Incentives, planning and government developmental activities, on the other hand, may be very potent forces in stimulating desired activity.

Incentive Controls

Incentive controls bring into play government's powers to tax and to spend. They are laws relating to metropolitan land uses which neither order nor direct action, but seek to achieve it by a conditional offer of some benefit. The benefit induces action; the condition regulates its form. This category includes guarantees, low interest loans, subsidies, grants-in-aid, tax advantages, and technical assistance. The basic idea is not new. The guarantee, for example, was used by the federal government during the depression of the thirties to help small home owners secure mortgage money. But it is only during recent years that the whole battery of techniques has begun to be used on a large scale in furtherance of planning proposals relating to housing, highways, and other matters affecting urban shape.

Controls operate between levels of government as well as between government and individuals. One important influence in the direction of greater use of incentive controls is the tripartite structure of our government and the respective functions and financial strength of each level. The federal government has been getting an ever larger share of the tax dollar. The states and their subdivisions have been charged historically with responsibilities for schools, roads, such public housing as was constructed, and the like; demand for such construction has increased far beyond the financial capacity of the states. Hence while they may resent what they regard as federal intrusion in this area they are not in general reluctant to accept federal financial aid. The delicacy of intergovernmental relationship renders it more expedient for the federal government to act indirectly and to protect its investment by strings and conditions, rather than to attempt to take over direct control of these functions.

Analogous interrelated pressures are at work between government and private enterprise and conduce toward the same result. Politically also, it is far easier to confer a benefit subject to conditions than to achieve the same result through the overtly coercive force of police powers.

It may perhaps be argued that while, in theory, housing, zoning, and subdivision controls are a direct control almost of a rationing and licensing nature, in practice, mostly by the process of overzoning, sometimes through variances, exceptions, generally lax administration and inspection, they have not operated as such a curtailment of property rights. But the argument becomes less persuasive the closer we move towards fine pinpoint zoning, performance standards, floating zones, detailed handling of subdivision problems, the granting of broad discretions, spot rehabilitation, and the like. By contrast, control through incentive and subsidy may be regarded as permitting liberty of action. A system of government control which operates through the indirect effects of fiscal and monetary policy can be regarded as impinging less on the individual than do direct controls.

These considerations may explain the modification of those doctrines limiting the use of incentive controls where the alternative was resort to police powers. Thus public use, a requirement for the valid exercise of the eminent domain power, has been judicially transmuted

from the restrictive public purpose or employment to public advantage or benefit, with benefit being given a broad rather than a narrow construction. The Massachusetts Opinion of the Justices in 1955, that where justification for a redevelopment plan was sought in existing conditions there must be a full-blown residential slum, reflects a more restrictive view which was the earlier consensus. Its survival is attested to by decisions such as the Opinion of the Justices in Maine, considering a bill to condemn land for industrial development, and *Hogue* v. *Port of Seattle,* in Washington, reviewing a bill to take legally blighted lands, also for industrial development. Both decisions hold that the exercise of the power may not be justified on the public benefit to be derived from industrial expansion. The Washington decision additionally rejects the elimination of blight-productive defects in legal title.

These decisions, however, are contrary to the tide of judicial opinion toward the broader horizons opened by the United States Supreme Court decisions in *Berman* v. *Parker.* Among others, Connecticut, Illinois, Massachusetts, and Pennsylvania courts are part of the new judicial consensus that holds that the elimination of blight—whether residential, industrial or undeveloped—and the provision of industrial areas satisfy the requirement of public use.

Planning controls

Planning activity can be a direct control where the regulatory measure is made part of the plan; a direct control once removed where the regulatory measure controls individuals, but the plan controls the regulatory measures; or an indirect control where it influences, but does not coerce, development decisions.

Where incentives exercise control by changing the attractions of a specific development, hortatory planning exerts control by revealing already existing attractions. Rather than dictating what the planner deems to be desirable—which seems to be a common misconception among laity—the aim of planning may be to eliminate the inefficiencies of the market mechanism. The survey and plan thus provide a basis for rational decisions, and thereby foster rational development. Public planning collects and pulls together a host of information about economics, population, industrial tax space, and the rest which is not available to the ordinary entrepreneur —especially in a field like real estate where small business predominates. The effect may be to expose certain gaps in the existing fabric of land and housing to a man looking about for a field in which to produce.

By projecting probable development, the master plan furnishes a clue to the future of an area and, therefore, to the risk involved in making particular kinds of investments in that locale. The educational process of the plan, the sense of participation in the values of the community on whose resources the plan is to operate, and the setting of a general framework to maximize individual choice in the operations of the market mechanism are the means. This type of reconciliation of public and private purpose makes appropriate General Motors' use of the word "planning" in its planning division at the same time that, in the public field, a misconception sometimes fostered by planners themselves makes its use by a Conservative Ministry of Town and Country Planning almost improper.

If the level of planning activity is lower than desirable, it is not because legal barriers prevent it from rising; it is that the state laws which enable planning activities permit rather than direct. The laws exert no compulsion upon a city which does not choose to prepare a master plan for itself, or to join with other localities in the preparation of a regional plan. Even gentler prods of self interest are used sparingly. Urban renewal and redevelopment acts very frequently require the preparation of a plan before the benefits of the act can be had. But regulatory powers are generally not conditioned on or co-ordinated with any planning. Most zoning enabling laws do require a "comprehensive plan." But the overwhelming weight of judicial authority is that the requirement of the zoning law does not refer to the master plan of the same state's planning law, and, moreover, that it may be satisfied by the zoning ordinance itself. Thus zoning, the oldest land use control and the one still most widely employed, may be exercised without a guiding master plan, or, what is even more absurd, in disregard of such guidance where it is available.

At least one state, New Jersey, has taken a contrary view as to subdivision controls. The terms of the relevant enabling act do not specifically subject the delegation to a condition that its exercise be preceded by preparation of a master plan. Nevertheless, the condition has been inferred by courts which did not even have the question thrust on them. While this may render its dictum in legal jargon, the fact that the court reached out for the question may reflect its lack of doubt as to the proper answer.

Logically, the failure, even in New Jersey, to reach a parallel conclusion as to the relation of zoning and planning may seem indefensible. But subdivision control powers are generally delegated in the same act or at the same time as planning powers, whereas zoning powers usually precede both. In view of this embarrassing time sequence, it is hard to see how the courts could have reached any other conclusion with respect to zoning, and harder still to see how they could rationalize overruling their established precedent. If this should be changed—as does seem desirable—the onus is on the planning profession to make the necessity known to legislators.

As long as enabling acts are permissive, the potential benefits of planning will often remain unrealized. But the most disappointing experience has been with regional planning laws. In Wisconsin, for example, three years after the state legislature had authorized regional planning, not a single regional commission had been formed. Most of the reasons for planning inactivity on the smaller local level probably apply to the larger area of the region.

In addition, there is the obstacle of local government's jealousy of its power. Local government has accepted the idea of regulating the present use of land, transforming harmful areas, and planning future beneficial development. Thus far, at any rate, there is no evidence of similar acceptance of the idea of metropolitan government. Despite the pleas of several intellectuals and a few of the elite leaders such as the Regional Plan Association group in New York, the core's suburbs continue to exercise what land use measures have been delegated to them under state enabling legislation in at best a roughly co-ordinated fashion. Only the emergence of a greater common menace seems to induce voluntary co-operative action. This was recently demonstrated in Ohio. There the ordinarily home-rule-minded municipalities acted together through a regional planning association to oppose the greater danger of incursion into their powers by a commission having state-wide jurisdiction. But such emergency coalitions tend to disintegrate once the original raison d'être no longer exists.

Here again the difficulties in the way of a judicial solution make it unlikely that one will be found. Some years ago the New Jersey courts appeared to be making an effort in this direction. The foundation was laid in *Duffcon Concrete Products* v. *Borough of Cresskill,* which presented the question of whether a municipality had power to exclude all industry from its boundaries; the court deduced this

power from the statutory direction to encourage the "appropriate use" of land. While the municipal zoning enabling act under which the case arose limited its sights to the area of the municipality, the court took a broader view. "What may be the most appropriate use of any particular property depends not only on all the conditions, physical, economic and social, prevailing within the municipality and its needs, but also on the nature of the entire region in which the municipality is located and the use to which the land in that region has been or may be put most advantageously." This was in 1949. In 1954 the credo was reaffirmed in the battle of the boroughs reported in *Borough of Cresskill* v. *Borough of Dumont.*

Concerted action by a professional organization of planners, analogous to that undertaken by the American Civil Liberties Union in its field of interest, may be as important as getting legislation enacted. In *Duffcon Concrete Products,* which contains probably the best judicial statement on regional planning, the court had the benefit of an *amicus curiae* brief filed by the Joint Council of Municipal Planning Boards in Essex County, New Jersey. The court's sophistication on the regional issue almost certainly owes much to that source.

The doctrine of *Duffcon* is fine as an article of faith but, given the best will in the world, it was still only an attitude and not a guide to an answer in particular cases. If, in addition, the court had a master plan for the region, framed by the proper public body, it would have both the will and the means. It is doubtful whether the court can or will, or for that matter should, make the planning decisions which would properly be part of a regional master plan. Until some means are devised for requiring the preparation of such plans and for getting them before the court whenever regional questions are present, legal impetus to regional planning will be minimal.

Nevertheless, and even without changes in state legislation, the future will almost unquestionably see a substantial increase in planning, locally and perhaps even more regionally. A tremendous impetus is being given to such activity by the federal government aid programs which stress the necessity of planning, and, often, planning on a regional scale. Thus the President's 1962 Message to Congress requesting federal aid for urban mass transportation attributed "key importance" to "area-wide transportation planning and comprehensive development planning for metropolitan and large urban areas."

For this increased planning activity to result in proportionately greater indirect controls, the plans, including the underlying factual survey, must be generally available. This is not always the case, and often the unavailability is advertent, perhaps due to vestiges of the view of some early planners that the plan was purely a tool for the commission. To function properly, it had to have the utmost flexibility, and hence was certainly not to be enacted into law, and, for preference, it was not even to be a public document. This is a planning concept, not a legal one, and the initiative for any change must properly come from the planners.

Some fear that such designations may produce blight because the owner who knows his property is to be acquired for public purposes lacks incentive to expend money to keep it in good repair. To the extent that these dangers exist or there is a fear that they do, safety is being purchased at a needlessly high price. The benefits of a publicized plan without legal or factual blight can be had by the simple expedient of stating the plan in terms of principles and goals, rather than general locations.

Another desideratum is that public development adhere to the plan. The private developer in making his decision is hardly going to give much weight to the prophesies of a plan which experience has shown to be wrong in the very area where accuracy might most reasonably have been anticipated. Thus when, as is reported in a California case, the local authorities pick a site for public construction different from that recommended by their own plan, the self-fulfilling power of the plan with regard to the private sector is also weakened. The California court upheld the action of the municipality on the ground that the question was one governed by home rule rather than general law. It might with equal plausibility have held that although the question was within the home rule powers the municipality was bound by its own decision, as stated in its master plan, until it followed the prescribed procedure for changing that decision. It would nevertheless be a much harder result to reach because the court probably viewed the municipality's decision as a political matter and reversing it would be contrary to a very strong tradition.

Control through Development

Government development is both the most forthright of controls and an important indirect control. The government operates largely in spheres the private sector finds unprofitable to enter—schools, parks, roads, and selected forms of housing. New York City alone has over $1 billion invested in schools and a like amount in housing, redevelopment, and renewal projects. By way of perspective, the private construction boom in New York City amounted to $1 billion from mid-1940 to mid-1950, while during the same period the city spent about twice that amount for schools, hospitals, port facilities, parks, bridges, libraries, and other facilities.

The indirect control results from the inevitable repercussions in land uses, both publicly and privately owned, and on the whole setup of the metropolitan areas. For example, a highway program may remove land from the tax rolls, displace families, pump more cars into central cities, and constitute competition for a transit system already weak. But the same program can result in vast areas of slums being razed; federal aid may be made available for access roads and to channel traffic into and around the heart of the city; capital expenditures can provide catalytic agencies for private urban renewal investments.

One important factor in determining the amount of government development activity is the rate of population increase. A rapidly growing population makes demands for more schools, roads, park and recreation space; in short, more of all the goods and services traditionally furnished by government. If at the same time the standard of living is rising, the demand will be for new services as well. The extra-legal limiting factors are in general the same as those operating on incentive controls.

Legal institutions enter the picture at several points. One is with respect to compensation, a field of law which is, to put it most kindly, both confused and confusing. How much the government must pay to acquire the property it proposes to develop has a direct effect on how much development it can undertake. Part of this same question is how much property the government may acquire. If it may condemn in excess of its needs, it may be able to capture the increment its activities add to the value of surrounding properties. The effect is the same as a reduction in the cost of the project site. But, some jurisdictions hold this economy is beyond the pale of the Constitution. It may be that nothing short of an amendment to the Constitution will be able to effect a change.

The other point of contact is producing a most interesting legal accommodation. An attempt is being made, mostly in the context of open space, to reduce public costs by restricting purchases more closely to what is needed. The effort is resulting in the invention of new interests which can be carved out of the fee simple absolute. These include development rights, popularized by the British 1947 Planning Act, and conservation easements, which is California's contribution. Massachusetts has taken this idea and woven it into an interesting new combination with zoning and tax controls. A 1957 act authorizes the owner of land zoned for agricultural, forest, or open space use to apply for classification for tax purposes as open land. This entitles him to a tax rebate of 90 percent during the first three years, 70 percent for the next seven years, and 50 percent during the remaining years that the land is so classified.

Private Policies

Although not generally regarded as such, many private acts or policies are in effect semipublic enactments affecting land use. The line between private and public is by no means rigid; variations occur from day to day and from place to place.

Covenants and Conditions

Covenants are one of the earliest forms of land use control known to the common law. Agreements to use property for residential purposes only were lawful when the weight of authority still regarded zoning as unconstitutional. And since, under proper circumstances, such agreements would be enforced by equity, their provisions in a very real sense were law as to the convenanting parties. With the final validation and increasing use of zoning, resort to covenants probably declined. Now, however, there appears to be a resurgence brought about by the use of such agreements to control development of large subdivisions.

One criticism of the law of covenants has been that it permits one generation to fetter too severely the power of succeeding generations to deal with land. A remedial measure recently adopted in Massachusetts sets up two categories of agreements: (1) those imposed as part of a common scheme, i.e., private planning, and (2) others; it then establishes the period of their legal duration and provides for their recordation. It also prescribes the test to be applied by the courts in litigation seeking to enforce a covenant. Enforcement is to be denied unless the claimants actually benefit substantially by reason of it. Within the framework of the new statute, an able and experienced conveyancer, however, will probably be able to achieve the same objectives and with a degree of certainty not possible under purely case law regulation. Nevertheless, the provisions as to enforceability may tend to facilitate a more rational land use pattern.

The Massachusetts test of enforceability adopts the common law rule. Courts of equity in many jurisdictions have refused to enforce restrictive agreements that have outlived the conditions under which they were appropriate, and no longer serve a useful purpose. The criteria used by many of the cases are very much those of planning. What is the neighborhood affected? How long does it have to be in a use inconsistent with the covenant to be deemed a change in use? How does one know what is a "predominantly residential" purpose if that is the wording of the covenant? How does one decide what the traffic generation impact on a building is so that a present covenant for quiet no longer serves any useful purpose?

A basic question under our present legal structure is whether the judiciary or an administrative agency should make decisions concerning change in neighborhood, new needs, technology, and interrelationships of land use. If the decisions are to be made by the courts, private developers, who usually launch the arrangements, will also have the power to initiate proceedings looking to change. What criteria are to be applied to deciding the particular case and how can the results be correlated with what is happening in the administrative and planning branches of government? What, for example, should be the relationship of covenants to zoning? The old zoning ordinances often confer immunity on existing covenants. This may not give rise to much conflict under the cumulative type of zoning ordinance. But with the growing use of exclusive zoning ordinances providing for noncumulative uses in particular districts, conflicts are bound to grow apace. Will the courts say that the private power to dispose of land should prevail? Or will the contract right be put on a higher level of immunity from the reach of the police power, as was done so strongly by the New York Court of Appeals in the prior lien case of *Central Savings Bank* v. *City of New York*. Many of the zoning ordinances do not even purport to deal with covenants. If zoners live apart from the world of real property, and blissfully do not provide for recording variances or exceptions in the registry of deeds, and if planners survey, analyze, and project existing conditions of traffic and industrial uses, but utterly ignore the pattern established by conditions, determinable fees, covenants, and easements, what should be the court reaction? Should it say that this was not thought of by the agency and therefore it has to supply an artificial legislative intent, or should it assume that the zoning was meant to override the particular restriction in issue? What weight should a court give to the existence of a zoning ordinance? Should it simply disregard the zoning as not relevant for its common law adjudication? Should it regard zoning as conclusive upon it? Should it simply be regarded as evidence? Nor is this a tedious unraveling of alternatives; these are all views that have been taken by different jurisdictions. The problem from the point of view of achieving rational land use is not legal doctrine, but procedure.

These and similar issues are raised in litigation between two private parties, with no representation of the public considerations. Often the zoning ordinance is simply ignored or not argued by counsel. Planning principles may similarly not be brought to the court's attention. Yet such private litigation has tremendous land use effects. It may, for example, modify an entire zoning pattern either by starting new nonconforming uses, by encouraging further deviation from the plan, or by not permitting the kind of development which would be the most rational and best organized for that particular district.[3]

The need for much more thoughtful reformulation of related planning and property controls is apparent in the land disposition contract pushed on to the stage by urban renewal. In order to obtain detailed control of design, open space, and shape and placement of buildings, generalities of a zoning ordinance have proven inadequate. Detailed covenants and easements therefore have come into play. Assurance of the type of developer, the positive implementation of an architectural plan, non-speculation in redevelopment futures also require a resort to new property controls. What is the relationship between a zoning ordinance, which has to be in accordance with a comprehensive plan, and the redevelopment plan which has to be in accordance with the comprehensive plan or a master plan? What if the redevelopment plan is amended from time to time? What if the zoning ordinance is revised from time to time? How can we fit in the one lesson learned from land use controls—that time keeps wearing away at man's intentions, that one generation needs a power of appointment over the preceding one's assets, and that technology and man's knowledge are always expanding as are his desires? Since both the redevelopment plan and the zoning ordinance are adopted by the local legislative body, is it simply a ques-

tion of the more recent one prevailing should the two conflict? Conflicts are likely to arise, for the subsidy element in urban renewal means a demand for greater public controls, such as density or open space standards which in a zoning ordinance would give rise to claims of a taking of private property.

Private Institutional Policies

Just as covenants represent the primarily private counterpart of public planning enactments, the policies pursued by title companies are in some respects an important private counterpart of public enforcement in this area. In fact the zeal of title companies may exceed that of public enforcement, as in the period following the widespread invalidation of official mapping statutes. Contemporaries report that even after these decisions title companies were refusing to insure titles which violated the integrity of an official map.

For some reason, however, the title companies adopted a contrary approach to violations of zoning or subdivision laws; an exception to them is part of the "boiler plate" on every insurance binder. It is small comfort, as some Massachusetts land owners discovered, to find that you have a perfect "title," but cannot make the intended use of the land because it would violate the subdivision law. A similar unsatisfactory result may obtain with respect to bulk uses control, especially in the new guise of flexible floor area ratios; often the same open land is counted for the floor area ratio for two different parcels so far as the deed of chain of title is concerned, without cognizance being taken of the planning significance.

A recent pamphlet by the Home Title Insurance Company indicates that conservative conveyancers are increasingly aware of the necessary intertwining of private and public land use controls. Considerable impetus was given this development in Denver by a requirement to record all non-conforming uses. The result was swift enforcement through the action of mortgagees. Mortgagees—and after all, it is credit which is the life-blood of land development in this country—generally and their attorneys, too, are beginning to be more aware of the significance of subdivision and other land use controls.

This may have a great deal of significance in enforcement—that constant bugaboo of planning controls. It could greatly reduce the need for planning and building inspectors and local district attorneys as the enforcement arms of a government planning system. Policing by way of title and conveyancing may raise serious issues as to delegation of power to private groups, but its effectiveness in the day-to-day ordering of men's affairs can be little doubted, and the precedents of easements, covenants, and the like should ease acceptance.

A GLANCE AT THE FUTURE

This survey of selected land use controls depicts an over-all situation which in one sense might best be described as unexciting. A planner may wander through the entire domain and, unless he owes as much to Cervantes as to AIP, he would not meet with as much as one legal dragon belching forth proposal-consuming flames. This is not attributable to the fact that the selection is a mere fraction of the whole, because in this respect at least, it is a fairly representative sampling.

Private property, which not very long ago might have seemed nearly, though never quite, dragonesque, is now a relatively tame creature—civilized, if not socialized. A proposal portending substantial new restraints might show that there is still some fight left, but at present no great battles are being fought, only minor skirmishes.

Even as to these skirmishes how much constitutes a real, if lesser, conflict

between planning on the one hand and legal institutions on the other depends on how planning is defined. If, for example, every proposal to control land use automatically enters the ranks of planning, the instances of conflict would add up to a very large figure.

If, on the other hand, a proposal for controlling land use must have the unanimous support of the planning profession before legal veto of the proposal ranked as conflict, the picture would be one of perfect but meaningless rapprochement. Since our goal is the creation neither of a fool's paradise nor of a planner's inferno, the only reasonable approach seems to be to require some substantial consensus, short of unanimity. For present purposes, "substantial" is as precise as we need get.

With this as the yardstick, some tensions are discernible, more are inevitable. If suitable land were so plentiful that each individual could have all he desired without conflict with any other person, there would be no need for a law of real property. But where land is scarce in relation to demand, decisions must be made as to who gets what, and when, and the body of law grows because it is needed to assist in this decisional process.

Obviously the supply of suitable land in this country is less than the demand, but how much less is the subject of continuing dispute. Many people are fond of stating that the U.S. population could be sheltered at a figure of twelve houses to the acre in the state of Kansas. Others answer, "Who wants to live there?" and point to the shortage of land in metropolitan areas. The evaluation is complicated by the fact that neither element in the equation is a constant, a fact sometimes overlooked when inventorying supply. Right now, for example, we are in the process of discovering uses for urban space which lay idle because of lack of technological know-how and creative imagination. In the air space over the Franklin Roosevelt Drive in New York City there have recently risen high-rise luxury co-operative houses. A motel is rising in the air space over the New York Central's freight yards on the west side of the same city. The changes in living-working patterns wrought by the automobile after the First World War may be dwarfed by changes brought about by the airplane or some device not yet born.

Nevertheless, present indications are that demand will outrun supply. This situation makes for a growth in the law because scarcity is simply a shorthand way of saying that some needs are not being satisfied. These may be expected to create the pressures which are a major wellspring for proposals dealing with urban space, proposals to rearrange relations, to modify existing rights and duties. Every remedial law—and these formal enactments must come into being or the proposals will remain just so much talk—displeases someone. Such measures, therefore, contain within themselves the potential of conflict. Part of that potential will never be realized, but part will. Thus, it can be assumed that the near future will see many legal innovations attempted, with the usual proportion gradually gaining legal acceptance.

Incentive Controls

Prominent among the legal innovations will be more extensive resort to incentive controls: guaranties, low interest loans, subsidies, grants-in-aid, land assembly, tax advantages, and technical assistance. This means that positive aspects of development will be emphasized; above all, it signifies state and especially, since it is the fountain of credit, federal entry into the land use control field on a far larger scale.

One reason for this development is the dispute as to the scope of the police power, a dispute which goes back into common law history, probably even to

the time where "The memory of man runneth not," but is not perceptibly nearer solution for all its years. The police power was the issue in the struggle which accompanied the introduction of zoning, and it emerged triumphant in the debate among planners and lawyers as to the proper theory on which to base land use controls. Proponents were vindicated by the same Supreme Court which had invalidated minimum wages for women as an undue interference with property rights.

Today the most disputed subject matter is open space, whether park, playground, recreation, or simply undeveloped land. The effort to achieve it through the police power has taken many forms. In *Osteicher* v. *Wolcott,* an Ohio case, the technique was simply withholding subdivision approval. In *Forston Investment Co.* v. *Oklahoma City,* the device was a condition precedent to subdivision approval that a fee be paid into a general park fund. In a recent New Jersey case, the device was zoning the subject land for park, recreation, and school purposes. In all these cases, the courts expressed their sympathy with the open space objective and the concern for the common weal which inspired the government action. But they were also in accord that the police power could not constitutionally be utilized for the task.

Most recent attention has focused on development rights, with some planners arguing that such rights can be acquired or, more accurately perhaps, frozen through the exercise of the police power. The issue has not yet been presented to any court in this context. Even if, in a development rights case, the judiciary could be persuaded that the foregoing cases were distinguishable, and need not be followed as a matter of authority, the issue would remain a question of policy. Compensation allows greater, more intimate, and additional individual controls. There is a growing recognition that the money lubricant needs to be added to the machinery of land use controls in order to achieve greater flexibility. More important, perhaps, the affluence of our society may make subsidies and controls for the benefit of upper income groups politically palatable under a "filtering down" philosophy. Compensation also accords more precisely with accepted notions of fairness. In other words, even though a court would regard a control as a proper regulation under the police power, in fairness to the individual as well as on grounds of acceptability to the community it is appropriate to redress and spread the loss. Thus the recently proposed Pennsylvania law of open space, combining zoning and eminent domain, represents a legislative decision not to drive regulatory aspects too far. To a large extent this approach, if adopted, will be made possible by moving away from the limited property tax base through appropriations and subsidies by the state or federal government.

The considerations applying to open space resemble those mounted in the early years of zoning, but it has long been recognized that at some point differences in degree become, for practical purposes, indistinguishable from differences in kind. Thus the older regulation, even ignoring the effects of inflation on the values of real property, had a far deeper and wider bite, and the public, if it had had to pay the cost, would have prevented imposition of the control. This is proably not true as to development rights.

Each legal accommodation is bound to raise fresh problems. In the context of willingness to pay, the issue will arise of whether the benefits of planning traceable to the restriction should not be recaptured from those who benefit by planning. This, in turn, can be analyzed in another fashion: instead of paying through eminent domain—a burden on the general taxpayer—should not the cost be assumed by that district which is going to benefit primarily from the control? We can anticipate conflicts between the benefited neighboring group and the general taxpayer. There may be newer techniques aimed at recoupment, excess taking, and incremental taxation. As awareness grows of who is subsidizing whom, we can anticipate the invention of new kinds of transfer mechanism and new subsidies.

Mandatory Controls

However much incentive controls are expanded and improved, direct controls will continue to play an important role. The mandatory planning control of tomorrow will be a quite different animal from its predecessors of 1916–26. As has already been noted, mandatory control is now in a process of change. Two lines of development stand out, and both tend in the direction of greater flexibility. Carried to the extreme, the result could be that every change of use must be preceded by administrative authorization reminiscent of English development permission, with a transition of the zoning system to a licensing system through such techniques as special exceptions, special use districts, and floating districts.

The other vulnerable area of mandatory controls emerges when the concepts of racial, religious, and perhaps economic equality run counter to the use of controls to upgrade residential areas, provide parks, or gain other planning goals. The relationship between planning controls and discrimination, since the Supreme Court's decision in the School Cases, has been subjected to increasing judicial scrutiny. Coming after some years during which attention focused elsewhere, these issues tend to appear more novel than they are. Such early leading cases as *Spann* v. *Dallas* bottomed their opposition to the then infant control in very large part on the grounds that zoning was or could be used to perpetuate racial discrimination.

And *Buchanan* v. *Warley* condemned in 1917 a zoning ordinance making it unlawful for a white person to reside in a block where the residences were occupied by Negroes and for a Negro person to reside in a block where the residences were occupied by whites.

The verdict of the intervening years has been almost without exception in favor of the planning controls. The decisions never rejected the values of racial equality, equality of housing opportunity, and the like; the rationale was rather that the particular control did not entrench on them. *Town of Harrison* v. *Sunny Ridge Builders* is fairly typical. In issue was an upzoning from ½ to 1 acre minimum lots, which, the petitioners argued, would create an economic barrier which none but the wealthy would be able to surmount. The court vigorously asserted the impropriety of such a barrier as a planning goal. It upheld the zoning, however, pointing out that the subject area contained some of the most desirable residential sites in the community.

Today the result might well be different. The reason is not a shift in values. Rather there appears to be a heightened awareness of the realities of the situation, and a willingness to face up to them rather than to skirt the issue by resting on the theoretical or possible effect of the challenged action. This view, or renewed consciousness, is not limited to zoning, but probably will soon permeate the entire gamut of land use controls.

Here again there is a twofold question. One view is that if the control can be justified as advancing any proper planning goal it should be upheld regardless of its actual, probable, or intended purpose. But doubtless many planners would shun association with any measure motivated by discrimination.

The division in the planning ranks may well be such as to eliminate those controls from the category of conflict by definition. But even so, the new judicial sensitivity to discriminatory implications casts doubt on the propriety of far more defensible controls. These include most obviously zoning, but also all controls which have any tendency toward the prohibited effect, however innocent their purpose.

Real Property Devices

Still a third major innovation probably will occur in development of new legal concepts based on property conveyancing. New, more precise interests in property will be created—California's conservation rights and Minnesota's development rights point the way—making it possible for governments to acquire only that which they deem necessary and to compensate more often those injured by the acquistion. Experiments will be made in combining estate concepts, new and old, partial police power, eminent domain, and special tax theories, in enforcement of planning controls through the machinery of property conveyancing rather than through public government. There will be greater attention paid to the joint venture, to the relation between public and private energies. It is because of this spirit of experimentation, this willingness to regard the law of property as simply a tool which this age, like past ages, must reshape to meet its needs, that the American common law of property will probably continue to satisfy the needs of contemporary society.

Reviewability: The Legal Framework for Reasonableness

All three of the developments, by pushing hard the theory of controls, frame sharp issues for judicial review of land use decisions and of public and private relationships. An important factor in the resolution of many of them may be a suspicion that the new developments are probably more susceptible of abuse than the older controls by regulatory law. While the bulk of controls will continue to be upheld, some will not; the problem is to identify the factors which will determine validity. Some are quite clear.

In subdivision controls the rule has been fairly well crystallized that subdivision approval may be conditioned on the developer's assumption of the social costs occasioned by his activity. Similarly, in zoning it is now relatively clear that exclusionary zoining is not *per se* unreasonable and therefore illegal although specific instances might be. But as to other, newer issues, the courts have not yet had an opportunity to work out rules to determine legality. Hence the only determinant is the judicial distillation of what is reasonable in the circumstances. Since precise rules have not yet crystallized, these new issues will be handled in the common law fashion; generalized but accepted notions of reasonableness and fairness will furnish crude guideposts to future decisions.

Those aspects of fairness and justice denoted by equality of treatment and impartiality of procedure can be regarded as law ends which on occasion clash with physical planning ends, but essentially they are values shared by a consensus of society and expressed in a statute or decision. But even the state courts, which retain greater scrutiny than the federal courts, seem reluctant to interpose the Constitution against proposed solutions of urgent metropolitan problems. In fact, the constitutional role, which the layman tends to stress as the prime manifestation of United States planning law, has become so narrowed since the end of World War II that it is a minor constraint to the planner. One by-product is the need for a substitute for the tests of constitutionality that so often have been substituted for considerations of wisdom. But the typical judicial stress of balancing property rights against planning need underlines a major point. At the constitutional level law tends to focus on the relation between means and ends—in fact, the classic definition of the police power is "Whether the means employed . . . have a substantial relation to the public welfare." This concern with a testing of this relationship feeds into a concern over the intermeshing of goals so that even at the level of the legislative draftsman this search for co-ordination, which I have earlier referred to as rationality, is a natural inquiry into any planning proposal.

However, the planner, as much as the lawyer, has tended to rely too much on court review. Judicial invalidation of an enactment does not mean a reactionary brake; judicial vindication is not necessarily a victory for wise planning. The positive contribution of the restraints upon imprudent action has sometimes obsured the fact that judicial processes are somewhat helpless to induce rationality or even, at technical points, to review it. Given properly stated objectives, courts can be relied upon to review challenged actions to ascertain consistency with the avowed purpose for delegating the power being exercised. But it would be unrealistic in the extreme to rely on judicial review to ascertain whether the avowed purpose of one measure is in harmony with the stated goals and objectives of other interrelated measures. It is a job beyond the competence of the judiciary—beyond the scope of the type of knowledge an adversary system can present to a court, as well as beyond the remedies which a court can formulate or enforce. These difficulties are infinitely greater when the interacting measures are the product of different legislative bodies, whether on the same governmental level, as two cities, or different levels, as the federal government and municipalities. Equally important, both courts and legislature would almost certainly regard such judicial review as a rank usurpation of legislative powers by the judiciary. Hence, the ultimate conclusion: the pressing need is the guidance of a plan formulated and adopted by the local legislature, or, on the regional level, by the state legislature.

. . . . . .

Present urban problems can be analyzed solely in terms of particular fact clusters, for example: What is the best planning machinery for the region? Are gray areas eradicable? Do planning officials, generally non-elective, exercise more power than is consistent with democracy? Is flexible zoning better or worse than traditional zoning? This analysis may be adequate where the aim is amelioration of a particular evil. But the goal of rational development aspires to more and thus requires a different analysis. "Rational," in this context, implies that the goals and their consequences are known and that policies are adopted and reviewed in the light of that knowledge. Furthermore, rationality implies the articulation and harmonizing of the relationships of these goals and policies. This approach is not a substitute for fact studies; it is a framework for their analysis. The lack of such a framework is a serious aspect of the urban problem facing American society; its construction is one of the most interesting challenges in an area replete with them.

In this hammering out of a framework for goal clarification and alternatives, there will be a need for (1) local master plans of generalized statements of objectives, to which public developments and public controls over land uses must accord; (2) an articulation of federal policies and programs—those within a future Department of Urban Affairs as well as those without—which affect the pattern of metropolitan land uses; (3) a stress on the private dynamics of land development so that planning and controls can tap those energies which build and develop cities; (4) new relationships between private controls judicially administered through common law channels and public controls; and (5) new state-wide agencies both for administration and adjudication.

Law is only one profession which faces this challenge. In conjunction with other concerned groups, a legal framework can be devised for planning which can express the community consensus on planning objectives and means. This framework can also provide a system for articulating and testing these objectives and means as well as make possible community acceptance of proposals for attaining a rational utilization of urban space.

NOTES

1. See, e.g., the recent report to the Massachusetts legislature asserting that, because of abdication on the part of legislative bodies or overzealousness on the part of appointive planners, planning commissions were in fact wielding powers properly exercised only by elective bodies.

2. This quotation is from case 176 N.E. 2d at 802 (1961).— Editors' Note

3. Nuisance litigation raises the same issue. If a use permitted by a zoning ordinance is nevertheless claimed to be a common law nuisance by a legislator, what weight should the court give to the ordinance? How does public legislation of land controls, in general, fit in with the "private" side of the legal system where the courts are formulating what John Chipman Gray in his *Casebook on Property* described as the law of the "proper place"?

A SOCIAL CRITIC'S PERSPECTIVE

SOCIAL JUSTICE
AND SPATIAL SYSTEMS
DAVID HARVEY

Urban institutions are themselves subject to change and, says Harvey, such changes must consider more than the efficacy of existing social processes: they must be guided by principles of justice. Admittedly, "justice" is an elusive concept. But it is only by addressing it directly that its impact can be felt and, for Harvey, the recognition of a value such as justice is the crucial step in the humanizing of our urban areas.

Reprinted from *Antipode Monographs in Social Geography*, No. 1 (1972): 87–106, by permission of the publisher and the author.

Normative thinking has an important role to play in geographical analysis. Social justice is a normative concept and it is surprising, therefore, to find that considerations of social justice have not been incorporated into geographical methods of analysis. The reason is not far to seek. The normative tools characteristically used by geographers to examine location problems are derived from classical location theory. Such theories are generally Pareto-optimal since they define an optimal location pattern as one in which no one individual can move without the advantages gained from such a move being offset by some loss to another individual. Location theory has therefore characteristically relied upon the criterion of *efficiency* for its specification. Efficiency may be defined in a variety of ways, of course, but in location theory it usually amounts to minimizing the aggregate costs of movement (subject to demand and supply constraints) within a particular spatial system. Models of this type pay no attention to the consequences of location decisions for the distribution of income. Geographers have thus followed

economists into a style of thinking in which questions of distribution are laid aside (mainly because they involve unwelcome ethical and political judgments), while efficient "optimal" location patterns are determined with a particular income distribution assumed. This approach obviously lacks something. In part the reaction away from normative thinking towards behavioral and empirical formulations may be attributed to the search for a more satisfying approach to location problems. This reaction has been healthy, of course, but partly misplaced. It is not normative modelling which is at fault but the *kind* of norms built into such models. In this chapter, therefore, I want to diverge from the usual mode of normative analysis and look at the possibility of constructing a normative theory of spatial or territorial allocation based on principles of social justice. I do not propose this as an alternative framework to that of efficiency. In the long run it will be mostly beneficial if efficiency and distribution are explored jointly. The reasons for so doing are evident. If, in the short run, we simply pursue efficiency and ignore the social cost, then those individuals or groups who bear the brunt of that cost are likely to be a source of long-run inefficiency either through decline in what Liebenstein (1966) calls "x-efficiency" (those intangibles that motivate people to cooperate and participate in the social process of production) or through forms of antisocial behavior (such as crime and drug addiction) which will necessitate the diversion of productive investment towards their correction. The same comment can be made about the single-minded pursuit of social justice. It is counter-productive in the long-run to devise a socially just distribution if the size of the product to be distributed shrinks markedly through the inefficient use of scarce resources. In the long-long-run, therefore social justice and efficiency are very much the same thing. But since questions of social justice have been neglected (except in political rhetoric) and there is a persistent tendency to lay them aside in short run analysis, I shall do the opposite and lay aside questions of efficiency. This should not be taken to imply, however, that efficiency is irrelevant or unimportant.

The concept of social justice is not an all-inclusive one in which we encapsulate our vision of the good society. It is rather more limited. Justice is essentially to be thought of as a principle (or set of principles) for resolving conflicting claims. These conflicts may arise in many ways. Social justice is a particular application of just principles to conflicts which arise out of the necessity for social cooperation in seeking individual advancement. Through the division of labor it is possible to increase production: the question then arises as to how the fruits of that production shall be distributed among those who cooperate in the process. The principle of social justice therefore applies to the division of benefits and the allocation of burdens arising out of the process of undertaking joint labor. The principle also relates to the social and institutional arrangements associated with the activity of production and distribution. It may thus be extended to consider conflicts over the locus of power and decision-making authority, the distribution of influence, the bestowal of social status, the institutions set up to regulate and control activity, and so on. The essential characteristic in all such cases, however, is that we are seeking a principle which will allow us to evaluate the distributions arrived at as they apply to individuals, groups, organizations, and territories, as well as to evaluate the mechanisms which are used to accomplish this distribution. We are seeking, in short, a specification of a just distribution justly arrived at.

Unfortunately there is no one generally accepted principle of social justice to which we can appeal. Yet the notion of social justice underpins social philosophical thought from Aristotle's *Ethics* onwards. Its two most important forms are derivative of the social contract (initially formulated by Hume and Rousseau) and utilitarianism (initially formulated by Bentham and Mill). Recently, there has been a resurgence of interest in these principles resulting in modern versions of them which seem much more acceptable for a number of reasons—the work of Rawls (1969; 1971), Rescher (1966) and Runciman (1966), being outstanding in this respect. There are other strands to this thinking of course. The detailed discussion of the concept of equality by writers such as Tawney (1931), and the now voluminous literature on the question of the proper distribution of income in society have added their weight to the argument. I do not wish to review this literature here, however, and I shall confine myself to one possible argument concerning social justice and endeavor to show how it can be formulated in a manner that is geographically relevant and useful.

The principle of social justice which

I shall explore starts with the skeleton concept of "a just distribution justly arrived at." The main task of this chapter is to put flesh on this skeleton and to formulate its geographic variant. Two preliminary questions may be asked about it:

What are we distributing? It is easy enough to say that we are distributing the benefits to be had from social cooperation but it is very much more difficult to specify what those benefits are, particularly as they relate to individual preferences and values. For the purpose of this paper I shall leave this question unanswered and merely call whatever it is that we are distributing "income." This indicates a very general definition of income—such as Titmuss's (1962) "command over society's scarce resources" or an even more general one such as that proposed by Miller and Roby (1970). I shall assume here that we can devise a socially just definition of income—for it would indeed be a net injustice to devise a socially just distribution of something defined in an unjust manner!

Among whom or what are we distributing it? There is general agreement that the ultimate unit with which we should be concerned is the human individual. For convenience it will often be necessary to discuss distribution as it occurs among groups, organizations, territories, and so on. Geographers are particularly interested in the territorial or regional organization of society and it will be convenient to work at that level of aggregation. But we know enough about the various forms of ecological fallacy (see Alker, 1969) to know that a just distribution across a set of territories defined at one scale does not necessarily mean a just distribution achieved at another scale or a just distribution among individuals. This scale or aggregation problem poses some thorny methodological difficulties. In principle, we may hold that distribution made at any scale or across any aggregates should be accountable to distribution as it occurs at the individual level of analysis. This is difficult to do, but for present purposes I shall assume that justice achieved at a territorial level of analysis implies justice achieved for the individual, even though I am too aware that this is not necessarily the case.

"A JUST DISTRIBUTION"

Having assumed away two rather important questions, I shall now undertake an analysis of the principle of social justice. This can be split into two parts and here I shall seek an understanding of what is meant by a "just distribution." To do this I must first establish a basis for that distribution. This is, of course, an ethical problem which cannot be resolved without making important moral decisions. These decisions essentially concern what it is that justifies individuals making claims upon the product of the society in which they live, work, and have their being. Several criteria have been suggested (see Rawls, 1969; 1971; Rescher, 1966).

1. *Inherent equality*—all individuals have equal claims on benefits irrespective of their contribution.
2. *Valuation of services in terms of supply and demand*—individuals who command scarce and needed resources have a greater claim than do others. It is perhaps important to differentiate here between situations in which scarcity arises naturally (inherent brain and muscle power) and situations in which it is artificially created (through the inheritance of resources or through socially organized restrictions on entry into certain occupations).
3. *Need*—individuals have rights to equal levels of benefit which means that there is an unequal allocation according to need.
4. *Inherited rights*—individuals have claims according to the property or other rights

which have been passed on to them from preceding generations.

5. *Merit*—claims may be based on the degree of difficulty to be overcome in contributing to production (those who undertake dangerous or unpleasant tasks—such as mining—and those who undertake long periods of training—such as surgeons—have greater claims than do others).

6. *Contribution to common good*—those individuals whose activities benefit most people have a higher claim than do those whose activities benefit few people.

7. *Actual productive contribution*—individuals who produce more output—measured in some appropriate way—have a greater claim than do those who produce a lesser output.

8. *Efforts and sacrifices*—individuals who make a greater effort or incur a greater sacrifice relative to their innate capacity should be rewarded more than those who make little effort and incur few sacrifices.

These eight criteria are not mutually exclusive and they obviously require much more detailed interpretation and analysis. I shall follow Runciman (1966) and suggest that the essence of social justice can be embodied in a weak ordering of three of these criteria so that *need* is the most important, *contribution to common good* is the second and *merit* is the third. I shall not argue the case for this decision. It necessarily rests, however, on an appeal to certain controversial and ethical arguments. But as will become apparent in what follows, the issues raised in the detailed examination of these three criteria are sufficiently comprehensive to subsume many of the issues which could legitimately be raised under the other headings. These three criteria could be examined in detail in a variety of contexts. I choose at this juncture to introduce the geographic aspect to the argument and examine how they might be formulated in the context of a set of territories or regions. For pur-

poses of exposition I shall mainly consider the problem as one of a central authority allocating scarce resources over a set of territories in such a way that social justice is maximized. As I have already stated, I shall assume that territorial distributive justice automatically implies individual justice.

TERRITORIAL DISTRIBUTIVE JUSTICE

The first step in formulating a principle of territorial distributive justice lies in determining what each of the three criteria—need, contribution to common good, and merit—means in the context of a set of territories or regions. Procedures may then be devised to evaluate and measure distribution according to each criterion. The combination of the three measures (presumably weighted in some way) provides a hypothetical figure for the allocation of resources to regions. This figure can then be used, as happens in most normative analysis, to evaluate existing distributions or to devise policies which will improve existing allocations. A measure of territorial justice can be devised by correlating the actual allocation of resources with the hypothetical allocations. Such a procedure allows the identification of those territories which depart most from the norms suggested by standards of social justice: but this is not, of course, easy. Bleddyn Davies (1968), who first coined the term "territorial justice" has published a pioneering work on the subject, which indicates some of the problems involved.

1. Need

Need is a relative concept. Needs are not constant for they are categories of human consciousness and as society is transformed so the consciousness of need is transformed. The problem is to define exactly what it is that need is relative to and to obtain an understanding of how needs arise. Needs can be defined with respect to a number of different categories of activity—these remain fairly constant over time and we can list nine of them:

1. food
2. housing
3. medical care
4. education
5. social and environmental service
6. consumer goods
7. recreational opportunities
8. neighborhood amenities
9. transport facilities

Within each of these categories we can set about defining those minimum quantities and qualities which we would equate with needs. This minimum will vary according to the social norms at a given time. There will also be a variety of ways of fulfilling such needs. The need for housing can be met in a number of ways but at this time these would presumably not include living in shacks, mud-huts, tents, crumbling houses, and the like. This raises a whole host of issues which I can best examine in the context of a particular category—medical services.

Nobody, presumably, would deny that medical care is a legitimate form of need. Yet that need is not easily defined and measured. If we are to obtain a normative measure of social justice we have first to define and measure need in a socially just way. For example, the category "health services" comprises a multitude of subcategories some of which, such as cosmetic surgery and back massages, can reasonably be regarded (in our present society at least) as non-essential. An initial decision has to be made, therefore, on which subcategories should be regarded as "needs" and which should not. Decisions then have to be made as to what are reasonable standards of need within each subcategory. Let us consider some of the methods for doing this.

(i) Need can be determined through looking at *market demand.* Wherever facilities are working very close to capacity we may take it that there is an unfulfilled need in the population and thereby justify the allocation of more resources to expand medical services. This procedure is only acceptable if we can reasonably assume that nothing is inhibiting demand (such as lack of money or lack of access to facilities). To accept market demand as a socially just measure of need requires that the other conditions prevailing in society (affecting both demand and supply) are themselves socially just. This is usually not the case and this method of determining need is therefore likely to be socially unjust.

(ii) *Latent demand* may be assessed through an investigation of relative deprivation as it exists among individuals in a set of regions. Individuals would be relatively deprived if (1) they do not receive a service (2) they see other people (including themselves at a previous or an expected time) receiving it (3) they want it, and (4) they regard it as feasible that they should receive it (Runciman, 1966, 10). The concept of relative deprivation (basically similar to perceived or felt need) has been associated in the literature with the concept of a reference group (a group against which an individual measures his or her own expectations). The reference group may be socially determined—i.e., all blacks or all blue-collar workers—or spatially determined—i.e., everybody in a neighborhood or even in a large region. The difference between the expectations of the group for health care and actual services received provides a measure of relative deprivation. This measure can be obtained either by direct survey data, or if we know something about reference groups we can calculate likely relative deprivation by looking at variance in provision within different groups. The advantages of the latter approach are that it incorporates a behavioral element so that legitimate differences in group preferences can be expressed, while also providing a measure of dissatisfaction and therefore an indicator of likely political pressure. Its disadvantage is that it assumes that "real" needs are reflected by felt needs. This is often not the case. Very poorly served groups often have very low standards of felt need. Also, all kinds of social inequities are likely to be incorporated into the measure of need if, as is usually the case in class differentiated and (or) segregated societies, the reference group structure is itself a response to conditions of social injustice.

(iii) *Potential demand* can be evaluated by an analysis of the factors which generate particular kinds of health problem. Population totals and characteristics will have an important impact on territorial needs. Health problems can be related to age, life-cycle, amount of migration, and so on. In addition there are special problems which may relate to occupational characteristics (such as mining), to sociological and cultural circumstances, as well as to income levels. Health problems can also be related to local environmental conditions (density of population, local ecology, air and water quality, and so on). If we knew enough about all of these relationships we should be able to predict the volume and incidence of health care problems across a set of territories. This requires, however, a far more sophisticated understanding of relationships than we currently possess; even so, various attempts have been made to employ this method. Its attraction, of course, is that it does provide a reasonably objective method for measuring potential demand for health care. Unfortunately, we are still left with the problem of converting this demand into a measure of need, which in this case requires that we determine appropriate forms and levels of response to these statistically determined potential demands. The response usually amounts to setting standards, which is usually done with a given quantity of resources in mind.

(iv) We could also seek to determine needs through *consultation* with experts in the field. Experts tend to determine need with one eye on available resources. But those who have lived and worked in a community for a long period of time can often draw upon their experience to provide subjective assessments which are nevertheless good indicators of need. The resolution of opinions provided by judiciously selected experts in the health field (health planners, hospital administrators, physicians, community groups, social workers, welfare rights groups, and so on) may provide a socially just determination of need. The method relies upon the subjective judgments of a selected set of individuals, but it has the considerable benefit of drawing directly upon the experience of those who have been most concerned with the health care problem. The disadvantage, of course, lies in the possibility that the experts are selected on the basis of socially unjust criteria— for example, to place the determination of need in the hands of a committee of the American Medical Association would at present be disastrous from the point of view of social justice.

We must select among the various methods for determining need in such a way that we maximize on the social justice of the result. In the current circumstances I would discard (i) altogether in the health field and I would only accept (ii) if I felt that legitimate variations in preference were being expressed rather than variations in a felt need arising out of a socially unjust social situation or out of ignorance or false consciousness. Both (iii) and (iv) provide possible methods for establishing needs in the health field, but neither are easy to employ and both contain within them the possibility of a socially unjust determination of need.

If need is a primary criterion for assessing the social justice of a distribution of resources across a set of territories, then we are first obliged to establish a socially just definition and measurement system for it. The various methods (and their attendant difficulties) outlined in the medical care case can be applied to each of the categories—education, recreation, housing, consumer goods, and so on. It is not easy to decide upon a socially just definition of need within each category. The appropriate method may also vary from category to category —it may be best do determine consumer need through conventional supply and demand analysis, recreational needs through relative deprivation analysis, housing needs through statistical analysis, and medical care needs through resolution of expert opinion. These, however, are open questions. Defining social justice in terms of need thrusts onto us the whole uncomfortable question of what is meant by need and how it should be measured. It is imperative that we make socially just decisions on these issues. Otherwise our pursuit of a principle of social justice for evaluating geographic distributions will be worthless.

2. Contribution to Common Good

The concept of contribution to common good can be translated into existing geographic concepts with relative ease. We are here concerned with how an allocation of resources to one territory affects conditions in another. A technology exists to handle some of these questions in the work on interregional multiplier analysis, growth poles and externalities. The spread effects may be good or bad— pollution being an example of the latter. The notion of contribution to common good (or common "bad" in the case of pollution) suggests that our existing

technology should be used to extend our understanding of interregional income transfers, interregional linkages, spatial spread effects and so on, insofar as these have actual or potential consequences for the distribution of income in society. This is not an easy task, as is demonstrated by the problems which have plagued the attempt to evaluate the benefits of urban renewal (Rothenberg, 1967). There are two rather different aspects to this problem. We can seek to improve on existing allocations given the existing pattern of interregional multipliers or we can take a more radical approach and seek to restructure the pattern of interregional multipliers by reorganizing the spatial system itself. If we take the latter approach we seek a form of spatial organization which will make the greatest contribution to fulfilling needs through the multiplier and spread effects generated by a particular pattern of regional investment. Common good may have a second component to it, that of increasing the total aggregate product. In this case contribution to common good comes close to the usual efficiency and growth criteria with externalities and side-effects incorporated into the analysis. In the search for social justice this sense of contributing to the common good should remain subsidiary to the concern for distributive consequences.

3. Merit

I shall translate the concept of "merit" into a geographical concept which relates to the degree of environmental difficulty. Such difficulties may arise out of circumstances in the physical environment. Certain hazards, such as drought, flood, earthquakes and so on, pose extra difficulty to human activity. If there is a need for a facility (say a port in an area subject to hurricane damage) then extra resources should be allocated to counter this hazard. In terms of the weak ordering that I have imposed on the criteria for social justice, this means that if a facility is needed, if it contributes to the common good in some way, *then and only then* would we be justified in allocating extra resources for its support. If people live in flood plains when they have no need to live in flood plains and if they contribute nothing to the common good by living there, then under the principle of social justice they ought not to be compensated for damage incurred by living there. If, however, individuals are forced by circumstances (such as lack of alternative choice) to live there then the primary criterion of need may be used to justify compensation. The same remarks apply to problems which arise in the social environment. Hazards posed by crimes against property, fire and riot damage, and the like, vary according to the social circumstances. Individuals need adequate security if they are to be able to contribute meaningfully to the common good and if they are to be able to allocate their productive capacity to fulfill needs. Under a principle of social justice it can therefore be argued that society at large should underwrite the higher costs of insurance in areas of high social risk. To do so would be socially just. The same argument can be applied to the allocation of extra resources to reach groups who are particularly difficult to service—as Davies (1968, 18) points out "it may be desirable to over-provide needy groups with services since they have not had access to them in the past and have not formed the habit of consuming them." This issue arises particularly with respect to the education and health care facilities extended to very poor groups, recent immigrants, and the like. Merit can therefore be translated in a geographical context as an allocation of extra resources to compensate for the degree of social and natural environmental difficulty.

The principles of social justice as they apply to geographical situations can be summarized as follows:

1. The spatial organization and the pattern of regional investment should be such as to fulfill the needs of the population. This requires that we first establish socially just methods for determining and measuring needs. The difference between needs and actual allocations provides us with an initial evaluation of the degree of territorial injustice in an existing system.

2. A spatial organization and pattern of territorial resource allocation which provides extra benefits in the form of need fulfillment (primarily) and aggregate output (secondarily) in other territories through spillover effects, multiplier effects, and the like, is a "better" form of spatial organization and allocation.

3. Deviations in the pattern of territorial investment may be tolerated if they are designed to overcome specific environmental difficulties which would otherwise prevent the evolution of a system which would meet need or contribute to the common good.

These principles can be used to evaluate existing spatial distributions. They provide the beginnings of a normative theory of spatial organization based on territorial distributive justice. There will be enormous difficulties in elaborating them in detail and there will be even greater difficulties in translating them into concrete situations. We have some of the technology at hand to do this. It needs to be directed towards an understanding of just distributions in spatial systems.

TO ACHIEVE A DISTRIBUTION JUSTLY

There are those who claim that a necessary and sufficient condition for attaining a just distribution of income lies in devising socially just means for arriving at that distribution. Curiously enough this view prevails at both ends of the political spectrum. Buchanan and Tullock (1965)—conservative libertarians in viewpoint—thus suggest that in a properly organized constitutional democracy the most efficient way to organize redistribution is to do nothing about it. Marx (*A Critique of the Gotha Programme*, 11) attacked those "vulgar socialists" who thought that questions of distribution could be considered and resolved independent of the prevailing mechanisms governing production and distribution. Marx and constitutional democrats have a basic assumption in common—that if socially just mechanisms can be devised then questions of achieving social justice in distribution will look after themselves. In the literature on social justice (and in the arena of practical policy determination) there is a varied emphasis on "means" and "ends" with liberal and some socialist opinion apparently believing that social justice in the latter can be achieved without necessarily tampering with the former. But most writers indicate that it is foolhardy to expect socially just ends to be achieved by socially unjust means. It is instructive to follow Rawls's (1969) argument in this respect:

. . . the basic structure of the social system affects the life prospects of typical individuals according to their initial places in society. . . . The fundamental problem of distributive justice concerns the differences in life-prospects which come about in this way. We . . . hold that these differences are just if and only if the greater expectations of the more advantaged, when playing a part in the working of the social system, improve the expectations of the least advantaged. The basic structure is just throughout when the advantages of the more fortunate promote the well-being of the least fortunate. . . . *The basic structure is perfectly just when the prospects of the least fortunate are as great as they can be.* (Emphasis mine.)

The problem then, is to find a social, economic and political organization in which this condition is attained and maintained. Marxists would claim, with considerable justification, that the only hope for achieving Rawls's objective would be to ensure the least fortunate always has the final say. From Rawls's initial position it is not difficult by a fairly simple logical argument to arrive at a "dictatorship of the proletariat" type of solution. Rawls tries to construct a path towards a different solution:

. . . if law and government act effectively to keep markets competitive, resources fully employed, property and wealth widely distributed over time, and to maintain the appropriate social minimum, then if there is equality of opportunity underwritten by education for all, the resulting distribution will be just.

To achieve this Rawls proposes a four-fold division in government in which an allocation branch acts to keep the market working competitively while correcting for market failure where necessary; a stabilization branch maintains full employment and prevents waste in the use of resources; a transfer branch sees to it that individual needs are met; and a distribution branch looks after the provision of public goods and prevents (by proper taxation) any undue concentration of power or wealth over time. From Rawls's initial position it is possible to arrive, therefore, at a Marx or a Milton Friedman, but in no way can we arrive at the liberal or socialist solutions. That this is a sensible conclusion is attested by the fact that the socialist programs of post-war Britain appear to have had little or no impact upon the distribution of real income in society, while the liberal anti-poverty programs in the United States have been conspicuous for their lack of success. The reason should be obvious: programs which seek to alter distribution without altering the capitalist market structure within which income and wealth are generated and distributed, are doomed to failure.

Most of the evidence we have on group decision-making bargaining, the control of central government, democracy, bureaucracy, and the like, also indicates that *any* social, economic and political organization which attains any permanence is liable to cooptation and subversion by special interest groups. In a constitutional democracy this is usually accomplished by small well-organized interest groups who have accumulated the necessary resources to influence decision-making. A dictatorship of the proletariat solution is likewise subject to bureaucratic subversion as the Russian experience all too readily demonstrates. An awareness of this problem has led good constitutional democrats, such as Jefferson, to look favorably on an occasional revolution to keep the body politic healthy. One of the practical effects of the sequence of revolutions in China since 1949 (and some have attributed this to Mao's conscious design) has been to prevent what Max Weber (1947) long ago called the "routinization of charisma." The question of the appropriate form of social, economic and political organization and its maintenance for the purpose of achieving social justice is beyond the scope of this essay. Yet the way in which it is resolved effectively determines both the mode and likelihood of achieving territorial justice. I shall therefore confine myself to considering how considerations of the means of achieving distribution take on a specific form in the territorial context.

The geographical problem is to design a form of spatial organization which maximizes the prospects of the least fortunate region. A necessary initial condition, for example, is that we have a socially just way of determining the boundaries of territories and a just way of allocating resources among them. The former problem lies in the traditional field of "regionalizing" in geography, but in this case with the criterion of social justice put foremost. The experience of gerrymandering indicates only too well that territorial aggregates can be determined in a socially unjust way. Boundaries can be placed so that the least advantaged groups are so distributed with respect to the more advantaged groups in a set of territorial aggre-

gates that whatever the formula devised for allocation of resources the latter always benefit more than the former. It should be possible to devise territorial boundaries to favor the least advantaged groups—in which case social justice in allocation becomes the normative criterion for regionalization. In the actual allocation of resources we may take Rawls's objective to mean that the prospects for the least advantaged territory should be as great as they can be. How to determine when this condition exists is itself an intriguing problem, but the prospects for its achievement are presumably contingent upon the way in which a central authority decides on the territorial disposition of the resources under its control. Since poor areas are often politically weak, we are forced to rely on the sense of social justice prevailing in *all* territories (and it takes an assumption of only mild self-interest to counter that hope), upon the existence of a benevolent dictator or a benevolent bureaucracy at the center (the latter perhaps prevails in Scandinavia), or upon a constitutional mechanism in which the least advantaged territories have the power of veto over all decisions. Exactly what arrangements are made for arbitrating among the demands of political territories (demands which do not necessarily reflect need) and for negotiating between a central authority and its constituent territories are obviously crucial for the prospect of achieving territorial justice. It is arguable, for example, whether a greater centralization of decision-making (which has the potential for ironing out differences between territories) should prevail over a greater decentralization (which has the merit of being able to prevent the exploitation of disadvantaged territories by the richer territories). The answer to this probably depends upon the initial conditions. When they are characterized by exploitation (as they appear to be in the United States), a tactical decentralization may be called for as an initial step; when exploitation is not so important (as in Scandinavia), centralization may be more appropriate. Advocacy of metropolitan control or neighborhood government should be seen in this light.

Similar kinds of problem arise if we examine the impact of the highly decentralized decisions over capital investment characteristic of a freely working capitalist economy. Leaving aside the problems inherent in the tendency for modern capital to congeal into monopoly forms of control, it is useful to examine how an individualistic capitalist system typically operates with respect to territorial justice. Under such a system it is accepted as rational and good for capital to flow to wherever the rate of return is highest. Some (Borts and Stein, 1964) argue that this process will continue until rates of return are equalized over all territories, while others (Myrdal, 1957) suggest that circular and cumulative causation will lead to growing imbalances. Whatever the long term implications of this process are for growth, capital clearly will flow in a way which bears little relationship to need or to the condition of the least advantaged territory. The result will be the creation of localized pockets of high unfulfilled need, such as those now found in Appalachia or many inner city areas. Most societies accept some responsibility for diverting the natural stream of capital flow to deal with these problems. To do so without basically altering the *whole* capital flow process seems impossible however. Consider, as an example, the problems arising out of the housing situation in inner city areas of British and American cities. It is no longer profitable for private capital to flow into the inner city rental housing market. In London in 1965 a return of nine percent or more would have been necessary to encourage private investment and conditions were such that there was no hope of obtaining such a return by reasonable

or legal means (Milner-Holland Report, 1965). In Baltimore in 1969 a rate of twelve to fifteen percent would be required but actual rates were probably nearer six to nine percent (Grigsby et al., 1971). It is hardly surprising that the private inner city rental housing market has collapsed in most cities as capital is withdrawn, buildings have depreciated, and capital has been transferred to other sectors or out to the much more profitable private building market in the suburban ring. Thus arises the paradox of capital withdrawing from areas of greatest need to provide for the demands of relatively affluent suburban communities. Under capitalism this is good and rational behavior—it is what the market requires for the "optimal" allocation of resources.

Is it possible to reverse this flow using capitalist tools? Government can (and often does) intervene to make up the difference between what is now earned in the inner city and what could be earned elsewhere. It can do this in a number of ways (rent supplements to tenants, negative income taxes, direct grants to financial institutions, etc.). But whatever the means chosen the effect is to bribe financial institutions back into the inner city rental market where the government would otherwise have to take over responsibility for provision (through public housing). The first solution initially appears attractive, but it has certain flaws. If we bribe financial institutions, one effect will be to create a greater relative scarcity of capital funds for (say) suburban development. The more advantaged suburbs will adjust the rate of return they offer upwards to bring back the capital flow. The net effect of this process will be a rise in the overall rates of return which is obviously to the advantage of financial institutions—most of which are owned, operated and managed by people who live in the suburbs anyway! Thus there appears to be a built-in tendency for the capitalist market system to counteract any attempt to divert the flow of funds away from the most profitable territories. More specifically, it is impossible to induce action in one sector or territory without restricting it at the same time in other sectors and territories. Nothing short of comprehensive government control can do this effectively.

What this suggests is that "capitalist means invariably serve their own capitalist, ends" (Huberman and Sweezy, 1969), and that these capitalist ends are not consistent with the objectives of social justice. An argument can be formulated in support of this contention. The market system functions on the basis of exchange values and exchange values can exist only if there is relative scarcity of the goods and services being exchanged. The concept of scarcity is not an easy one to comprehend although we are constantly making reference to it when we talk of the allocation of scarce resources. It is questionable, for example, whether there is any such thing as a naturally arising scarcity. Pearson thus writes:

the concept of scarcity will be fruitful only if the natural fact of limited means leads to a sequence of choices regarding the use of these means, and this situation is possible only if there is alternativity to the uses of means and there are preferentially graded ends. But these latter conditions are socially determined; they do not depend in any simple way upon the facts of nature. To postulate scarcity as an absolute condition from which all economic institutions derive is therefore to employ an abstraction which serves only to obscure the question of how economic activity is organized. (1957, 320.)

The concept of scarcity, like the concept of a resource, only takes on meaning in a particular social and cultural context. It is erroneous to think that markets simply arise to deal with scarcity. In sophisticated economies scarcity is socially organized in order to permit the market to function. We say that jobs are scarce when there is plenty of work to do, that space is restricted when land lies empty, that food is scarce when farmers are being paid not to produce. Scarcity must be produced and controlled in society because without it price fixing markets could not function. This takes place through a fairly strict control over access to the means of production and a control over the flow of resources into the productive process. The distribution of the output has likewise to be controlled in order for scarcity to be maintained. This is achieved by appropriative arrangements which prevent the elimination of scarcity and preserve the integrity of exchange values in the market place. If it is accepted that the maintenance of scarcity is essential for the functioning of the market system, then it follows that deprivation, appropriation and exploitation are also necessary concomitants of the market system. In a spatial system this implies (the ecological fallacy permitting) that there will be a series of appropriative movements between territories which leads some territories to exploit and some to be exploited. This phenomenon is most clearly present in urban systems, since urbanism, as any historian of the phenomenon will tell us, is founded on the appropriation of surplus product.

Certain benefits stem from the operation of the market mechanism. The price system can successfully coordinate a vast number of decentralized decisions and it can consequently integrate a vast array of activities into a coherent social and spatial system. The competition for access to scarce resources, on which the capitalistic market system rests, also encourages and facilitates technological innovation. The market system therefore helps to increase, immeasurably, the total product available to society. It is also expert at promoting overall growth, and this has led some to argue that, since the market mechanism successfully promotes growth, it follows as a matter of course that the prospects for the least fortunate territory are naturally as great as they possibly can be. Appropriation obviously takes place but this appropriation, it is held, should not be characterized as exploitation because the appropriated product is put to good use and is the source of benefits which flow back into the territories from which it was initially exacted. Appropriative movements which occur under the price system are therefore justified because of the long-term benefits which they generate. This argument cannot be rejected out of hand. But to concede that appropriation is justifiable under certain conditions is not to concede that the appropriation achieved under the market mechanism is socially just. In any economy appropriation and the creation of a social surplus product is necessary, but the pattern achieved under the market economy is not in many respects a necessary one unless the internal logic of the market economy itself is regarded as a form of justification. In a capitalist market economy an enormous concentration of surplus product (at the present time this is mainly located in large corporations) has to be absorbed in ways which do not threaten the continuance of that scarcity upon which the market economy is itself based. Hence the surplus product is consumed in socially undesirable ways (conspicuous consumption, conspicuous construction in urban areas, militarism, waste): the market system cannot dispose of the socially won surplus product in socially just ways. It therefore seems necessary, from the point of view of social justice, to increase total social product without the use of the price-fixing market mechanism. In this regard the Chinese and Cuban efforts to promote growth with social justice are probably the most significant so far undertaken. The third world is otherwise presumably doomed to repeat the experience of individual or state capitalism in which growth is achieved at huge social and human cost.

In contemporary "advanced" societies the problem is to devise alternatives to the market mechanism which allow the transference of productive power and the distribution of surplus to sectors and territories where the social necessities are so patently obvious. Thus we need to move to a new pattern of organization in which the market is replaced (probably by a decentralized planning process), scarcity and deprivation systematically eliminated wherever possible, and a degrading wage system steadily reduced as an incentive to work, without in any way diminishing the total productive power available to society. To find such a form of organization is a great challenge, but unfortunately the enormous vested interest associated with the patterns of exploitation and privilege built up through the operation of the market mechanism, wields all of its influence to prevent the replacement of the market and even to preclude a reasoned discussion of the possible alternatives to it. Under conditions of social justice, for example, an unequal allocation of resources to territories and appropriative movements would be permissible if (and only if) those territories favored were able, through their physical and social circumstances and through their connections with other territories, to contribute to the common good of all territories. This pattern of appropriation will obviously be different to that achieved under the market mechanism for the latter is institutionally bound to maintain patterns of appropriation, deprivation, and scarcity, and institutionally incapable of distributing according to need or of contribution to common good. The social organization of scarcity and deprivation associated with price-fixing markets makes the market mechanism automatically antagonistic to any principle of social justice. Whether the market mechanism can be justified on grounds of efficiency and growth depends on how it compares with those alternatives which most are not prepared even to discuss.

A JUST DISTRIBUTION JUSTLY ACHIEVED: TERRITORIAL SOCIAL JUSTICE

From this examination of the principles of social justice we can arrive at the sense of *territorial social justice* as follows:

1. The distribution of income should be such that (a) the needs of the population within each territory are met, (b) resources are so allocated to maximize interterritorial multiplier effects, and (c) extra resources are allocated to help overcome special difficulties stemming from the physical and social environment.
2. The mechanisms (institutional, organizational, political and economic) should be such that the prospects of the least advantaged territory are as great as they possibly can be.

If these conditions are fulfilled there will be a just distribution justly arrived at.

I recognize that this general characterization of the principles of territorial social justice leaves much to be desired and that it will take a much more detailed examination of these principles before we are in a position to build some kind of theory of location and regional allocation around them. It took many years and an incredible application of intellectual resources to get to even a satisfactory beginning point for specifying a location theory based on efficiency and there is still no general theory of location—indeed we do not even known what it means to say that we are "maximizing the spatial organization of the city" for there is no way to maximize on the multiplicity of objectives contained in potential city forms. In the examination of distribution, therefore, we can anticipate breaking down the objectives into component parts. The component parts are as follows:

1. How do we specify need in a set of territories in accord with socially just principles, and how do we calculate the degree of need fulfillment in an existing system with an existing allocation of resources?
2. How can we identify interregional multipliers and spread effects (a topic which has already some theoretical base)?
3. How do we assess social and physical environment difficulty and when is it socially just to respond to it in some way?
4. How do we regionalize to maximize social justice?
5. What kinds of allocative mechanisms are there to ensure that the prospects of the poorest region are maximized and how do the various existing mechanisms perform in this respect?
6. What kinds of rules should govern the pattern of interterritorial negotiation, the pattern of territorial political power, and so on, so that the prospects of the poorest area are as great as they can be?

These are the sorts of questions which we can begin to work on in some kind of single-minded way. To work on them will undoubtedly involve us in making difficult ethical and moral decisions concerning the rights and wrongs of certain principles for justifying claims upon the scarce product of society. We cannot afford to ignore these questions for to do so amounts to one of those strategic non-decisions, so prevalent in politics, by which we achieve a tacit endorsement of the *status quo*. Not to decide on these issues is to decide. The single-minded exploration of efficiency has at best amounted to a tacit endorsement of the *status quo* in distribution. To criticize those who have pursued efficiency for this reason is not to deny the importance of analysis based on efficiency itself. As I indicated at the beginning of this chapter, we need to explore efficiency and distribution jointly. But to do so we first need a detailed exploration of those questions of distribution which have for so long been left in limbo.

REFERENCES

Alker, H. 1969. A typology of ecological fallacies. In M. Dogan and S. Rokan (eds.), *Quantitative ecological analysis in the social sciences.* Cambridge, Mass.: M.I.T. Press.

Borts, G. H. and Stein, J. L. 1964. *Economic growth in a free market.* New York: Columbia University Press.

Buchanan, J. M. and Tullock, G. 1965. *The calculus of consent.* Ann Arbor: University of Michigan Press.

Davies, B. 1968. *Social needs and resources in local services.* London.

Grigsby, W. C., Rosenberg, L., Stegman, M., and Taylor, J. 1971. *Housing and poverty.* Philadelphia: University of Pennsylvania, Institute of Environmental Studies.

Huberman, L. and Sweezy, P. 1969. *Socialism in Cuba.* New York: Monthly Review Press.

Liebenstein, H. 1966. Allocative efficiency versus x-efficiency. *American Economic Review* 61: 392–415.

Marx, K. 1938. *Critique of the Gotha Programme.* New York: International Publishers Edition.

Miller, S. M. and Roby, P. 1970. *The future of inequality.* New York: Basic Books.

Milner-Holland Report. 1965. *Report of the committee on housing in greater London.* London: HMSO, Cmnd, 2605.

Myrdal, G. 1957. *Economic theory and under-developed regions.* London.

Pearson, H. 1957. The economy has no surplus: A critique of a theory of development. In K. Polanyi, C. M. Arensberg, and H. W. Pearson (eds.), *Trade and market in early empires.* New York: The Free Press.

Rawls, J. 1969. Distributive justice. In P. Laslett and W. G. Runciman (eds.), *Philosophy, politics, and society.*

———. 1971. *A theory of justice.* Cambridge, Mass.: Harvard University Press.

Rescher, N. 1966. *Distributive justice.* Indianapolis: Bobbs Merrill.

Rothenberg, J. 1967. *Economic evaluation of urban renewal.* Washington, D.C.: Brookings Institution.

Runciman, W. G. 1966. *Relative deprivation and social justice.* Los Angeles: University of California Press.

Tawney, R. H. 1931. *Equality.* London.

Titmuss, R. M. 1962. *Income distribution and social change.* London.

Weber, M. 1947. *The theory of economic and social organization.* New York: Oxford University Press.

PART TWO **The Urban Infrastructure**

Introduction
To Part Two

The first Part of this collection offers some perspectives on the nature of urban space and its implications for problem analysis. The geographer, the economist, the political scientist, the sociologist, the planner, the social critic, and the lawyer all have varying perspectives which are derived both from the kinds of problems they face and the tools which they have at their command. In each of these views, however, it is evident that the spatial characteristics of our metropolitan areas are subject to substantial influence and manipulation by a variety of different institutions. The range of legal and administrative instruments available to planners and policy makers permits widespread control over both the use of land and the occupancy of housing even at the local level. The act of locating an expressway or school generates direct spatial impacts which are highly localized and often discriminatory. The market exercises its influence through control over access to financial resources and through specific construction and development decisions in the private sector. Political fragmentation leads to a myriad of overlapping decision units, each with its own power structure and pattern of local laws.

For a great number of decisions involving changes in physical stock, social conditions, or service provision, it is thus critical that we understand the relationships between the spatial structure of urban areas and the institutions which affect the decision-making process itself. In Part Two we focus explicitly on those decisions taken by public and private institutions which influence the arrangement and use of physical and service components of the urban system. Typical examples are not hard to find. Where is a new expressway to be located? Which schools in the inner city should be renovated and which should be closed? Shall we build low-income units throughout the city on a "fair-share" basis or shall we concentrate them in certain sub-areas? Can more balanced development be achieved by changes in current zoning practices? In short, we maintain that if we can appreciate the ways in which such decisions are made and their respective consequences, then we have made substantial progress toward a better understanding of both the existing structure of metropolitan areas and the implications of alternative approaches to future planning.

As stated in the Introduction to Part One, much of the current writing on urban areas stresses the influence of economic forces, particularly the cost of accessibility and its impact on the value of land. But this is clearly not the whole picture. The zoning of land for industrial or for single-family residential uses is a legal and administrative procedure which severely constrains the paths of future development. The willingness of banks to lend money to some members of the community and not to others is an important mechanism in the private sector for promoting or containing the spread of specific sub-groups of the population. Similarly, the decision to invest money in a so-called "magnet" school in one district or to bus children between other districts has an impact on the residential choices of households as well as on the collective future of their children. All of these are institutional issues which are capable of being described and analyzed and, more significantly, they are also instrumental criteria which are used to design the future urban environment. Although work in this area has not been sufficient to identify the principles underlying such decisions, there is little doubt as to their presence and impact on the space around us.

To bring the argument into stronger focus, we have organized Part Two around three themes relating to public housing, transportation, and the provision of public services (the latter particularly in the areas of health and education). Although these sectors are of obvious importance in themselves, they are also selected as being illustrative of a wide spectrum of issues. What is said about institutional influences on housing choice, for example, can be readily extended to broader classes of land-use controls. In the same way that zoning ordinances specifying single-family housing as the only permissible land use affects the character of an area, so do related ordinances specifying light manufacturing or commercial activities affect the character of others. Similarly, although we limit the consideration of public services to health and education, the ideas presented are easily expanded to encompass police systems, library services, refuse collection, and the wealth of other demands made on local government. The usefulness of these readings should thus be regarded as more than case studies on the specific issues addressed; the same general ideas can be carried beyond the immediate context of the authors' concerns and applied to a wide variety of similar issues.

Four related themes underly the readings we have selected, each exemplifying a specific kind of relationship between institutional forces and urban spatial structure. Although the examples are specific, each facet finds its expression in many different spheres of public action.

(i) *Rules and regulations, in both the public and private sectors, restrict access to resources and thereby modify the influence of the usual market processes.*

Locational decisions frequently involve a major financial outlay by the individual or corporate entity engaged in the transaction. In the case of housing, many attempts to analyze patterns of residential location have simplified this decision so that all households, both owners and renters, can be included within a single framework. The decision is treated in terms of the direct economic relation between the recurrent costs of housing and the household's budget. For the renter, the treatment of cost is straightforward, being merely the payments for the use of the dwelling; for the owner, housing costs are translated into an average carrying cost of the investment in the house, taxes, and utility payments on a yearly or monthly basis. However, this conceptualization almost totally ignores the institutional environment of such decisions. In this Part, Harvey provides a strong counter to conventional arguments in his analysis of the influence of financial and governmental institutions on the spatial structure of the housing market: he sees both neighborhood structure and neighborhood change arising out of attempts by investors to realize "class-monopoly rent," and the lending policies of various public and private agencies play a major part in this process. In particular, discriminatory lending policies with regard to mortgage money have had a strong influence on community development in many large American cities.

The actions of public institutions have produced policies which are equally selective. Not only have FHA mortgages and the HUD sponsored section 235 and 236 housing programs had great impact on suburban development of lower-income housing but, as the selections from the Report of the National Commission on Urban Problems and Clawson's paper point out, current income tax policies also greatly favor the suburban growth of middle- and upper-income housing.

While the case of housing is paramount, similar principles apply in other sectors as well. For example, the continued decline, the stabilization, or the rehabilitation of inner city neighborhoods is dependent in part upon the ability of small businesses to obtain financial backing and adequate insurance coverage. Indeed, the differential availability of these resources, which has such considerable impact on the possible paths of change in many sectors within our urban areas, is a function not only of the kinds of institutions involved but also of the roles which these institutions see themselves playing within limited space economies.

(ii) *In the public sector, a wide variety of local regulations serve as further constraints on locational choices in a manner which is relatively independent of economic resources.*

Haar's discussion in Part One has pointed to the range of legal and administrative mechanisms which exist to constrain the location and nature of uses of urban land. In this Part, the papers by Foley and by Kaiser and Weiss illustrate the range and effectiveness of these regulations from two different perspectives. Foley shows how instruments such as zoning, sub-division control, and the master plan can be used to restrict the housing choice of minorities. Moreover, as Kaiser and Weiss point out in their examination of the institutional influences on residential developers, this manipulation applies not only to demand but to the supply as well. Developers themselves are responsive to pressures exerted by local zoning ordinances and by the framework established by local master plans.

In a similar manner, the distribution of industry in metropolitan areas, particularly in growing suburban communities, is strongly influenced by the willingness of such communities to set aside land for those uses. Given the general unwillingness of planners to zone land adjacent to industrial uses for higher-income housing and for developers to build such housing, the decisions regarding zoning thus have substantial and long-lasting implications for the spatial form of the metropolitan area.

These observations illustrate the most obvious aspects of the influence of public regulations. More searching questions can be raised with regard to the principles underlying the kinds of decisions on which particular zoning ordinances are based. Yet, even at the simplest level it is not clear to what extent zoning decisions and master plans are themselves responsive to the usual considerations of accessibility costs as stressed by the economists, nor is it clear how the configuration of accessibility costs are manipulated by decisions concerning the extension of the transportation network. For example, individual communities can exert political pressure to influence the location of expressway interchanges according to their desires to promote or restrain expansion of commercial and industrial enterprise within their own jurisdictions. Writing in this area tends to be anecdotal, however, and a deeper understanding of these problems awaits integration of theories of economic, social, and political processes within an urban setting.

(iii) *The character of urban space is substantially modified by specific locational decisions made within the public sector.*

Vast amounts of public monies are devoted to public projects which are locationally specific. Expressways, airports, hospitals, schools, sewage systems, and public utility networks all have impacts which must be evaluated in terms of specific locational advantages and disadvantages. As the contributions by both Kaiser and Weiss and of Harvey suggest, the presence of a given configuration of public facilities in an area is an important element of its residential attractiveness or unattractiveness. Thus, not only can facility packages be designed to meet certain local needs but they can also act as instruments of design, as forces which promote or constrain the development of the social, economic, and demographic characteristics of a community.

There are a number of different components to the general theme. The act of locating a public facility such as a school, hospital, or library must result, for example, in differential degrees of accessibility for members of the community: those in close proximity to a facility are likely to be affected quite differently from those farther away. This realization has led directly to one goal of public policy which is to develop a system of facilities which provides what may be viewed as an "optimum" degree of accessibility from the societal viewpoint within the constraints of a given budget. A system which achieves this state is deemed to be "efficient" in the technical sense of the term. However, as the analysis pursued by Morrill and Earickson in this Part suggests, criteria which are related only to efficiency are often simplistic; although optimization criteria can be used as initial benchmarks, in reality numerous factors serve to distort accessibility patterns. Once we recognize that every hospital, school, or public library does not provide the identical bundle of services, that the service needs of each part of the population are not the same and that these needs vary considerably over time, the very notion of efficiency becomes elusive. The paper by Dear elaborates this argument by considering the cases of sub-groups of the population who have been discriminated against in the pursuit of efficiency by public agencies. Dear argues for a complete restructuring of the approach to facility location using a criterion of equity rather than efficiency. However, as Harvey points out in Part One, while it may be easy to recognize the needs of groups who have received harsh treatment in the past, it is still not clear how such recognition is to be parlayed into a set of priorities and related criteria which provide sound guidelines for the development of metropolitan-wide systems of public facilities in the future.

The second element in this theme is that public resources may be allocated to existing facilities within a system in such a way as to generate differential quality of local service provision over and above that due to pure distance effects. Such differentials in school spending in Chicago form the basis of Baron's contribution, differentials which lead to further variation in teacher experience, expenditures on books and supplies, and in the nature of extra-curricula activities. Although federal legislation during the 1960s attempted to reduce the magnitude of such disparities, they persist nonetheless and serve to reinforce the diversity in the spatial character of service provision throughout the city.

Most facilities which come under public control provide not only positive benefits related to their primary function, but also generate indirect effects or externalities which may be either positive or negative. Thus expressways, which increase levels of physical accessibility within the metropolitan area, frequently generate positive side effects in terms of increasing land values in adjacent areas and negative effects in terms of increased noise levels, air pollution, and traffic build-up in nearby residential districts. Similar effects are observed for other facilities such as airports, sewage farms, and garbage dumps. Even institutions which provide substantial benefits on a regional level, such as hospitals, mental institutions, and drug rehabilitation centers, generate local impacts which some members of the community find offensive. The paper by the Wolperts provides a disturbing look at a recent variant on this problem. The restructuring of mental health programs in California has resulted in an increased rate of release for patients in state mental hospitals. However, many communities have been quick to create institutional barriers such as zoning against board-and-care centers which effectively discourage the return of these patients to their former home areas. The result of such actions is an increasing concentration of ex-mental patients in a new form of inner city ghetto.

In more general terms problems arise as a result of the localization of spatial side effects of public action. Although benefits from a facility may reach a broad segment of the population, the externalities, particularly those which are undesirable, have to be borne by the few. Frequently, the ones who suffer the most are those already disadvantaged, the poor, the black, and the elderly groups who have little power to question or influence such locational decisions. The contribution by Pavlos paints a typical picture of the discriminatory impacts of urban expressway construction in the sixties and the problems of effective planning to incorporate the needs and desires of local communities directly affected by public actions. The degree of conflict generated by such decisions and the perceived inequity of earlier decision-making procedures have increased markedly in the last decade. These trends are making public decisions increasingly difficult, particularly since the law stands firmly on the side of the rights of individuals. The number of thwarted projects grows even larger: the Spadina Expressway in Toronto, I-95 in Philadelphia, and the Crosstown and Fox River Freeways in Chicago are notable items among the many. Although one cannot deny the validity of the concerns in many such cases, one must question whether planning can ever be effective within such a system, particularly insofar as decisions which are oriented toward the public good are almost inevitably discriminatory for some group of individuals.

Although the most common concern is with the selectivity of the negative side effects of public projects, even the positive side effects and direct benefits may be discriminatory. An area which has received much attention concerns the accessibility provided to different population subgroups by public transit systems. It can be argued, for example, that those who are most in need of such systems are those segments of society who cannot afford private means of transportation. Yet, as the Davies and Albaum study in Indianapolis shows, public transit often does little to satisfy their needs. Particularly as jobs continue to suburbanize, the problems of access to employment for the inner city poor increase and special efforts are required to solve them. These include not only the provision of better transit linkages between the city and suburb but also a decentralization of low-income housing and the support of business activities in inner city areas, particularly those with minority ownership.

Even when the needs of the inner city poor are recognized and funds appropriated for transit development, there is no guarantee that the outcome will be beneficial to the most needy groups. In Washington, D.C., the rapid transit system, which was promoted in terms of its benefits to the poor, resulted in far greater returns to middle- and upper-income suburban residents. In his contribution Brittain shows how this situation arose from the fact that the central city had virtually no political power when faced with the coalition of suburban communities. As is so often the case, the distribution of benefits was ultimately governed by territorially-based political power rather than the distribution of need.

(iv) *The character of local areas within the metropolis is modified by the territorial structure of organizations which provide public services.*

In Part One, Soja's perspective on urban space stressed both its territorial and its hierarchical elements. One aspect of this with which we are all familiar concerns the impact of separate jurisdictions within metropolitan areas: the multitude of suburban communities surrounding most major cities creates many discontinuities, disparities, and inefficiencies in the provision of services. However, within the central city itself, the nature of many service activities such as hospital service areas, school districts, and police precincts requires a hierarchical structure of districts and subdistricts to facilitate administration and delivery of that service.

We noted above that the character of services provided at a particular location is an important part of the residential attractiveness of that location. In many instances, however, the nature of these services depends on assignment to a particular territorial unit. The apparently simple act of redrawing service area boundaries can and does have profound impacts on the value placed on a location by a household: the value of a suburban dwelling is drastically altered by inclusion in or exclusion from the water and sewage systems of the adjacent urban area. More subtly, change in school boundaries many cause an individual to re-evaluate his location both from the viewpoint of physical accessibility and of the social milieu of the new school to which his children are assigned.

School districting perhaps provides the most dramatic contemporary example of this territorial influence. Not only does the assignment to specific school districts affect an individual's locational evaluation, but redrawing of boundaries can be used to achieve other effects of both an educational and community nature. Redistricting can be used to encourage or discourage integration of black students by appropriate boundary choices. These same principles are readily extended to other situations. Thus we are not surprised to find community pressures for reassignment of students used in the attempt to maintain the middle-class integrity of specific sub-areas in the face of encroachment of lower-income households into the neighborhood.

While the impact of redrawing specific boundaries can be documented, as we noted in the Introduction to Part One, criteria for boundary definition on a system-wide basis are not so readily established. The number of possible ways of drawing boundaries for a given number of facilities in an urban area is usually extremely large even with an acceptable criteria for boundary definition. How are administrators to choose between such a vast array of alternatives? Should districts be formed so as to guarantee equality of numbers, to promote integration of minority groups, or to minimize the number of children who have to take public transport to school? Resolution of this issue must emanate from some set of stated goals on the part of elected officials and planners, but we must all be aware that such administrative reorganization of school boundaries can have many side effects over and above those which might be stated as the goals of the exercise.

* * * * *

In Part Two, each of these four themes is illustrated within the context of the three substantive areas of housing, transportation, and the provision of public services. It is important, though, that we do not forget our general perspective on the nature of the problems which are identified in each area. Many planning and policy issues are not fundamentally spatial. In some cases the spatial perspective enters through the side door as locational and territorial influences are recognized as important in understanding certain aspects of the problem or in formulating strategies which are directed toward broader nonspatial goals.

Educational planning provides a good example of the role of the spatial perspective. The primary task of a school board is to provide as high quality education as possible to all students within its jurisdiction. This task involves many difficult decisions, not the least of which may be the process by which the jurisdictions are selected. Beyond this, for any given jurisdiction, the available resources must be allocated between the conflicting demands of salaries, buildings, equipment, and supplies. Curricula must be designed to meet the needs of children of different ages, backgrounds and interests, and an efficient means must be found for administering the business of the board. We have emphasized the strong spatial overtones of some of these decisions. However, we cannot regard the evaluation of these spatial impacts as an end in itself; they must be placed in the broader context of the attempt to achieve higher quality educational programs.

In an attempt to provide a suitable perspective for evaluating the arguments about the role of space, we have included in each substantive area one or more overview papers which sketch the range of the more general issues. This is achieved in the area of housing with a selection by Harvey, followed by an excerpt from the National Commission on Urban Problems, and a paper from the National Advisory Commission on Civil Disorders. On the issue of transportation, Meyer presents the first overview paper, followed by a contribution from Owen; on health, we include a paper by Roemer and Kisch, and finally, on the subject of education, a general overview by Campbell and Meranto.

In the same way that we must view the nature of problems as being multi-faceted, we must also be careful that we do not assume that problems in particular substantive areas have unitary solutions. This error is found in many public debates on strategies for solving specific problems. In the case of central city unemployment, for example, one finds separate protagonists for construction of central city-suburban transit systems, for dispersal of low-income housing, and for public support of minority businesses. Yet, the magnitude and complexity of the problems are often so great that no single strategy can be totally effective. We must search for appropriate mixes of different strategies to achieve our goals. The papers in our three selected areas of public action reflect this perspective. In separate contributions Rubinowitz and Zelder discuss a variety of approaches to the problems of housing the poor, ranging from ways of encouraging suburban communities to promote low-income housing to subsidies for rehabilitation, while Gans in his paper directs attention to the need for governmental reorientation in the provision of housing services to low-income families. Similar broad-ranging treatments are provided by Owen's examination of future transportation needs and their implications for planning, by Langer's discussion of medical programs in Denver, and by Kirp and Cohen in their evaluation of the potential impact of local government reform on the provision of educational services.

The fundamental lesson to be drawn from these discussions is that, while we may abstract our arguments in order to simplify the process of understanding, the real test of our understanding is the ability to synthesize our knowledge to provide solutions to complex problems.

HOUSING

Overview: Housing Needs and Problems

The Nature of Housing
David Harvey

Housing Needs
National Commission on Urban Problems

Housing in the Central Cities
National Advisory Commission on Civil Disorders

Analysis

Class-Monopoly Rent, Finance Capital and the Urban Revolution
David Harvey

Institutional and Contextual Factors Affecting the Housing Choice of Minority Residents
Donald L. Foley

Factors Affecting Suburbanization in the Postwar Years
Marion Clawson

Public Policy and the Residential Development Process
Edward J. Kaiser and Shirley F. Weiss

Strategy

The Failure of Urban Renewal: A Critique and Some Proposals
Herbert J. Gans

Low-Income Housing: Suburban Strategies
Leonard S. Rubinowitz

Poverty, Housing, and Market Processes
Raymond E. Zelder

THE NATURE OF HOUSING
DAVID HARVEY

The dwelling unit is a complex commodity constituting a major item of expenditure for most urban households, whether owners or renters. Harvey draws a basic distinction between the "use-value" of a dwelling which is specific to the occupants at a given time and the "exchange-value" which reflects the return on a sale under current market conditions. The distinction between these two concepts is important to the analysis of many decisions in the housing market.

Reprinted from David Harvey, *Society, The City and the Space-Economy of Urbanism,* Resource Paper No. 18, Commission on College Geography (Washington, D.C.: Association of American Geographers, 1972), pp. 15–16, by permission of the Association of American Geographers and the author. This is an edited version of the original publication, and a new title has been added.

What does a person get when he or she rents or purchases a house or apartment? We can begin by making a list:

1. Shelter
2. A quantity of space for the exclusive use of the purchaser or renter. This quantity is made up of the interior living space and the exterior living space.
3. A relative location which is
   a. Accessible to
      (i) work place
      (ii) retail opportunities
      (iii) social services (schools, hospitals, etc.)
      (iv) entertainment and recreational facilities
      (v) family and friends (people you like)
   b. Proximate to
      (i) sources of pollution (noxious facilities)
      (ii) areas of congestion
      (iii) sources of crime, fire hazard, noise, etc.
      (iv) people you don't like
4. A neighborhood which is characterized by:
   (i) people of a certain sort
   (ii) a physical environment of a certain sort
   (iii) an address which indicates prestige or social status
5. An absolute location with respect to
   (i) other absolute locations around you
   (ii) the total transport network as it exists around you at a given point in time.

Each of the things mentioned above is an important consideration for the purchaser or renter of the house or apartment although the categories are not necessarily mutually exclusive of each other. What we have described above is really the set of *uses* to which the house or apartment is put by the *user* and we shall refer to all of these things together as the *USE-VALUE OF THE DWELLING UNIT.*

Before exploring other kinds of value it is as well to remark that this use-value is not the same for all people nor is it constant for the same person at different points in time. Thus the use-value varies according to certain characteristics of the users. One of the most important of these characteristics is what is called "life-cycle stage" for clearly swinging singles, young married couples with children, old retired people, etc., have very different needs and therefore will measure their use-values very differently. Also the employment status will be important since those who are not in the work force (too young or too old or disabled) will not value access to employment. There will also be special factors arising; the chronically sick will value access to health services while the healthy will not be concerned. Finally there is the question of taste and preference (for neighborhood characteristics for example) and this obviously will vary among different groups and between individuals, according to their aspiration, preferences, and so on. So the use value is really defined by the meeting up of these individual or family characteristics with the list of relevant features which we outlined. It is important to notice that this use value contains all kinds of features which can be related to reciprocity as a mode of economic integration (particularly in the neighborhood setting); so in some respects the individual purchases or rents opportunities to integrate through reciprocity. The individual also purchases and rents with respect to redistributive features in economic organization, particularly with respect to status and rank neighborhoods and accessibility and proximity to those services supplied by government.

What of market exchange? There is a housing market and therefore housing has an *EXCHANGE VALUE* as well as a use value. It is crucial to understand the relationships between use-value and exchange value. Obviously, useless things will have no exchange value, but it does not automatically follow that use values are accurately represented by exchange values. Unfortunately, it is normally assumed in economics that these values are equivalent *at the margin* by which is meant that the purchaser or renter will,

in determining exchange-value, bid exactly that extra quantity of money which represents the value to him or her of obtaining an extra quantity of use value (an extra amount of space, for example, or a slightly better neighborhood). This assumption is only reasonable if we have a market situation which is kept in a perfectly well-ordered state. There are many good reasons for not thinking of housing in these terms because the market cannot possibly be perfect. First, a house is not a commodity which can be moved around at will (except mobile homes of course, but even most of these are rather immobile). It is therefore a very different commodity from things like wheat, iron ore, Cadillacs, stereo sets, and the like. It is fixed in space because it has an absolute location. Second, a house is a commodity which changes hands infrequently and most of the population will purchase a house only once or twice in a lifetime (although the rate of change is increasing). Also, when a purchase is made there are very high transaction costs to be borne so that the marketing mechanism contains a barrier to free exchange. Third, shelter is something which no individual can do without and it is therefore impossible to substitute housing against apples in the way that apples can be substituted for oranges in our food supply. This means that every individual will have to purchase housing no matter what its price. Fourth, the house has many uses and it therefore possesses a multitude of values compared with apples which are only for eating, automobiles which are almost entirely for driving, and utensils which are only for cooking. Finally, because housing is such a permanent feature in the built form of the city it is itself a form of stored wealth which people use to preserve their own equity. The implications of this last point are legion. It means, for example, that the purchase of a house is not geared simply to use values, but to the future market exchange value of the property. For the individual who purchases a house, it becomes important to preserve the market value of the house because this represents much of his lifetime savings. It also means that a certain proportion of the housing stock will be "used" by investors, landlords, real estate operators, and the like, to generate income or to increase their net worth. This is a very different use from that described under "use value" and it implies that money is to be made through market operations with respect to housing. Thus the housing market is penetrated at many points by market exchange considerations (the most obvious points of penetration are the rental sector and the exchange market). Hence, mortgage rates, interest rates, tax depreciation laws, future expectations with respect to use values, speculation, and the like, all affect the housing market in ways which have nothing necessarily to do with the actual use-value to the person living in a property here and now.

A house is, therefore, a special commodity. It is fixed in geographic space, it changes hands infrequently, it is a commodity which we cannot do without, and it is a form of stored wealth which is subject to speculative activities in the market and the object of use by capital itself as a means for reaping income or for increasing capital value. In addition, the house has various forms of value to the user and above all it is the point from which the user relates to every other aspect of the urban scene.

HOUSING NEEDS
NATIONAL COMMISSION ON URBAN PROBLEMS

The formulation of policies to satisfy housing needs necessitates both a definition of need and measures to assess the extent to which needs are not met. Although it is a well known fact that federal housing programs greatly favor the middle-class homeowner, the degree to which the poor have suffered under these policies is difficult to assess because of the deficiencies of existing data. This Report particularly stresses the weaknesses in Census data as a basis for evaluating housing needs.

Reprinted from the Douglas Commission, Report of the National Commission on Urban Problems, *Building the American City* (Washington, D.C.: Government Printing Office, 1969), pp. 66–69. This is an edited version of the original publication.

One of the most enduring sources of controversy and misunderstanding in urban affairs has been the issue of *housing needs*. At bottom they are, at any moment of time, the needs of the families and other households who do not have what the Congress, in the Housing Act of 1949, called "a decent home and a suitable living environment." Overwhelmingly, these households are among the poor, the near poor, and the lower economic middle class.

Much of the controversy comes on two points: (1) In more concrete terms, what is a *decent* home and what is a *suitable* living environment? (2) What of needs beyond those of the present moment? How many more households will be formed over the coming 5, 10, or 25 years? What will they be able to spend on housing? Where will they want to live? Will internal migration of our physically mobile population result in surpluses of decent housing in some localities and serious shortages in others? How many presently acceptable houses will slide into the substandard category through the ravages of age, neglected maintenance and repair, and shifting land uses in our many growing and ever-changing urban areas?

TWENTY YEARS OF MIDDLE AND UPPER INCOME HOUSING

The nation has made a phenomenal record over the last two decades in building housing for the middle and affluent classes, mainly at the edges of the central cities and in the suburbs. The efforts of private enterprise account for most of this construction, but government policy has provided significant incentives and help through mortgage guarantees, secondary credit facilities, and Federal income tax deductions for interest payments and local property taxes. The intent of government policy—and its effect—has been to increase substantially the rate of homeownership.

The extent to which government policy has subsidized the private homeowner is not generally recognized or acknowledged. The homeowner who deducts interest and property taxes as costs in computing his Federal tax return is not required to include the imputed value of rent as a part of his income. This generous but generally unacknowledged Federal subsidy to the affluent or middle-class homeowner needs to be emphasized in view of the self-righteous opposition often expressed toward subsidized housing for the poor.[1]

SCANTY AID FOR LOW-COST HOUSING

In contrast to its truly amazing record in housing construction for the upper half of America's income groups, the nation has made an inexcusably inadequate record in building or upgrading housing for the poor to provide them with decent, standard housing at rents and prices they can afford.

Low-rent public housing built since the 1930s does provide housing for about 2.4 million people and includes an inventory of almost 700,000 units. But today, even by the most liberal calculations, less than 100,000 units a year of all kinds are built or "made available" under low-rent housing programs—newly constructed public housing, rehabilitation, leased housing units, rent supplements, rent certificates, and other programs. And this small annual total has only been reached in the most recent years.

Even under these programs, the very poor have virtually been excluded. The amounts of subsidy available under the most generous programs often are insufficient to help them. The most needy also are rejected by the administrators of programs and the managers of projects because these poor bring with them so many problems.

It is in part for this reason that a disproportionate share of the units built or made available under public housing in recent years—more than half—has gone to the less troublesome elderly. While not enough is presently built either for them or for other needy groups, families

living in poverty have had very little help under existing housing programs.

In addition, with very few exceptions, little has been built for poor families in the large central cities, for much of the small amounts of public housing built for families has gone to middle-sized cities.[2] Further, very few units of three or more bedrooms have been built at all, so that a huge housing gap for the large, poor family exists not only in the larger cities, but nearly everywhere.

Furthermore, over the last decades, government action through urban renewal, highway programs, demolitions on public housing sites, code enforcement, and other programs has destroyed more housing for the poor than government at all levels has built for them.

Meanwhile, in the past, relocation assistance to persons and businesses displaced through federal, state, and local public works programs has been inadequate, nonuniform, and for some programs—completely absent.

While public housing, its related programs, and the 221 (d) (3) program for moderate-income groups have been of some slight help [3] in meeting the housing needs of the poorer half of the population, urban renewal has essentially been irrelevant to the housing needs of the poor. While the centers of some of our cities have been transformed by urban renewal into attractive business and higher income residential districts with a consequent strengthening of local tax base, very little low-income housing has been built on renewal sites. Fierce arguments may ensue as to whether this was by design or the result of the administration of the program. But few would dispute the fact that to date it has not served to help house the poor.

Finally other provisions of housing and urban legislation by which local agencies have bought and preserved open space, improved some mass transit systems, and built needed community facilities may well have improved the living environment of urban areas, but this benefit is largely general—that is, it is largely unrelated to the critical housing needs of specific segments of the urban population.

These facts make a strong moral case for action to help the most needy now. It justified the passage of the Housing Act of 1968 and, most importantly, it calls for carrying out the goals of the act on schedule.

It should be repeated that this responsibility is based not only on need. It is a moral requirement for the nation. Having built generously for the most prosperous half of the nation, and having destroyed more housing for the poor than we have built, we now owe a special effort to provide decent housing for those who have in the past largely been left out.

INADEQUACY OF DATA

Today, more than a generation after the federal government began to undertake various programs to influence housing production and housing conditions, and decades after improved housing was at least an objective of public regulation by local and state governments, there has been no satisfactory analysis of present housing needs and a similar estimate of probable future needs as guides for housing policy and programs. Aside from the hazards in predicting birth and fertility rates, the *basic facts* for such studies, in reasonable detail and refinement, are not available. In some respects this is the most damning indictment against the public concern, including but by no means limited to governmental concern, with housing in this country.

There are not even good working definitions of a *decent* home and a *suitable* living environment, the supposed anchor points of our national housing goal, used in what statistics are being gathered. Still more elusive, therefore, are the complex questions such as:

How many presently acceptable houses will slide into the substandard category through the ravages of age, neglect, and shifting land uses?

How many presently substandard houses could be made acceptable through rehabilitation?

What is the best balance between public and private investment in housing?

The only reasonably comprehensive data on housing conditions or quality are those of the Bureau of the Census. To say that the available data are inadequate is no adverse criticism of the Bureau, which has worked hard and intelligently on housing. A nationwide, decennial census, however, cannot supply the complete range of facts needed to judge housing quality. The Bureau knows this prefectly well. Its 1960 Census of Housing says:

The combination of data on condition and plumbing facilities is considered one measure of housing quality. It takes account of the physical characteristics of the unit—the structural condition and the presence of basic plumbing facilities (water supply, toilet facilities, and bathing facilities). Although such factors as light, ventilation, and neighborhood also reflect quality, particularly in urban areas, it is not feasible to measure them in large scale census enumeration. These elements, however, often are closely associated with condition and plumbing facilities.[4]

The Commission warns against the common tendency to read into the census housing data more than is there. Visible condition of building (which the census classifies as *sound, deteriorating, and dilapidated*) and plumbing facilities in combination are indeed, as the Census puts it, "one measure of housing quality," but only one—and a crude one at that. Quite surely it is on the conservative side—that is, it results in a lower estimate of the volume of substandard housing than most reasonable persons would arrive at on the basis of careful local studies. This seems doubly likely for the housing in older, large, central cities and industrial suburbs of metropolitan areas.

And how is the data related to environment? Commission members saw rehabilitated housing in the blighted areas of St. Louis, New York City, Philadelphia, and Baltimore, among other cities, which met the local code standard. But the housing was surrounded by areas with inadequate city services for their special needs, areas which were deteriorating, or where freeways were scheduled to be built nearby. In many cases these circumstances will make it difficult for the rehabilitated housing to remain in good repair, as was the case in the early Baltimore experiments.

This Commission inspected one housing area where the noxious fumes from a giant chemical company plant nearby led the local housing expert to remark that if such a level of air pollution were found inside a factory the state would either require gas masks or shut down the plant. But human beings lived in that environment unprotected by local or state law because the company has carved out its separate municiple jurisdiction, thus avoiding both its fiscal and social responsibility to the larger community. Would even a $50,000 house in that environment be "standard" or "decent" housing?

Is a unit correctly defined as standard under available data if the lot next door is littered with garbage; if police protection is limited; if street lights are not provided; if the sidewalk is buckled; if the street is full of potholes; if a liquor store is found on each corner; if sewers are nonexistent or inadequate; if the noise level is excessive; or if a rendering works is found in the block (as is true along the waterfront in the otherwise exclusive Georgetown area of Washington D.C.)?

The Commission saw large sections of cities where, at the time of our examination, most of the dwellings did not rank very low on the census measures of housing quality but where, nevertheless, insurance companies would not write the usual forms of property insurance, banks and savings and loan associations would not lend on mortgages, and where the FHA would not insure. These areas, in the parlance of the trade, were "red-lined." People there were out of the ball game that has resulted in the improvement of many less needy areas in recent years.

The Commission in this discussion of available facts on urban housing emphatically is *not* saying or implying two things:

It is *not* saying that more data will decide for us what is acceptable housing what is substandard. All standards, whether in housing or automobiles, require human judgment. "Scientific standards," if anyone wishes to use the term, are simply those based on carefully determined facts rather than on rule-of-thumb or mere opinion. Such facts are indispendable to sound judgment, but they are not a substitute for it.

Neither is the Commission suggesting that no changes be made in housing policy and programs until more adequate data are at hand. Quite the opposite. The need for more decent housing in American cities is so great, so pressing, and so obvious that much larger and more vigorous efforts to meet it are urgently needed. These efforts can and should be started at once, as the Housing Act of 1968 contemplates, using existing tools and programs, plus modifications and additions as experience to date justifies. If the refinement of housing facts is undertaken promptly, the results would soon be available to light the way for even more effective action toward a "decent home and a suitable living environment for every American family."

NOTES

1. Alvin L. Schorr, "National Community and Housing Policy," *Social Service Review* 39, 4 (Chicago: University of Chicago Press, December 1965).

2. New York and Chicago are among the most notable exceptions.

3. Instituted under the 1961 Housing Act, the 221 (d) (3) program has only begun to achieve its housing con-struction goals in the last few years.

4. F. S. Kristof, *Urban Housing Needs Through the 1980's*, Research Report No. 10, National Commission on Urban Problems, 1968.

HOUSING IN THE CENTRAL CITIES
NATIONAL ADVISORY COMMISSION ON CIVIL DISORDERS

Within the limits of existing data sources, the main dimensions of the disparity between white and nonwhite housing are outlined. Major differences between the two groups are identified with respect to age of housing, condition, and degree of overcrowding. Data are also provided which strongly suggest that nonwhites pay more than whites for comparable housing, at least in the larger metropolitan areas at the turn of the sixties.

Reprinted from the Kerner Commission, *Report* of the National Advisory Commission on Civil Disorders (Washington, D.C.: Government Printing Office, 1968), pp. 257–59. This is an edited version of the original publication.

The passage of the National Housing Act in 1934 signalled a new federal commitment to provide housing for the nation's citizens. Fifteen years later Congress made the commitment explicit in the Housing Act of 1949, establishing as a national goal the realization of "a decent home and suitable environment for every American family."

Today, after more than three decades of fragmented and grossly under-funded federal housing programs, decent housing remains a chronic problem for the disadvantaged urban household. Fifty-six percent of the country's nonwhite families live in central cities today, and of these, nearly two-thirds live in neighborhoods marked by substandard [1] housing and general urban blight. For these citizens, condemned by segregation and poverty to live in the decaying slums of our central cities, the goal of a decent home and suitable environment is as far distant as ever.

During the decade of the 1950s, when vast numbers of Negroes were migrating to the cities, only 4 million of the 16.8 million new housing units constructed throughout the nation were built in the central cities. These addi-tions were counterbalanced by the loss of 1.5 million central-city units through demolition and other means. The result was that the number of nonwhites living in substandard housing increased from 1.4 to 1.8 million, even though the number of substandard units declined.

Statistics available for the period since 1960 indicate that the trend is continuing. There has been virtually no decline in the number of occupied dilapidated units in metropolitan areas, and surveys in New York City and Watts actually show an increase in the number of such units. These statistics have led the Department of Housing and Urban Development to conclude that while the trend in the country as a whole is toward less substandard housing, "There are individual neighborhoods and areas within many cities where the housing situation continues to deteriorate." [2]

Inadequate housing is not limited to Negroes. Even in the central cities the problem affects two and a half times as many white as nonwhite households. Nationally, over 4 million of the nearly 6 million occupied substandard units in 1966 were occupied by whites.

It is also true that Negro housing in

large cities is significantly better than that in most rural areas—especially in the South. Good quality housing has become available to Negro city dwellers at an increasing rate since the mid-1950s when the postwar housing shortage ended in most metropolitan areas.

Nevertheless, in the Negro ghetto, grossly inadequate housing continues to be a critical problem.

SUBSTANDARD, OLD, AND OVERCROWDED STRUCTURES

Nationwide, 25 percent of all nonwhites living in central cities occupied sub-

units classified as deteriorating, dilapidated, or lacking full plumbing in 1960 (the latest date for which figures are available), were as shown in Table 1.

Conditions were far worse than these citywide averages in many specific disadvantaged neighborhoods. For example, a study of housing in Newark, New Jersey, before the 1967 disorders, showed, as seen in Table 2, the situation in certain predominantly Negro neighborhoods as of 1960. These three areas contained 30 percent of the total population of Newark in 1960, and 62 percent of its nonwhite population.

City	Percentage of Nonwhite Occupied Housing Units Classified Deteriorating or Dilapidated, 1960	Percentage of Nonwhite Occupied Housing Units Classified Deteriorating, Dilapidated, or Sound but Without Full Plumbing, 1960
New York	33.8%	42.4%
Chicago	32.1%	42.8%
Los Angeles	14.7%	18.1%
Philadelphia	28.6%	32.0%
Detroit	27.9%	30.1%
Baltimore	30.5%	31.7%
Houston	30.1%	36.7%
Cleveland	29.9%	33.9%
Washington, D.C.	15.2%	20.8%
St. Louis	40.3%	51.6%
San Francisco	21.3%	34.0%
Dallas	41.3%	45.9%
New Orleans	44.3%	56.9%
Pittsburgh	49.1%	58.9%

TABLE 1. Nonwhite Housing in 14 Cities
Source: U.S. Department of Commerce, Bureau of the Census

standard units in 1960 compared to 8 percent of all whites. Preliminary Census Bureau data indicate that by 1966, the figures had dropped to 16 and 5 percent respectively. However, if "deteriorating" units and units with serious housing code violations are added, the percentage of nonwhites living in inadequate housing in 1966 becomes much greater.

In 14 of the largest U.S. cities, the proportions of all nonwhite housing

The Commission carried out special analyses of 1960 housing conditions in three cities, concentrating on all Census Tracts with 1960 median incomes of under $3,000 for both families and individuals. It also analyzed housing conditions in Watts. The results showed that the vast majority of people living in the poorest areas of these cities were Negroes, and that a high proportion lived in inadequate housing. (See Table 3.)

Area Number	Population	Percentage Nonwhite	Percentage of All Housing Units Dilapidated or Deteriorating
1	25,300	75.5%	91.0%
2	48,200	64.5%	63.8%
3A	48,300	74.8%	43.1%

TABLE 2. Percentage of Housing Units Dilapidated or Deteriorated in Selected Areas of Newark, 1960
Source: Adapted from George Sternlieb, *The Tenement Landlord* (New Brunswick, N.J.: Rutgers University Press, 1966), pp. 238–41.

Item	Detroit	Washington, D.C.	· Memphis	Watts Area of Los Angeles
Total population of study area	162,375	97,084	150,827	49,074
Percentage of study area nonwhite	67.5%	74.5%	74.0%	87.3%
Percentage of housing units in study area:				
—Substandard by HUD definition	32.7%	23.9%	35.0%	10.5%
—Dilapidated, deteriorating or sound but lacking full plumbing	53.1%	37.3%	46.5%	29.1%

TABLE 3
Source: U.S. Department of Commerce, Bureau of the Census

Negroes, on the average, also occupy much older housing than whites. In each of ten metropolitan areas analyzed by the Commission, substantially higher percentages of nonwhites than whites occupied units built prior to 1939. (See Table 4.)

Finally, Negro housing units are far more likely to be overcrowded than those occupied by whites. In U.S. metropolitan areas in 1960, 25 percent of all nonwhite units were overcrowded by the standard measure (that is, they contained 1.01 or more persons per room). Only 8 percent of all white-occupied units were in this category. Moreover, 11 percent of all non-white occupied units were seriously overcrowded (1.51 or more persons per room), compared with 2 percent for white-occupied units. The figures were as shown in Table 5 in the

Metropolitan Area	White Occupied Units	Nonwhite Occupied Units
Cleveland	33.2	90.6
Dallas	31.9	52.7
Detroit	46.2	86.1
Kansas City	54.4	89.9
Los Angeles— Long Beach	36.6	62.4
New Orleans	52.9	62.2
Philadelphia	62.0	90.8
Saint Louis	57.9	84.7
San Francisco— Oakland	51.3	67.6
Washington, D.C.	31.9	64.9

TABLE 4. Percentage of White and Nonwhite Occupied Housing Units Built Prior to 1939 in Selected Metropolitan Areas
Source: U.S. Department of Commerce, Bureau of the Census

ten metropolitan areas analyzed by the Commission.

Metropolitan Area	White Occupied Units	Nonwhite Occupied Units
Cleveland	6.9	19.3
Dallas	9.3	28.8
Detroit	8.6	17.5
Kansas City	8.7	18.0
Los Angeles— Long Beach	8.0	17.4
New Orleans	12.0	36.1
Philadelphia	4.9	16.3
Saint Louis	11.8	28.0
San Francisco— Oakland	6.0	19.7
Washington, D.C.	6.2	22.6

TABLE 5. Percentage of White and Nonwhite Occupied Units with 1.01 or More Persons Per Room in Selected Metropolitan Areas
Source: U.S. Department of Commerce, Bureau of the Census

HIGHER RENTS FOR POORER HOUSING

Negroes in large cities are often forced to pay the same rents as whites and receive less for their money, or pay higher rents for the same accommodations.

The first type of discriminatory effect —paying the same amount but receiving less—is illustrated by data from the 1960 Census for Chicago and Detroit.

In certain Chicago census tracts, both whites and nonwhites paid median rents of $88, and the proportions paying various specific rents below that median were almost identical. But the units rented by nonwhites were typically:

——Smaller (the median number of rooms was 3.35 for nonwhites versus 3.95 for whites).

——In worse condition (30.7 percent of all nonwhite units were deteriorated or dilapidated units versus 11.6 percent for whites).

——Occupied by more people (the median household size was 3.53 for nonwhites versus 2.88 for whites).

——More likely to be overcrowded (27.4 percent of nonwhite units had 1.01 or more persons per room versus 7.9 percent for whites).

In Detroit, whites paid a median rental of $77 as compared to $76 among nonwhites. Yet 27.0 percent of nonwhite units were deteriorating or dilapidated, as compared to only 10.3 percent for all white units.

The second type of discriminatory effect—paying more for similar housing —is illustrated by data from a study of housing conditions in disadvantaged neighborhoods in Newark, New Jersey. In four areas of that city (including the three areas cited previously), nonwhites with housing essentially similar to that of whites paid rents that were from 8.1 percent to 16.8 percent higher. Though the typically larger size of nonwhite households, with consequent harder wear and tear, may partially justify the difference in rental, the study found that nonwhites were paying a definite "color tax" of apparently well over 10 percent on housing. This condition prevails in most racial ghettos.

The combination of high rents and low incomes forces many Negroes to pay an excessively high proportion of their income for housing. This is shown dramatically in Table 6, showing the percentage of renter households paying over 35 percent of their incomes for rent in ten metropolitan areas.

The high proportion of income that must go for rent leaves less money in such households for other expenses. Undoubtedly, this hardship is a major reason many Negro households regard housing as one of their worst problems.

Metropolitan Area	White Occupied Units	Nonwhite Occupied Units
Cleveland	8.6	33.8
Dallas	19.2	33.8
Detroit	21.2	40.5
Kansas City	20.2	40.0
Los Angeles— Long Beach	23.4	28.4
New Orleans	16.6	30.5
Philadelphia	19.3	32.1
Saint Louis	18.5	36.7
San Francisco— Oakland	21.2	25.1
Washington, D.C.	18.5	28.3

TABLE 6. Percentages of White and Non-white Occupied Units with Households Paying 35 Percent or More of their Income for Rent in Selected Metropolitan Areas
Source: U.S. Department of Commerce, Bureau of the Census

NOTES

1. The Department of Housing and Urban Development classifies substandard housing as that housing reported by the United States Census Bureau as (1) sound but lacking full plumbing, (2) deteriorating and lacking full plumbing, or (3) dilapidated.
2. Hearings before the Subcommittee on Executive Reorganization of the Committee on Government Operations, United States Senate, 89th Congress, 2nd Session, August 16, 1966, p. 148.

CLASS-MONOPOLY RENT, FINANCE CAPITAL AND THE URBAN REVOLUTION
DAVID HARVEY

Harvey focuses directly on the institutional issue. His paper provides a strong counter to the conventional explanations of residential differentiation phrased in terms of individual or groups preferences for specific types of housing and socio-economic milieu. In this provocative paper, he argues that a major contribution to this process is made by financial and governmental institutions with the active agent being the investor seeking to realize "class-monopoly rent." This concept refers to the rate of return to a class of providers of an urban resource (such as housing) arising from a conflict with a class of consumers of that resource. The importance of this notion in examining neighborhood structure and neighborhood change is illustrated by his empirical analysis in the city of Baltimore. Of greatest importance, however, is his argument that these types of influences are necessary corollaries of the urbanization process in a capitalist society.

Reprinted from *Regional Studies* 8 (1974): 239–55, by permission of Pergamon Press and the author.

The author would like to acknowledge the helpful criticism provided in seminars at Darwin College, University of Kent, Department of Planning, The University of Toronto as well as the critical discussion of these ideas by various individuals associated with The Johns Hopkins University or from the Baltimore community.

In a stimulating and provocative work, Lefebvre argues that we ought to interpret the industrial revolution of the nineteenth century as a precursor to the "urban revolution" of the twentieth. He explains that by "urban revolution" he means:

the total ensemble of transformations which run throughout contemporary society and which serve to bring about the change from a period in which questions of economic growth and industrialization predominate to the period in which the urban problematic becomes decisive. (Lefebvre, 1970, p. 13.)

Lefebvre is not explicit as to what is meant by "the ensemble of transformations" nor does he explain how and why capitalism is transformed so that questions of urbanization come to replace questions of economic growth and industrialization. Nor is Lefebvre very explicit when he argues that "the proportion of global surplus value formed and realized in industry declines" while the proportion realized "in speculation, construction and real estate development grows" (Lefebvre, 1970, p. 212). The thesis that this "secondary circuit of capital" is supplanting "the primary circuit of capital in production" is startling in its implications and obviously requires very careful consideration before being accepted or rejected. In this paper, therefore, I shall attempt to shed some light on Lefebvre's hypotheses by examining how rent, and in particular class-monopoly rent, arises in the context of the urbanization process.

1. THE CONCEPT OF RENT IN AN URBANIZED WORLD

I take it as axiomatic that *value* arises out of those processes that convert naturally occurring materials and forces into objects and powers of utility to individuals in specific social and natural environments. In its simplest form, we can say that value arises out of production and is realized in consumption (Marx, 1967 edn.). But production and distribution cannot take place without (1) an elaborate social structure (encompassing the division of labor, the provision of socially necessary services, and so on), (2) a structure of social institutions through which individual and group activities can be coordinated, and (3) a certain minimum of physical infrastructure (communication links, utilities and the like). Any system of production and distribution requires, consequently, certain transfer payments to be made out of value produced to support socially necessary institutions, services and physical infrastructures.

The history of the rental concept is strewn with arguments for and against the legitimacy of the transfer payment that rent represents (Keiper et al., 1961). In recent years, however, many appear to have been persuaded that rent is a kind of rationing device through which a scarce factor of production—land and its associated resources—is rationally and efficiently allocated to meet the productive needs of society (Wicksteed, 1894). Rent is justified, according to this view, as a necessary coordinating device for the efficient production of value. The problem with this neoclassical argument is, however, that rent is regarded as a payment to a scarce "factor" (which is a "thing" concept) rather than as an actual payment to people. This reification may be convenient for purposes of analysis but actual payments are made to real live people and not to pieces of land. Tenants are not easily convinced that the rent collector merely represents a scarce

factor of production. The social consequences of rent are important and cannot be ignored simply because rent appears so innocently in the neoclassical doctrine of social harmony through competition (Barnbrock, 1974).

There is a further point to be considered. In order for payments to be made certain basic institutions are required. In our own society, private property arrangements are crucial; rent is, in effect, a transfer payment realized through the monopoly power over land and resources conferred by the institution of private property. Consequently, any examination of how rent originates and is realized cannot proceed without evaluating the performance of these supportive institutions.

But what is rent a payment for? The simplest answer is that it is a payment made by a user for the privilege of using a scarce productive resource which is owned by somebody else. But how does scarcity arise? Ever since production began to be organized systematically, human societies have recognized that many natural resources (understood as technical and cultural evaluations of nature [Firey, 1960; Spoehr, 1956]) are limited. There is a tendency, therefore, to think of scarcity as something inherent in nature and on this basis we may be willing to concede that more should be charged for the use of productive fields and mines than for fields and mines of average productivity. On reflection, however, this conception of "natural wealth" and "scarcity" appears less satisfactory. There is little "natural wealth" that has not been prepared prior to production—the field has to be cleared and the mineshaft has to be dug. Relatively permanent improvements—such as the terracing of hillsides, the building up of soil fertility and the draining of marshlands, may with time come to be regarded as "natural" resources for human use. In an urbanized world this problem becomes even more serious.

Urbanization creates relatively permanent, man-made resource systems (Harvey, 1973, Chapter 2). Human effort is, as it were, incorporated into the land as fixed and immobile capital assets that may last hundreds of years. Consequently, the high rent for a piece of land in the center of London may be due to its higher productivity, but that productivity has been *created* by the construction of the vast man-made resource system that is London. Because these relatively permanent fixed capital assets are highly localized in their distribution, the urbanization process has created scarcity where there was none before. If rent is a transfer payment to a scarce factor of production, then the urbanization process has also multiplied the opportunities for realizing rent.

The blurring of the distinction between natural and artificially created scarcity, makes it difficult to distinguish between rent and profit. Are houses, for example, to be regarded as relatively permanent improvements incorporated into the value of the land or are they better regarded as commodities commanding a profit on the capital outlay required to produce them? The answer to this question depends on what is meant by "relatively permanent." Housing has to be produced and it has to be paid for as a commodity. Once this is done, however, the house may be regarded as a relatively permanent improvement incorporated into the value of the land. Buckingham Palace is a permanent improvement whereas the suburban house just built is not yet in that happy state. It seems reasonable to think in similar fashion about other elements in the built form of the city—offices, shops, transport links, and so on.

The distinction between a mere transfer payment—rent—and profit on productive capital investment is difficult to keep in mind. The individual investor does not particularly care about the distinction; the overall rate of return on financial outlays is what matters. Money is put, therefore, where the rate of return is highest irrespective of whether productive activity is involved or not. If rates or return are high in the real estate and property markets, then investment will shift from the primary productive circuit of capital to this secondary circuit in a manner that would be consistent with Lefebvre's thesis. From the investor's point of view there is nothing to prevent such a shift. What has to be explained, however, is how returns can be higher on the secondary circuit over any length of time. For the fact that the distinction between productive and unproductive investment has disappeared from the investor's calculus does not negate the significance of such a distinction as a social fact. If all capital chases rent and no capital goes into production, then no value will be produced out of which the transfer payment that rent represents can come.

2. CLASS-MONOPOLY RENT, URBANIZATION AND CLASS-MONOPOLY POWER

Rent can be charged for a variety of reasons. Marx's categories of differential, absolute and monopoly rent, to which Walker has recently added redistributive rent, are useful if only because they force us to consider the different kinds of situations out of which rent can arise (Harvey, 1973, Chapter 5; Walker, 1974). In this paper I will be concerned with what I shall call "class-monopoly rent." Whether this form of rent should be included in Marx's categories of absolute or monopoly rent is not clear. The resolution of this question depends upon the solution of the celebrated "transformation problem" which arises out of the relationship between values and prices in the Marxian schema.[1] I am of the opinion that class-monopoly rent is best treated as one form of absolute rent. But since this is a contentious and as-yet unresolved problem I will stick to the neutral term "class-monopoly rent" in what follows.

Class-monopoly rents arise because there exists a class of owners of "resource units"—the land and the relatively permanent improvements incorporated in it—who are willing to release the units under their command only if they receive a positive return above some arbitrary level (Marx, 1967 edn., Chapter 45). As a class these owners have the power always to achieve some minimum rate of return. The key concept here is *class power*. If landlords could not or would not behave in accordance with a well-defined class interest, then class-monopoly rents would not be realized. Landlords gain their class power in part from the fact that individually they can survive quite well without releasing all of the resource units under their command.

In nineteenth century Europe landlord power was essentially a residual from feudalism. Marx observed that it would be very much in the interest of the capitalist class to bring land and other productive resources under state ownership since this would relieve the capitalist of the obligation of making any transfer payment to landed property (Marx, 1968 edn., Part 2). It was unlikely, however, that capitalists would challenge the private property arrangements that allowed rent to be realized (and which provided the basis for the class power of landlords) since these arrangements also provided the necessary legal framework for entrepreneurial activity. But in an urbanized world, the distinction between capitalist and landlord has blurred concomitantly with the blurring of the distinctions between land and capital and rent and profit. We need, therefore, to adapt our categories to deal with the new complexities of extensive man-made resource systems. But the same questions arise: are there owners of resource units (be they natural or artificial) who can and

do behave so as to make it possible to realize rent? If so, what is the basis of their class power, how are they defining "class interest" and how are we to interpret their role in relation to the structure of social class in society as a whole? We can begin to answer these questions by examining two examples that clarify the meaning of "class interest" in the sense in which that term is being used here.[2]

(a) *Landlords versus low-income tenants*
Suppose there exists a class of people who, by virtue of their income, social status, credit-worthiness and eligibility for public assistance, are incapable of finding accommodation as homeowners or as residents in public housing. The existence of such a class is readily demonstrable in any large American or European city. This class of people has no alternative but to seek accommodation in the low-income rental market; they are trapped within a particular housing sub-market. The needs of this class are provided for by a class of landlords. Landlordism varies, of course, from the old lady who rents an attic to the large scale professional business operation. For purposes of exposition, let us assume that all rental accommodation is provided by a class of professional landlord-managers. This class has certain options as to where it puts its money but much of its capital exists in the form of housing. On the basis of the potential yield of money on the capital market, professional landlords may set their expected rate of return on the estimated market value of their fixed capital assets at, say, 15 percent per annum. Suppose there is an abundance of low-income units in a particular city for some reason and that rates of return are in fact as low as 5 percent. A rational landlord strategy is to reduce maintenance, milk properties of value and actively disinvest, using the money so extracted on the capital market where it earns, say, 15 percent. With declining maintenance, the hous-

ing deteriorates in quality and eventually the worst units will be taken out of use— scarcity is successfully produced. Rents will gradually rise until the 15 percent rate of return is obtained (and there is nothing to stop rents going higher if circumstances allow). The class interest of the landlord is to obtain a minimum of 15 percent or else to find some way to get out of the market.

The class interests of landlord and tenant are clearly opposed to each other. If the quality of housing deteriorates and rents rise, tenants may seek accommodation elsewhere, but since they are, for the most part, trapped in this sub-market their power is limited in this respect. If they have some political power, they may seek to offset the class-monopoly power of landlords by imposing minimum housing standards or rent controls. If the effect of such legislation is to reduce landlord profits, landlords will respond by trying to transform the fixed capital (the house) into money to be used on the capital market. If prices are low it will not be worthwhile to sell. Social, legal and political pressures may make it difficult for the landlord to disinvest without severe social and fiscal penalties. Under these conditions the landlord may well compromise and settle for a much lower rate of return. The tenants will then have achieved some kind of partial victory vis-à-vis the class-monopoly power of landlords. If, on the other hand, tenants are politically weak, there is a shortage of suitable accommodation (because of in-migration or redevelopment) and if landlords can easily sell or transform to different uses (e.g., upper-income tenancies), then the landlord class will have very considerable power and will be able to raise their rate of return to well above 15 percent. With rising rents eating into an already limited disposable income, low-income tenants can respond only by subdividing space with the inevitable consequences —over-crowding and slum formation.

Class-interest conflict of this sort between tenants and landlords can be documented in any capitalist city (Chatterjee, 1973; Sternlieb, 1966; Milner-Holland Report, 1965). The rate of return set through the working out of this conflict is best interpreted as a class-monopoly rent even though the landlord usually thinks of it as a rate of return on capital investment. The realization of this rent depends upon the ability of one class-interest group to exercise its power over another class-interest group and thereby to assure for itself a certain minimum rate of return.

(b) *Speculator-developers and suburban middle- and upper-income groups*

We now turn to a case that is rather more complex but which indicates that class-monopoly rents can be realized in all sectors of the housing market. Upper-income groups have a wide range of choice of housing as far as their income is concerned. But if their sense of social status and prestige is highly developed, then the producers of housing (who actively promote such thoughts on the part of the buyer) have an opportunity to realize a class-monopoly rent as these consumers vie with each other for prestigious housing in the "right" neighborhoods. Middle-income groups may have less choice. In many American cities, for example, they have moved to suburbia in part because they were hooked on the suburban dream, but also because social changes in the city—the influx of a low-income "lumpen-proletariat," the decline of city services, falling property values, the withdrawal of financial support for whole neighborhoods, and declining employment opportunities—have given them a hefty push by a process that I have elsewhere dubbed "blow-out" (Harvey, 1973, Chapter 5).

The realization of a class-monopoly rent depends, however, on the existence of a class of speculator-developers who have the power to capture it.[3] In a free market economy, speculator developers perform a positive service. They promote an optimal timing of land-use change, ensure that the current value of land and housing reflects expected future returns, seek to organize externalities to enhance the value of their existing developments, and generally perform a co-ordinating and stabilizing function in the face of considerable market uncertainty (Neutze, 1968; Hall et al., 1973). The role of speculator-developer is, in fact, integral and essential to the workings of a capitalist economy. Since the urbanization process relates to economic growth in general, the speculator-developer who is, in effect, the promoter of urbanization, plays a vital role in promoting economic growth. Certain institutional supports are necessary, however, if this role is to be performed effectively. The exact nature of these supports will vary from country to country but they must do two things: (1) they must reduce the uncertainty in land-use competition usually through some form of governmental regulation—planning or zoning controls, provision of infrastructure, etc.; and (2) they must encourage wealthy groups—those who can afford to wait for land to "ripen"—to participate as speculator-developers usually by offering convenient and advantageous tax arrangements. The first support permits speculator-developers to form reasonable expectations about the future, while the second ensures that only people with sufficient resources undertake the task of coordinating and stabilizing land-use change.

Class-monopoly rents can be realized by speculator-developers only if they possess mechanisms for expressing their collective class interest. The necessary institutional supports in fact provide these mechanisms. In the United States, for example, speculator-developers usually realize monopoly-rents through the manipulation of zoning decisions. Politi-cal control of suburban jurisdictions by speculator-developers is quite general in the United States; as Gaffney notes, suburban jurisdictions provide one of the most effective of all cartel arrangements with respect to land-use decisions (Gaffney, 1973). Political corruption also plays a role which, in a market economy, can be viewed positively since it frequently loosens up the supply of land from the excessive rigidities of land-use regulation by bureaucratic fiat. Without a certain minimum of governmental regulation and institutional support, however, the speculator-developer could not perform the vital function of promoter, co-ordinator, and stabilizer of land-use change. Without such an interest group to perform these functions, suburban development would degenerate into chaos and finance capital would be forced to withdraw investment from the suburbanization process. The effect of such a withdrawal upon economic growth in general, effective demand in general and the capitalist market system as a whole would, of course, be catastrophic.

The level of class-monopoly rent realized by speculator-developers depends upon the outcome of the conflict of interest between them and the various consumer groups who confront them in the market. If the speculator-developer can persuade upper-income groups of the virtues of a certain kind of housing in a particular neighborhood, gain complete control over the political process, and so on, then the advantage lies with the speculator-developer. If consumers are unimpressed by the blandishments of the speculator-developers and have firm control over the political mechanisms for land-use regulation and the provision of infrastructure, then the class-monopoly power of the speculator-developers will be contained. But if certain minimum rates of return are not realized, the speculator-developer will pull out of the business until rates of return rise. What the minimum must be is difficult to say—but in the United States a 40 percent rate of return is not regarded as abnormal.

The two cases we have examined—the landlord versus the low-income tenant and the speculator-developer versus the middle- and upper-income consumer—provide us with certain insights into the meaning of class-monopoly rent and class-monopoly power in the context of urbanization. Firstly, this form of rent appears inevitable in capitalistically organized land and housing markets. Second, the transfer payments that result from class-monopoly rents are structured in certain important respects. Suppose the landlord lives in suburbia and as a resident there gives up a class-monopoly rent to the speculator-developer? Notice, that the rent realized from a low-income tenant has been passed on, in this example, to the speculator-developer via the landlord. It is unlikely, bordering on the impossible, for rent realized by the speculator-developer to be passed on to the low-income tenant. It seems reasonable to postulate, therefore, an hierarchical structure of some sort through which class-monopoly rents percolate upwards but not downwards. At the top of this hierarchy sit the financial institutions. And so the question arises, how does this hierarchy arise and what is its *raison d'être*?

3. THE HIERARCHICAL INSTITUTIONAL FRAMEWORK FOR CO-ORDINATING ACTIVITIES IN THE HOUSING MARKET

I shall begin by stating a general proposition: the hierarchical institutional structure through which class monopoly rents are realized is a necessity if housing market activity is to be co-ordinated in a way that helps to avoid economic crisis. The problem with seeking to validate this proposition is that institutional arrangements vary markedly from country to country. But all capitalist economies must, of necessity, possess elaborate devices to integrate national and local aspects of economies, to integrate individual decisions with the needs of society as a whole. Any society must possess, in short, formalized human practices which resolve the social aggregation problem (Harvey and Chatterjee, 1974). These formalized human practices are manifest in a structure of financial and governmental institutions which, I shall argue, create the basis for class-monopoly power in the land and property markets. To explore this proposition I will examine institutional structures in the United States and consider how these affect events in Baltimore in particular..

National institutions of government and finance do not operate without a purpose; they seek, by and large, to ensure the reproduction of society and to deal with any problems that may arise in an orderly and non-disruptive manner. In a capitalist society this means a policy directed towards the orderly accumulation of capital, economic growth and the reproduction of the basic social and political relationships of a capitalist society. In the housing market these general concerns are translated into three typical concerns for national housing policy:

1. To ensure orderly relationships between construction, economic growth and new household formation;
2. To ensure short-run stability and iron out cyclical swings in the economy at large by using the construction industry and the housing sector as a partial Keynesian regulator; and
3. To ensure domestic peace and tranquility by managing the distribution of welfare in society through the provision of housing.

In the United States these concerns have been embedded in policy goals which have, by and large, been successfully met since 1930.[4] Economic growth has been accompanied and to some degree accomplished by rapid suburbanization—a process that has been facilitated by national housing policies conducted through the Federal Housing Administration. Much of the growth in GNP, both absolute and *per capita,* since the 1930s has been wrapped up in the suburbanization process (taking into account the construction of highways and utilities, housing, the effective demand for automobiles, gasoline and so on). Cyclical swings in the economy have been broadly contained since the 1930s and the construction industry appears to have functioned effectively as a major counter-cyclical tool. The evident social discontent of the 1930s has largely been defused by a government policy which has created a large wedge of middle-income people who are now "debt-encumbered homeowners" and consequently unlikely to rock the boat. The discontent of the 1960s exhibited by the blacks and the urban poor, provoked a similar political response in the housing sector—a response that has not provided a "decent house in a decent living environment" (as Congressional legislation perennially puts it) for many of the poor but which has successfully created a debt-encumbered class of black homeowners; the social instability of the 1960s certainly appears to have been defused. It appears, then, that national policies are designed to maintain the existing structure of society intact in its basic configurations, while facilitating economic growth and capitalist accumulation, eliminating cyclical influences and defusing social discontent.

How are these national policies transmitted to the locality and how do individuals come to incorporate them into their decisions? Federal, State and local government from a three-tiered

political hierarchy and an independent bureaucracy is attached to each level. The Federal bureaucracy is itself hierarchically organized, however, so that it is in a position to relate national policies to local housing markets. The Federal Housing Administration (FHA) administers a wide range of government programs and operates autonomously from bureaucracies created at the State and local levels. But in the United States the main mechanism for co-ordinating national and local, individual and societal activities lies in the hierarchical structure of financial institutions operating under governmental regulation. This structure is exceedingly complex and I shall not attempt to detail it here.[5] It is important to note one feature of it, however. Certain kinds of institution—the State and Federally chartered savings and loan institutions—operate solely in the housing sector. They were initially designed to "promote the thrift of people locally to finance their own homes and the homes of their neighbors." [6] Some of these institutions are community-based, depositor controlled and operate on a non-profit basis. They are, of course, affected by money market conditions and govern conditions and government regulation. These institutions contrast with the mortgage banks, savings banks and commercial banks which are oriented to profits or to the expansion of their business. All of these institutions, however, operate together to relate national policies to local and individual decisions and, in the process create localized structures within which class-monopoly rents can be realized.

The Baltimore situation demonstrates the point. The metropolitan area has a population of approximately two million; 900,000 live in Baltimore City and 600,000 live in the largest suburban jurisdiction—Baltimore County—which surrounds Baltimore City on almost all sides. The political machine in Baltimore County has been dominated by speculator-developer interests who have, until recently, been able to manipulate the zoning laws more or less at will in order to realize speculative gains. Political corruption is usual (Agnew was once County Executive). All that is neccessary for the realization of class-monopoly rents is some generally sustained demand for new housing (through population increase or new household formation). There is a further point to be considered, however. The investment climate is radically different in Baltimore County and Baltimore City. All of the institutions look collectively on the former as an area of growth and expansion compared to the City which is looked upon as an area that is at best stable and at worst in the process of rapid decline. The consequent channelling of investment funds to the County and the general reluctance to invest in the City turns out to be a self-fulfilling prediction to which middle-income groups are forced to respond by migrating from the City to the County, where the speculator-developer eagerly awaits them. In this fashion the conflict between city and suburb in the United States contributes to the realization of class-monopoly rents on the suburban fringe.

But there is also a geographical structure to the housing market in Baltimore City which further contributes to the potential for realizing class-monopoly rents. This geographical structure is produced by the interacting policies of financial and governmental institutions. To demonstrate this point Baltimore City is divided into 13 submarkets which can be further aggregated into eight sub-market types (see Figure 1). Data concerning the financing of housing in each of these sub-markets, together with some socio-economic information, is presented in Tables 1 and 2. It is evident that the housing market in Baltimore City is highly structured geographically with respect to the type of institutional

involvement as well as with respect to the insurance of home purchases by the Federal Housing Administration (FHA). Let us consider the main features of this structure.

(i) The *inner city* is dominated by cash and private loan transactions with scarcely a vestige of institutional or governmental involvement in the used housing market. This sub-market is the locus of that conflict between landlord and low-income tenant to which we have already alluded. There is currently a surplus of housing in this sub-market which is leading to active disinvestment (there are several thousand vacant structures in this sub-market. Professional landlords are anxious to disinvest but they still manage to get a rate of return around 13 percent (Chatterjee, 1973). The tenants are low-income and for the most part black. They are poorly organized, exercise little political control and are effectively trapped in this sub-market. Class-monopoly rents are here realized by professional landlords who calculate their rate of return to match the opportunity cost of their capital.

(ii) The white *ethnic areas* are dominated by home-ownership which is financed mainly by small community-based, savings and loan institutions which operate without a strong profit orientation and which really do offer a community service. As a consequence little class-monopoly rent is realized in this sub-market and reasonably good housing is obtained at fairly low purchase price, considering the fairly low incomes of the residents.

(iii) The black residential area of *West Baltimore* was essentially a creation of the 1960s. Low- to moderate-income blacks did not possess local savings and loan associations, were regarded with suspicion by all other financial institutions and in the early 1960s were dis-

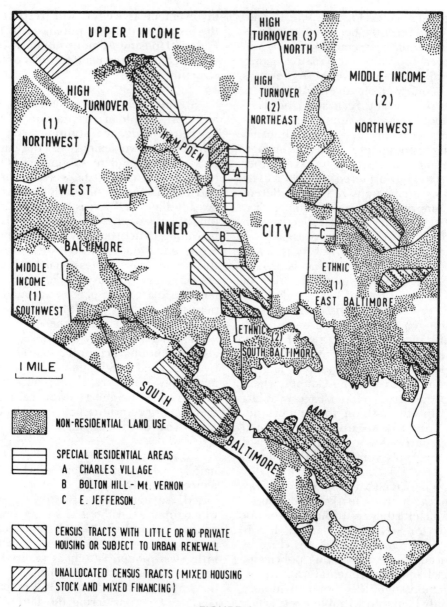

I MILE

NON-RESIDENTIAL LAND USE

SPECIAL RESIDENTIAL AREAS
A CHARLES VILLAGE
B BOLTON HILL - Mt. VERNON
C E. JEFFERSON.

CENSUS TRACTS WITH LITTLE OR NO PRIVATE HOUSING OR SUBJECT TO URBAN RENEWAL.

UNALLOCATED CENSUS TRACTS (MIXED HOUSING STOCK AND MIXED FINANCING)

FIGURE 1

criminated against by the FHA. The only way in which this group could become homeowners was by way of something called a "land-instalment contract" which works as follows. A speculator purchases a house for, say, $7,000, adds a purchase and sales commission, various financing charges and overhead costs, renovates and redecorates the property and finally adds a gross profit margin of, say, 20 percent. The house is then sold for, say, $13,000. To finance the transaction, the speculator interposes his credit rating between that of the purchaser and the financial institutions, takes out a conventional mortgage up to the appraised value of the house (say, $9,000), borrows another $4,000, and then, packages a $13,000 loan for the buyer. The speculator retains title to the property to secure the risk but permits the "buyer" immediate possession. The monthly payments cover the interest charges on the $13,000 plus the administrative charges and a small part is put to redeeming the principle. When the purchaser has redeemed $4,000 (after, say, 10 or 15 years) a conventional mortgage at the appraised value of $9,000 may be obtained. At that juncture the purchaser will get title and can start to build equity in the house.[7]

This procedure is perfectly legal and it was in effect the only way in which low- or moderate-income blacks could become home-owners in the early 1960s. There were many transactions of this sort in West Baltimore. The problem was that a comparable house sold to a person in a comparable income bracket in white ethnic areas cost $7,000 compared to the $13,000 registered in the black community. Blacks consequently regarded themselves as exploited and paying "the black tax," which was nothing more nor less than class-monopoly rent realized by speculators as they took advantage of a particular mix of financial and governmental policies compounded by problems of racial discrimination. But

a new sub-market was formed in West Baltimore by means of the land-instalment contract; and in the process strong pressures were exerted on white middle class groups to move to suburbia where the speculator-developers waited, all too willing and able to accommodate them.

The political conflict over the use of the land-instalment contract in Baltimore came to a head in the late 1960s. In the process the black communities learned that the speculator was creeping in where financial and governmental institutions refused to tread and that the problems of speculation could not be divorced from the activities of the financial and governmental institutions. Since the 1960s the land-instalment contract has declined as a form of financing. But the speculator has not disappeared from the scene; rather, he now has other instrumentalities at his disposal.

(iv) The areas of *High Turnover* are serviced mainly by a combination of mortgage banker finance and FHA insurance which were doing in 1970 what the land instalment contract did in the 1960s. Various programs were initiated in the late 1960s to try and create a debt-encumbered, socially stable class of home-owners amongst the black and the urban poor. These programs, together with administrative directives to end discriminatory practices against blacks, led to the creation of an FHA insured, mainly black, fairly low income, housing sub-market. The main tool in Baltimore was the FHA 221 (d) (2) program (D2s) which permits the financing of home-ownership for low- or moderate-income groups who have no money for a down-payment. FHA insurance in Baltimore in 1970 was, for the most part, of the D2 variety (see Table 1).

In the high turnover sub-markets created by these programs there are plenty of opportunities for the speculator to realize a class-monopoly rent. Operating through the D2 programs

TABLE 1. Housing Sub-Markets—Baltimore City, 1970

| | Total houses sold | Sales per 100 properties | % Transactions by source of funds: | | | | | | | | % Sales insured | | Average sale price ($)† |
			Cash	pvt	Federal S. & L.	State S. & L.	Mortgage Bank	Community Bank	Savings Bank	Other*	FHA	VA	
Inner city	1199	1·86	65·7	15·0	3·0	12·0	2·2	0·5	0·2	1·7	2·9	1·1	3498
1. East	646	2·33	64·7	15·0	2·2	14·3	2·2	0·5	0·1	1·2	3·4	1·4	3437
2. West	553	1·51	67·0	15·1	4·0	9·2	2·3	0·4	0·4	2·2	2·3	0·6	3568
Ethnic	760	3·34	39·9	5·5	6·1	43·2	2·0	0·8	0·9	2·2	2·6	0·7	6372
1. East Baltimore	579	3·40	39·7	4·8	5·5	43·7	2·4	1·0	1·2	2·2	3·2	0·7	6769
2. South Baltimore	181	3·20	40·3	7·7	7·7	41·4	0·6	—	—	2·2	0·6	0·6	5102
Hampden	99	2·40	40·4	8·1	18·2	26·3	4·0	—	3·0	—	14·1	2·0	7059
West Baltimore	497	2·32	30·6	12·5	12·1	11·7	22·3	1·6	3·1	6·0	25·8	4·2	8664
South Baltimore	322	3·16	28·3	7·4	22·7	13·4	13·4	1·9	4·0	9·0	22·7	10·6	8751
High turnover	2072	5·28	19·1	6·1	13·6	14·9	32·8	1·2	5·7	6·2	38·2	9·5	992
1. North-West	1071	5·42	20·0	7·2	9·7	13·8	40·9	1·1	2·9	4·5	46·8	7·4	9312
2. North-East	693	5·07	20·6	6·4	14·4	16·5	29·0	1·4	5·6	5·9	34·5	10·2	9779
3. North	308	5·35	12·7	1·4	25·3	18·1	13·3	0·7	15·9	12·7	31·5	15·5	12,330
Middle income	1077	3·15	20·8	4·4	29·8	17·0	8·6	1·9	8·7	9·0	17·7	11·1	12,760
1. South-West	212	3·46	17·0	6·6	29·2	8·5	15·1	1·0	10·8	11·7	30·2	17·0	12,848
2. North-East	865	3·09	21·7	3·8	30·0	19·2	7·0	2·0	8·2	8·2	14·7	9·7	12,751
Upper income	361	3·84	19·4	6·9	23·5	10·5	8·6	7·2	21·1	2·8	11·9	3·6	27,413

* Assumed mortgages and subject to mortgage.
† Ground rent is sometimes included in the sale price and this distorts the averages in certain respects.
The relative differentials between the sub-markets are of the right order however.
Source: City Planning Department Tabulations from Lusk Reports

makes it less easy to extract the "black tax" but if whites move (as they are likely to do if a low-income black family moves in), speculators can pick up houses cheaper than appraised value, put in some cosmetic repairs to meet FHA quality standards, and sell through the D2 program. If FHA quality control standards are poor (or if speculators can corrupt the administration of them) then class-monopoly rents can be realized as a white "exit tax" and a black or low-income "entry tax." In some cities, such as Detroit, New York and Philadelphia, the windfall profits to speculators have been enormous largely through the corruption of FHA programs (Boyer, 1973). In Baltimore, the sub-market created by the land-instalment contract in the 1960s is now being extended in areas of high turnover by speculator activity in conjunction with mortgage banker finance and the FHA D2 programs.

(v) The *middle-income* sub-markets of North-East and South-West Baltimore are typically the creation of the FHA programs of the 1930s. By the 1960s home-ownership was being financed conventionally by Federal savings and loan institutions and some of the smaller ethnic savings and loan institutions which have helped to finance migration from the older ethnic areas of the city to the newer housing of North-East Baltimore. The inner edge of this sub-market is under some pressure, however, and financial institutions are extremely sensitive about risks in these areas. As a consequence they tend to withdraw support from an area if they perceive it to be threatened in any way. By so doing they create a vacuum in housing finance into which the speculator moves backed by the FHA programs and mortgage banker finance. There is a good deal of political friction in these boundary zones

	Median income*	% Black occupied d.u.'s	% Units owner occupied	Mean $ value of owner occupied	% Renter occupied	Mean monthly rent
Inner city	6259	72·2	28·5	6259	71·5	77·5
1. East	6201	65·1	29·3	6380	70·7	75·2
2. West	6297	76·9	27·9	6963	72·1	78·9
Ethnic	8822	1·0	66·0	8005	34·0	76·8
1. East Baltimore	8836	1·2	66·3	8368	33·7	78·7
2. South Baltimore	8785	0·2	64·7	6504	35·3	69·6
Hampden	8730	0·3	58·8	7860	41·2	76·8
West Baltimore	9566	84·1	50·0	13,842	50·0	103·7
South Baltimore	8941	0·1	56·9	9741	43·1	82·0
High turnover	10,413	34·3	53·5	11,886	46·5	113·8
1. North-West	9483	55·4	49·3	11,867	50·7	110·6
2. North-East	10,753	30·4	58·5	11,533	41·5	111·5
3. North	11,510	1·3	49·0	12,726	51·0	125·1
Middle income	10,639	2·8	62·6	13,221	37·5	104·1
1. South-West	10,655	4·4	48·8	13,470	51·2	108·1
2. North-East	10,634	2·3	66·2	13,174	33·8	103·0
Upper income	17,577	1·7	50·8	27,097	49·2	141·4

TABLE 2. Housing Sub-Markets—Baltimore City, 1970 (Census Data)
* Weighted average of median incomes for census tracts in sub-market.
Source: 1970 Census

and a political struggle to preserve the middle-income sub-markets from erosion at the edges—an erosion that inevitably leads middle income groups to search for housing opportunities in the suburbs.

(vi) The more affluent groups make use of savings banks and commercial banks to much greater degree and rarely resort to FHA guarantees. Such groups usually have the political and economic power to fend off speculative incursions and it is unlikely that they will move except as the result of their own changing preferences or from declining services. Class-monopoly rents are realized in this sub-market largely because of prestige and status considerations.

This geographical structure of sub-markets in Baltimore forms a decision environment in the context of which individual households make housing choices. These choices are likely, by and large, to conform to the structure and to reinforce it. The structure itself is a product of history. In the long-run we find that the geographic structure of the city is continuously being transformed by conflicts and struggles generated by the ebb and flow of market forces, the operations of speculators, landlords and developers, the changing policies of governmental and financial institutions, changing tastes, and the like. But in the short run the geographic structure is rather fixed and it is this rigidity which permits class-monopoly rents to be realized within sub-markets (as classes of providers face classes of consumers) and between sub-markets as a variety of processes seek to erode the boundaries of the sub-markets themselves (every sub-market has its speculator-developer fringe). In some parts of the city these conflicts may be dormant at times— boundaries may be stabilized (often with the help of natural or artificial barriers) and accommodation between opposing forces may be reached within sub-mar-

kets. But it would be rare indeed to find a city in which no such conflicts were occurring.

4. CLASS-MONOPOLY RENT, ABSOLUTE SPACE AND URBAN STRUCTURE

Class-monopoly rents arise because the owners of resource units have the power always to exact a positive return. Ricardo thought that *absolute* rent could exist only on an island where all resource units were employed and on which there was an absolute scarcity. The Baltimore materials indicate that the man-made resource system created by urbanization is, in effect, a series of man-made islands on which class monopolies produce absolute scarcities. Absolute spaces, created by human practices, are essential, it seems, to the realization of class-monopoly rent. Absolute spaces can be constructed by dividing space up into parcels and segments each of which can then be regarded as a "thing in itself" independent of other things (Harvey, 1973, Chapter 5). The private property relation is, of course, the most basic institution by means of which absolute spaces are formally created. Political jurisdictions define collective absolute spaces which may then be carved up by the bureaucratic regulation of land use. All of these forms of absolute space create the possibility to realize class-monopoly rents. But it is primarily through the informally structured absolute spaces of sub-markets that such rents are realized.

The implications of this for residential structure are of interest. Residential differentiation in urban areas has long been explained in terms of social ecological processes, consumer preferences, utility-maximizing behaviors on the part of individuals, and the like. The Baltimore evidence suggests that financial and governmental institutions play an active role in shaping residential differentiation and that the active agent in the process is an investor seeking to realize a class-monopoly rent. The relationship between traditional explanations of urban residential differentiation and this interpretation is complex. The small neighborhood savings and loan institution in Baltimore, for example, is in effect a community institution that fits neatly into a social ecological view of urban community structure. But most housing finance comes from institutions seeking profits or the expansion of business. Faced with a choice between supporting a risk-absorbing landlord operation and a vulnerable home-owner in the inner city, business rationality dictates support of the former at the expense of the latter. Not all financial institutions exhibit a totally cold market rationality— they will grant personal favors (usually to people of the same social class, however) and they will sometimes actively support neighborhoods (often to procure a desirable stability in a particular sub-market). But the options of the profit-maximizing or expansion-conscious financial institution are limited. The hidden hand, and in particular the prospects for realizing class-monopoly rents, will inexorably guide them in certain directions. And as a result these institutions become a fundamental force in shaping the residential structure of the city.

This is not to say that considerations of race and ethnicity, social status and prestige, life-style aspirations, community and neighborhood solidarity, and the like, are irrelevant to understanding residential differentiation. Ironically, all of these features *increase* the potential for realizing class-monopoly rent because they help to maintain the island-like structure, to create the absolute space of the parochially-minded community. Indeed, a strong case can be made for regarding consumer preferences as being produced systematically rather than as arising spontaneously (as neo-classical

economic doctrines appear to envisage via the myth of consumer sovereignty). The simplest manifestation of this is the use of techniques of persuasion to convince upper-income people of the virtues of living in a "smart" house in the "right" neighborhood. But there is a deeper process at work. Financial institutions and government manage the urbanization process to achieve economic growth, economic stability and to defuse social discontent (see Section 3). If these aims are to be realized, then new modes of consumption and new social wants and needs will have to be produced whether people like it or not. If these new modes of consumption and new social wants and needs do not arise spontaneously, in a manner that fits with the overall necessities of capitalist society, then people will have to be forced or cajoled to accept them. The urbanization process achieves this end quite successfully. By structuring and restructuring the choices open to people, by creating distinctive decision environments, the urbanization process forces new kinds of choice independently of spontaneously arising predilictions.

If the dynamic of urbanization is powered by financial and governmental institutions, mediated by speculator-developers and speculator-landlords in pursuit of class-monopoly rent, and necessitated by the over-riding requirement to reproduce the capitalist order, then it may not be too fanciful to suggest that distinctive "consumption classes," "distributive groupings" or even "housing classes" may be produced at the same time (see Giddens, 1973; Rex and Moore, 1967). Individuals can, of course, strive or choose to join one or other "distributive grouping " or shift (if they can) from one "consumption class" to another. In like manner they can strive or choose (depending on their circumstances) to move from one housing sub-market to another. What individuals cannot choose, however, is the structure of the distributive grouping or the structure of the housing sub-markets—these are dictated by forces far removed from the realms of consumer sovereignty. The general proposition we are here led to is an intriguing one: in producing new modes of consumption and new social wants and needs, the urbanization process concomitantly produces new distributive groupings or consumption classes which may crystallize into distinctive communities within the overall urban structure. This topic will be taken up again in Section 5.

The Baltimore materials suggest another startling conclusion. The class-monopoly rent gained in one sub-market is not independent of its realization elsewhere and certain strong multiplier effects can be detected. Suppose, for example, that there is a speculative boom in the inner city through which new sub-markets are formed out of existing neighborhoods and that the old residents of these neighborhoods are forced to seek housing opportunities in suburbia. Then, the greater the class-monopoly rent earned by the inner-city speculator, the greater the opportunity to realize rent on the suburban fringe. Multiplier effects of this sort may be captured by the same financial institutions or, in some cases, by the same entrepreneur. If there is no conscious collusion to generate the multiplier effect, the calculus of profits and losses, of expectations and perceived risks, will function as a hiddenhand regulator to achieve the same results.

These conclusions are, of course, geographically and institutionally specific to Baltimore and the United States. But a cursory examination of the literature suggests that they may be generalized to all advanced capitalist nations.[8] Whether or not this is the case must be proved by future research. It seems likely, however, that the processes are general but that the mainfestations are particular because the institutional, geographical, cultural and historical situations vary a great deal from place to place. In other words, the processes are general, but the circumstances are unique to each case and so, consequently, are the results.

If the multiplier effects to the realization of class-monopoly rents are general, then we have a partial explanation of how investment can shift continuously over time from the primary to the secondary circuit of capital as Lefebvre hypotheses. Governmental and financial institutions are forced to operate in certain ways if individual behaviors are to be co-ordinated and integrated with national and societal requirements. Urbanization, itself a product of these requirements, creates islands of opportunities for realizing class-monopoly rents. And the quest for this rent generates a multiplier effect that makes it even more profitable in the short run to shift investment into the land, housing and property markets. Such a shift helps to explain the industrial stagnation, particularly evident since the late 1960s, in the advanced capitalist nations as investment shifts from the production of value to the attempt to realize it. In the short run such a shift is possible because it is possible to milk value produced in past periods for purposes of current realization (which means, however, a continuous decay in the quality of urban environments). But in the long run such a shift is doomed to failure for if value is not produced, then how can it possibly be realized?

5. CLASS SYSTEM, CLASS STRUCTURE, CLASS INTEREST IN THE POLITICAL ECONOMY OF URBANISM

We will now consider the relationship between the concept of class interest as it arises in the context of urbanization (and as it is used in this paper) and more general concepts of class structure and class antagonism. It is useful to distinguish at the outset between the concept of *subjective* class which describes the consciousness which different groups have of their position within a social structure and the concept of *objective* class which, in Marx's schema, describes a basic division within capitalism between a class of producers and a class of appropriators of surplus value (for a recent discussion on this topic, see Giddens, 1973). The former class includes both productive labor and that labor which is socially necessary but unproductive (for example, labor contributing to circulation, realization, administration and the provision of socially necessary services). The meaning attached to class interest in this paper stems from the fact of certain conflicts around the realization of class-monopoly rent. We are, therefore, working at the level of subjective class interest and the task is to relate these diverse class interests to the concept of objective class.

Traditionally, rent is viewed as a transfer payment from capitalist producers to a rentier class which gains its power as a residual of feudalism. But we are here concerned with rent extracted from the community out of the consumption process rather than out of the production process. This extraction generates a species of community conflict which has become widespread with the progress of urbanization in advanced capitalist countries. This kind of conflict contrasts, superficially at least, with the more traditional work-based conflicts over the immediate production of value. We can observe as a consequence some curious dichotomies. Community-based organizations rarely offer support in a work-based conflict (such as a strike) and work-based organizations (such as the trade unions) rarely offer active support to community groups in conflict over, for example, the realization of class-monopoly rent. Individuals may in fact switch roles with respect to such conflicts

—a work-based radical may be a community-based conservative and vice versa. The place of work also tends to be male-dominated space compared with the female-dominated residential space. Sex roles may get intertwined as a male work-based radical acts conservatively with respect to a female community-based radical. Such conflicts may be internalized within the family. The geography of human activity within large metropolitan areas appears to generate curious transformations and inversions to create a complex geography of subjective class consciousness. The expression of class interest around community issues cannot, therefore, be interpreted as a simple reflection of class interest at the point of production.

Yet class interest can be equally strong and express analogous goals at the point of production and within the community. Workers may seek for worker-control while residents may seek for community control. Both goals express a basic felt need on the part of individuals to control the social conditions of their existence. But under urbanization the two goals become divorced from each other. A far more cohesive basis for political power exists when community-based and work-based interests coincide (for example, in mining communities and in other situations characterized by *industrial* rather than *advanced urban* forms of social organization). Marx thought that large concentrations of population would heighten class-awareness. But under urbanization class-consciousness appears to have become fragmented.

Community-based class interest always tends to be parochialist in its perspectives. The community is regarded as a "thing-in-itself" independent of other things—it is regarded as an absolute space, as something to be preserved and defended against external threat. From such a standpoint flows a form of community conflict which is essentially internecine—it pits community against community so that the average condition of communities is not altered one wit. What one community gains another loses. The sequence of wins and losses merely serves to perpetuate the defensiveness and competitiveness of the communities concerned—a situation which permits even more class-monopoly rents to be realized since speculators so easily feed off community antagonisms. Parochialist community-based class interest can never be an adequate surrogate for objective social class for it ignores the essential fact that the survival of the community depends, given the enormous complexity in the division of labor, upon commodity exchanges on a global scale and because it ignores the links in the production and circulation of value in society.

Yet certain kinds of community-conflict lead to the formation of non-parochialist horizons. In Baltimore, for example, community groups enraged at the use of the land-instalment contract, gradually came to realize that financial institutions, by denying conventional mortgage funds while financing speculator-landlords, were the controlling influence in the situation. The community group began to unravel the skein of argument presented in this paper through a process of political exploration. And at the end of the road, the community came face to face with what appears to be the dominant power of finance capital.

Curiously enough, there are hints that work-based conflict may lead to the same confrontation. The traditional conflict between worker and industrialist is being ameliorated in certain sectors by the growing integration of workers into management leading, perhaps, to worker control under certain conditions. But worker control over the factory, brings the worker face to face with the power of finance capital to exercise an external control over the activities of industrial enterprise. In much the same

way that Marx thought it possible (but unlikely) that land and resources could be brought under state ownership to the advantage of the capitalist, so it appears possible (but unlikely) to nationalize industrial production, introduce decentralized worker control, without in any way necessarily touching or diminishing the power of finance capital. Worker control has to be viewed, therefore, as a transitional step that fails unless finance capital is also controlled.

The conclusion from the standpoint of both the community and the work place is that the ultimate power to organize the production and realization of value in society lies in the hands of finance capital. To sustain this conclusion, however, we have to show the necessity for an inner transformation of capitalism such that finance capital comes to exercise a hegemonic power over industrial production as well as all other aspects of life. All that I have space to do here, is to provide some clues as to where we might look for the logic of such an inner transformation.

The changing role of money itself provides one such clue. Without money there could be no integrated commodity production, no elaborate division of labor, no price-fixing markets, no universalized exchange values, no medium for the accumulation of capital, no urbanization, and so on. Money in its role of mediator of exchange consequently mediates all significant social interactions. Marx argued that:

The need for exchange and for the transformation of product into pure exchange value progresses in step with the division of labour, i.e. with the increasingly social character of production. But as the latter grows, so grows the power of money, i.e. the exchange relation establishes itself as a power external to and independent of producers. What originally appeared as a means to promote production becomes a relation alien to producers. As the producers become more dependent on exchange, exchange appears to become independent of them, and the gap between the product as product and the product as exchange value appears to widen. Money does not create these antitheses and contradictions; it is, rather, the development of these contradictions and antitheses which creates the transcendental power of money. (Marx, 1973 edn. *The Grundrisse*).

The "increasingly social character of production" (the increasingly complex division of labor), the constant expansion of capitalist social relations and the increasing integration of society on a world-wide basis, have, since Marx's time, greatly increased the "transcendental power of money." But this power, if it is to be exercised, requires an institutional framework for its expression and a class of people willing and able to make use of it. Marx again provides a clue to the former when he argues that the joint stock company is an institutional response to the inherent instability of competitive capitalism— an instability which required the concentration of first, industrial, and later, finance capital. This new arrangement transforms "the actually functioning capitalist into a mere manager, administrator of other people's capital and . . . the owner of capital into a mere owner, a mere money capitalist" (Marx, 1967 edn., Vol. 3, p. 436). As a result, interest—"the mere compensation for owning capital that now is entirely divorced from the actual process of reproduction"—is substituted for profit. Marx saw all this creating a transitional mode of production in which new institutions would be increasingly social in character:

This is the abolition of the capitalist mode of production within the capitalist mode of production itself, and hence a self-dissolving contradiction, which *prima facie* represents a mere phase of transition to a new form of production. . . . It establishes a monopoly in certain spheres and thereby requires state interference. It reproduces a new financial aristocracy, a new variety of parasites, in the shape of promoters, speculators, and simply nominal directors. . . . It is private production without the control of private property." (Marx, 1967 edn., Volume 3, p. 438).

Marx did not elaborate much on these remarks but history has. Industrial corporations have attempted to maintain their independence of financial institutions by generating funds internally, but this has led them to diversify and to take on many characteristics of financial institutions—ITT is almost purely a financial holding company now and General Motors is steadily moving in that direction. Financial institutions equal and perhaps surpass the industrial corporations in economic power (U.S. House of Representatives, 1968, 1971; Herman, 1973). State power has grown remarkably and functions to support, by appropriate budgetary, fiscal and monetary policies, the operations of finance capital. The State is also active in managing both production and consumption (Miliband, 1969). Finance capital, operating through State, corporate and financial institutions, effectively co-ordinates all social activity into one coherent whole. An industrial capitalism based merely on the immediate production of goods has evolved to a finance form of capitalism which seeks to create and appropriate value through the production, not only of goods, but of new modes of production and new social wants and needs (see the important passages on this point in Marx, 1973 edn., p. 92). But in so doing, new institutions are founded on the power of money, which is the appearance but not the substance of wealth. Hence arises, in Marx's view, the contradictory character of finance capitalism and its historical necessity as a transitional form.

Financial institutions can accumulate by a variety of techniques. Operating competitively they frequently try to accumulate off each other (by takeovers, asset-stripping and the like). In aggregate, however, finance capital accumulates out of production in the immediate sense (a work-based exploitation), out of the production of new modes of consumption and the production of new social wants and needs (both of which lead to community-based exploitation). And as finance capital seeks to manage and control the totality of the production process so there emerges a certain indifference as to whether accumulation takes place by keeping wages down in the immediate production process or by manipulations in the consumption sphere (varying from the manipulation of pension funds to accumulation by means of the processes described in this paper).

We have already suggested (Sections 3 and 4) that urbanization serves to produce new modes of consumption and new social wants and needs. The roles of speculator-landlord and speculator-developer are crucial to the dynamics of urbanization and therefore to the maintenance of effective demand; and a structure of sub-markets through which class-monopoly rents can be realized provides the necessary incentive to play these roles with profit. But at the same time the potential to realize these rents provides the possibility for rapid accumulation of capital out of the land and property markets when the occasion demands it. When industrial demand lags and industrial profits decline, financial institutions will compensate by moving into the land and property markets (ITT has extracted millions out of the Florida real estate boom, for example). But many communities will resist these external forces controlling the conditions of their existence—hence the community conflict typical of advanced urban societies. This analysis suggests a certain underlying unity to community-based and work-based conflict and herein may lie a clue to the definition of objective classes under advanced urbanization. If objective classes are still to be defined in terms of the production and appropriation or surplus value, then it is now production as a totality (including the production of new modes of consumption and new social wants and needs) rather than immediate production which defines the division between producers and

appropriators and surplus value. Marx's theory of surplus value is founded in the analysis of immediate production (with modes of consumption and wants and needs held constant) (see Marx, 1973 edn., Vol. 1). Exploitation can arise out of the creation of new modes of consumption and the imposition of new social wants and needs—whether or not this exploitation can be interpreted in terms of the surplus value concept or not is a matter of debate (I am inclined to the view that the theory of surplus value ought to be embedded in a general theory of exploitation). But we are on safer ground when we assert that the growing hegemonic power of finance capital over the totality of production, circulation and realization of value in society, produces a dichotomy between work-based and community-based conflict at the same time as it demonstrates its underlying unity.

This view is reinforced when we turn back to the possibility, broached in Section 4, that the processes described in this paper also serve to generate specific "distributive groupings" or "consumption classes" which in turn define community characteristics in housing sub-markets. It is also the case that the production and reproduction of labor power occurs in the community (Giddens, 1973, pp. 109–110; Bunge, 1973). The reproduction of the social relations of capitalism requires the production of a population which, from the standpoint of employment opportunities and the wages system, will ultimately become fragmented into subjective classes, each prepared to take on certain social roles and to acquire certain technical skills, appropriate to its particular position within the overall social structure of a constantly expanding capitalist society. The structure of "consumption classes" and "distributive groupings" may, in this fashion, become related to the production of a stratified labor force. All urban areas exhibit considerable variation in opportunity to acquire education, social status, social services, and the like (to acquire what Giddens calls "market capacity") (1973, pp. 103–110). And while there may be considerable individual mobility, it appears that the structure of sub-markets which we have identified and the distinctive distributive groupings that occupy them, when combined with the differential distribution of resources to acquire market capacity within the urban system,[9] function to reproduce the social relations of labor under capitalism. These social relations achieve a greater stability precisely because communities, differentiated by social relations, become self-replicating. Objective classes have to be defined, therefore, in terms of a totality of the production process which includes (1) the immediate production of value, (2) the production of new modes of consumption, (3) the production of new social wants and needs, (4) the production and reproduction of labor power, and (5) the production and reproduction of the social relations of capitalism.

6. FINANCE CAPITAL AND THE URBAN REVOLUTION— A CONCLUSION

We are now in a position to reflect back upon Lefebvre's fundamental thesis. We can provide a comprehensible inner logic for Lefebvre's "ensemble of transformations" through which industrial society comes to be superceded by urban society. In the early years of capitalism, production in particular (the organization of industrial production) was the main focus of attention. In late capitalism, production in all of its facets predictably becomes more and more important. Since the industrialist is adept at immediate production but has little control over the totality of production, finance capital (operating through industrial, financial and governmental institutions) has emerged as the hege-

monic force in advanced capitalist societies. Urbanism has consequently been transformed from an expression of the production needs of the industrialist to an expression of the controlled power of finance capital, backed by the power of the State, over the totality of the production process. Herein lies the significance of urbanization as a mode of consumption and as a producer of new social wants and needs. Concomitantly, the urban realm becomes the locus for the controlled reproduction of the social relations of capitalism. But there also emerges a new definition of objective class interest which is manifest both in work-based and community-based conflicts. In the community these conflicts are over the production of new modes of consumption, new social wants and needs, and over the production and reproduction of both labor power and the social relations of capitalism. It seems, however, that the finance form of capitalism, which has emerged as a response to the inherent contradictions in the competitive industrial form, is itself unstable and beset by contradictory tendencies. Of necessity, it treats money as a "thing in itself" and thereby constantly tends to undermine the production of value in pursuit of the form rather than the substance of wealth. The alien but "transcendental" power of money and the institutions created to facilitate the operation of finance capital are not tied to the production of value and hence we may explain the shift of investment into the secondary circuit of capital at the expense of the primary productive circuit. The perpetual tendency to try to realize value without producing it is, in fact, the central contradiction of the finance form of capitalism. And the tangible manifestations of this central contradiction are writ large in the urban landscapes of the advanced capitalist nations.

The ensemble of transformations of which Lefebvre speaks are far more complex than he imagines. But then so also are the processes of transformation in capitalist society when compared to our ability to grasp them. This complexity cannot be used as an excuse, however, for our almost studied ignorance on the crucial interconnections between the processes of urbanization, economic growth and capitalist accumulation and the structuring of social classes in advanced capitalist societies. This gap in our thinking is quite odd when the literature on the Third World is so explicit in its dealing with these kinds of relationships. It is rather as if we have succumbed to the illusion that because we are both "advanced" and "urbanized" there is no need to examine the crucial relations through which we arrived in our contemporary state and *which also serve to sustain us in it.* To make these relations more explicit is an urgent task to which this paper seeks to make a modest beginning.

NOTES

1. There is an extensive literature on "the transformation problem" most of which is cited in Laibman (1973); the relationship between this transformation and rent is spelled out by Marx (1967 edn., Vol. 3, chapter 45), and critically examined by Emmanuel (1972).

2. It may be objected to that I am using the concepts "class" and "class interest" far too freely and loosely. In what follows I will use these concepts to refer to any group that has a clearly defined common interest in the struggle to command scarce resources in society. I will use the phrase *social class* or *class structure* when referring to more general concepts of class in society. The notion of class-monopoly is made use of by Marx (1967 edn., Vol. 3, pp. 194–5).

3. The term "speculator-developer" is here used generically to refer to all those individuals and institutions that operate in the land and property markets with a view to realizing gains through ultimate sale or change in land use. In practice there may be considerable division of labor in this activity, while different institutions operate under different constraints (see, for example, the difference between entrepreneurs and the relics of the feudal order—the Crown, the Church, etc.—described in C.I.S. Anti-Report on the Property Developers. 1973, *The Recurrent Crisis of London* (London).

4. The views expressed in this paragraph can be documented in detail from The Douglas Commission Report (1968).

5. More detail is provided in Harvey and Chatterjee (1974).

6. Ibid.

7. The details of this are explained in Grigsby et al., (1971, chapter 6).

8. For comparable materials on London see, for example, Hall et al., (1973), *The Milner-Holland Report* (1965), Pahl (1970), C.I.S. (1973) and Marriott (1967). The point here is, of course, that the large number of vacant houses in the center of Baltimore is a vivid contrast with the situation in London; but the process of "gentrification" in London is as much a manifestation of the process of realizing class-monopoly rent as is the land-instalment contract and speculation with the D2's in Baltimore.

9. For more on these points, see Harvey (1973, chapter 2).

REFERENCES

Barnbrock, J. 1974. Prologomenon to a debate on location theory: The case of Von Thunen. *Antipode* 6, no. 1: 59–66.

Boyer, B. D. 1973. *Cities destroyed for cash.* New York.

Bunge, W. 1973. The point of reproduction (unpublished). Department of Geography, York University, Ontario, Canada.

Chatterjee, L. 1973. Real estate investment and deterioration of housing in Baltimore. Ph.D. Dissertation, Department of Geography and Environmental Engineering, The Johns Hopkins University, Baltimore.

C.I.S. 1973. Anti-Report on the Property Developers, *The recurrent crisis of London.*

Douglas Commission Report. 1968. *Building the American city.* Washington, D.C.

Emmanuel, A. 1972. *Unequal exchange: A study of the imperialism of trade.* New York.

Firey, W. 1960. *Man, mind and the land: A theory of resource use.* Glencoe, Ill.

Gaffney, M. 1973. Releasing land to serve demand via fiscal disaggregation. In M. Clawson (ed.), *Modernizing urban land use policy.* Washington, D.C.

Giddens, A. 1973. *The class structure of the advanced societies.* London.

Grigsby, W., Rosenberg, L., Stegman, M., and Taylor, J. 1971. *Housing and poverty,* Chapter 6. Institute for Environmental Studies, University of Pennsylvania, Philadelphia.

Hall. P., Gracey, H., Drewett, R., and Thomas, R. 1973. *The containment of urban England,* Vol. 2, Chapter 6. London.

Harvey, D. 1973. *Social justice and the city,* Chapter 2. London.

Harvey, D. and Chatterjee, L. 1974. Absolute rent and the structuring of space by financial institutions. *Antipode* 6, no. 1: 22–36.

Herman, E. 1973. Do bankers control corporations? *Monthly Review* 25, no. 2: 12–29.

Keiper, J. S., Kurnow, E., Clark, C. D., and Segal, H. H. 1961. *Theory and measurement of rent.* Philadelphia.

Laibman, D. 1973. Values and prices of production: The political economy of the transformation problem. *Science and Society* 37: 404–36.

Lefebvre, H. 1970. *La revolution urbaine*, p. 13. Paris.

Marriott, O. 1967. *The property boom*. London.

Marx, K. 1967 Edition. *Capital* (Three Volumes). International Publishers: New York.

Marx, K. 1968 Edition. *Theories of surplus value*, Part 2, p. 44. Moscow.

Marx, K. 1973 Edition. *The Grundrisse*, p. 146. Penguin. Harmondsworth.

Miliband, R. 1969. *The state in capitalist society*. London.

Milner-Holland Report. 1965. *Report of the committee on housing in greater London*. H.M.S.O, Cmnd. 2605. London.

Neutze, M. 1968. *The suburban apartment boom*. Baltimore.

Pahl, R. E. 1970. *Whose city?* London.

Rex, J. and Moore, R. 1967. *Race, community and conflict.* London.

Spoehr, A. 1956. Cultural differences in the interpretation of natural resources. In W. Thomas (ed.), *Man's role in changing the face of the earth.* Chicago.

Sternlieb, G. 1966. *The tenement landlord.* New Brunswick: New Jersey.

United States House of Representatives. 1968. Committee on Banking (Staff Report). *Trust banking in the United States.* (The Wright-Patman Report). Washington, D.C.

United States House of Representatives. 1971. Judiciary Committee (Staff Report). *Report on conglomerates.* Washington, D.C.

Walker, R. A. 1974. Urban ground rent: Building a new conceptual framework. *Antipode* 6, no. 1: 51–58.

Wicksteed, P. H. 1894. *The co-ordination of the laws of distribution.* London.

INSTITUTIONAL AND CONTEXTUAL FACTORS AFFECTING THE HOUSING CHOICE OF MINORITY RESIDENTS

DONALD L. FOLEY

The separation of racial and ethnic groups is one of the most marked attributes of modern American cities. While the previous reading illustrates the spatial influence of one institutional element, Foley's essay identifies the broad range of public and private controls which serve to promote and to reinforce segregation. Not only do these comments relate to central cities but also to the larger scale issue of the general exclusion of minorities from suburban environments.

Reprinted from A. H. Hawley and V. P. Rock, eds., *Segregation in Residential Areas,* Publication No. 0–309–02042–5, Division of Behavioral Sciences (Washington, D.C.: National Academy of Sciences—National Research Council, 1973), pp. 85–147, by permission of the publisher and the author. This is an edited version of the original publication.

PRIVATE INSTITUTIONAL PRACTICES IN THE RENTAL, SALE, AND FINANCING OF HOUSING FOR MINORITY FAMILIES

Rental Housing

Various studies support the conclusion that Negroes and other minorities have the greatest difficulty in obtaining rental housing outside established minority areas (Denton [1970]; Watts et al., 1964; NCDH, 1970; Meyer et al., 1965). A 1965 mail questionnaire, to which 164 members of the Greater Pittsburgh Board of Realtors responded, found that 72 percent of these realtors had never shown housing to, and 79 percent had never completed rental arrangements with, black prospects in predominantly white areas (Biochel et al., 1969).

In part, this reflects the selectivity of landlords, apartment managers, and real estate agents, whether or not in non-minority residential areas. For example, a 1960 survey in Schenectady, New York, reported the following objections stated by 200 landlords of vacant apartments: 65 percent objected to renting to Negroes (compared with 75 percent, 1951 survey of same city), of which 36 percent would "under no circumstances" rent to Negroes and 29 percent would prefer not to rent to Negroes; 55 percent objected to renting to families with children; 53 percent objected to renting to families with pets; and 6 percent objected to renting to non-Christians (Mercer, 1962, p. 49). Landlords, either apartment owners or managers, may be gatekeepers to their apartment building and the immediate neighborhood for various reasons: They may live there themselves and wish to screen their own prospective neighbors; they may seek to protect what they take to be the interests of present or prospective majority-white tenants; they may be unfavorably influenced by stereotypes about housing maintenance by minority tenants; and they may believe that minority households, once admitted, will stimulate pressures for further minority tenancy.

A great increase in construction of new apartments has taken place in the suburbs since the late 1950s. This has meant that new rental housing has become readily available in the suburbs; such housing has often been attractively designed and located, sometimes in well-landscaped settings. Better housing and more services for the rental dollar were offered than were available in the central city. Generally, however, such apartments, located in predominantly or all majority-white residential areas, are even more likely to discriminate against prospective minority tenants than older apartment buildings in or closer to the inner city (Neutze, 1968).

Our conclusion from our research is that the vast majority [of apartment owners] discriminate, and almost all believe that their white tenants will leave if they rent any of their apartments to minority families. Their usual tactics for avoiding integration are delay and red tape, i.e., the minority prospect gets delay and red tape and the white prospect gets the apartment. Where housing is as tight as it is in the Bay Area, discrimination becomes very difficult to prove and easy to practice. If a minority prospect can be held off for as little as four hours, it is usually time to get a bona fide white tenant signed up in time. . . .

Time is bought in all kinds of ways by setting requirements almost no one can meet: by forms; by demanding references; by myriad uncertainties, even by failing to call back when an initial phone inquiry suggests that the prospect may be of a minority ethnic group. . . . Actually, most minority prospects are easily turned away. They are too proud to force the issue, and also very worried about the amount of time it takes to follow through a complaint.

Some of the data suggests that because of their determination to discriminate, more mamma-poppa operations are using agents than was formerly the case. The obvious reason is that [real estate] brokers have developed skills to fend off minority prospects and can do this more clearly than an owner. Moreover, where all else fails, it can turn out that "the owner had already rented the apartment and forgotten to tell the broker." . . . (Denton, 1970, p. Jb23–Jb24.)

As will be further discussed below, the broker has become more sophisticated in the performance of this "service" in the face of fair-housing laws and other anti-discrimination legislation (NCDH, 1970; Denton, 1970).

It is essential for minority households that the rental market be opened up. Because of severe housing shortages, fierce competition for rental housing, and the restrictions imposed by discriminatory practice, minority households are victims of an unusually tight market or submarket. It has long been understood that minority households get less housing for the money than do majority households, and this discrepancy may be widening (Abrams, 1965; Kerner Commission, 1968; Douglas Commission, 1969; Kaiser Committee, 1968; U.S. Commission on Civil Rights, 1967; New York City Rand Institute, 1970; Grebler et al., 1970, Ch. 11). No matter how advantageous and desirable home ownership may be in the long run, rental housing remains the immediate prospect for most minority families. Available rental housing in the suburbs could facilitate the staging of moves, so that the family could face up to the spatial move before taking the next step of a tenure change. Moreover, a rental base in an outer locality would provide an advantageous base for the search for a house to buy.

Sale of Older Housing

Most slum clearance and relocation transactions are handled through real estate brokers. The broker paired with an owner may provide a formidable gatekeeping arrangement. The seller may feel a sense of responsibility on behalf of his majority-white neighbors and may determine, almost as a matter of course, to instruct the realtor not to consider "undesirable" prospects. The real estate broker, in addition to a loyalty to the seller, may have an eye to future business and may interpret such a dictum as his "professional" responsibility to maintain the stability of the neighborhood. While the National Association of Real Estate Boards (NAREB) has openly stated that all realtors are expected to conform to the fair-housing laws, there is evidence that the brokers have continued their screening responsibilities, but with greater care in order not to be caught openly in violation of the new legislation.

In the San Francisco Bay Area study, Denton (1970, p. Jb5) concluded:

> . . . by and large, the vast majority of realtors still believe in residential segregation and believe that to maintain their control of the market for used homes they must find ways to prevent minority prospects from finding housing in all-white neighborhoods.

Of the sample of Pittsburgh realtors studied in 1965, 53 percent had never shown housing for sale and 79 percent had never completed housing sales to black prospects in predominantly white areas (Biochel et al., 1969). In the Washington, D.C., area, realtors had at one time been instructed not to sell (or rent) to "colored people." Later this instruction was modified, but the realtors still tend to urge sellers to specify terms of the sale as to whom they would not want to sell or would not sell (Simpson & Yinger, 1965, p. 332).

In understanding discriminatory practices in the sale of houses, it is essential to distinguish between specific mechanisms and the underlying spirit and outlook that pervade the setting in which transactions are carried through. Regarding these transactions, Denton (1970, p. Jb6–Jb7) reports:

> Our conclusion about how discrimination takes place is that every routine act, every bit of ritual in the sale or rental of a dwelling unit can be performed in a way calculated to make it either difficult or impossible to consummate a deal. Everyone in real estate recognizes how easily deals are killed by poor salesmanship, ignorance and ineptitude on the part of the intermediaries, failure to show property to good advantage, and other non-purposive errors. Yet no one has made an analysis of how these devices are intentionally used to destroy the interest of minority people in looking for housing in all-white neighborhoods. Perhaps this is because most of these devices can not be reached by law. . . .

> Since brokers almost invariably act as agents for landlords and homesellers, the general rule of law is that they are under no obligation to renters or buyers to offer them service. Theoretically, California solved this problem with the Unruh Act, passed in 1959, which requires all business . . . to provide every prospective customer with the same services. However, in recent years, there has been so little attempt to enforce this act, that we discovered that many salesmen and brokers make frank verbal avowals of their unwillingness to serve minority prospects. It should be noted that we found no evidence of outright refusals, but we think this is a specious difference. . . .

Denton goes on to show that since negotiated bargaining is so crucial to the typical real estate transaction, it is difficult for a minority client (or for someone seeking to police fair-housing laws) to know whether the broker has at critical points failed to represent the client's interest with integrity. It is safe to speculate that minority buyers are more likely to settle for the full asking price rather than jeopardize the purchase by bargaining.

Majority-white persons are able to spend a long period searching for housing and can expect the cooperation of a real estate broker; they are not screened until financial negotiations begin. Minority prospects, however, may be screened at the very start before a broker even expresses willingness to be of direct assistance. Various discouraging or delaying tactics may be employed by the broker; if delaying tactics fail, the broker may delay the submission of a client's order or find technical difficulties (Denton, 1970; NCDH, 1970; McEntire, 1960; Helper, 1969).

Real estate brokers are also in a position to foster "panic" selling, although this may be more characteristic of the central city than the suburbs (Leacock et al., 1965, p. 32).

When it becomes apparent that a particular neighborhood is undergoing change, [real estate agents] are in a position either to speed up or slow down the process. It has been the pattern throughout the country for real estate interests to play an extremely destructive role in relation to interracial communities. They spread mis-information about declining values in changing neighborhoods, using it to manipulate desegregation and "re-segregation" by causing a rapid turnover once Negro families have started to move in. In some cases they simply do not show houses in one section to prospective Negro buyers, nor houses in another section to whites; at times they use genuine scare tactics to speed up turnover to their own advantage.

The Sale of New Housing

In earlier periods, the sale of new housing, particularly tract housing built by large developers, was also subject to prevalent discriminatory practices. The cases of exclusion of minorities from the Levitt's large suburban developments are generally known; once forced, the New Jersey Levittown was smoothly integrated (Gans, 1967; [U.S.] HHFA, 1964). Large firms of homebuilders, in particular have been changing their practices. The Denton survey in the Bay Area (1970, p. Jb20)

. . . tends to show that minority prospects get much better treatment from tract builders with their own sales forces than from realtors. To some extent this is due to the differences in marketing factors, i.e.,
   1) the prospect transports himself to the site and needs very little service from the sales agent on the premises.
   2) the price and terms are usually fixed and widely advertised, so that there is very little room for bargaining.
In addition, there seems to be no organized resistance from the homebuilding industry, as there obviously is within the fields dominated by NAREB. In our judgment, the different attitudes of white realtors and white homebuilders is at least partially a reflection of the fact that the National Association of Homebuilders has a more favorable attitude toward residential integration than does NAREB. . . . [We] made trips to new subdivisions and were pleasantly surprised to find that most of those in modest price brackets had at least a few minority homeowners. . . .

New homes for sale are increasingly provided in large-scale tracts and, as we have just indicated, there is evidence that practices have shifted considerably during the past few years. But most of the general research literature is based on earlier studies and may provide outdated conclusions. Ten years ago the McEntire study (1960, p. 176–177) could report:

The combination of large-scale building methods with racial discrimination has given rise to the phenomenon of the totally white community. . . . [The] developer has the power and generally uses it, to exclude unwanted minority groups completely.

But just as the large developers had the monolithic power to exclude, so, too, have they the power to institute changes in policy. We judge this to be a needed area of research; it is important to monitor the practices and experiences of the tract builders. Indeed, it would be valuable to know about their initial sales to minority households and to follow through the impact of the pattern thus created on attitudes and practices with respect to resales in subsequent years. McEntire reported (1960, p. 177), ". . . as several experiences have demonstrated, a pattern of total minority exclusion, once established, is extremely difficult to change." We could hypothesize, alternatively, that a pattern of racial mixture, once established, would make it more likely that integration within the development would continue.

We need to research the role and effectiveness of black builders and contractors. This should include information on types and location of housing built, marketing and financing arrangements, and the characteristics for the buyers. Does this lead to black enclaves? Does it promote dispersal to suburban areas?

One additional research approach deserves particular note. In this approach, a sample survey of the sale of new homes is coupled with an analysis of the chain of moves into the housing successively left vacant. This approach was suggested in earlier work by Kristof (1965) and used in a significant national study by Lansing and his associates (1969). The Lansing study concluded that only six tenths of the number of Negroes that one would predict on the basis of income actually occupied new dwellings. In the national sample, of all the Negro families moving into new homes, only one third moved into owned homes, whereas of all white families moving into new homes, over one half moved into owned homes. This lower fraction for Negro families appears to reflect both a relative dearth of assets among Negro families and the impact of discrimination. Applying the filter theory of housing, the Lansing study concluded that the building of new housing is of less indirect help to Negro families than to white families in opening up other vacancies along chain-of-moves paths and that it is of even less assistance to poor families (of either race).

Real estate boards cut across real estate brokers' involvement in the rental of housing and in the sale of both old and new homes. They have typically resisted taking in minority persons as brokers. In the San Francisco Bay Area, real estate board membership has gradually opened to minorities in the core cities (only after law suits, however, still pending as recently as 1966), but memberships have not been generally available "to nonresident minority brokers in all-white suburban real estate boards" (Denton, 1970).

Sale of housing to minorities is also affected by the multiple-listing practices of real estate boards. In the San Francisco Bay Area, at least, a broker is on the distribution list for listings produced by his own real estate board, but he only has access to the listings produced by other boards if he can establish his own reciprocity with brokers in these other boards or if he can take out a nonresident membership in these areas. A minority broker who is a member of a core-city real estate board thus may find it difficult or impossible to have access to listings of suburban real estate boards. He therefore has great difficulty in providing the full range of listings in suburban areas to a minority client, and the client is at the mercy of majority-white brokers in these suburbs. In Denton's words (1970, p. Ja31),

The conclusion we have drawn from our survey of listing practices is that they effectively bar minority people looking for housing from having access to indispensible information about what is offered. Moreover, so long as multiple listing is voluntary in most Bay Area cities there is no way it can be made into area wide "exchange" of homes for sale. . . .

Restrictive Covenant or Deed Restriction

Probably no institutional device has been more insidiously woven into the web of practices bearing on the rental and sale of real estate than the restrictive covenant or deed restriction. Weaver (1948), for example, was able to show that in the period just before and after World War II these covenants carried much, and probably the brunt of, discriminatory restrictions. A very large number of urban and suburban residential properties were at that time covered by covenants. Real estate boards and property owners' associations had vigorously campaigned to get signatures or resignatures on the covenants. That very year, the Supreme Court in *Shelley* v. *Kraemer* withdrew any role for courts in enforcing restrictive covenants, although it did not outlaw the covenants as such. We lack full up-to-date evidence about how these millions upon millions of covenants, still part of deeds, are interpreted by prospective sellers and buyers and by the real estate brokers and others involved in the complex process of transferring property. Some participants may act as though the covenants had no force. Some participants who believe in fair-housing and integration may avoid the purchase of such properties or take pains when selling to see that an open market is maintained. But it is quite possible that a large number of persons use the covenants to maintain discrimination. Drawing upon a report issued in 1962 by the U.S. Commission on Civil Rights, Simpson and Yinger (1965, p. 331) argued that covenants were still being effectively used:

In the Washington D.C. area, builders in at least 13 communities utilize [restrictive covenants]. Their effectiveness is seen in the racial composition of the census tracts covering these communities. It is not clear why they continue to be effective despite the fact that they are no longer enforceable in the courts, but one possibility is that some homeowners are not aware of the 1948 Supreme Court decision. Also, it has been suggested that those who have entered into these agreements feel under moral pressure to keep them. The U.S. Commission on Civil Rights thinks that the best explanation for the effectiveness of these covenants in the District of Columbia and environs is that simple exclusion is used to enforce the policy they declare.

Perhaps beyond the purview of social scientific research—for it involves judicial and political considerations—is the question of whether it is reasonable that restrictive covenants be permitted to persist. Although *Shelley* v. *Kraemer* implied that such covenants based on race, creed, or color were legal, critical differences in views remain. One observer has said, "Most commentators today are of the opinion that such a covenant is illegal and should be so regarded, rather than accepting the incongruous fiction that it is legal but unenforceable" (Robinson, 1964, p. 36). We believe research should be done on covenants—their prevalence, their use in new housing, and their meaning to the various persons concerned with the sale and rental of housing and the sale and development of residential land.

Mortgage Financing

In 1960, McEntire reported (p. 218–219):

Mortgage credit is the key to acquisition of good housing via home ownership. . . . Whites and nonwhites of comparable economic status and owning similar properties seem to receive, on the whole, similar treatment from most lending agencies, with the crucial exception: institutional lenders traditionally have required properties for nonwhite occupancy to be located in recognized minority residence areas, and many lenders continue to enforce this special requirement. By making mortgage credit available to minorities in certain areas and withholding it in others, lending agencies help to maintain segregation.

Simpson and Yinger (1965, p. 332), drawing upon evidence submitted to the U.S. Commission on Civil Rights (1962 report) suggested that this practice was continuing:

A spokesman for the Mortgage Bankers Association of Metropolitan Washington wrote [to the Commission]: "Applications from minority groups are not generally considered in areas that are not recognized as being racially mixed, on the premise that such an investment would not be attractive to institutional lenders."

Denton, in his recent San Francisco Bay area study, said (1970, p. Jb32):

Based on our discussions with black brokers and fair housing brokers we believe it is fair to say that minority people trying to move out of the ghetto have *even* more trouble than formerly in obtaining mortgage loans. Earmarking "minority mortgage money" for loans on so-called ghetto property means that minority applicants are more likely than ever to find it hard to get loans for purchase in suburban areas.

He stresses that, just as there are no minority suburban real estate firms, there are no Bay area minority-group mortgage bankers. He doubts that there are any in the entire United States, but he is careful to state he lacks conclusive evidence.

Real Estate Appraisers

It is reported that in the Bay area there are very few minority real estate appraisers of minority status. We presume this may also be the national situation; we found no other relevant studies. Admission to the American Institute of Real Estate Appraisers is contingent upon approval by a mail ballot sent to every member; this system clearly offers an opportunity for black-balling. The theory and interpretations of real estate appraisers strongly influence the channeling of minority loans into areas where minority families already live. Title companies, in the San Francisco Bay area, still have a very small percentage of minority work force, although one major company now has at least one black office manager (Denton, 1970).

We have sought to identify separate phases of the operation of the market for residential real estate and to report on different groups of functionaries and institutional mechanisms. It is important to remember, however, that discrimination results from the interaction of a number of attitudes and practices. Change in the total situation requires more than change in specific single factors. In a spirit similar to that pervading the Kerner Commission report, Carter (1965, p. 108–109) provides this summary of his impressions:

Discrimination against Negroes was and is a part of the fabric of American life in New York, Chicago, and San Francisco, as well as in Jackson, Mississippi; Little Rock, Arkansas; and Birmingham, Alabama. It inheres in the housing market and service of real estate brokers, landlords, builders, developers (private and public), city planners, banks, and mortgage loan companies. . . . Past practices have virtually solidified housing segregation in the North, and as yet no major break in the iron ring enclosing the Negro ghetto has been effected.

Denton pessimistically concludes (1970, p. Jb40) ". . . that by preventing the minority person from being able to shop for housing in the way that is normal for his white peers, a permanent barrier to residential desegregation has been created which may be beyond the power of positive law to reach."

PUBLIC INSTITUTIONAL PRACTICES IN URBAN PLANNING AND LAND USE CONTROLS, IN URBAN RENEWAL, AND IN THE FINANCING, DEVELOPMENT, AND MANAGEMENT OF HOUSING

We must necessarily be selective in discussing the many governmental policies and practices that affect the housing choices open to minority families. Our main presentation will be in this order: (a) land use plans and general development policy; (b) zoning and other precise land use and building regulations; (c) urban renewal; (d) support or incentives for private housing; (e) public housing; (f) fair-housing regulations; and (g) public taxation.

Certain very broad questions rise out of these facets of governmental institutional practices. The first question is whether residents and citizens get from their local governments what they want. This is not easy to determine, but there are few signs of serious dissatisfaction. Ironically, perhaps, our system of suburban government tends to give its residents a remarkably direct voice in policy determination (Wood, 1958; Davidoff et al., 1970).

A second question is whether each local government can take into account regional considerations as well as its own more provincial interests. The general conclusion is that it can not. This raises difficult problems as to providing a broader policy framework and establishing review procedures. Planning and fiscal issues, in particular, call for vigorous exploration of possible regional government and for the determination of appropriate state and federal roles in urban and regional affairs. Until recently, at least, there has been a tendency to assume the validity of local self-determination, but this is increasingly coming under legislative and judicial review (Douglas Commission, 1968; Hawley & Zimmer, 1970).

A third question, and the one that probably relates most directly to our inquiry, is how the rights of minorities can be fully protected and, equally important, how the twin objectives of dispersal from inner-city minority areas and integration into other areas within the metropolis can be carried into effect. We conclude that to account for these urgent social objectives, traditional public institutional mechanisms must be changed (Kerner Commission, 1968; Kaiser Committee, 1968).

We are not certain how helpful social scientific knowledge about public institutional practices can be in bringing about attitudinal changes and political changes. In situations where the practices (e.g., exclusionary zoning or an unwillingness to create a public housing authority) are what the residents want, it will take far more than knowledge of institutional practices to bring about basic changes. Ironically, citizens and politicians may appropriate institutional practices introduced at earlier times by civic reformers and change them into mechanisms for preserving majority and status-quo interests. This has particularly been true of zoning (Babcock, 1966; Piven, 1970; Brooks, 1970; Toll, 1969; Ylvisaker, 1970). Indeed, it must be recognized that urban planning has sometimes become a handmaiden for the stabilizers. On the other hand, urban planning has been caught squarely in the middle of battles among irreconcilable parties and interests—aggressive developers, ambitious elected officials, career-concerned professional staff members, and a diverse citizenry. City planners have often sought valiantly to control development under heavy pressures and within a political setting reflecting all of the crossfires of contemporary America (Scott, 1969; Fraser, 1970). In such a context, the vigorous introduction of changes designed to open up suburban communities adds a further set of pressures to the political battlefield (Lilley, 1970).

Land Use Plans and Development Policy

The land use plan of a municipality, a county, or a metropolitan-level government or quasi-government identifies certain community or regional goals (possibly social and political as well as physical) and presents a maplike diagram of the arrangement of future land uses that will foster or incorporate these goals. It may suggest a program and time table for working toward the goals (Kent, 1964). As of 1968, there were within U.S. metropolitan areas the following local governments with planning boards and with plans as presented in Table 1. About 65 percent of suburban governments have fewer than 5,000 residents. Of communities with 5,000 or more population, about 9 out of 10 planning boards, and 2 out of 3 have land use plans. The smaller communities are less apt to have planning boards.

There is relatively little careful research on the character and impact of suburban land use plans, and it would seem particularly relevant to the purposes of this paper that systematic studies of these plans be undertaken. We conclude from such studies of land use plans as have been made (whether or not suburban communities) that, except for unusual and recent examples, these plans have focused almost completely on physical objectives, and that social and political presumptions and goals have not been openly stated or related to the physical plans (Altshuler, 1965; Gans, 1967). Further, most metropolitan planning efforts have not been any more explicit in openly identifying social policy

Governments within SMSA's (1960 population)	No. of Governments	Percent with Planning Boards	Percent with Land Use Plans	
			Of All Governments	Of Governments with Planning Boards
Total	7,609	65.2	n.d.	n.d.
County governments	404	80.0	n.d.	n.d.
Municipalities				
50,000+ population	314	98.4	87.6	89.0
5,000–49,999	1,303	92.9	65.8	70.8
Under 5,000	3,360	54.9	n.d.	n.d.
New England-type townships				
5,000+ population	765	79.1	58.7	74.2
Under 5,000	1,463	45.7	n.d.	n.d.
Total municipalities and New England-type townships				
5,000+ population	2,382	89.2	66.4	74.4

TABLE 1. Local Governments—Planning Boards and Plans (Within Metropolitan Areas as of 1968)
Source: Adapted from Manvel (1968, p. 24, 31)

objectives or in working toward them (Downs, 1970; Dunleavy and Associates, 1970). We also conclude that many plans suffer from undue generality, jargon, and lack of specific proposals about how they might be carried out (Spatt, 1970; Altshuler, 1965). Land use plans may not be taken seriously by most residents, since the plans appear to be advisory in tone and sometimes not even submitted for the approval of the city council or other elected body (Denton, 1970).

Most land use plans appear to represent established interests and to take either a conserving or preserving approach. Land use plans may concentrate on the major goal of "orderly development" and such further subgoals as the control of residential densities, the preservation of open space, and the deliberate containment of commercial and industrial land uses (Davidoff, 1965; Marcuse, 1969). Either deliberately or by default, the plans have rarely sought to contend with the serious housing situation confronting disadvantaged families. This may reflect various reasons: (a) community sentiment and leaders' commitment to prevent the influx of minority households or, perhaps more common, to discourage the influx of low- and even moderate-income households; (b) the structure of local government in which a housing authority and

a renewal agency may be operating relatively independently from the planning department in such a situation, the planning department may leave it to the other agencies to promote or introduce appropriate housing; (c) a tendency of land use plans to be more concerned with the elimination of blight than with the positive provision of housing for families not well served by the private housing market (Altshuler, 1965).

As a result of these shortcomings in land use plans, the Housing and Urban Development Act of 1968 required all local communities to identify and to take into account "the housing needs of both the region and the local communities," with a subgoal of encouraging each community to do it share in providing housing for disadvantaged households. It will be particularly important to examine whether the preparation of these housing element reports brings substantial change to the land use plans and, subsequently, to the outlook and programs of the community. There is some initial evidence that suburban communities will continue to protect the status quo (Denton, 1970). It will also be important to pay careful attention to HUD-sponsored research that is coordinated by the National Association of Housing and Redevelopment Officials (NAHRO) (Nenno, 1969; Spicer, 1970; Beckman, 1970).

Zoning and Other Precise Regulations

Zoning is unquestionably at the very center of the process of land use control (Leary, 1968). It is thus at the center of major value conflicts, for, as some gain what they seek, others must lose (ASPO, 1968). Zoning has been so completely incorporated into the local political process and has become so well understood by the citizenry (at least with respect to its broad possibilities) that it is probably the major mode of land use regulation relied on by politicians and residents (see Table 2).

A slightly larger number of communities have zoning ordinances than have planning boards and a considerably larger number have zoning ordinances than have land use plans. Of those local governments with population 5,000 or more that do have zoning ordinances, 42.9 percent passed their first zoning ordinance after 1950, 33.0 percent have at least some use districts prescribing residential lots with minimum size of one acre or more, and 14.8 percent do not permit any new apartments (of three units or more).

Zoning is certainly the suburban community's perfect tool if it wants to maintain essentially single-family housing and if it wants to exclude other land uses (and, as we shall discuss, to exclude various types of households) (Babcock, 1966). Zoning purports to control the character of physical development and to ensure orderly development on behalf of the community as a whole. Thus it regulates type of land use, lot size, setback, parking requirements, etc. Indirectly, it controls density of development and thus assists in ensuring that services can be properly related, that traffic can be accommodated, and that timing of development can be effectively controlled. By its very nature, zoning is exclusory: A zoning ordinance excludes various land uses, permitting only designated land uses, within any given district of a community. Most studies rank zoning as a very significant device for exclusion, pointing particularly to zoning ordiances that prohibit residential development on lots of less, say, than an acre or a half acre (Brooks, 1970; Babcock, 1966; NCDH, 1970; Funnyé, 1970). Only Denton (1970, p. Jc6) concludes that in the San Francisco Bay area, large-lot zoning, at least, does not seem to be a serious discriminatory tool, except in a few bedroom communities.

Particularly, in exurbia, residents may be antagonistic to development of any sort. In one study (Raymond and May Associates, 1968, p. 71) it was found that

Governments within SMSA's (1960 population)	No.	Precent with Zoning Ordinance	Percent with First Ordinance since 1950	Percent with Any 1-Acre Minimum Lot Size	Percent Not Permitting Any New Apartments
Total	7,609	68.3	n.d.	n.d.	n.d.
County governments	404	49.3	n.d.	n.d.	n.d.
Municipalities					
50,000+ population	314	98.7	16.7	24.2	3.5
5,000–49,999	1,303	97.0	45.2	24.0	11.0
Under 5,000	3,360	54.0	n.d.	n.d.	n.d.
New England-type townships					
5,000+ population	765	81.0	51.4	54.6	28.2
Under 5,000	1,463	44.8	n.d.	n.d.	n.d.
Total municipalities and townships					
5,000+ population	2,382	92.1	42.9	33.0	14.8

TABLE 2. The Extent of Zoning, as of 1968, among Local Governments in Metropolitan Areas in the United States
Source: Adapted from Manvel (1968, p. 24, 31–32)

They frequently sought a secluded natural environment in spite of the increased costs in travel, time, and discomforts. Any invasion or change is therefore actively resisted. Clustering is viewed as an invasion and destruction of the security which large-lot zoning has created. This innate opposition to urbanization of any sort is generally as storng, and sometimes an even stronger factor in such areas than fear of invasion by lower-income groups or nonwhites. In such areas, a significant proportion of the resident population is composed of older residents who are farm laborers, craftsmen, factory workers, etc. . . .

The nature of zoning is such that it is difficult to disentangle its control over physical development and land use, per se, from its influence over the economic status of prospective residents and its use to discriminate against specific ethnic or racial groups (ASPO, 1968, p. 36–37):

Discrimination through the use of zoning at present must be done by indirect means. It is difficult to prove that discrimination is an objective of the zoning action. For obvious reasons, exclusion of a particular ethnic group will never appear in any record nor will it be admitted by responsible public officials. Intemperate remarks by citizens at public hearings will be the only overt indications that might be discovered. . . .

. . . because true racial zoning is forbidden, the exclusion has been *de facto* and based on economic status—against families with low income. Economic discrimination will operate against any disdvantaged minority. . . .

Perhaps the most significant clues to the use of land-use controls for discrimination are public statements of intent to "preserve the character" of the community by "maintaining high standards"; occasional frank statements about not wanting low-income families who will create a "tax burden"; and moves to prevent construction of nondiscriminatory developments in exclusively white communities. . . .

The zoning device most frequently cited as one used for racial exclusion is the specification of unusually large lots. However, this is the common device for economic exclusion. Large lots are also used for limiting urban expansion or for setting up holding zones.

Another zoning action that can be used to exclude minority groups is the prohibition of industry, especially heavy industry, from a community. . . .

In any event, a certain amount of double talk can be expected. For example, prevention of apartment construction can be a way of excluding certain types of households. The "shouted" reasons for opposing apartment developments in the suburbs include the following: Apartments will not pay their way in taxes; apartments will cut off light and air; apartments will turn into slums; apartments will reduce property values; apartments will injure the character of the community. The "whispered" reasons are that the apartments will attract lower-class tenants, transient households not in the community's interest, and Negroes (Babcock & Bosselman, 1963). Judicial review has legitimized zoning on such bases as detrimental effects of apartments on single-family uses and harmful impact on property values. Babcock concludes (1966, p. 185) his long treatment of zoning with the judgment that ". . . social influences, far more than economic considerations, motivate the public decision-makers in zoning matters."

Zoning, along with other institutional devices used by local governments, is often justified by fiscal necessity (Brooks, 1970, p. 3):

Most suburban governments contend that their intention is not to exclude low-income families but to cope with fiscal reality. Because of their heavy dependence on local property taxes, suburban governments have traditionally sought land uses which yield higher taxes and require fewer public dollars to service. Whether or not the intent is to meet fiscal reality, the contention of the suburbs is no longer being accepted at face value. Suburban governments are being challenged to broaden the narrow considerations they have used in making land-use decisions by considering problems in both regional and socio-economic terms. These challenges take different forms, with a number aimed at the practice of exclusionary zoning.
. . . For purposes of this report, exclusionary zoning is defined not in terms of intent or motive, but in terms of results.

Traditionally, as we have already indicated, the right of a community to determine its own land use has been accepted. This has meant that its zoning could be completely local in outlook [Anderson (1970) quoted in Brooks (1970, p. 18)].

The cases are rare which expressly require that the zoning municipality consider the extraterritorial effect of a zoning restriction. Indeed, the very propriety of such consideration may be questioned. . . . [M]ost courts have respected the power of each municipality to seek its own solutions, to fashion its own character, and to prescribe its own exclusions, without regard (or with small regard) to the needs of its neighbors of its larger community. . . .

It may also be difficult (Raymond and May Associates, 1968, p. 47) for individual suburban communities to

. . . deal effectively with social problems of a metropolitan scope. The problem is the result of general housing discrimination against Negroes in the metropolitan area. In the few suburban areas where housing, such as these apartments [in the case study of authors present], is open to Negroes the rapid influx of Negroes creates massive fears and resentments, as expressed in some of the interviews.

As we have noted, an acknowledged problem is how to create the intergovernmental arrangements by which a broad policy framework can be estab-lished into which local community zoning could be expected to fit.

Another important type of land use control used by local governments is subdivision regulation. The planning commission must approve of the proposed design of a subdivision; thus, it can exercise control over the process by which land is converted into building sites (Green, 1968). Something over 80 percent of the communities having zoning also have subdivision regulations (see Table 3).

Although it is recognized that subdivision regulations are part of the family of regulations controlling new subdivision and construction, there is little direct research evidence on the impact of subdivision regulations, as such, on housing opportunities for minority families. As noted by Green (1968, p. 449), restrictive covenants or deed restrictions

. . . are of interest to the agency regulating subdivisions, because they are customarily filed with the plat of a subdivision. Knowing this, the plat approval agency may through a process of negotiation persuade a developer to include detailed regulations governing the siting of structures, landscaping, architectual design, and so forth, tailored to the particular needs of his subdivision, which it

Governments within SMSA's (1960 population)	No.	Percent with Subdivision Regulations
Total	7,609	59.3
County governments	404	62.9
Municipalities		
50,000+ population	314	92.7
5,000–49,999	1,303	90.0
Under 5,000	3,360	47.7
New England-type townships		
5,000+ population	765	74.0
Under 5,000	1,463	44.0

TABLE 3. The Extent of Subdivision Control, as of 1968, among Local Governments in Metropolitan Areas in the United States
Source: Adapted from Manvel (1968, p. 24)

could not easily require in its general [public] regulations.

We need to research the attitudes of local officials and planning staffs, in particular, toward covenants that restrict ownership or tenancy to majority whites and how these covenants have been handled in the process of subdivision control.

Literature identifying regulations contributing to discrimination against minority families typically mentions building and housing codes. Probably their main impact is to promote economic discrimination. Codes may prevent or discourage the greatest possible economies in housing construction and maintenance. It is alleged that inspectors are in a position to block construction. Banfield and Grodzins (1958, p. 97) concluded:

Local [building] inspectors sometimes use the [building] code as a weapon against builders who do not "play ball" with a political machine, who sell to Negroes or other "undesirables," or who are felt to be outsiders creating unwarranted or unfair competition. The inspector's unquestioning acceptance of the canons of the local community and especially of its dominant builders is as likely as venality to be the problem here.

Schermer and Levin reported (1968, p. 14) more recently that:

[L]arge city zoning and licensing officials were not found to be particularly obstructive because of racial policy. But there is almost universal feeling that such officials in white suburban areas can and do effectively impede developments that are likely to be integrated.

The Manvel–U.S. Census Bureau survey (Manvel, 1968) showed in considerable detail the recency of codes and the proportion of local jurisdictions that have adopted various standardized codes. The direct bearing on discrimination against minorities is, however, unclear.

REFERENCES

Abrams, C. 1965. *The city is the frontier.* New York: Harper & Row.

Altshuler, A. A. 1965. *The city planning process: A political analysis.* Ithaca: Cornell University Press.

American Society of Planning Officials (ASPO). 1968. *Problems of zoning and land-use regulation.* Research Report No. 2 for the U.S. National Commission on Urban Problems. Washington, D.C.: Government Printing Office.

Anderson, M. 1964. *The federal bulldozer.* New York: McGraw-Hill Paperbacks.

Babcock, R. F. 1966. *The zoning game: Municipal practices and policies.* Madison: University of Wisconsin Press.

Babcock, R. F., and Bosselman, F. P. 1963. Suburban zoning and the apartment boom. *University of Pennsylvania Law Review* 3: 1040–91.

Banfield, E. C., and Grodzins, M. 1958. *Government and housing in metropolitan areas.* New York: McGraw-Hill.

Beckman, N. 1970. Legislation review—1968–1969: Planning and urban development. *Journal of the American Institute of Planners* 36: 345–59.

Biochel, M. R., Aurbach, H. A., Bakerman, T., and Elliott, D. H. 1969. Exposure, experience and attitudes: Realtors and open occupancy. *Phylon* 30: 325–37.

Brooks, M. 1970. *Exclusionary zoning.* Chicago: American Society of Planning Officials.

Carter, R. L., Kenyon, D., Marcuse, P., and Miller, L. 1965. *Equality.* New York: Pantheon Books.

Davidoff, P. 1965. Advocacy and pluralism in planning. *Journal of the American Institute of Planners* 31: 331–38.

Davidoff, P., Davidoff, L., and Gold, N. N. 1970. Suburban action: Advocate planning for an open society. *Journal of the American Institute of Planners* 36: 12–21.

Denton, J. H. 1970. *Report of consultant.* San Francisco: National Committee against Discrimination in Housing. Appendix J of summary report by NCDH.

Douglas Commission. See (U.S.) National Commission on Urban Problems.

Downs, A. 1970. Alternative forms of future urban growth in the United States. *Journal of the American Institute of Planners* 36: 3–11.

Dunleavy, Hal, and Associates. 1970. *Research report: Population, housing, jobs.* San Francisco: National Committee against Discrimination in Housing. Appendix H of summary report by NCDH.

Fraser, J. B. 1970. In Santa Clara Valley: The debris of development. *City* 4: 21–30.

Funnyé, C. 1970. Zoning: The new battleground. *Architectural Forum* 132: 62–65.

Gans, H. J. 1967. *The Levittowners.* New York: Pantheon Books.

Grebler, L., Moore, J. W., and Gusman, R. C. 1970. *The Mexican-American people.* New York: The Free Press.

Green P. P., Jr. 1968. Land subdivision. In W. I. Goodman and E. C. Freund (eds.), *Principles and practice of urban planning.* Chicago: International City Managers Assoc., pp. 443–48.

Hawley A. H., and Zimmer, B. G. 1970. *The metropolitan community: Its people and its government.* Beverly Hills: Sage Publications.

Helper, R. 1969. *Racial policies and practices of real estate brokers.* Minneapolis: University of Minneapolis Press.

Kaiser Committee. See (U.S.) President's Committee on Urban Housing.

Kent, T. J., Jr. 1964. *The urban general plan.* San Francisco: Chandler.

Kerner Commission. See (U.S.) National Advisory Commission on Civil Disorders.

Kristof, F. S. 1965. Housing policy goals and the turnover of housing. *Journal of the American Institute of Planners* 31: 232–45.

Lansing, J. B., Clinton, C. W., and Morgan, J. N. 1969. *New homes and poor people: A study of chains of moves.* Ann Arbor: Institute of Social Research, University of Michigan.

Leacock, E., Deutsch, M., and Fishman, J. H. 1965. *Toward integration in suburban housing: The Bridgeview study.* New York: Anti-Defamation League of B'nai B'rith.

Leary, R. M. 1968. Zoning. In W. I. Goodman and E. C. Freund (eds.), *Principles and practice of urban planning.* Chicago: International City Managers Assoc., pp. 403–42.

Lilley, W., III. 1970. Housing report: Romney faces political perils with plan to integrate suburbs. *National Journal* 2: 2251–63.

Manvel, A. D. 1968. *Local land and building regulation: How many agencies? What practices? How much personnel?* Research Report No. 6. for the U.S. National Commission on Urban Problems. Washington, D.C.: Government Printing Office.

Marcuse, P. 1969. Integration and the planner. *Journal of the American Institute of Planners* 35: 113–7.

McEntire, D. 1960. *Residence and race.* Berkeley and Los Angeles: University of California Press.

Mercer, N. A. 1962. Discrimination in rental housing: A study of resistance of landlords to non-white tenants. *Phylon* 23: 47–54.

Meyer, J. R., Kain, J. F., and Wohl, M. 1965. *The urban transportation problem.* Cambridge, Mass.: Harvard University Press.

National Committee against Discrimination in Housing (NCDH). 1970. *Jobs and housing: A study of employment and housing opportunities for racial minorities in suburban areas of the New York metropolitan region.* New York: NCDH.

Nenno, M. K. 1969. Planning and programming for housing and community development. In *Planning 1969.* Chicago: American Society of Planning Officials, pp. 59–66.

Neutze, M. 1968. *The suburban apartment boom.* Washington, D.C.: Resources for the Future. (Distributed by Johns Hopkins Press.)

New York City Rand Institute. 1970. *Rental housing in New York City.* Vol. 1. *Confronting the crisis.* New York.

Piven, F. F. 1970. Comprehensive social planning: Curriculum reform or professional imperialism. *Journal of the American Institute of Planners* 36: 226–8.

Raymond and May Associates. 1968. *Zoning controversies in the suburbs: Three case studies.* Research Report No. 11 for U.S. National Commission on Urban Problems. Washington, D.C.: Government Printing Office.

Robinson, N. 1964. Civil rights and property rights reexamined. In J. Denton (ed.), *Race and property.* Berkeley: Diablo Press, pp. 35–41.

Schermer, G., and Levin, A. J. 1968. *Housing guide to equal opportunity: Affirmative practices for integrated housing.* Washington, D.C.: Potomac Institute.

Scott, M. 1969. *American city planning since 1890.* Berkeley and Los Angeles: University of California Press.

Simpson, G. E., and Yinger, J. M. 1965. *Racial and cultural minorities: An analysis of prejudice and discrimination.* (3rd ed.) New York: Harper & Row.

Spatt, B. M. 1970. A report on the New York plan. *Journal of the American Institute of Planners* 36: 438–44.

Spicer, R. B. 1970. Housing elements are taking shape. *ASPO Planning* 36: 95–96.

Toll, S. I. 1969. *Zoned America.* New York: Grossman Publishers.

U.S. Commission on Civil Rights. 1969. *For all the people . . . by all the people: A report on equal opportunity in state and local government employment.* Washington, D.C.: Government Printing Office.

(U.S.) Housing and Home Finance Agency (HHFA). 1964. Changing a racial policy, Levittown, N. J. In *Equal opportunity in housing.* Washington, D.C.: HHFA, pp. 17–27.

(U.S.) National Advisory Commission on Civil Disorders (the Kerner Commission). 1968. *Report.* Washington, D.C.: Government Printing Office.

(U.S.) National Commission on Urban Problems (the Douglas Commission). 1969. *Building the American city.* Washington, D.C.: Government Printing Office.

(U.S.) President's Committee on Urban Housing (the Kaiser Committee). 1968. *A decent home.* Washington, D.C.: Government Printing Office.

Watts, L. G., et al. 1964. *The middle income Negro family faces urban renewal.* Boston: Research Center of the Florence Heller Graduate School for Advanced Studies in Social Welfare, Brandeis University.

Weaver, R. 1948. *The Negro ghetto.* New York: Harcourt Brace.

Wood, R. C. 1958. *Suburbia: Its people and their policies.* Boston: Houghton Mifflin.

Ylvisaker, P. N. 1970. Utter chaos or simple complexity. In *Planning 1970.* Chicago: American Society of Planning Officials, pp. 6–16.

FACTORS AFFECTING SUBURBANIZATION IN THE POSTWAR YEARS
MARION CLAWSON

Suburban expansion has been the dominant element in post-war urban development. It has not been solely a function of a burgeoning urban population nor a desire of the middle-classes to escape from the environment of the central city. It also reflects complex pressures on the housing market in the post-war era, pressures which led to quite specific federal programs which supported and even accelerated the suburbanization process.

Reprinted from Marion Clawson, *Suburban Land Conversion in the United States: An Economic and Governmental Process* (Baltimore: The Johns Hopkins Press for Resources for the Future, Inc., 1971), pp. 33–46, by permission of the publisher. This is an edited version of the original publication. Notes have been renumbered, and a new title has been added.

The conjunction of several factors has produced the massive postwar suburbanization in the United States. In the decade beginning with 1948, more than 10 million new households were formed, partly because of a high marriage rate, partly because of the accumulated backlog of unfilled or potential demand for separate households that had built up through depression and war. In many older cities there was relatively little vacant land on which new residential structures could be built—or the land available was not suitable for residential building. Urban renewal, whether public or private, would have been too slow in assembling and clearing sites and in building new apartments. Destruction of old housing, however poor as long as it was at all livable, would have created still more serious housing difficulties. The obvious direction to go, in providing the new housing, was toward the suburbs. The additional households simply had to be located somewhere, and neither farms nor old city centers were in good positions to absorb them.

At the same time, industrial, commercial and other trends were all in the direction of concentration in cities. These urbanization forces worked in different degrees in different parts of the country. One major aspect of the postwar growth has been the trend toward "amenity" regions, particularly the Southwest, California, and Florida.

While these economic and other forces were pulling people out of the small towns, off the farms, and away from the countryside (unless each of these was within commuting distance of a larger city), there were other forces pushing toward decentralization within each metropolitan or urban region. Postwar cars and postwar highways went far toward freeing an urban worker from the necessity of living near his job. He could live nearly anywhere within the urban area and work at any other location, if he really wished to do so. True, there are added costs to some locations as compared with others. Some parts of the total labor force have earnings so low that automobile ownership—and hence travel by car—is difficult or impossible. The cost of housing and zoning restrictions keep low- and moderate-income workers out of the suburbs. But an enormous flexibility in location of home and job has become possible for the majority of households in the United States today.

At the same time, changes under way in industrial plants tended to take them to the suburbs. Many plants were old at the end of the war. New methods of materials handling required larger areas and were more easily managed on ground level only. In addition, there has been a considerable tendency to build industrial plants with moderately extensive grounds, for aesthetic reasons, for parking, and as a margin for future growth. Location near major express highways is providing advantages that once were associated with location on railroad spurs. As the factories moved from city center out to suburban locations, there was a strong tendency for the labor force to follow. Thus industrial employment has shrunk in the older parts of the city.

The central downtown business district in many cities is no longer as important for manufacturing or trade. Instead, the downtown district is increasingly becoming the location of business, of offices, and of services allied to business. Total downtown employment may remain constant or even rise, but the relative importance of different kinds of jobs changes. New York City illustrates these shifts very well. The shift from manufacturing to office employment in downtown New York has continued, at least until 1965.

Downtown districts of many larger cities have experienced a postwar boom in office building. It is the white-collar workers who commute from suburb to downtown office. The blue-collar worker may live in an older city section and commute to a suburban job or live in one suburb and commute to another.

At the same time, retail shopping stores and districts moved from downtown to the suburbs. The large shopping center, with stores on one or two levels and with ample parking space, has become a major feature in many suburban areas. Movement of customers to the suburbs induced many department stores to open suburban branches, and the availability of convenient shopping areas certainly was another force leading families to move to the suburbs.

This combination of shifts in job location, changes in transportation, and development of new modes of communication has led toward a major expansion of the city at the periphery. This expansion conceivably could have been in a relatively solid and blocked-up fashion. It was not—discontinuity and dispersion were its marked characteristics.

FEDERAL PROGRAMS AS A STIMULUS TO SUBURBANIZATION

Since the early New Deal days, the federal government has supported the home-building industry and has helped its citizens to buy homes or to retain homes previously bought. This support to home ownership has greatly stimulated the rate and process of suburbanization.[1]

In the depression of the early 1930s, defaults on mortgages on homes became serious and building of new homes fell to a very low level. As early as 1932, the Federal Home Loan Bank Act was passed.[2] Under the New Deal, assistance in financing of existing mortgages and federal mortgage insurance stimulated home construction. The practice of requiring relatively low down payments (generally 10 to 20 percent of purchase price) and of regular monthly payments for interest, amortization, and taxes became firmly established on a wide scale. The federal government, in return for a small charge added to the monthly payment on the mortgages, insured the lenders against loss from mortgage defaults except for part of the foreclosure costs.

In order to provide such insurance without excessive losses, the federal agencies imposed standards of home building, of home appraisal, and of financial management by builders and lenders which have had enormous impact on home-building over the years. One successful private builder has stated to the author that all his homes must meet Federal Housing Administration standards for loans, even though he has arranged his financing without FHA help, simply because it is too difficult to sell houses which do not have or cannot get FHA loan approval. Thus, the federal standards have tended to become standards for the whole industry, in spite of the fact that FHA loans have financed only about 16 percent of home building.

The slow but impressive resumption of building of housing units during the latter 1930s was very much due to these federal aids. A substantial part of this building was in suburban areas. Yet, the number of housing units built during the entire decade from 1933 to 1942 totalled only 3½ million—about two years' output today.

With the end of the war, federal stimulation to house and apartment construction became great and influential. In addition to financing through FHA, a special home-buying program for veterans was extended through the Veterans Administration. Down payments were further reduced (sometimes to zero) while guarantees to lenders were increased. Easy money became national policy and further stimulated a flow of capital into the housing industry. The federal programs were supplemented in some states, notably in California and Connecticut, with state programs to help veterans buy homes.

Beginning in 1946, a series of steps were taken to accelerate the rate at which

commercial and rental housing property (apartments, particularly) could be depreciated faster under federal tax accounting procedures. One result was the creation of a tax-free cash throw-off, since the depreciation allowance exceeded amortization of principal on the mortgage. These tax arrangements have been particularly stimulating to development of suburban shopping centers and to construction of apartments.

Federal income tax laws, as they apply to the individual, also encourage home purchase. Income tax encouragement to home ownership takes three forms:

1. The imputed rent of the owner's dwelling does not have to be included as part of his income, for federal income tax purposes.
2. Payments for real extate taxes may be deducted from gross income.
3. Interest on home mortgages may also be deducted.

A homeowner receives a substantial part of his income from his own home, in the form of housing, but this income does not have to be included in his income tax return. Slitor has calculated that these three aids to home ownership in 1958 amounted to $3.2 billion, or about $100 per owner-occupied dwelling.[3] These financial advantages to home ownership tend to become more important, even on a relative basis, as personal incomes rise, in part because of the higher tax rates on larger incomes. On the basis of rather typical income and housing conditions, the federal income tax under current income tax rates is reduced by from 14 to 31 percent of the interest and tax payments on the home (see Table 1). This is obviously a substantial incentive to home purchase.

The economics of owning vs. renting a home has long been discussed, and obviously depends in part upon economic conditions generally.[4] Shelton argues

	Annual salary before taxes					
	$5,000	$10,000	$15,000	$20,000	$25,000	$30,000
Tax exemption plus deductions[1]	2,900	3,400	3,900	4,400	4,900	5,400
Taxable income	2,100	6,600	11,100	15,600	20,100	24,600
Income tax, 1967 rates (joint return)	306	1,114	2,062	3,160	4,412	5,876
Marginal rate of tax[2]	16%	19%	22%	25%	32%	36%
Net income, after tax	4,694	8,886	12,938	16,840	20,588	24,124
Price of house[3]	9,400	17,800	25,900	33,700	41,200	48,200
Annual payment to lender[4]	649	1,228	1,788	2,325	2,843	3,326
Interest payment first year[4]	423	801	1,166	1,516	1,854	2,169
Annual real estate taxes[4]	141	267	389	505	618	723
Interest and taxes paid, first year	564	1,068	1,555	2,021	2,472	2,882
Reduction in income tax[5]	90	203	342	505	791	1,038
As percent of net income	2	2	3	3	4	4
As percent of income tax	29	18	17	16	18	18
As percent of payments to lender	14	17	19	22	27	31

TABLE 1. Extent to which Federal Income Tax Provisions Assist Home Ownership
[1] Assuming 4 dependents at $600 each, plus 10 percent for miscellaneous deductions.
[2] Rate applicable to last income earned.
[3] Assuming double net income after taxes, rounded upward to nearest $100.
[4] Assuming 5 percent interest, 1 percent for amortization and mortgage insurance, for 90 percent loan plus local real estate taxes at $1.50 per $100 full value.
[5] On assumption interest and taxes are net additions to deductions and that marginal rate applies.

that, under essentially static economic conditions, the annual net advantage of ownership is equal to about 2 percent of the value of the house

While Shelton's analysis is quite careful and considers the various components of cost, it greatly understates the advantages of home ownership in the past 25 years, when the general price level was constantly rising. The purchase of a home, especially with a low down payment, provided a hedge against inflation for the full price of the house. While it was true that the seller would have to pay a more or less equally inflated price for any other house he bought, if or when he sold his house, he also received favorable income tax treatment on the nominal capital gain and—more importantly—his previous purchase of a house provided the necessary down payment for the new one.

The effect of these various programs was to stimulate the building of single-family homes for sale to home buyers.

The low down payments, low monthly payments (made possible in part because of the low interest rates flowing out of an easy money policy), and the income tax reductions, all combined to stimulate purchase of homes. In total, the scales were steeply tipped toward home purchase, as against purchase of cooperative apartments or as against rental. The single-family home on its separate lot is a voracious consumer of suburban land, and thus the federal measures to stimulate this type of house building indirectly strongly stimulated suburbanization.

It is true that various federal programs also stimulated apartment construction during these same years. There was easy money for apartment construction and also accelerated depreciation, with its substantial tax-free cash spin-off. These programs stimulated the apartment builder, or developer, or owner; but they did not aid the apartment tenant unless the owner passed on these favorable financial arrangements. In a great many cases a family could buy a house with a low down payment and with monthly costs (payments on loan, taxes and insurance, upkeep, etc.) no greater, and often less, than it would have to pay as rental for equivalent space.

The strong demand for houses naturally led to an active home-building industry in the postwar years. There was money to be made in building homes quickly, and concern lest the boom market not continue. Since the builder was typically under some pressure to acquire building sites quickly, he frequently purchased a distant site that was immediately available rather than spend time negotiating for a more favorably located one. The sites available were usually influenced by prior use of the land—for example, whole farms now would go on the market. The same booming market for housing encouraged the landowner to hold his land for further increases in price. These forces accentuated the more or less normal tendency for suburban development to move erratically outward, and the result was the sprawl and discontinuity of settlement which has been so widely discussed.

In the postwar years, until nearly 1960, about 80 percent of all housing units built in the United States were detached single-family dwellings. For reasons not entirely clear, the building of apartments then began to accelerate, particularly in suburban areas, so that by 1964, 39 percent of all housing units built were apartments.[5] The changing age distribution (toward more older people), more general purchase of apartments on a condominium basis (so that tax- and inflation-hedge benefits accrued to apartments as well as to houses), and a wider range of sizes and styles were all factors. Neutze feels that some part of the suburban apartment boom was not explained by these factors, and may have been due to a shift in consumer tastes. Some disillusion-

ment with owning one's own home in the suburbs is altogether possible.

Nearly all the major SMSAs experienced this boom in apartment building, including suburban apartments, but with somewhat different timing and at different levels in relation to building of single-family homes. In the Washington SMSA, apartment house building has varied much more from year to year in recent years than has the building of single-family homes. In 1955, apartments were less than a fourth of the total, but in 1965 they were two-thirds of the total.[6] In several SMSAs the apartment boom seems to have peaked in the mid-1960s and to have receded somewhat; high interests rates in recent years have been especially discouraging to the building of apartments as rental property. But activity in apartments seems to have been resumed again in 1968 and 1969.

ECONOMIC BASES OF THE FLIGHT TO SUBURBIA

The postwar suburbanization, with its relatively large demands for land, may be looked at from the viewpoint of those families—typically young couples with small children—who bought homes and settled in suburbs. Why did they buy these homes, rather than live in suburban apartments or in houses or apartments in the older parts of the city?

The statement is commonly made that the postwar rush to the suburbs reflected a different demand for housing, a desire for a different life style, a different set of personal values, than was dominant a generation or more earlier. The role of higher incomes, of the auto as a more flexible individual form of transportation, and above all of a new approach toward life and new demands for a different style of living, are stressed in popular and professional publications. These may well be factors, and the present generation of young married couples may indeed have different standards of living than their parents and grandparents had. Before one comes to the conventional conclusions on this point, it may be helpful to look at the various factors which seem likely to have influenced the decisions of those locating in the suburbs since the war. The financial terms, particularly to an economist, on which different alternatives are available are significant.

Quite apart from the fact that houses and apartments in older parts of the city were simply not available on a net increase basis, the young couple with children who bought a house in the suburbs found a good many advantages in doing so.

1. The suburban house was new—clean, fresh, full of modern gadgets—although it might be shoddily built and subject to rapid deterioration.

2. It offered a way *out of* the ills of downtown or older residential areas and *into* a congenial community with desirable services, such as schools. The heavy concentration of suburban settlers in the above-average income group, in the young marriage stage of the life cycle, and with very similar backgrounds might lead to an unbalanced community from the sociologist's point of view. But this very unbalance was often attractive to the new settlers. The reality of suburban life may not have lived up to the dream, but the dream was surely a factor in leading young couples to settle there.[7]

3. The suburban new house could be purchased for a relatively low initial outlay. Down payments and various settlement charges generally were a fourth of a year's income for the purchaser and often less; with high and rising incomes for the salaried class, savings of such magnitude were not very difficult to achieve. The down payment on the house, if spread over five years or even less, would often be no greater than the difference between monthly purchase payments on

this house and monthly rentals for similar housing. Purchase of older housing could not be financed so readily. The demand for housing is highly sensitive to the size of the down payment; small reductions in the payment open up the possibility of home purchase to relatively large groups whose incomes are modest or low.[8]

4. The monthly payments were offset to a significant degree by the federal (and usually state) income tax provisions, which permitted deduction of interest and local real estate tax payments. Such subsidies extended to ownership of older homes also, but occupants of such homes were more likely to be out of debt on their home; such subsidies did not extend at all to renters of houses or of apartments.

5. Lastly, purchase of a home was a magnificent hedge against inflation; in fact, for the low down payment, the buyer had a hedge against inflation on the total price of his home. With the steadily rising cost of new housing, the selling prices of older houses often has risen also. A family has been known to buy a house, occupy it for some years, and sell at a price which has meant (in current dollars) that it had cost them nothing to live in the house for several years. Moreover, federal income tax policy has treated such capital gains with great tenderness; if another home of equal or greater cost was purchased within six months capital gains tax was postponed.

With these very powerful financial incentives toward purchase of a new separate dwelling in the suburbs, it is no wonder that suburbanization has proceeded rapidly since the war, and that suburbanization has taken a lot of land. In view of these incentives, one may reasonably ask: Just how different are the preferences and the living styles of the present generation of young married couples, as compared with their parents and grandparents? Had the latter enjoyed the same opportunities and incentives, might they not have responded in the same way?

Or, to put it differently had national policy been different, how much of the postwar suburban settlement with its nearly total reliance on purchase of single-family dwellings might have been directed toward rental instead of purchase of living space, or toward suburban apartments instead of suburban houses, or toward building apartments in the older residential areas or the downtown? Suppose, for example, federal income tax law were changed to allow an individual to deduct apartment rental payments from his gross income. What difference would this have made? Suppose that renters had somehow been given a guarantee against inflation, not only in their monthly rentals but of their capital assets, comparable to that which home purchase provided. What difference would this have made? Or, alternatively, suppose that mortgages on homes had been geared to an index of general price level with both principal and monthly payment rising during inflationary periods. Suppose that rehabilitation or rebuilding of older housing had been given substantial financial incentive, operating through the building industry and the householder as contrasted to public urban renewal; or that credit had been as favorable for restoration of old dwellings as for buying new ones. What difference might this have had?

Such questions suggest that the direction, pace, and extent of suburbanization since the the war has been, to a substantial degree, an outcome of federal housing and income tax policy. If past suburbanization has reflected past federal policy, then future urbanization might equally be affected by future federal policies.

NOTES

1. I am indebted to Mortimer Kaplan, formerly of the U.S. Department of Housing and Urban Development, for some of the ideas in this section.
2. A good source for description of these and related programs is A.M. Weimer and H. Hoyt, *Real Estate,* 5th ed., (New York: Ronald Press, 1966). See also S. Maisel, *Financing Real Estate* (New York: McGraw-Hill, 1965).
3. R. E. Slitor, *The Federal Income Tax in Relation to Housing,* National Commission on Urban Problems Research Report No. 5 (Washington, D.C.: Government Printing Office, 1968).
4. J. P. Shelton, "The Cost of Renting Versus Owning a Home," *Land Economics* (February, 1968).
5. M. Neutze, *The Suburban Apartment Boom* (Washington, D. C.: Resources for the Future, 1968), p. 9.
6. *Washington Post,* December 28, 1968, p. E 1.
7. Contrasting views of suburban life are presented by J. Keats, *The Crack in the Picture Window* (Boston: Houghton Mifflin, 1957) and H. J. Gans, *The Levittowners* (New York: Pantheon, 1967).
8. J. E. Gelfand, "The Credit Elasticity of Lower-middle Income Housing Demand," *Land Economics* (November, 1966) shows that the potential market demand in this income class is highly sensitive to size of down payment but only modestly sensitive to either length of mortgage period or to interest rate.

¹14

PUBLIC POLICY
AND THE RESIDENTIAL
DEVELOPMENT PROCESS
EDWARD J. KAISER
SHIRLEY F. WEISS

If policies are to be formulated which direct and control future patterns of urban development, then we must understand the nature of the influences on the developer himself. Accessibility does not appear to be an important consideration in the decision to develop, whereas the nature of zoning, of public facility policy, and the confidence in the quality of local development planning exert a much stronger influence on where new development is likely to occur.

Reprinted from the *Journal of the American Institute of Planners* 36, no. 1 (1970): 30–37, by permission of the publisher and the authors. This is an edited version of the original publication.

The research was financed in part by the Environmental Engineering Policies and Urban Development Project, Public Health Service Research Grant EC 00142–07 of the Environmental Control Administration.

If public policy is to be effective in guiding patterns of new urban growth, it must be based on a realistic understanding of the development process. Our conceptualization of the development process is based on empirical research as well as supporting literature.[1] The research included in-depth interviews with decision agents and field data from North Carolina Piedmont cities along with some nationally representative data. We focused on the predevelopment landowner, the developer, and consumers of various classifications including white and nonwhite as well as buyers and renters. We feel that the basic ideas about the residential process, the role of public policy, and the modeling approach could be widely applicable. However, the specific relationships found in the analyses and models calibrated on individual cities cannot be generalized to the same extent.

AN OVERVIEW OF RESIDENTIAL LAND CONVERSION

The transition of a unit of land on the periphery of an urban area can be traced from an initial state of non-urban use through several stages of development to a state of active residential use by a household. Such a conception of the land conversion process is illustrated in the top row of Figure 1. Thus, the land could be considered as (1) acquiring interest for urban use; (2) being actively considered by an entrepreneur for purchase and development; (3) being programmed for actual development; (4) being developed; and, finally (5) being purchased and inhabited by a household. Local public policies might be conceived as attempts to control the probabilities of units of land changing from one state to another. That is, the planner could attempt to lower probabilities for development decisions in some areas of the planning jurisdiction (thereby discouraging and postponing development) while increasing the probabilities in other areas (encouraging or accelerating the transition from nonurban to urban use).

Land Transition Decisions

Underlying land conversion is a complex set of decisions by assorted individuals and groups, each guided by his own incentives—the household by basic needs and preferences, the developer-entrepreneur by the profit motive, the predevelopment landowner by a mixture of pecuniary and personal motives. These decisions, shown on the second row of Figure 1, are the ones that land use controls must influence if local government is to affect the pattern of change.

Decisions of the Predevelopment Landowner[2]

Land assumes the state of *urban interest* when someone considers it to have urban development potential. At this point, determination of the land's value is based on the prevailing, usually agricultural, use as well as the potential urban use. The existing land use then becomes transitional.[3] Sometimes the transitional nature of the use is obvious, for example, junk yards and used car lots. But sometimes it is disguised as the previous rural use—this is carried on to help the landowner through the transitional period. Meanwhile the old use is becoming increasingly obsolete, due to nearby existing and anticipated urban development.

The landowner's decision to hold or sell the land depends upon income and satisfaction received from the land and his expectations about the land's future value compared to its present market value.[4] The income aspect of the landowner's decision includes such things as net annual holding cost of the land, costs that would be incurred in shifting to another investment, opportunity costs of capital, and time period of the investment.[5] In addition, the landowner's decision also depends on his relative satisfaction from such qualitative aspects as farming as a way of life, the land as a residence, love of the land, or privacy and status.[6] It appears that these motives are too important to be ignored in the explanation of the predevelopment landowner's decision to hold or sell.[7]

The Developer's Locational Decision[8]

At the next stage, the developer becomes the key decisionmaker, taking the initiative by deciding to develop the land as a means of profit rather than relying on land value appreciation for capital gain. If the developer feels that (1) a site may generally fill the specifications for the market he chooses to meet, or (2) there exists a potential demand for housing appropriate to a specific tract and if he can obtain a tentative agreement from one or more landowners to sell, he options the land and proceeds to a purchase decision. This purchase decision represents the most crucial step. The prior decision to consider the land is anticipatory; the latter decision to develop the land is anticlimactic to this decision, for development typically follows within less than five years and probably in a form not much different than the development programmed at the time of purchase.[9]

The Household's Decisions[10]

In the course of development into residential packages, the unit of property is divided into smaller parcels to accommodate individual dwelling structures. The number of decisionmakers involved in this stage of the development process is many times greater than the number involved in earlier stages, but each decision has a smaller impact on the total. However, in the aggregate this step determines the population that will reside in a particular sector of a community's

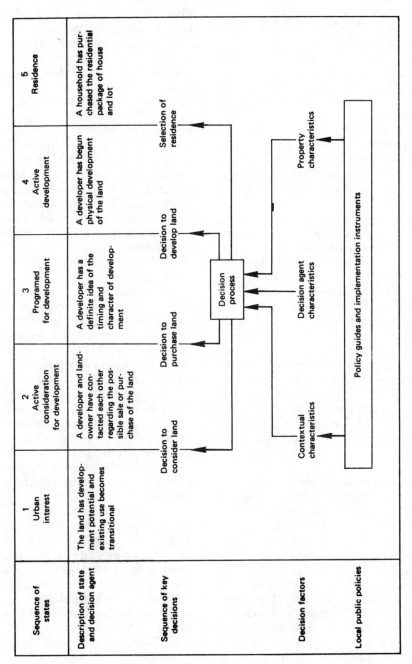

FIGURE 1. The Residential Land Conversion Process

space. By implication, it determines the relative success of the developer's locational decisions in terms of whether the subdivision development proceeds swiftly, slowly, or stalls. It determines, in part, the nature of the demand for urban services. Finally, it establishes linkages, particularly movement linkages, to other spatial, social, and economic sectors of the community.

The household's selection of a residence is actually the second of two related decisions in the residential mobility process. The first is the decision to move. It almost always precedes the selection of a residence in a relatively independent manner. An understanding of the decision to move and its correlations with previous dwelling unit characteristics, geographic divisions within the urban area, and household characteristics can give the planner an estimate of the areas of the city where outmoving and replacement in-moving will occur and where used housing stock will be vacant or turned over and will, at the same time, produce estimates of the composition of households in the market for housing. The second decision, selection of a residence, provides the opportunity to link the residential mobility process with the land conversion process.

Factors Influencing Decisions

Referring to Figure 1, and going one step deeper into our conceptual framework, we introduce three types of decision factors (from interviews, literature search, and statistical tests) to clarify the decisions which explain the transition of property through the land conversion and development process. The lower portion of Figure 1 shows the three types of decision factors: contextual, decision agent, and property characteristics. Each type influences the decision process of each decision agent in an unique way.

Contextual factors include considerations that limit and determine the overall rate and type of change in the urban community and the general structure of decision agent and property characteristics. Contextual characteristics are of two types—socioeconomic and public policy. Some of the socioeconomic contextual factors suggested are economic structure and growth prospects of the urban area, community leadership, condition of local housing market, local development industry concentration and competition, and the prevailing psychology of the period. The public policy context includes annexation powers and the exercise of these powers; capital improvement and services policies affecting quality, gross spatial pattern, and costs of transportation, water, sewerage, and schools; and subdivision regulations, building codes, zoning, and land use plans.

Property characteristics provide an operational means to describe the units of land (sites, parcels, zones, blocks, grid cells) about which decisions are made. It has been useful to distinguish three types of property characteristics. *Physical* characteristics, such as topography and soil conditions, are inherent in the land and cannot be changed except by direct modification of the site itself. *Locational* characteristics, on the other hand, are not inherent in the land but are derived solely from the relative location of the site within the spatial pattern of urban activities. Accessibility to employment areas is an example. Changes in locational characteristics depend on spatial shifts in the surrounding context of community activities and values since the site itself is fixed in space. The third category, *institutional* site characteristics, represents attributes that are applied directly to the site, but that are not inherent in the site. Imposed by social institutions, they include such things as the site's zoning category.

Property characteristics can be changed during the residential development process, so they are not necessarily the same for each decision along the way. For example, the developer in his manufacturing process may change the zoning, or he may build or provide a site for a school, shopping center, or industrial operation, thus changing the locational characteristics of the site. Construction of dwelling units and other improvements adds completely new property variables, such as size of the dwelling unit, type of dwelling unit, and environmental amenity afforded. These were nonexistent for the predevelopment landowner. They became part of the intended market strategy for the developer when he made his locational decision. To the household they are probably the most important of the property characteristics.

Decision agent characteristics, including those of the landowner, developer, and household, are the third important set of factors influencing location of residential development. Decision agent characteristics cannot be directly influenced by public policy in the way contextual factors and property characteristics can, but they are too important to be ignored in a discussion of policy-making and the development process, because they play a large role in determining the direction and the strength of the impact of contextual and property characteristics, and hence of public policy, on residential development.

PUBLIC POLICY, DECISION FACTORS, AND THE DEVELOPMENT PROCESS

The influence of local public policies on the evolution of land is indirect since it is channeled through contextual and property characteristics, as shown at the bottom of Figure 1. The important aspects of public policy are its content, differentiation of the application of this content to properties over space and time, and finally expected variation among different types of decisionmak-

ers' reactions to the policy content. These aspects bear on the decision of the predevelopment landowner to hold or to sell, the locational decision of the developer to develop a property or to look for another location, and the household's decision to move and its selection of a residence.

The Landowner's Decision to Hold or Sell

Public policy appears to affect the transition of land through predevelopment landowner selling by influencing (1) the landowner's estimated future stream of income and expenses; and (2) the present or future market value of the land. By decreasing estimated incomes and/or increasing expenses, a policy will lower the value of land to the owner and hence increase the probability that its value to him is less than the current market value. That would, of course, increase the probability that the landowner will either sell or change the use to one creating higher income relative to expenses.

Perhaps the strongest local policy influence on annual expenses is *taxation.*[11] Taxes on raw land may often represent the major cost in holding it as an investment. Smith found that cost of taxes more often than not exceeds current income, even though taxes as a percentage of the land's market value may be minimal.[12] In addition, the impact of taxes is direct; each year the landowner must find the funds to meet this cost. The impact of local policy on the landowner's income is felt through zoning limitations affecting the property's economic use. However, findings from Smith's study suggest that current income considerations are usually not as important as expenses in the transitional landowner's calculus.

The impact of local policy on the estimated future value of the land is less direct than its influence on current income and expenses. Both present and future market values greatly depend on locational characteristics, such as prestige level of the location, as well as accessibility and institutional characteristics, such as zoning protection, availability of public services, and their relationship to subdivision regulations. In general, if all these exist, the present market value may compare very well with the expected future market value.

Because of interactions between decision factors, effectiveness of policy as an influence on transition of land to urban use will depend very much on other contextual and property characteristics as well as on decision agent characteristics. For example, effectiveness of tax policy will depend on general rate of land value appreciation in the area, spatial distribution of decision agent income, and importance of nonpecuniary motives for holding land. First, "in areas with very rapid rates of appreciation, say on the order of 20 percent, only very heavy taxes on land would eliminate the investment potential" of holding land.[13] Second, the impact of heavy taxes on wealthy landowners is not as great because the rate of return on alternative investments may be lower. Third, the impact will be less strong on landowners who have significant nonpecuniary motives in addition to their pecuniary motives for holding land, because these intangible motives increase the present value to the landowner but do not affect market value.

Statistical analyses bear out the importance of decision agent characteristics as a key factor in land sales. In fact, our statistical analyses indicate they are even more important than property characteristics. Least likely to sell are those living on the land, those who are not retired, those who own the land singly, and those who at the start of the study period had held the land longer than ten years but less than forty years. Most likely to sell are absentee owners, along with owners who are retired, own the land jointly, or have had their land

either for a very short time or for a very long time.[14] Property characteristics do have some effect—land contiguous to urban development is more likely to be sold than land not so situated. Also, the effect of landowner characteristics is stronger for tracts on the fringe of the urbanized area than it is for tracts within the built-up area or tracts further out.

The Developer's Locational Decision

Again, the influence of local public policy on the residential developer's decision process is primarily channeled through contextual factors and property characteristics. But, just as in landowner and consumer decisions, the developer's characteristics affect his reaction to property characteristics and contextual factors. Public policy can affect the developer's expected costs, expected revenues, and risk of the investment.

Our study indicates that the effect of contextual, property, and developer characteristics on marketability and revenue tends to make cost considerations secondary to the developer. If this is generally true, local public policy that affects revenues would tend to have more leverage than policy that affects costs. Our interviews indicated that, as an influence in the locational decision, estimated effects of property characteristics on marketability of the residential product far outweigh estimated effects on the cost of producing the product. One reason may be that cost implications for various sites are not as uncertain to the developer nor do they tend to vary as much from site to site. In general, the higher the price range, the more important are the estimated marketability effects of the site characteristics as opposed to cost considerations.

Of the property characteristics affecting marketability, locational and institutional characteristics are clearly the most important. Both the statistical analyses and the reply "location, location, and location" (to the interview question about the three most important factors in the land purchase decision) support the importance of locational characteristics. Of these, social prestige level, a variable little affected by public policy other than school location and quality, is clearly the most important. Local public policy may have a substantial effect over a period of time on the accessibility of the site either directly through governmental investment policies concerning transportation improvements and school and recreation facilities, or indirectly through zoning for shopping and employment activities, but these are not as important as social location. More encouraging to the planner is the finding that institutional characteristics imposed by local public actions, such as availability of urban services, zoning protection, and school district lines that tend to reflect differential standards, appear significant in some developer decisions.

Despite the greater importance of the estimated marketability effects of site characteristics in our study area, the developer cannot afford to concentrate on marketability at any cost. The locational decision still requires weighing of the costs; thus it is possible for public policy to influence locational decisions by affecting change in the spatial pattern of land and physical development costs. This is illustrated by the fact that in spite of the developer's greater concern for marketability, the most influential public policy affecting developer decisions in our major study city, Greensboro, was public facility policy affecting the developer's costs. The city of Greensboro will install streets and water and sewerage systems in residential subdivisions within the city limits for the developer "at cost," up to a maximum charge. If actual costs to the city exceed that maximum charge, the city absorbs the overcost. Further, the city effectively finances the developer within the city limits by allowing up to five years to pay at a nominal interest rate. The effect of this overall policy on residential growth in Greensboro is reduction of scatteration by encouraging a more compact development pattern. Such a policy also tends to eliminate the influence of topographic and soil conditions on subdivision location within the city limits by absorbing the cost of adverse construction conditions.

The developer's assessments of costs, revenues, and marketability are tempered by his consideration of investment risk. A substantial portion of the developer's entrepreneurial activity and strategy while holding an option and considering purchase is directed toward ascertaining and reducing these risks. Part of the risk in the development industry stems from the general rule that analysis of marketability is unsystematic and the facts are weak. This appears especially true of the controlling factors—those concerning estimates of the level of market demand and the proper mixture of house, lot, physical neighborhood, and location to meet consumer preferences in that market.[15] Intensifying the developer's concern with risk are his generally low level of available capital within the firm and the correspondingly strong need for financing by inherently conservative financial intermediaries, first for development and later for homebuying.

Unclear and changeable policies concerning annexation, school district boundaries, extension of public utilities, enforcement or changes in subdivision regulations, zoning regulations, building codes, health codes, and taxation and assessment practices can increase risk, thereby discouraging any but the most conservative type of development and encouraging scatteration. At the same time, clear and relatively stable policies can have the more desirable effect of distinguishing areas where development is to be encouraged from areas where it will be discouraged, rewarding appropriate innovation and reducing some of the fluctuation between shortage and excess in various apartment and single-family housing markets. In addition to stable and clear policies, Wheaton and others have suggested the additional possibilities of information collection, analysis, and dissemination to assist the many decision agents in reducing risks in the city building industry.[16] There is even the more direct approach illustrated by the development participation policy of Greensboro which reduces uncertainty about the cost of improvements by placing an upper limit on the developer's costs.

Developer characteristics, such as size of firm, entrepreneurial approach, and nature of the production process used, influence locational behavior under similar property and contextual factors by affecting the relative attraction of different kinds of sites. In our empirical tests and modeling efforts, we have found significant differences between the locational decisions of large-scale developers (those developing over 100 lots per year) and the locational behavior of small-scale developers. While both are influenced by property characteristics, large developers are much more responsive to them and therefore to public policy than small developers.[17] Further, the two categories almost appear to be looking for very different combinations of site characteristics. For example, large developers tend to choose sites closer to the CBD, an elementary school, and employment centers, with public utilities available. Small developers tend to select the opposite kind of site.[18]

The price market preferred by the developer also influences his selection of site characteristics and hence the location of his subdivisions. Tests relating site characteristics to the price range of houses indicate that higher priced subdivisions are more sensitive to socioeconomic prestige level of the site than lower priced subdivisions, while middle and lower priced subdivisions are more sensitive to zoning, availability of public utilities, and amount of nearby development.[19]

Policy and the Household's Decision

In a private market economy the influence of local governmental policies on household decisions is not readily apparent. Exceptions are open housing laws discouraging private market discrimination practices, therefore removing constraints that affect household locational choice, and financial aids in the form of rent subsidies or mortgage insurance. Also, local public policy can affect the course of change in a developed neighborhood through the level of services provided, housing and health codes, and zoning changes in the vicinity. By providing services, protecting the area from incongruous uses, and discouraging neglect of physical improvements, local government encourages maintenance of a residential area and discourages mobility. However, much of the potential for maintenance or deterioration is incorporated in the quality of construction and planning of the original development, and much of the force for change is beyond control of local public policy especially in the socioeconomic context that governs the area's economic vitality, residential and population trends, and federal and state policy regarding financing for used and new housing.

The limited effectiveness of public intervention in the household's decisions suggests that governmental influence could be more effectively applied toward the developer's choice of types of residential packages to be produced in various locations through zoning, for example. Especially important are the developer's decisions about characteristics of the dwelling unit because much of the consumer's moving decision and housing choice appears to be based on the dwelling unit and the neighborhood as opposed to the accessibility portion of the residential package.

Although distance to work is a factor in some planned moves, in our research no difference was noted between prospective movers and stayers in regard to current accessibility in minutes to such services and amenities as grocery stores, shopping centers, downtown, doctor's offices, hospitals or clinics, parks, playgrounds, and elementary schools.[20] With respect to accessibilities of the residences after the moves, there appears to be little difference in time distance to work or services between central city residents and suburbanites, rich and poor, or renters and owners, although there is some between white and nonwhite. The findings relating to the limited role of accessibility in consumer choice suggest two possibilities.

First, that modeling and policy-making based on these research findings would differ substantially from many existing land use planning models in the deemphasis of accessibility as a determinant of residential location. Second, linking the developer and consumer model implies that some of these additional housing characteristics should be part of the description of the developer model output in order to facilitate residential choice, since consumers appear more concerned with the dwelling unit and neighborhood than with accessibility.

CONCLUSIONS

While recognizing the geographic limitations of the empirical data on which much of this paper is based, we are convinced that a decision agent orientation to studying and modeling residential growth can be extremely useful. It provides an alternative modeling outlook to the more common aggregation of the development process. Using population projection methodology as an analogy, we see the decision agent modeling approach as disaggregating the residential growth process into important components, just as the cohort-survival method of population projection disaggregates the components of population change for separate examinations of the parts and a better understanding of the whole. Further, we feel that this emphasis on disaggregation of the residential growth process will provide insights particularly well-suited to the problem of planning and coordinating local public policies. In the end, it is the moving and investment decisions by individuals and organizations that must be influenced if public actions and policies are to effect changes in urban spatial structure.

Along this line, the research suggests that the planner should look toward *mixes* of policies, some of which are aimed at landowners, some at developers, some at consumer households in already built-up areas, and some at households in the housing market. For example, a taxation policy that encourages selling may not necessarily lead to urban residential use of the land unless the site is also made profitable for residential development by other policies. Also, the research suggests that for landowners, policies that affect expenses have more leverage than policies that affect current income, while the reverse is true for developers. Furthermore, property characteristics that seem to have little impact on the predevelopment landowner's inclination to sell have considerable influence on the developer in his purchase decisions.

Analysis of the actions and attitudes of the owners, producers, and consumers of residential land reveals an extremely interdependent pattern, similar to a sort of three-dimensional spiderweb that can be moved by impact in any corner. Local public policies and implementation devices to influence urban residential growth must be determined in terms of a *chain of decisions,* responding to many direct and indirect channels of influence.

NOTES

1. For discussion of the nature of the urban land development process, see: W. L. C. Wheaton, "Public and Private Agents of Change in Urban Expansion," *Explorations into Urban Structure* (Philadelphia: University of Pennsylvania Press, 1964); Twin Cities Metropolitan Planning Commission, *Determinants of Residential Development,* Background Document No. 1, Series on Determinants of Urban Development (St. Paul: March, 1962); R. C. Martin et al., *Decisions in Syracuse: A Metropolitan Action Study* (Garden City, N.Y.: Anchor Books, Doubleday and Company, Inc., 1965); and S. F. Weiss, J. E. Smith, E. J. Kaiser, and K. B. Kenney, *Residential Developer Decisions: A Focused View of the Urban Growth Process,* Urban Studies Research Monograph (Chapel Hill: Center for Urban and Regional Studies, Institute for Research in Social Science, University of North Carolina, 1966).

2. See J. E. Smith, "Toward a Theory of Landowner Behavior on the Urban Periphery" (M.R.P. thesis, University of North Carolina, 1966); E. J. Kaiser, R. W. Massie, S. F. Weiss, and J. E. Smith, "Predicting the Behavior of Predevelopment Landowners on the Urban Fringe," *Journal of the American Institute of Planners* 34, no. 5 (September, 1968): 328–33.

3. See J. Lessinger, "The Determinants of Land Use in Rural-Urban Transition Areas: A Case Study of Santa Clara County, California" (Ph.D. diss., University of California, 1957).

4. J. E. Smith, "Toward a Theory of Landowner Behavior on the Urban Periphery," chapter 3.

5. Ibid., pp. 32–46.

6. Ibid., p. 54.

7. For research on income aspects, see S. J. Maisel, "Land Costs for Single-Family Housing," in *California Housing Studies* (Berkeley: Center for Planning and Development Research, University of California, 1963), and J. Lessinger, "The Determinants of Land Use in Rural-Urban Transition Areas."
   For research on other motives, see K. B. Kenney, "Predevelopment Land Ownership Factors and Their Influence on Residential Development," Research Memorandum submitted to Center for Urban and Regional Studies, Institute for Research in Social Science, University of North Carolina, September 21, 1965; and R. W. Bahl, *A Bluegrass Leapfrog* (Lexington: Bureau of Business Research, University of Kentucky, 1963).

8. The basic ideas of the developer in this paper are derived from Weiss, Smith, Kaiser, and Kenney, *Residential Developer Decisions;* E. J. Kaiser, *A Producer Model for Residential Growth: Analyzing and Predicting the Location of Residential Subdivisions,* Urban Studies Research Monograph (Chapel Hill: Center for Urban and Regional Studies, Institute for Research in Social Science, University of North Carolina, 1968); and W. L. C. Wheaton, "Public and Private Agents of Change in Urban Expansion."

9. See Weiss, Smith, Kaiser, and Kenney, *Residential Developer Decisions,* p. 58 for the experience in the Piedmont Cities of North Carolina; and G. Milgram, *The City Expands* (Institute for Environmental Studies, University of Pennsylvania, March, 1967), pp. 287–9, for the experience in northeast Philadelphia.

10. The main sources for this paper's ideas concerning the household's residential decisions are: E. W. Butler and E. J. Kaiser, "Prediction of Residential Movement and Spatial Allocation," A Paper presented at the Annual Meeting of the Population Association of America, Atlantic City, N.J., April 11, 1969 (Mimeographed); The Research Team: E. W. Butler, F. S. Chapin, Jr., G. C. Hemmens, E. J. Kaiser, M. A. Stegman, and S. F. Weiss, *Moving Behavior and Residential Choice: A National Survey* (Chapel Hill: Center for Urban and Regional Studies, Institute for Research in Social Science, University of North Carolina, in cooperation with the Highway Research Board, National Academy of Sciences, March 1968); L. E. Armiger, Jr., "Toward a Model of the Residential Location Decisions: A Study of Recent and Prospective Buyers of New and Used Homes" (M.R.P. thesis, University of North Carolina, 1966); and P. H. Rossi, *Why Families Move* (Glencoe, Illinois: The Free Press, 1955).

11. A. A. Schmid, *Converting Land from Rural to Urban Uses* (Baltimore: The Johns Hopkins University Press, 1968), pp. 43–46.

12. J. E. Smith, "Toward a Theory of Landowner Behavior," p. 47.

13. Ibid., pp. 74–78, Table 2, pp. 99–100.

14. Kaiser, Massie, Weiss, and Smith, "Predicting the Behavior of Predevelopment Landowners," pp. 329–30.

15. This unsystematic approach to decisions by development entrepreneurs appears to be a definite characteristic of the industry. In addition to our interviews, see W. L. C. Wheaton, "Public and Private Agents of Change," p. 168; and Twin Cities Metropolitan Planning Commission, *Determinants of Residential Development,* p. 31.

16. W. L. C. Wheaton, "Public and Private Agents of Change," p. 194–5.

17. Kaiser, *A Producer Model for Residential Growth,* p. 44.

18. Ibid., pp. 27–31.

19. Ibid., p. 44.

20. The Research Team, *Moving Behavior and Residential Choice,* p. 281.

THE FAILURE OF URBAN RENEWAL:
A CRITIQUE AND SOME PROPOSALS
HERBERT J. GANS

Even after ten years, Gans' view of the problems associated with urban renewal programs of the sixties provides an insightful perspective as to the grounds for a critical evaluation of housing strategies. The issue goes beyond mere consideration of physical structures and even of the social and economic needs of low-income families; it embraces the much broader questions of the viability of a government-supported and -regulated housing industry and the nature of requirements for integrated societal planning.

Reprinted from *Commentary* 39, no. 4 (April, 1965): 29–37, by permission of the American Jewish Committee and the author. Copyright © 1965 by the American Jewish Committee.

I

Suppose that the government decided that jalopies were a menace to public safety and a blight on the beauty of our highways and therefore took them away from their drivers. Suppose, then, that to replenish the supply of automobiles, it gave these drivers a hundred dollars each to buy a good used car and also made special grants to General Motors, Ford, and Chrysler to lower the cost—although not necessarily the price—of Cadillacs, Lincolns, and Imperials by a few hundred dollars. Absurd as this may sound, change the jalopies to slum housing, and I have described, with only slight poetic license, the first fifteen years of a federal program called urban renewal.

Since 1949, this program has provided local renewal agencies with federal funds and the power of eminent domain to condemn slum neighborhoods, tear down the buildings, and resell the cleared land to private developers at a reduced price. In addition to relocating the slum dwellers in "decent, safe, and sanitary" housing, the program was in-tended to stimulate large-scale private rebuilding, add new tax revenues to the dwindling coffers of the cities, revitalize their downtown areas, and halt the exodus of middle-class whites to the suburbs.

For some time now, a few city planners and housing experts have been pointing out that urban renewal was not achieving its general aims, and social scientists have produced a number of critical studies of individual renewal projects. These critiques, however, have mostly appeared in academic books and journals; otherwise there has been remarkably little public discussion of the federal program. Slum dwellers whose homes were to be torn down have indeed protested bitterly, but their outcries have been limited to particular projects; and because such outcries have rarely been supported by the local press, they have been easily brushed aside by the political power of the supporters of the projects in question. In the last few years, the civil-rights movement has backed protesting slum dwellers, though again only at the local level, while rightists have opposed the use of eminent domain to take private property from one owner in order to give it to another (especially when the new one is likely to be from out of town and financed by New York capital).

Slum clearance has also come under fire from several prominent architectural and social critics, led by Jane Jacobs, who have been struggling to preserve neighborhoods like Greenwich Village, with their brownstones, lofts, and small apartment houses, against the encroachment of the large, high-rise projects built for the luxury market and the poor alike. But these efforts have been directed mainly at private clearance outside the federal program, and their intent has been to save the city for people (intellectuals and artists, for example) who, like tourists, want jumbled diversity, antique "charm," and narrow streets for visual adventure and aesthetic pleasure. (Norman Mailer carried such thinking to its furthest point in his recent attack in *The New York Times* magazine section on the physical and social sterility of high-rise housing; Mailer's attack was also accompanied by an entirely reasonable suggestion—in fact, the only viable one that could be made in this context—that the advantages of brownstone living be incorporated into skyscraper projects.)

II

But if criticism of the urban-renewal program has in the past been spotty and sporadic, there are signs that the program as a whole is now beginning to be seriously and tellingly evaluated. At least two comprehensive studies, by Charles Abrams and Scott Greer, are nearing publication,[1] and one highly negative analysis—by an ultraconservative economist and often free-swinging polemicist—has already appeared: Martin Anderson's *The Federal Bulldozer*.[2] Ironically

enough, Anderson's data are based largely on statistics collected by the Urban Renewal Administration. What, according to these and other data, has the program accomplished? It has cleared slums to make room for many luxury-housing and a few middle-income projects, and it has also provided inexpensive land for the expansion of colleges, hospitals, libraries, shopping areas, and other such institutions located in slum areas. As of March 1961, 126,000 dwelling units had been demolished and about 28,000 new ones built. The median monthly rental of all those erected during 1960 came to $158, and in 1962, to $192—a staggering figure for any area outside of Manhattan.

Needless to say, none of the slum dwellers who were dispossessed in the process could afford to move into these new apartments. Local renewal agencies were supposed to relocate the dispossessed tenants in "standard" housing within their means before demolition began, but such vacant housing is scarce in most cities and altogether unavailable in some. And since the agencies were under strong pressure to clear the land and get renewal projects going, the relocation of the tenants was impatiently, if not ruthlessly, handled. Thus, a 1961 study of renewal projects in 41 cities showed that 60 percent of the dispossessed tenants were merely relocated in other slums; and in big cities, the proportion was even higher (over 70 percent in Philadelphia, according to a 1958 study). Renewal sometimes even created new slums by pushing relocatees into areas and buildings which then became overcrowded and deteriorated rapidly. This has principally been the case with Negroes who, for both economic and racial reasons, have been forced to double up in other ghettos. Indeed, because almost two-thirds of the cleared slum units have been occupied by Negroes, the urban-renewal program has often been characterized as Negro clearance, and in too many cities this has been its intent.

Moreover, those dispossessed tenants who found better housing usually had to pay more rent than they could afford. In his careful study of relocation in Boston's heavily Italian West End,[3] Chester Hartman shows that 41 percent of the West Enders lived in good housing in this so-called slum (thus suggesting that much of it should not have been torn down) and that 73 percent were relocated in good housing—thanks in part to the fact that the West Enders were white. This improvement was achieved at a heavy price, however, for median rents rose from $41 to $71 per month after the move.

According to renewal officials, 80 percent of all persons relocated now live in good housing, and rent increases were justified because many had been paying unduly low rent before. Hartman's study was the first to compare these official statistics with housing realities, and his figure of 73 percent challenges the official claim that 97 percent of the Boston West Enders were properly rehoused. This discrepancy may arise from two facts: renewal officials collected their data after the poorest of the uprooted tenants had fled in panic to other slums; and officials also tended toward a rather lenient evaluation of the relocation housing of those actually studied in order to make a good record for their agency. (On the other hand, when they were certifying areas for clearance, these officials often exaggerated the degree of "blight" in order to prove their case.)

As for the substandard rents paid by slum dwellers, these are factual in only a small proportion of cases, and then mostly among whites. Real-estate economists argue that families should pay at least 20 percent of their income for housing, but what is manageable for middle-income people is a burden to those with low incomes who pay a higher share of their earnings for food and other necessities. Yet even so, low-income Negroes generally have to devote about 30 percent of their income to housing, and a Chicago study cited by Hartman reports that among nonwhite families earning less than $3,000 a year, median rent rose from 35 percent of income before relocation to 46 percent afterward.

To compound the failure of urban renewal to help the poor, many clearance areas (Boston's West End is an example) were chosen, as Anderson points out, not because they had the worst slums, but because they offered the best sites for luxury housing—housing which would have been built whether the urban-renewal program existed or not. Since public funds were used to clear the slums and to make the land available to private builders at reduced costs, the low-income population was in effect subsidizing its own removal for the benefit of the wealthy. What was done for the slum dwellers in return is starkly suggested by the following statistic: *only one-half of 1 percent* of all federal expenditures for urban renewal between 1949 and 1964 was spent on relocation of families and individuals, and 2 percent if payments to businesses are included.

Finally, because the policy has been to clear a district of all slums at once in order to assemble large sites to attract private developers, entire neighborhoods have frequently been destroyed, uprooting people who had lived there for decades, closing down their institutions, ruining small businesses by the hundreds, and scattering families and friends all over the city. By removing the structure of social and emotional support provided by the neighborhood, and by forcing people to rebuild their lives separately and amid strangers elsewhere, slum clearance has often come at a serious psychological as well as financial cost to its supposed beneficiaries. Marc Fried, a clinical psychologist who studied the West Enders after relocation, reported that 46 percent of the women and 38 percent of the men "give evidence of a fairly severe grief reaction or worse" in response to questions about leaving their tight-knit community. Far from "adjusting" eventually to this trauma, 26 percent of the women remained sad or depressed even two years after they had been pushed out of the West End.[4]

People like the Italians or the Puerto Ricans who live in an intensely group-centered way among three-generation "extended families" and ethnic peers have naturally suffered greatly from the clearance of entire neighborhoods. It may well be, however, that slum clearance has inflicted yet graver emotional burdens on Negroes, despite the fact that they generally live in less cohesive and often disorganized neighborhoods. In fact, I suspect that Negroes who lack a stable family life and have trouble finding neighbors, shopkeepers, and institutions they can trust may have been hurt even more by forcible removal to new areas. This suspicion is supported by another of Fried's findings: that the socially marginal West Enders were more injured by relocation than those who had been integral members of the old neighborhood. Admittedly, some Negroes move very often on their own, but then they at least do so voluntarily and not in consequence of a public policy which is supposed to help them in the first place. Admittedly also, relocation has made it possible for social workers to help slum dwellers whom they could not reach until renewal brought them out in the open, so to speak. But then only a few cities have so far used social workers to make relocation a more humane process.

These high financial, social, and emotional costs paid by the slum dwellers have generally been written off as an unavoidable by-product of "progress," the price of helping cities to collect more taxes, bring back the middle class, make better use of downtown land, stimulate private investment, and restore civic pride. But as Anderson shows, urban renewal has hardly justified these claims either. For one thing, urban renewal is a slow process: the average project has taken twelve years to complete. Moreover, while the few areas suitable for luxury housing were quickly rebuilt, less desirable cleared land might lie vacant for many years because developers were—and are—unwilling to risk putting up high- and middle-income housing in areas still surrounded by slums. Frequently, they can be attracted only by promises of tax write-offs, which absorb the increased revenues that renewal is supposed to create for the city. Anderson reports that, instead of the anticipated four dollars for every public dollar, private investments have only just matched the public subsidies, and even the money for luxury housing has come forth largely because of federal subsidies. Thus, all too few of the new projects have produced tax gains and returned suburbanites or generated the magic rebuilding boom.

Anderson goes on to argue that during the fifteen years of the federal urban-renewal program, the private housing market has achieved what urban renewal has failed to do. Between 1950 and 1960, twelve million new dwelling units were built, and fully six million substandard ones disappeared—all without government action. The proportion of substandard housing in the total housing supply was reduced from 37 to 19 percent, and even among the dwelling units occupied by nonwhites, the proportion of substandard units has dropped from 72 to 44 percent. This comparison leads Anderson to the conclusion that the private market is much more effective than government action in removing slums and supplying new housing and that the urban-renewal program ought to be repealed.

III

It would appear that Anderson's findings and those of other studies I have cited make an excellent case for doing so. However, a less biased analysis of the figures and a less tendentious mode of evaluating them than Anderson's leads to a different conclusion. To begin with, Anderson's use of nationwide statistics misses the few good renewal projects, those which have helped both the slum dwellers and the cities, or those which brought in enough new taxes to finance other city services for the poor. Such projects can be found in small cities and especially in those where high vacancy rates assured sufficient relocation housing of standard quality. More important, all the studies I have mentioned deal with projects carried out during the 1950s and fail to take account of the improvements in urban-renewal practice under the Kennedy and Johnson administrations. Although Anderson's study supposedly covers the period up to 1963, many of his data go no further than 1960. Since then the federal bulldozer has moved into fewer neighborhoods, and the concept of rehabilitating rather than clearing blighted neighborhoods is more and more being underwritten by subsidized loans. A new housing subsidy program, known as 221 (d) (3), for families above the income ceiling for public housing has also been launched, and in 1964 Congress passed legislation for assistance to relocatees who cannot afford their new rents.

None of this is to say that Anderson would have had to revise his findings drastically if he had taken the pains to update them. These recent innovations have so far been small in scope—only 13,000 units were financed under 221 (d) (3) in the first two years—and they still do not provide subsidies sufficient to bring better housing within the price range of the slum residents. In addition, rehabilitation unaccompanied by new

construction is nearly useless because it does not eliminate overcrowding. And finally, some cities are still scheduling projects to clear away the nonwhite poor who stand in the path of the progress of private enterprise. Unfortunately, many cities pay little attention to federal pleas to improve the program, using the local initiative granted them by urban-renewal legislation to perpetuate the practices of the 1950s. Yet even with the legislation of the 1960s, the basic error in the original design of urban renewal remains: it is still a method for eliminating the slums in order to "renew" the city, rather than a program for properly rehousing slum dwellers.

Before going into this crucial distinction, we first need to be clear that private housing is not going to solve our slum problems. In the first place, Anderson conveniently ignores the fact that if urban renewal has benefited anyone, it is private enterprise. Bending to the pressure of the real-estate lobby, the legislation that launched urban renewal in effect required that private developers do the rebuilding, and most projects could therefore get off the drawing board only if they appeared to be financially attractive to a developer. Thus, his choice of a site and his rebuilding plans inevitably took priority over the needs of the slum dwellers.

It is true that Anderson is not defending private enterprise per se, but the free market, although he forgets that it only exists today as a concept in reactionary minds and dated economics tests. The costs of land, capital, and construction have long since made it impossible for private developers to build for anyone but the rich, and some form of subsidy is needed to house everyone else. The building boom of the 1950s which Anderson credits to the free market was subsidized by income-tax deductions to homeowners and by F.H.A. and V.A. mortgage insurance, not to mention the federal highway programs that have made the suburbs possible.

To be sure, these supports enabled private builders to put up a great deal of housing for middle-class whites. This in turn permitted well-employed workers, including some nonwhites, to improve their own situation by moving into the vacated neighborhoods. Anderson is quite right in arguing that if people earn good wages, they can obtain better housing more easily and cheaply in the not-quite-private market than through urban renewal. But this market is of little help to those employed at low or even factory wages, or the unemployed, or most Negroes who, whatever their earnings, cannot live in the suburbs. In consequence, 44 percent of all housing occupied by nonwhites in 1960 was still substandard, and even with present subsidies, private enterprise can do nothing for these people. As for laissez faire, it played a major role in creating the slums in the first place.

IV

The solution, then, is not to repeal urban renewal, but to transform it from a program of slum clearance and rehabilitation into a program of urban rehousing. This means, first, building low- and moderate-cost housing on vacant land in cities, suburbs, and new towns beyond the suburbs and also helping slum dwellers to move into existing housing outside the slums; and then, *after* a portion of the urban low-income population has left the slums, clearing and rehabilitating them through urban renewal. This approach is commonplace in many European countries, which have long since realized that private enterprise can no more house the population and eliminate slums than it can run the post office.

Of course, governments in Europe have a much easier task than ours in developing decent low-income projects. Because they take it for granted that housing is a national rather than a local responsibility, the government agencies are not hampered by the kind of real-estate and construction lobbies which can defeat or subvert American programs by charges of socialism. Moreover, their municipalities own a great deal of the vacant land and have greater control over the use of private land than do American cities. But perhaps their main advantage is the lack of popular opposition to moving the poor out of the slums and into the midst of the more affluent residents. Not only is housing desperately short for all income groups, but the European class structure, even in Western socialist countries, is still rigid enough so that low- and middle-income groups can live near each other if not next to each other and still "know their place."

In America, on the other hand, one's house and address are major signs of social status, and no one who has any say in the matter wants people of lower income or status in his neighborhood. Middle-class homeowners use zoning as a way of keeping out cheaper or less prestigious housing, while working-class communities employ less subtle forms of exclusion. Consequently, low-income groups, whatever their creed or color have been forced to live in slums or near-slums and to wait until they could acquire the means to move as a group, taking over better neighborhoods when the older occupants were ready to move on themselves.

For many years now, the only source of new housing for such people, and their only hope of escaping the worst slums, has been public housing. But this is no longer a practical alternative. Initiated during the Depression, public housing has always been a politically embattled program; its opponents, among whom the real-estate lobby looms large, first saddled it with restrictions and then effectively crippled it. Congress now permits only 35,000 units a year to be built in the entire country.

The irony is that public housing has declined because, intended only for the poor, it faithfully carried out its mandate. Originally, sites were obtained by slum clearance; after the war, however, in order to increase the supply of low-cost housing, cities sought to build public housing on vacant land. But limited as it was to low-income tenants and thus labeled and stigmatized as an institution of the dependent poor, public housing was kept out of vacant land in the better neighborhoods. This, plus the high cost of land and construction, left housing officials with no other choice but to build high-rise projects on whatever vacant land they could obtain, often next to factories or along railroad yards. Because tenants of public housing are ruled by a set of strict regulations—sometimes necessary, sometimes politically inspired, but always degrading—anyone who could afford housing in the private market shunned the public projects. During the early years of the program, when fewer citizens had that choice, public housing became respectable shelter for the working class and even for the unemployed middle class. After the war, federal officials decided, and rightly so, that public housing ought to be reserved for those who had no alternative and therefore set income limits that admitted only the really poor. Today, public housing is home for the underclass—families who earn less than $3,000 to $4,000 annually, many with unstable jobs or none at all, and most of them nonwhite.

Meanwhile the enthusiasm for public housing has been steadily dwindling and, with it, badly needed political support. Newspaper reports reinforce the popular image of public housing projects as huge nests of crime and delinquency—despite clear evidence to the contrary—and as the domicile of unregenerate and undeserving families whose children urinate only in the elevators. The position of public housing, particularly among liberal intellectuals,

has also been weakened by the slurs of the social and architectural aesthetes who condemn the projects' poor exterior designs as "sterile," "monotonous," and "dehumanizing," often in ignorance of the fact that the tightly restricted funds have been allocated mainly to make the apartments themselves as spacious and livable as possible and that the waiting lists among slum dwellers who want these apartments remain long. Be that as it may, suburban communities and urban neighborhoods with vacant land are as hostile to public housing as ever, and their opposition is partly responsible for the program's having been cut down to its present minuscule size.

The net result is that low-income people today cannot get out of the slums, either because they cannot afford the subsidized private market or because the project they could afford cannot be built on vacant land. There is only one way to break through this impasse, and that is to permit them equal access to new subsidized, privately built housing by adding another subsidy to make up the difference between the actual rent and what they can reasonably be expected to pay. Such a plan, giving them a chance to choose housing like all other citizens, would help to remove the stigma of poverty and inferiority placed on them by public housing. Many forms of rent subsidy have been proposed, but the best one, now being tried in New York, is to put low- and middle-income people in the same middle-income project, with the former getting the same apartments at smaller rentals.

Admittedly, this approach assumes that the poor can live with the middle class and that their presence and behavior will not threaten their neighbors' security or status. No one knows whether this is really possible, but experiments in education, job-training, and social-welfare programs do show that many low-income people, when once offered *genuine* opportunities to improve their lives and given help in making use of them, are able to shake off the hold of the culture of poverty. Despite the popular stereotype, the proportion of those whom Hylan Lewis calls the clinical poor, too ravaged emotionally by poverty and deprivation to adapt to new opportunities, seems to be small. As for the rest, they only reject programs offering spurious opportunities, like job-training schemes for nonexistent jobs. Further, anyone who has lived in a slum neighborhood can testify that whatever the condition of the building, most women keep their apartments clean by expenditures of time and effort inconceivable to the middle-class housewife. Moving to a better apartment would require little basic cultural change from these women, and rehousing is thus a type of new opportunity that stands a better chance of succeeding than, say, a program to inculcate new child-rearing techniques.

We have no way of telling how many slum dwellers would be willing to participate in such a plan. However poor the condition of the flat, the slum is home, and for many it provides the support of neighborhood relatives and friends and a cultural milieu in which everyone has the same problems and is therefore willing to overlook occasional disreputable behavior. A middle-income project cannot help but have a middle-class ethos, and some lower-class people may be fearful of risking what little stability they have achieved where they are now in exchange for something new, strange, demanding, and potentially hostile. It would be hard to imagine an unwed Negro mother moving her household to a middle-income project full of married couples and far removed from the mother, sisters, and aunts who play such an important role in the female-centered life of lower-class Negroes. However, there are today a large number of stable two-parent families who live in the slums

only because income and race exclude them from the better housing that is available. Families like these would surely be only too willing to leave the Harlems and Black Belts. They would have to be helped with loans to make the move and perhaps even with grants to buy new furniture so as not to feel ashamed in their new surroundings. They might be further encouraged by being offered income-tax relief for giving up the slums, just as we now offer such relief to people who give up being renters to become homeowners.

Undoubtedly there would be friction between the classes, and the more affluent residents would likely want to segregate themselves and their children from neighbors who did not toe the middle-class line, especially with respect to child-rearing. The new housing would therefore have to be planned to allow some voluntary social segregation for both groups, if only to make sure that enough middle-income families would move in (especially in cities where there was no shortage of housing for them). The proportion of middle- and low-income tenants would have to be regulated, not only to minimize the status fears of the former but also to give the latter enough peers to keep them from feeling socially isolated and without emotional support when problems arise. Fortunately, nonprofit and limited-dividend institutions, which do not have to worry about showing an immediate profit, are now being encouraged to build moderate-income housing; they can do a more careful job of planning the physical and social details of this approach than speculative private builders.

If the slums are really to be emptied and their residents properly housed elsewhere, the rehousing program will have to be extended beyond the city limits, for the simple reason that that is where most of the vacant land is located. This means admitting the low-income population to the suburbs; it also means creating new towns—self-contained communities with their own industry which would not, like the suburbs, be dependent on the city for employment opportunities and could therefore be situated in presently rural areas.

To be sure, white middle-class suburbanites and rural residents are not likely to welcome nonwhite low-income people into their communities, even if the latter are no longer clearly labeled as poor. The opposition to be expected in city neighborhoods chosen for mixed-income projects would be multiplied a hundredfold in outlying areas. Being politically autonomous, and having constituencies who are not about to support measures that will threaten their security or status in the slightest, the suburbs possess the political power to keep the rehousing program out of their own vacant lots, even if they cannot stop the federal legislation that would initiate it. On the other hand, experience with the federal highway program and with urban renewal itself has demonstrated that few communities can afford to turn down large amounts of federal money. For instance, New York City is likely to build a Lower Manhattan Expressway in the teeth of considerable local opposition, if only because the federal government will pay 90 percent of the cost and thus bring a huge sum into the city coffers. If the rehousing program were sufficiently large to put a sizable mixed-income project in every community, and if the federal government were to pick up at least 90 percent of the tab, while also strengthening the appeal of the program by helping to solve present transportation, school, and tax problems in the suburbs, enough political support might be generated to overcome the objections of segregationist and class-conscious whites.

Yet even if the outlying areas could be persuaded to co-operate, it is not at all certain that slum dwellers would leave the city. Urban-renewal experience has shown that for many slum dwellers there are more urgent needs than good housing. One is employment, and most of the opportunities for unskilled or semiskilled work are in the city. Another is money, and some New York City slum residents recently refused to let the government inspect, much less repair, their buildings because they would lose the rent reductions they had received previously. If leaving the city meant higher rents, more limited access to job possibilities, and also separation from people and institutions which give them stability, some slum residents might very well choose overcrowding and dilapidation as the lesser of two evils.

These problems would have to be considered in planning a rehousing program beyond the city limits. The current exodus of industry from the city would, of course, make jobs available to the new suburbanites. The trouble is that the industries now going into the suburbs, or those that would probably be attracted to the new towns, are often precisely the ones which use the most modern machinery and the fewest unskilled workers. Thus, our rehousing plan comes up against the same obstacle—the shortage of jobs—that has frustrated other programs to help the low income population and that will surely defeat the War on Poverty in its present form. Like so many other programs, rehousing is finally seen to depend on a step that American society is as yet unwilling to take: the deliberate creation of new jobs by government action. The building of new towns especially would have to be co-ordinated with measures aimed at attracting private industry to employ the prospective residents, at creating other job opportunities, and at offering intensive training for the unskilled after they have been hired. If they are not sure of a job before they leave the city, they simply will not leave.

The same social and cultural inhibitions that make slum residents hesitant to move into a mixed-income project in the city would, of course, be even stronger when it came to moving out of the city. These inhibitions might be relaxed by moving small groups of slum residents en masse or by getting those who move first to encourage their neighbors to follow. In any case, new social institutions and community facilities would have to be developed to help the erstwhile slum dweller feel comfortable in his new community, yet without labeling him as poor.

Despite its many virtues, a rehousing program based on the use of vacant land on either side of the city limits would not immediately clear the slums. Given suburban opposition and the occupational and social restraints on the slum dwellers themselves, it can be predicted that if such a program were set in motion it would be small in size and would pull out only the upwardly mobile—particularly the young people with stable families and incomes—who are at best a sizable minority among the poor. What can be done now to help the rest leave the slums?

The best solution is a public effort to encourage their moving into existing neighborhoods within the city and in older suburbs just beyond the city limits. Indeed, a direct rent subsidy like that now given to relocatees could enable people to obtain decent housing in these areas. This approach has several advantages. It would allow low-income people to be close to jobs and to move in groups, and it would probably attract the unwed mother who wanted to give her children a better chance in life. It would also be cheaper than building new housing, although the subsidies would have to be large enough to discourage low-incomes families from overcrowding —and thus deteriorating—the units in order to save on rent.

There are, however, some obvious disadvantages as well. For one thing, because nonwhite low-income people would be moving into presently white or partially integrated areas, the government would in effect be encouraging racial invasion. This approach would thus have the effect of pushing the white and middle-income people further toward the outer edge of the city or into the suburbs. Although some whites might decide to stay, many would surely want to move, and not all would be able to afford to do so. It would be necessary to help them with rent subsidies as well; indeed, they might become prospective middle-income tenants for rehousing projects on vacant land.

Undoubtedly, all this would bring us closer to the all-black city that has already been predicted. For this reason alone, a scheme that pushes the whites further out can be justified only when combined with a rehousing program on vacant land that would begin to integrate the suburbs. But even that could not prevent a further racial imbalance between cities and suburbs.

Yet would the predominantly nonwhite city really be so bad? It might be for the middle class which needs the jobs, shops, and culture that the city provides. Of course, the greater the suburban exodus, the more likely it would become that middle-class culture would also move to the suburbs. This is already happening in most American cities —obvious testimony to the fact that culture (at least of the middle-brow kind represented by tent theaters and art movie houses) does not need the city in order to flourish; and the artists who create high culture seem not to mind living among the poor even now.

Nonwhite low-income people might feel more positive about a city in which they were the majority, for if they had the votes, municipal services would be more attuned to their priorities than is now the case. To be sure, if poor people (of any color) were to dominate the city, its tax revenues would decrease even further, and cities would be less able than ever to supply the high-quality public services that the low-income population needs so much more urgently than the middle class. Consequently, new sources of municipal income not dependent on the property tax would have to be found; federal and state grants to cities (like those already paying half the public-school costs in several states) would probably be the principal form. Even under present conditions, in fact, new sources of municipal income must soon be located if the cities are not to collapse financially.

If nonwhites were to leave the slums en masse, new ghettos would eventually form in the areas to which they would move. Although this is undesirable by conventional liberal standards, the fact is that many low-income Negroes are not yet very enthusiastic about living among white neighbors. They do not favor segregation, of course; what they want is a free choice and then the ability to select predominantly nonwhite areas that are in better shape than the ones they live in now. If the suburbs were opened to nonwhites—to the upwardly mobile ones who want integration now—free choice would become available. If the new ghettos were decent neighborhoods with good schools, and if their occupants had jobs and other opportunities to bring stability into their lives, they would be training their children to want integration a generation hence.

In short, then, a workable rehousing scheme must provide new housing on both sides of the city limits for the upwardly mobile minority and encouragement to move into older areas for the remainder. If, in these ways, enough slum dwellers could be enabled and induced to leave the slums, it would then be possible to clear or rehabilitate the remaining slums. Once slum areas were less crowded and empty apartments were going begging, their profitability and market value would be reduced and urban renewal could take place far more cheaply and quickly. Relocation would be less of a problem, and with land values down, rebuilding and rehabilitation could be carried out to fit the resources of the low-income people who needed or wanted to remain in the city. A semi-suburban style of living that would be attractive to the upper-middle class could also be provided.

At this point, it would be possible to begin to remake the inner city into what it must eventually become: the hub of a vast metropolitan complex of urban neighborhoods, suburbs, and new towns in which the institutions and functions that have to be at the center—the specialized business districts, the civil and cultural facilities, and the great hospital complexes and university campuses—would be located.

Even in such a city, there would be slums—for people who wanted to live in them, for the clinical poor who would be unable to make it elsewhere, and for rural newcomers who would become urbanized in them before moving on. But it might also be possible to relocate many of these in a new kind of public housing in which quasi communities would be established to help those whose problems were soluble and to provide at least decent shelter for those who cannot be helped except by letting them live without harassment until we learn how to cure mental illness, addiction, and other forms of self-destructive behavior.

V

This massive program has much to recommend it, but we must clearly understand that moving the low-income population out of the slums would not eliminate poverty or the other problems that stem from it. A standard dwelling unit can make life more comfortable, and a decent neighborhood can discourage some antisocial behavior, but by themselves, neither can effect radical transformations. What poor people need most is decent incomes, proper jobs, better schools, and freedom from racial and class discrimination. Indeed, if the choice were between a program solely dedicated to rehousing and a program that kept the low-income population in the city slums for another generation but provided for these needs, the latter would be preferable, for it would produce people who were able to leave the slums under their own steam. Obviously, the ideal approach is one that coordinates the elimination of slums with the reduction of poverty.

As I have been indicating, an adequate rehousing program would be extremely costly and very difficult to carry out. But its complexity and expense can both be justified, however, on several grounds. Morally, it can be argued that no one in the Great Society should have to live in a slum, at least not involuntarily.

From a political point of view, it is urgently necessary to begin integrating the suburbs, and to improve housing conditions in the city before the latter becomes an ominous ghetto of poor and increasingly angry Negroes and Puerto Ricans and the suburbs become enclaves of affluent whites who commute fearfully to a downtown bastion of stores and offices. If the visible group tensions of recent years are allowed to expand and sharpen, another decade may very well see the beginning of open and often violent class and race warfare.

But the most persuasive argument for a rehousing program is economic. Between 50 and 60 percent of building costs go into wages and create work for the unskilled who are now increasingly unemployable elsewhere. A dwelling unit that costs $15,000 would thus provide as much as $9,000 in wages—one and a half years of respectably paid employment for a single worker. Adding four and a half million new low-cost housing units to rehouse half of those in substandard units in 1960 would provide almost seven million man-years of work, and the subsequent renewal of these and other substandard units yet more. Many additional jobs would also be created by the construction and operation of new shopping centers, schools, and other community facilities, as well as the highways and public transit systems that would be needed to serve the new suburbs and towns. If precedent must be cited for using a housing program to create jobs, it should be recalled that public housing was started in the Depression for precisely this reason.

The residential building industry (and the real-estate lobby) would have to be persuaded to give up their stubborn resistance to government housing programs, but the danger of future underemployment, and the opportunity of participating profitably in the rehousing scheme, should either convert present builders or attract new ones into the industry. As for the building-trades unions, they have always supported government housing programs, but they have been unwilling to admit nonwhites to membership. If, however, the rehousing effort were sizable enough to require many more workers than are now in the unions, the sheer demand for labor —and the enforcement of federal nondiscriminatory hiring policies for public works—would probably break down the color barriers without much difficulty.

While the federal government is tooling up to change the urban-renewal program into a rehousing scheme, it should also make immediate changes in current renewal practices to remove their economic and social cost from the shoulders of the slum dwellers. Future projects should be directed at the clearance of really harmful slums, instead of taking units that are run down but not demonstrably harmful out of the supply of low-cost housing, especially for downtown revitalization and other less pressing community-improvement schemes. Occupants of harmful slums, moreover, ought to be rehoused in decent units they can afford. For this purpose, more public housing and 221 (d) (3) projects must be built, and relocation and rent-assistance payments should be increased to eliminate the expense of moving for the slum dweller. Indeed, the simplest way out of the relocation impasse is to give every relocatee a sizable grant, like the five hundred dollars to one thousand dollars paid by private builders in New York City to get tenants out of existing structures quickly and painlessly. Such a grant is not only a real incentive to relocatees but a means of reducing opposition to urban renewal. By itself, however, it cannot reduce the shortage of relocation housing. Where such housing now exists in plentiful supply, renewal ought to move ahead more quickly, but where there is a shortage that cannot be appreciably reduced, it would be wise to eliminate or postpone clearance and rehabilitation projects that require a large amount of relocation.

VI

Nothing is easier than to suggest radical new programs to the overworked and relatively powerless officals of federal and local renewal agencies who must carry out the present law, badly written or not, and who are constantly pressured by influential private interests to make decisions in their favor. Many of these officials are as unhappy with what urban renewal has wrought as their armchair critics and would change the program if they could—that is, if they received encouragement from the White House, effective support in getting new legislation through Congress, and, equally important, political help at city halls to incorporate these innovations into local programs. But it should be noted that little

of what I have suggested is very radical, for none of the proposals involves conflict with the entrenched American practice of subsidizing private enterprise to carry out public works at a reasonable profit. The proposals are radical only in demanding an end to our no less entrenched practice of punishing the poor. Yet they also make sure that middle-class communities are rewarded financially for whatever discomfort they may have to endure.

Nor are these suggestions very new. Indeed, in March 1965 President Johnson sent a housing message to Congress which proposes the payment of rent subsidies as the principal method for improving housing conditions. It also requests federal financing of municipal services for tax-starved communities and aid toward the building of new towns. These represent bold and desirable steps toward the evolution of a federal rehousing program. Unfortunately, however, the message offers little help to those who need it most. Slum dwellers may be pleased that there will be no increase in urban-renewal activity and that relocation housing subsidies and other grants are being stepped up. But no expansion of public housing is being requested, and to make matters worse, the new rent subsidies will be available only to households above the income limits for public housing. Thus, the President's message offers no escape for the mass of the nonwhite low-income population from the ghetto slums; in fact it threatens to widen the gap between such people and the lower-middle-income population which will be eligible for rent subsidies.

On the other hand, as in the case of the War on Poverty, a new principle of government responsibility in housing is being established, and evidently the President's strategy is to obtain legislative approval for the principle by combining it with a minimal and a minimally controversial program for the first year. Once the principle has been accepted, however, the program must change quickly. It may have taken fifteen years for urban renewal even to begin providing some relief to the mass of slum dwellers, but it cannot take that long again to become a rehousing scheme that will give them significant help. The evolution of federal policies can no longer proceed in the leisurely fashion to which politicians, bureaucrats, and middle-class voters have become accustomed, for unemployment, racial discrimination, and the condition of our cities are becoming ever more critical problems, and those who suffer from them are now considerably less patient than they have been in the past.

NOTES

1. C. Abrams, *The City is the Froniter* (New York: Harper & Row, 1965); S. Greer, *Urban Renewal and American Cities* (Indianapolis: Bobbs Merrill, 1965).
2. M. Anderson, *The Federal Bulldozer* (Cambridge: M. I. T. Press, 1964).
3. C. Hartman, "The Housing of Relocated Families," *Journal of the American Institute of Planners* 30 (November, 1964): 266–86. This paper also reviews all other relocation research and is a more reliable study of the consequences of renewal than Anderson's work.
4. M. Fried, "Grieving for a Lost Home," in L. J. Duhl (ed.), *The Urban Condition* (New York: Basic Books, 1963), pp. 151–71.

16

LOW-INCOME HOUSING: SUBURBAN STRATEGIES
LEONARD S. RUBINOWITZ

The growth of low-income housing in the suburbs is considered by many analysts to be not only a desirable but also a necessary element of urban policy. Since many individual suburban communities are likely to resist such a step, it is necessary to explore the role that state and federal governments might play in implementation of this policy. Without such intervention it is unlikely that existing patterns of development will be changed.

Reprinted from Leonard S. Rubinowitz, *Low-Income Housing: Suburban Strategies* (Cambridge, Mass.: Ballinger Publishing Company, 1974), pp. 47–51, by permission of the publisher and the author. Copyright© 1974 by Ballinger Publishing Company. This is an edited version of the original publication.

This country faces a difficult and potentially disastrous dilemma. It is both just and necessary for lower-income people to have access to suburban housing. At the same time, suburban communities have long had the power to maintain an unjust, costly practice of economic exclusion. The log jam must be broken. Suburbs must not be able to keep people from living there because of their income. The question is how to open the doors of suburbia. What governmental and private strategies can succeed in overcoming the barriers to building low- and moderate-income housing in the suburbs?

First, what role can public bodies play in opening the suburbs? County governments, regional bodies, state governments and the federal government cannot be neutral on the question of suburban access. They are inextricably involved in the metropolitan development process. They encourage or carry out planning, provide resources to local communities, and undertake related regulation. In the past, governments at all levels have been part of the problem. They have presided over an exclusionary system. Federal, state and local laws, policies and practices have contributed to the exclusion of lower-income people from suburbia. While our articulated goals emphasize adequate housing supply and choice for all Americans, the actions and inactions of government at all levels have impeded the achievement of those goals. Land use controls obstruct or prevent development of housing for lower-income people outside the central city. Federal laws help to raise the wall still higher by granting localities veto power over subsidized developments.

Not only has government helped to exclude the poor from suburbia, it financed the development of the suburbs for affluent white Americans. While suburban FHA and VA mortgage guarantees, highways, schools, and water and sewer facilities were paid for by everyone's tax dollars, the benefits were maldistributed. Government at all levels has a responsibility to redress the balance. Public bodies must redress the past practice of taxing all for suburban development, while only the relatively well-to-do gain access to the benefits.

It would be folly to expect large numbers of individual communities to open their doors voluntarily to lower-income people. Localities perceive themselves as having strong incentives to maintain their exclusionary posture. They have had the power to keep out the poor for 50 years. Since the U.S. Supreme Court upheld zoning as a legitimate exercise of the police power in *Euclid* v. *Ambler Realty,* the use of land has been a matter of almost exclusively local control. It is clear that suburban communities, given continued free rein, would persist in closing their doors to low- and moderate-income people. Local autonomy is an important value, but it cannot be used to justify derogation of the rights of all Americans to choose where they wish to live. The independence of local communities needs to be limited to the extent necessary to guarantee free access to the suburbs.

In short, most suburban jurisdictions will keep doing their best to keep out housing for low- and moderate-income people. It is up to county and regional bodies, states, and the federal government to reverse this pattern. Changes require affirmative policies and programs at higher levels to provide lower-income groups the opportunity to live in suburbia. In the late 1960s public bodies began to take steps in that direction. In one part of the country, county governments passed ordinances requiring builders to include low- and moderate-income components in their housing developments. Although one of these promising ordinances was invalidated by the courts, the other still may be implemented. Moving to a larger geographical area, a number of metropolitan and regional agencies adopted housing allocation plans to facilitate suburban development of lower-income housing. These plans identify places where needed subsidized housing should be located. Several of the agencies have worked aggressively to implement these plans, to convert them from paper to real housing opportunities.

State governments have also tried to facilitate development of low- and moderate-income housing in suburbia. Many states have created housing finance agencies. These agencies sell tax-exempt bonds so they can make mortgage money available to housing developers. Because they are providing the financing, the agencies have a great voice in where the housing is to be located. A few housing finance agencies have focused on financing economically integrated suburban housing. However, none of these agencies has a mandate to build in the suburbs or authorization to eliminate or ignore the barriers suburbs have erected.

States have also reclaimed some of the power over land use that they have delegated for so long to localities. Increasingly, state legislatures are deciding that local governments should not be permitted to act totally autonomously in matters of regional and statewide concern. Although these laws generally emphasize environmental protection, one state has zeroed in on the problem of local exclusionary practices. The Massachusetts "anti-snob zoning" law sets limits on a locality's ability to deny necessary approvals for subsidized housing. Connecticut and Wisconsin have considered similar legislation.

Additional leverage is available to states (as well as to the federal government) through the "carrot and stick" process. State governments bestow benefits on local communities in many forms, including grants, loans and construction of state facilities. States can set particular kinds of actions by a locality as conditions for allocating these resources. For example, a state could give grants only to communities which eliminate the barriers to building low- and moderate-income housing. The Pennsylvania Department of Community Affairs has used this approach and has withheld grants to several suburbs which the department concluded were exclusionary. The state informed these communities that the state funds would be released when the localities had taken appropriate action to include lower-income housing.

Pennsylvania was also the first state to try litigation as a tool to open its suburban "creatures." The state joined a lawsuit against a large number of Philadelphia suburbs. The plaintiffs argued that these communities excluded housing for low- and moderate-income people and urged the court to require affirmative inclusionary actions by the localities.

Initial efforts to increase suburban access have not been confined to the county, regional and state levels. Even the slumbering federal giant has shown some signs of awakening to the problem. The "feds" have taken isolated actions which by no means amount to coherent policy in support of opening the suburbs to low- and moderate-income people. In fact, the president's 1971 Equal Housing Message placed the federal government in opposition to racial discrimination but abdicated all responsibility for dealing with economic exclusion. In two cases, the Justice Department sued suburban communities which refused to permit development of subsidized housing projects, but the suits alleged that racial discrimination was involved. The Justice Department made clear that it was acting pursuant to the president's message. Given this posture, the Justice Department is likely to sue only when a suburb practices blatant racial discrimination in keeping out lower-income housing.

In addition to litigation, the federal government has on occasion used its administrative authority to press for greater suburban housing opportunities. For example, HUD provides funds to metropolitan and regional planning agencies. In at least one instance, HUD conditioned a planning grant on the regional agency's commitment to develop a housing allocation plan of the kind described earlier. In several other cases, HUD used its "carrots" available to suburbs, such as open space and water and sewer grants, to encourage applicants for these funds to accept low- and moderate-income housing.

Perhaps the most visible federal effort in the early 1970s involved the administration of the subsidized housing programs. Early in 1972 HUD adopted regulations which encouraged development of subsidized housing outside of the inner city. These "project selection criteria" gave priority for the limited HUD funds to applicants who could open up new housing opportunities, including options in suburbia. In some areas, housing sponsors shifted their efforts to the suburbs. However, these regulations had only a short test, as the subsidy programs became the subject of first, a moratorium, and later, a planned phase-out.

Public strategies at all levels have taken one of two paths. Some approaches have focused on specific instances of exclusion or exclusionary practices. For example, the Massachusetts law provides a state review process which enables developers denied permits locally to seek state permission to build the housing. The suits brought by the state of Pennsylvania and the federal government have challenged specific suburban obstacles. Pennsylvania's suit related to a whole range of specific exclusionary practices, while the federal suits have dealt with the exclusion of individual subsidized housing projects.

Other governmental efforts have attempted to provide an "inclusionary" context or framework, rather than challenging particular local ordinances or practices. For example, housing allocation plans do not change zoning ordinances or practices directly, but their existence and widespread support for them may facilitate land use changes throughout individual communities or for particular subsidized housing projects.

THE POTENTIAL OF PUBLIC STRATEGIES

The efforts by public bodies outlined above represent cautious first steps to solve the problem of suburban exclusion. Government has far greater leverage to increase suburban access than has been tapped. The potential governmental influence is enormous, through regulation, litigation, financing of housing, planning, and conditioning funding to local communities.

State and federal regulatory powers which might be employed to increase suburban access, such as civil rights provisions, have scarcely been used. For example, enforcement of employment discrimination laws could include requirements that suburban employers see to it that housing is available for lower-income employees near the job site.

States could also reclaim more of their land use control powers. They could require, for example, that localities plan and zone affirmatively to provide for lower-income housing.

In addition, some of the regulatory approaches that have been used by one level of government could also be used by others. As states moved to carve out a role for themselves relative to land use, the Congress considered a number of national land use policy bills. These bills contemplate encouraging additional state involvement in regulating the use of land. Meanwhile, existing federal policy required areawide comprehensive planning, including housing planning,

as a precondition for a variety of federal grants. It was up to the responsible federal agencies to administer their planning grants and requirements to assure that there were ongoing efforts to open the suburbs before federal funds would flow.

Beyond expanding the scope of regulatory activities, public agencies have other mechanisms at their disposal. First, states and the federal government could pursue litigation strategies being used by private organizations. Second, although a couple of states have created subsidy programs on a limited scale, this area remains largely the domain of the federal government. More states could create subsidy programs and use these programs to increase suburban access. Third, although regional agencies have been the prime initiators of allocation plans, states could also do this job. Alternatively, states could require that metropolitan or regional agencies develop and implement allocation plans. Finally, the carrot and stick approach could be used aggressively by state and federal agencies to condition benefits bestowed on inclusionary actions taken by localities. This approach could be expanded in terms of the state and federal agencies involved and should emphasize the grants and facilities which have the most appeal for suburbanites.

In sum, the last few years have witnessed the development and implementation of a wide variety of public strategies for overcoming suburban hurdles to low- and moderate-income housing. Most of these activities are at an embryonic state. Many of the victories to date have been symbolic. Other efforts have met with defeat, at least temporarily. The resistance of the suburbs shows no sign of fading away. However, more public bodies are making efforts to increase suburban access each year.

POVERTY, HOUSING, AND MARKET PROCESSES
RAYMOND E. ZELDER

Although suburban growth of low-income housing is an important element in policies aimed at improving the welfare of the poor, one cannot depend on a single strategy. Zelder covers a broad spectrum of such strategies, each of which has different implications for the future distribution both of the poor and of the characteristics of housing.

Reprinted from Donald J. Reeb and James T. Kirk, Jr., eds., *Housing the Poor* (New York: Praeger Publishers, Inc., 1973), pp. 29–41, by permission of the publisher and the author. Copyright © 1973 by Praeger Publishers, Inc. This is an edited version of the original publication. Artwork has been renumbered.

Improving the quantity and quality of housing for low-income households has an almost irresistible appeal unless one is a curmudgeon (or perhaps an economist). The notion that a vast, if not overwhelming, scarcity of "satisfactory" housing confronts low-income families is viewed as so evident that no documentation is needed. Many quotations citing the obvious severity of the low-income housing problem could be presented. The following quotations are illustrative. The President's Committee on Urban Housing, in a 1968 report, noted that one of the "two major challenges to the Nation . . . [are] Measures to relieve the severe shortage of adequate housing for the poor." [1] The National Advisory Commission on Civil Disorders described the situation in the following terms: "Today after more than three decades of fragmented and grossly under-funded Federal housing programs, decent housing remains a chronic problem for the disadvantaged urban household." [2] *"The supply of housing suitable for low-income families should be expanded on a massive basis."* [3]

Some reflection suggests that the foregoing assessments do not adequately describe the low-income housing market nor can they account for developments in this market over the past decade. One is tempted to argue that almost just the reverse is the case; that is, the low-income market has been threatened by underlying conditions of chronic oversupply. At the same time, housing suppliers have had to cope with substantially increasing costs.

LOW-COST HOUSING AVAILABILITY

On the demand side, the dominant force has been a strong, persistent decline in the number of poor households. Between 1959 and 1969 the number of households (families and unrelated individuals) below the revised official poverty definition of 1969 decreased almost 3.5 million to 9.8 million, or 26 percent. (In 1970 a reversal of the downward trend of 436,000 was experienced, reflecting the impact of the recession.) Decreases were experienced by both whites and nonwhites. Even inside central cities the number of poverty households contracted, by more than 13 percent or approximately one-half the overall percentage decrease. Table 1 presents some summary data detailing the shrinkage in low-income households.

of market growth.

Although dramatic, obvious symptoms of the decrease in low-income demands may have been aborted, some

Poverty Population	1959	1969	1970	Percent Change
	(in thousands)			1959-69
Total Poverty Families and				
Unrelated Individuals	13,248	9,801	10,237	-26.0
White	10,226	7,517	7,822	-26.5
Nonwhite	3,022	2,284	2,416	-24.4
Households—Metropolitan				
Total	5,231	4,535		-13.3
Inside central cities	3,304	2,865		-13.3
White	2,315	1,933		-16.5
Negro	960	874		- 9.0
Outside central cities	1,927	1,670		-13.3

TABLE 1. Trends in Poverty Households
Source: Total Poverty Families and Unrelated Individuals: Bureau of the Census, *Current Population Reports*, P-60, No. 77, "Consumer Income."
Source: Households—Metropolitan: Bureau of the Census, *Current Population Reports*, P-23, No. 37, "Social and Economic Characteristics of the Population in Metropolitan and Non-Metropolitan Areas: 1970 and 1960."

centage decrease. Table 1 presents some summary data detailing the shrinkage in low-income households.

The normal impact of a decrease in demand against a relatively fixed standing stock, in the absence of offsetting factors, is rising vacancy rates and softening rentals. To some extent, evidence of these tendencies began to emerge in the first half of the 1960s. Vacancies generally ranged between 7.5 and 8.0 percent and reports of local neighborhood vacancy rates of 15 percent and higher were not infrequent. The sharp reductions in residential building after 1965 served to mask the contraction in low-income housing demand. If households with improving incomes are to vacate their lower quality for higher quality units, there must be a release or filtering of units. This release is dependent on the construction of new units in excess

less direct indications might be suggested. On an overall basis, and in a relative price sense, rents did decline during the past decade. The U.S. Consumer Price Index advanced 31.1 percent between 1960 and 1970, while the rent component increased only 20.1 percent. (The 1970 ratio of rents to all prices fell to .916 of the 1960 ratio.) This experience of relative decreases in rent was widespread, occurring in 22 of the 25 cities reported on by the Bureau of Labor Statistics. Direct observations on low-income rental trends would be useful. However, it can be noted that recent data show vacancy rates on low-rental units average 35 to 70 percent above the rates for all units, supporting the hypothesis of relatively weak low-income demand.[4]

Certain quality measures (persons per room, availability of plumbing facilities, urban population densities) also seem likely to reflect improvement for low-income households when 1970 Census results can be compared with the 1960 figures. Relatively recent Bureau of the Census estimates on housing not meeting specified criteria show marked

confront the landlord:

1. user costs (UC)—heat, janitorial services, other costs of operating
2. fixed costs (FC)—taxes, insurance, etc.
3. normal maintenance (NMC)—offsets to depreciation and obsolescence.

Number of Housing Units (thousands)	Meeting Specified Criteria		Not Meeting Specified Criteria	
	Nonwhites	Whites	Nonwhites	Whites
1960	2,881	41,668	2,263	6,210
1968	5,001	50,991	1,550	3,151
Change				
Number	+2,120	+ 9,323	-713	3,059
Percent	+ 74	+ 22	32	- 49

TABLE 2. Housing Quality Estimates
Source: Bureau of the Census, *Current Population Reports*, P-23, No. 29, "The Social and Economic Status of Negroes in the United States, 1969." Housing "meeting specified criteria" includes "units with all basic plumbing facilities *and* . . . not dilapidated." Ibid., p. 56.

overall gains in housing quality between 1960 and 1968. Table 2 contains an indication of the gains. Finally, the trend to building abandonments and commercial removals from the housing stock hardly seems consistent with a severe shortage interpretation.

With slum owners faced with a contraction in low-income housing demand, and the probable prospects of more in the future, what adjustment responses might be anticipated? I.S. Lowry's analysis of filtering points to the obvious mechanism of undermaintenance and accelerated deterioration. While the point of the Lowry article is to argue that expanding the housing stock would be a fruitless way to improve housing for lower income groups, his analysis can be applied readily to the case of decreasing demand. The critical factor in the analysis is the emergence of "a price-depressing surplus." [5]

A brief restatement of the Lowry analysis may be useful. Three basic costs

The first two costs may be viewed as relatively fixed so long as the units are used to supply housing. The major item of variable cost for Lowry is maintenance. So long as price covers all three costs, a given housing unit can be maintained more or less indefinitely in standard quality condition. But what happens when price falls below $UC + FC + NMC$ (see Figure 1) as occurs after T_1? Reductions will presumably be made in variable maintenance costs, beginning the process of quality erosion. Building abandonment occurs after T_2 when price is no longer sufficient to cover user costs.

The possibility of varying costs in categories 1 and 2 also needs to be taken into account. Janitorial services *can* be reduced; heating provided less abundantly; filth and trash accumulated. *In extremis* taxes can go unpaid on the road to building abandonment. The quickness with which a building can deteriorate, particularly if longer-run prospects

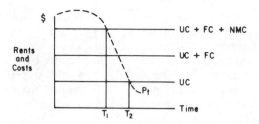

FIGURE 1. Illustration of Rental Housing Costs

are unfavorable, can be effectively documented from the experiences in New York City.

The Lowry analysis is primarily in a framework of stable costs. The upward trend in costs in the past decade also must have played a role in supplier responses, in addition to the downward trend in demand. The supposedly non-variable costs of taxes, insurance, janitorial wages, and implicit opportunity costs of capital all rose substantially more than rents in the 1960s. These types of costs rose 40 percent or more compared with the 20 percent advance in rents.[6] The impact of rising costs has been experienced not only in the privately operated sector of the housing market, but also among public housing authorities. They, too, have been compelled by financial constraints to undermaintain and deteriorate the housing stock.

The influence of cost increases can be introduced into Figure 1 by tilting the several cost schedules upward. This, of course, moves points T_1 and T_2 toward the y-axis in time. Deterioration occurs earlier and at a more rapid pace.

ALTERNATIVES FOR HOUSING IMPROVEMENT

The paradox of improving housing standards and the accompanying deterioration of the standing stock of housing poses an unusually difficult dilemma for central cities. The process of upgrading housing as income improves leaves in its wake newly emerging areas of deterioration and blight. At the same time, numerous higher-income households are crossing the urban frontier to suburbia. The emerging areas of deterioration and blight become the focal points of low-income housing units. Stopping or slowing the escape from poverty might serve to stem the spreading deterioration process; but such is hardly within the power of cities nor an acceptable goal of rational policy. Alternatively, heavily subsidized new units to house low-income families might be pursued with large-scale funding. But traditional low-income units on such lines have come under heavy attack; moreover, by adding to the emergent price-depressing surplus this process seems likely to accelerate the deterioration of the current standing stock.

What are the alternatives for improving the quantity of quality units for low-income households? Five potential approaches can be distinguished: (1) new construction, (2) antideterioration subsidies, (3) direct income subsidies, (4) development of lower-cost construction methods, and (5) demolition. Each of these strategies needs to be evaluated in the context of the housing market processes of shrinking poverty demands and expanding deterioration incentives.

New Construction

The building of many new housing units of current "high quality" standards is the obvious, intuitively appealing approach. It is also expensive; how expensive depends on characteristics of the program adopted. The larger the fraction of new units directed to low-income households, the more expensive the program is likely to be in terms of federal funding requirements. If one sought to eliminate all substandard units, such a program might involve $90 billion to $120 billion of direct construction expense (i.e., excluding land acquisition costs, demolition of existing structures, etc.). These estimates are based on a cost of $20,000 per unit multiplied by the figure of some 4.5 million units derivable from Table 2 and the six million units of low- to moderate-income housing projected in the President's Housing Report.[7] On a ten-year basis these direct costs would involve an annual expenditure rate of $9 billion to $12 billion. This would be enough to eliminate "official" poverty based on 1969 and 1970 estimates of the "aggregate income deficit" of $10.7 billion and $11.4 billion respectively.

This program would not be a one-time effort, for the standing stock would continue to deteriorate and at an accelerated rate. The newly constructed units would also begin to deteriorate with the passage of time. At what rates would new substandard units be produced? The rates would presumably be rather higher than before the construction program began and price-depressing surpluses emerged (or became anticipated). It would be useful to know something about the supply function for deteriorating units.

If the additions to the housing stock were sufficiently rapid to more than offset the accelerated rates of deterioration, somewhat better quality units (on the average) would become available at somewhat lower prices (on the average). But the improvement would not be maintained unless continuous injections of publicly supported new construction were to occur.

Rising incomes would, of course, permit quality improvements to be sustained; but that is because incomes are higher, not that subsidized construction has occurred. With no change in incomes, the preexistent quantity-quality equilibrium would tend to be restored. Net improvement depends on the maintenance of a housing market disequilibrium; and even continuous injections at a steady rate might not be a sufficient condition if deterioration rates were stimulated to expand to a compensating extent. The ultimate logic of repeated public construction programs might even be to eliminate private suppliers altogether, a situation that seems to be at hand in some segments of the New York housing market.

An alternative housing program, less expensive from a public funding viewpoint, might be devised based on new construction subsidies to middle-income families. If, for example, a $2,000 subsidy would stimulate the building of a new unit by a nonpoor household, the same aggregate impact on housing supply might be achieved at one-tenth the public outlay.[8] The stimulus to deterioration via market filtering cannot be avoided, however. The distribution of deterioration may be different, ranging more widely throughout the housing market. If concentrations of deterioration are lessened, perhaps the emergence of newly substandard units may be slowed. But this is all rather speculative in the absence of knowledge about the empirical relationships.

Antideterioration Subsidies

Stemming the rate of housing deterioration through some form of subsidy has a certain appeal given the deterioration-accelerating characteristics of new construction programs. From the viewpoint of central cities, the stopping and reversal of the deterioration of existing units would seem particularly desirable. S. Lebergott, in a provocative article, points to the significant gains that a slowing of the rate of deterioration might accomplish. By lowering the depreciation rate from 5 percent to 3 percent each year "we would add 100,000 units to the stock of acceptable housing."[9] While the validity of this speculative estimate is difficult to judge, there does appear to be considerable merit in his conclusion: "If the housing of the poor is to be improved significantly, therefore, we must keep the stock of low-income housing from sliding downhill at its present rate."[10]

Devising an operational subsidy to encourage the maintenance of existing structures presents a number of complexities. Both demand and supply deterioration are possible. Units used by low-income households may be subject to higher rates of deterioration; and landlords, both private and public, may face financial constraints that promote deterioration. Among the complexities faced by an antideterioration program are the problems of (1) defining the components of quality maintenance, (2) ensuring that subsidies are linked to performance at noninflated prices, and (3) coping with neighborhood effects.

A general subsidy to property owners to maintain "quality" is plagued by the multiple dimensions of the housing quality definition. Four more-or-less distinguishable aspects can be indicated: (1) plumbing and major appliances; (2) aesthetics maintenance (painting, cleanliness, etc.); (3) structural integrity; (4) tenant behavior. Suppose that some sort of maintenance standards can be established for items (1), (2), and (3). To whom should subsidies be extended? From the viewpoint of fiscal efficiency one would like to argue for subsidies (tax relief, incentive payments) for those who would not otherwise maintain their properties. But is there any way of identifying such landlords? Considerable naiveté would be required to accept property-owner declarations of nonintent. Some limitations of the program's scope might be attainable by restricting subsidies to units in which "poor" ten-

ants live. (Under such a restriction landlords might even vie for poverty tenants.)

Lebergott proposes an ingenious incentive plan to reward "good" tenant behavior. "Financial rewards would be given to any public housing tenant who generates less than average maintenance and repair costs. . . . Those who create above average costs could continue to go on their merry way."[11] The proposal is limited to public housing "since private owners know their self-interest,"[12] and Lebergott seems willing to accept the situation that "many private investors have abandoned hope for central-city multiple-unit ownership."[13] Perhaps this is so; but this means a very dreary housing future for the central city. Might not an altering of financial incentives have some impact in altering decisions to abandon the city?

The administrative difficulties of providing subsidies to maintain the existing stock of housing need to be recognized. An administratively easier, but less direct, route might be feasible through an expanded rent supplement program for low-income households. A concern about rent supplements is that they may lead to a bidding up of rents, particularly in the shorter run, without accompanying supplier improvements in housing quality. That quality will *not* improve seems debatable without further evidence. R.S. Muth finds that income has a significant impact in reducing the percentage of substandard housing, reporting implicit income elasticities ranging from -1.77 to -4.6.[14] "In general, a 10 percent increase in the incomes of a family in a given area reduces the fraction of housing units which are poor quality . . . by about a third."[15] While rent supplements do not constitute a general increase in income, there seems to be no reason to anticipate that the market processes that lie behind Muth's findings would not be operative for rent supplements.

The more critical difficulties are two-fold. First, rent supplements, like the general reduction in poverty in the 1960s, may serve to depress further the demand for low-income units, hastening the deterioration of some components of the central city housing stock. Further exodus to the suburbs may also be stimulated, although this trend, if it includes a greater proportion of nonwhite households, may be helpful in any effort to reduce residential segregation. Second, rent subsidies, and specific subsidies more generally, constitute no more than "second best" uses of resources if the basic objective is to alleviate poverty. The question is: Do we want to help housing or households?

Income Subsidies

If the emphasis shifts to eliminating the low incomes of poverty households, the program of appeal for economists ought to be direct income-maintenance transfers. Housing quality can be expected to rise, presuming low-income groups constitute the major component of demand for low-quality housing. As Muth has observed, "there is nothing very novel in an economist's suggesting that poor-quality housing is purchased by low-income households." [16] But he also notes: "Most arguments commonly given . . . ignore the basic cause of poor housing quality, which is the poverty or low-income of its inhabitants." [17]

The obvious criticism of income transfers is that generalized purchasing power can and will be spent on many other things (cars, TV sets, clothes, food, medical care) than housing directly. Such alternative uses of funds, however, may have broader effects in improving the quality of the recipients' lives. It is these broader dimensions that may really matter, or rather their absence, in the decline of neighborhoods and in the attempt to maintain urban housing of stable or improving quality.

Lower-Cost Construction Methods

The benefits of cost reduction in residential construction have long been sought. Whether Operation Breakthrough [18] places us any closer to the achievement of significant cost reductions in urban construction remains to be seen. In a sense a major cost "breakthrough" was achieved in the 1960s with the rapid expansion of mobile homes. The location of these "cheap" units has been largely at the urban periphery on marginal land. Whether they can be stacked, or combined in other ways, to make efficient use of higher-valued central city land is yet to be demonstrated.

The cost breakthrough of mobile homes hardly represents a significant technological step, but rather a shift in consumer acceptance. This underscores an often ignored dimension in urban housing: the insistence on the production of "high quality" new units. The emphasis on middle-class construction standards, as A. Downs points out, effectively limits the number and variety of new housing units that can be produced. [19] The choice of housing to serve low-income families is accordingly circumscribed.

One is almost tempted to argue that the setting of high-quality construction standards is part of the American urban problem. Older housing units wear out in a physical sense at a disconcertingly slow pace. They are expensive to tear down and relegate to the scrap pile. A consequence is that cities become "locked into" historical land use patterns that too readily wear down (but not out) into central city slums. Perhaps the shortest route to lower-cost construction is through the acceptance of cheaper, less durable units.

Demolition

Demolition of unsatisfactory units in cities completes the cataloging of alternatives. While demolition may hardly seem to be a policy unless new units are built to replace those torn down, J.W. Forrester has argued that demolition introduces just the disequilibrium that urban systems need.[20] Otherwise cities cannot avoid the fate of being the center of gravity for the poorest households. The building of new low-income units on vacated land only serves to block the entry of industry into the central city and to reduce measures for population redistribution throughout the SMSA (Standard Metropolitan Statistical Area).

DESEGREGATING HOUSING

Population redistributions within SMSAs are the key to residential desegregation and perhaps even more importantly to job availabilities and to coping with racial imbalance in education. It is easy, although probably not correct, to attribute a large part of the urban housing problem to segregation in housing markets. Segregation in this context means restriction of access to parts of the housing market based on race, *not* on economic criteria. A recent study by this author indicates that economic circumstances may play a considerably larger role in urban white/nonwhite residential patterns than the usual perceptions suggest.[21] The Taeubers, for example, find very high rates of segregation; but their basic index is a faulty measure of segregation.[22]

For the four cities investigated in my research (Chicago; Kalamazoo and Detroit, Michigan; and Rochester, New York) the "results obtained suggest that a minimum of 30 to 50 percent of racial patterns in housing can be attributed to differences in the economic status of households."[23] Economic differences, moreover, are probably understated in this investigation because of the reliance on the 1960 Census data on incomes. A number of factors contribute to the underestimation of white/nonwhite differentials in economic status. Among the factors involved are the underenumeration of nonwhite males of prime labor force age, the exclusion of important property incomes in the reported data, the influence of financial asset accumulations, and the importance of permanent income in housing expenditures.

The role of asset accumulations is an underexplored element in the ability to acquire housing. Since nonwhite households are considerably younger than white households, their expected asset holdings are likely to be significantly smaller. Despite popular illusion to the contrary, nonwhite households exhibit considerably lower rates of car ownership than white households even after households are classified within census income categories. Data on households without cars from the 1960 Census are contained in Table 3. Cars clearly constitute an important complement in the consumption of further-out housing.

Between 1960 and 1969, a rise from 52 percent to 63 percent in the relative income relationship occurred for the income of Negroes and other races as a percent of white income. One might anticipate only a relatively small change in housing desegregation from this improvement if asset holdings are important. Even full equalization of current income flows would not eliminate household wealth differentials. An alternative, less expensive, and perhaps politically more feasible approach than eliminating all differences in economic status might be accomplished by direct subsidies to households living in residentially integrated neighborhoods.

The cost of a "Homesteading Act" for pioneering types of the twentieth century might not be too large relative to projected expenditures for other social welfare/social reform programs. If the four-city 1960 average market segregation coefficients of 10.1 percent for whites and 69.5 percent for nonwhites are applied to 1970 metropolitan area data, the required movement of

Income (in dollars)	Chicago SMSA Whites	Chicago SMSA Nonwhites	Detroit SMSA Whites	Detroit SMSA Nonwhites	Kalamazoo SMSA Whites	Kalamazoo SMSA Nonwhites	Rochester SMSA Whites	Rochester SMSA Nonwhites
Less than 2,000	65.7	79.7	51.6	69.9	41.4	57.9	59.8	72.9
2,000 to 2,999	55.0	75.2	35.2	59.8	20.4	40.3	44.2	62.8
3,000 to 3,999	49.2	60.9	23.8	45.3	19.9	17.8	36.0	56.7
4,000 to 4,999	38.7	50.1	16.3	35.9	7.6	14.9	23.7	47.9
5,000 to 5,999	25.0	41.4	9.4	27.2	4.1	11.8	11.5	32.3
6,000 to 6,999	16.9	37.6	6.2	24.4	3.1	. . . [a]	9.2	17.7
7,000 to 9,999	11.6	31.3	3.4	17.9	4.1	3.6	13.1	17.0
10,000 or more	6.5	22.6	1.8	12.6	0.4	. . .	1.4	10.2

TABLE 3. Percent of Households Lacking Automobiles
[a] . . . = none reported without automobiles in Census household sample.
Source: U.S. Bureau of the Census, *U.S. Census of Housing: 1960*, Volume II, *Metropolitan Housing*, Parts 2, 3, and 5. U.S. Bureau of the Census, unpublished tabulations for Kalamazoo and Rochester.

households to achieve residential desegregation would involve the redirection of approximately 3.5 million white and 3.5 million nonwhite households.

What sort of subsidy might be required to achieve this redistribution of population? $1,000 per household? $2,000? If these are appropriate upper and lower limits, the initiation cost would fall between $7 billion and $14 billion. Or perhaps it could be argued that the costs would be halved, since only one of a pairing of households might need to be induced to move; the household of the other color (whether white or nonwhite) would be "forced" in a "musical-chairs" sense to live in the vacated unit of the moving household. In any event, what seems to be needed is information about the elasticity of prejudice functions. The social returns to such knowledge could be considerable.

NOTES

1. President's Committee on Urban Housing, *A Decent Home* (Washington, D.C.: Government Printing Office, 1968), p. 40.
2. *Report of the National Advisory Commission on Civil Disorders* (Washington, D.C.: Government Printing Office, 1968), p. 257.
3. Ibid., p. 260. Italicized in the original text.
4. U.S. Bureau of the Census, "Housing Vacancies,"

Current Housing Reports, Series H–111 (Washington, D.C.: Government Printing Office, 1970 and 1971 issues).
5. I.S. Lowry, "Filtering and Housing Standards: A Conceptual Analysis," *Land Economics* 36 (November, 1960): 363.
6. The Consumer Price Index categories are suggestive of the extent of the cost increases experienced from 1960 to 1970: property insurance rates, +47.5 percent; house maintenance and repairs, +46.6 percent; mortgage interest rates, +38.6 percent; and property taxes, +39.5 percent (in the seven-year period 1963–70). Opportunity costs of capital rose significantly more than the reported mortgage rate index: Aaa corporate bonds averaged 8.04 percent in 1970 compared with 4.41 percent in 1960, an increase of 82.3 percent over the decade.
7. President's Committee on Urban Housing, *A Decent Home*, p. 3.
8. A program along these lines has been previously suggested: I.H. Welfeld, "Toward a New Federal Housing Policy," *The Public Interest* 19 (Spring, 1970): 31–43; and R. E. Zelder, "Realism in Housing Policy," *Draft Statement to Kalamazoo City Commission*, January, 1970.
9. S. Lebergott, "Slum Housing: A Proposal," *Journal of Political Economy* 78 (November/December, 1970): 1362.
10. Ibid.
11. Ibid.
12. Ibid., p. 1365.
13. Ibid.
14. R. S. Muth, *Cities and Housing* (Chicago: University of Chicago Press, 1969), pp. 199 and 278.
15. _____, "The Economics of Slum Housing," in W. D. Gardner (ed.), *America's Cities* (Ann Arbor: Bureau of Business Research, Michigan Business Papers, no. 54, 1970), p. 28.
16. Muth, *Cities and Housing*, p. 126.
17. Ibid., p. 115.
18. Operation Breakthrough is the federal government's

latest program to introduce new technology into our housing programs and to aggregate markets on a scale that makes it economically feasible for manufacturers to operate plants.

19. A. Downs, "Housing the Urban Poor: The Economics of Various Strategies," *American Economic Review* 59 (September, 1969): 646–51.

20. J. W. Forrester, *Urban Dynamics* (Cambridge: M. I. T. Press, 1969), passim.

21. R. E. Zelder, "Racial Segregation in Urban Housing Markets," *Journal of Regional Science* 10 (April, 1970): 93–105.

22. K. E. Taeuber and A. R. Taeuber, *Negroes in Cities* (Chicago: Aldine Publishing Co., 1965). Conceptual and analytical defects of their segregation index are dealt with in R. E. Zelder, "Residential Desegregation: Can Nothing Be Accomplished?," *Urban Affairs Quarterly* 5 (March, 1970): 265–77.

23. Zelder, "Racial Segregation in Urban Housing Markets." p. 94.

TRANSPORTATION

Overview

Urban Transportation
John R. Meyer

The Metropolitan Transportation Problem
Wilfred Owen

Analysis

Metro: Rapid Transit for Suburban Washington
Willard W. Brittain

The Mobility Problems of the Poor in Indianapolis
Christopher S. Davies and Melvin Albaum

Chicago's Crosstown: A Case Study in Urban Expressways
Elliott Arthur Pavlos

Strategy

Planning for Future Systems
Wilfred Owen

URBAN TRANSPORTATION
JOHN R. MEYER

This general review of the transportation situation in American cities provides a counter to many of the crisis-oriented discussions of the issue. It is argued that automobile-dominated systems are an efficient response to the low density characteristics of the majority of urban areas. Although recognizing that social costs arise in the development of such systems, the prime concept underlying the presentation is that of efficiency rather than equity. As such, it provides a good background against which to contrast the subsequent papers in the section.

Reprinted from Daniel P. Moynihan, ed., *Toward a National Urban Policy* (New York: Basic Books, Inc., 1970), pp. 66–73, by permission of the publisher and the author. Copyright © 1970 by Basic Books, Inc., Publishers New York.

The popular view when discussing urban transportation in American cities today is to decry its sorry state. Newspapers and journals are filled with talk of an "urban transportation crisis," of the "difficulties of getting from here to there," and so on at great length. Matters are reported to be getting worse—and very quickly. Everyone has his own favorite traumatic experience to report: of the occasion when many of the switches froze on New York's commuter railroads; of the sneak snowstorm in Boston that converted thirty-minute commuter trips into seven hour ordeals; of the New York transit strike of January 1966 that converted Manhattan Island into a traffic nightmare; of the extreme difficulties in Chicago and other Midwestern cities when some particularly heavy and successive snowstorms were endured.

There is, of course, always some danger in generalizing on the basis of casual observation or the isolated experience. Urban transportation is no exception. Thus, when one compares actual figures on the performance of urban transportation systems in the United States today and yesterday, one generally discovers some slow but steady improvement. The numbers are few and scanty but nevertheless systematically point toward a better situation now than previously. Data on the time required to travel between two points in American cities during rush hours today and, say, ten or fifteen years ago almost invariably suggest that the time required to make a trip has decreased slightly, usually in the vicinity of 10 to 20 percent. Or, alternatively, the average highway vehicle speed during rush hours in the central parts of American cities has slowly but surely climbed upward over the last ten years from approximately 15 to 25 miles an hour to somewhere in the vicinity of 25 to 30 miles per hour or slightly more. Needless to say, the figures vary widely from one set of circumstances to another. Moreover, there are some isolated but important cases where there has been deterioration, either in service levels or in actual performance.

That some improvement has occurred is hardly surprising. Americans have been spending a good deal of money recently to improve their urban transportation systems. First, they have made large private investments in automobiles: since 1945 the number of passenger cars registered in the United States has increased from just under 26 million to well over 70 million. Billions of dollars have also been invested by federal, state, and local governments in new highways, the current rate of expenditure being about 3 billion dollars per year on urban highways alone. Transit systems have also been improved. For example, the total number of buses registered in the U.S. has increased from approximately 112,000 in 1945 to over 150,000 today. Some extensions and improvements have also been made in rail mass transit systems. About the only major deterioration in urban transportation facilities in American cities in the postwar period has been of rail commuter trains, which provide high-performance express services between central business districts and suburban communities.

Improved speeds should not, however, be confused with any shortening of the time required to perform a typical commuter trip in American cities. Actually, on the basis of limited data available, the time required for the typical or average commuter trips seems to have remained more or less constant. The explanation, of course, is that the distance of the average commuter trip is longer today than it was a few years ago. This lengthening of commuter trips reflects an increasing tendency of Americans to live relatively more in single-family dwellings in the suburbs and less in multiple-family or apartment house dwellings in the central city. This choice of single-family dwellings means that Americans live at lower residential densities and, as long as everything else remains equal, must commute a great distance to reach their jobs.

Actually, not everything else has remained equal. In particular, workplaces have also dispersed to a considerable extent in American cities. On the whole, this dispersal has meant a removal of jobs from central business districts or urban core areas to the suburbs. This dispersal of jobs toward suburban locations has tended to offset some effects of the residential dispersal, making it possible for many workers to find the kind of housing they seek while living closer to their jobs. Nevertheless, these locational trends, dispersal of workplaces and jobs, have not been completely offsetting. The typical trip to work is clearly of somewhat greater distance in the American city now than ten years or so ago and just sufficiently longer, seemingly, to offset whatever slight improvement has been made in the performance speed of urban commuter transport.

One reason, then, for the talk of an urban transportation crisis in the United States today perhaps lies in a failure to meet anticipations. Many commuters expected to reduce their commuting times as systems improved, but instead found themselves barely able to maintain the status quo in terms of time requirements. Another reason for talk of crisis, almost certainly, is that the rate of improvement in the performance of urban transportation systems during rush hours has been markedly inferior to that experienced during off-peak hours. Specifically, the ability to move quickly about American cities during nonrush hours has improved in a truly phenomenal fashion. Using limited-access urban expressways, or freeways as they are called in the Western part of the United States, one can easily achieve speeds of 55 miles an hour or more.

It is, of course, an exhilarating experience to move through a congested urban area at such speed, with relative safety and comfort. The contrast between these high-performance speeds during nonrush hours and the relatively slow 25 to 30 miles an hour experienced during peak commuter periods can be disheartening. Quite humanly, the commuter would like to duplicate his off-peak speeds and experiences. The difficulty is that to accommodate these wishes, particularly if most commuters decide to go individually in private automobiles, would require a truly remarkable amount of highway capacity. While there has been a good deal of loose talk about how paved-over American cities are or have become, accommodation of most commuter needs by private automobile at high speed would require new expressway construction in or near central business districts that would pale previous efforts.

Otherwise, the automobile and the urban expressway generally economize on land requirements for transport purposes in urban areas. A common fallacy is to believe that reliance upon private automobiles as the basic mode of urban transportation necessarily results in a higher percentage of urban land being allocated to street and highway use.

Perspective can be obtained on land use requirements for transportation by looking at the entire urban area, including residential neighborhoods. In the over-all picture, the major land needs for highways and streets are attributable to local streets. Moreover, good local street access is required for police and fire protection, sanitation, local deliveries, and so forth, however one decides to organize the longer distance commuter transportation system. Local streets can require from 15 percent or so of total land in a residential area to as much as 30 to 35 percent. In American cities the lower percentages for local streets have been achieved in newer residential areas built on the premise that most households would have an automobile to serve their transportation requirements. Under such circumstances, long rectangular blocks can be used which economize on the total amount of land allocated to streets. By contrast, in the denser neighborhoods of older cit-

ies, where it is expected that most people must walk to and use public transportation, smaller, square blocks are typical. In these neighborhoods streets can account for as much as 30 or even 40 percent of total land use. Of course, residential densities will also be higher in these communities as a rule, so that these older cities remain relatively more compact than the newer, highway-oriented cities.

Major arterial highways, freeways, and expressways generally require relatively small amounts of land. Even in Los Angeles, which has what is probably the most ambitious and fully developed expressway system in the United States, the total space required for the freeway system when it is completed will be only about 2 to 3 percent of the entire land area of the city. One can dispute and debate about the specific amounts of land required for expressway systems, but rarely should the total amount of land for high-performance highway systems exceed three percent of total land or about one-sixth or one-seventh of the land required for local access streets. The total land requirement for all kinds of streets and highways in urban areas, therefore, is likely to run between 20 and 35 percent of total available land. Again, the lower percentage is far more likely to be achieved where the street design is specifically laid out on the premise of widespread auto ownership. Not only can more efficient block layouts be achieved under such a premise, but it should also be noted that high-performance expressways or freeways tend to move many more cars per hour per unit of space than lower performance facilities. That is, specialization of highway facilities achieves economies in land use.

There are other ways in which highways and highway vehicles represent an efficient adaptation to American circumstances. Specifically, under United States cost conditions, it is rather difficult to design a good public transit service at low cost except where very large volumes of people move along a common corridor. At corridor volumes of approximately 5,000 to 7,000 per hour or less and equivalent levels of service, public transit costs will be approximately equal to private automobile costs. Even then, only a bus transit system would be cost competitive with the automobile at such volumes. Generally speaking, a rail transit system becomes as low in cost as a bus system only at volumes of 18,000 to 20,000 people or more per rush hour along a corridor. Only New York and Chicago have transit corridors that record volumes much in excess of 25,000 per hour, and only Boston and Philadelphia have corridors that approach the 20,000 to 25,000 volume range per hour. With dispersal of jobs and residences, of course, there are many commuter trips increasingly performed along corridors with very low volumes, well under the 5,000 or so required to equalize public transit and automobile costs of equivalent services.

Private automobile transport in the United States derives some advantages from labor and capital costs, as well as from reduced residential and workplace densities. Specifically, automobile commuting is essentially a "do-it-yourself" activity. It requires little or no hired operating labor. The public transit system, on the other hand, usually does need hired operating labor. Therefore, it is rather in the position of the domestic servant in American society competing against washing machines, electric dishwashers, vacuum cleaners, and other consumer durables. The automobile, in short, is in keeping with the American pattern of responding to ever higher labor costs by substituting one's own labor and capital (in the form of consumer durables) for hired labor.

While the automobile, complemented by public transit buses, is probably a fairly efficient accommodation to urban transportation requirements in many if not most American cities, it carries with it many dislocations and traumas. In particular, efficient use of automobiles and other highway vehicles in many older American cities requires that large high-performance highways be built right into and through already heavily populated central areas. This, of course, means that many people and workplaces must be displaced to make room for the new highway construction. Though these new highways may require only a small percentage of total space in the city, this does not lessen the impact on those who are forced to leave their homes and relocate their businesses because of the highway construction. Thus, though the construction of these new highway facilities may be broadly justified by the gains to society as a whole, it is quite clear that the incidence of cost and trauma on those individuals who are displaced can be very high indeed. Unfortunately, American society has not yet developed adequate mechanisms for compensating these individuals.

Often, other social costs are also incurred because of new highway construction. For example, highway engineers have found that it sometimes reduces local community objections if they can find routes that minimize the number of houses that must be taken for construction of new highways. Furthermore, the total cost of the whole enterprise can sometimes be reduced if one can keep the highway in open and unoccupied land that is already in the public domain. An unoccupied urban area in the public domain well describes a public park, and so there has been a certain attraction on the part of highway builders for routing new urban expressways through and around the fringes of park lands. The difficulty, of course, is that reduction of available park and playground space tends to reduce the amenities of urban living in important ways. Thus, if the highway builder attempts to avoid household and workplace displacement by staying away from built-up congested areas, he in turn very often imposes a new kind of social cost on the society.

Sometimes, too, highway builders have shown a remarkable insensitivity to other urban needs and requirements. For example, they have been known to build urban expressways and interchanges to the same specifications used in rural areas. This usually means that a great deal of land is consumed for interchanges, median strips, and other highway embellishments which on close calculation might not be strictly necessary or even terribly functional in urban areas. When one considers the additional fact that most urban trips are relatively short, well under ten miles, it is not entirely clear that very much is gained by designing urban highways to sustain peak-performance speeds of 60 or even 70 miles per hour as opposed to only 40 or 50 miles per hour.

New expressways may often be rather poorly located as well. For example, some new facilities have divided what were previously relatively homogeneous and well articulated communities. A badly placed highway can thus disrupt community life in an unfortunate way. On the other hand, the construction of new high-performance highway facilities also drains traffic off neighboring parallel streets, so that some offset is achieved in the sense that the older streets become safer and less traversed.

Still another difficulty is that under certain climatic and topological conditions, (such as those found in Los Angeles, Salt Lake City, and a few other American cities) highway vehicles can create a most offensive and dangerous smog. Indeed, smog nuisances have been created even under relatively conventional North American climatic and topological conditions. Smog control devices and programs to reduce these

hazards are therefore under development. Some considerable progress has been made, but there is still much to be done. It should be observed that Europeans may never encounter quite these same difficulties, since European cars tend to be smaller and burn less fuel; smog created by operation of a vehicle is not strictly proportional to horsepower, but reduction of total horsepower does alleviate the problem.

Safety and noise problems can also be created by automobiles and new urban expressways. Here, however, the picture is somewhat more complex. For example, other things being equal, high-performance expressways reduce pedestrian deaths caused by automobiles in urban areas. In general, high-performance limited-access expressways tend to have a relatively good safety record in terms of accidents per million miles of travel when compared with conventional streets or highways. On the other hand, high-performance expressways are likely to increase the total miles traveled and the speed at which those miles are traveled. Similarly, there are pluses and minuses on the noise problem attached to use of automobiles or trucks in place of horsedrawn or other vehicles or the use of high-performance expressways in lieu of conventional streets and highways.

The preceding discussion has obviously concentrated on the highway and the automobile as major modes of urban transportation in the United States today. Such a concentration is easy to justify. About 64 percent of American commuter or work trips are made in private automobiles. Another 14 percent or so are performed entirely by buses on highways. Rail transit and walking account for only about 10 percent each. For other trips, that is for shopping, recreation, and personal business, the automobile is even more dominant. Thus, as even the casual observer of the American urban scene quickly recognizes, the automobile is certainly a fixture, at least for the moment.

And as the previous discussion suggests, the reasons are not hard to find. The automobile, though a noisy, smelly, and somewhat unsafe monster, is also a highly efficient transportation mode given the lower residential densities, increasingly dispersed workplaces, higher labor costs, and relatively low capital costs that characterize the American scene. The real question about urban transportation in the United States today is whether we will have the good sense, self-discipline, and social organization to mitigate the many bad effects of the automobile while still retaining its many advantages.

THE METROPOLITAN
TRANSPORTATION PROBLEM
WILFRED OWEN

Owen provides a gloomy contrast to Meyer. He does not believe that highway expansion has kept pace with needs, particularly when one considers the enormous concentration of flows within narrowly-defined peak-hour periods. More important in his perspective, however, is the rapid deterioration in mass transit systems. Faced with increasing costs and declining patronage, they are unable to provide adequate service either in low density suburbs or in the central city where the deterioration is hardest felt by the poor and the aged. The fundamental conflict is between the economic survival of the carriers and the interest of the community in the availability of service.

Reprinted from Wilfred Owen, *The Metropolitan Transportation Problem,* 2nd ed. (Washington, D.C.: The Brookings Institution, 1966), pp. 210–25, by permission of the publisher and the author. Copyright © 1956, 1966 by The Brookings Institution. This is an edited version of the original publication.

America's cities and their sprawling suburbs have been unable to adapt effectively to the revolutionary changes in transportation that have made us a nation on wheels. Expansion of automotive transportation has outstripped the provision of highway and terminal facilities and created conditions of congestion that have become a serious threat to the urban economy. At the same time public transportation has suffered from declining patronage and changing conditions of use that have resulted in financial embarrassment and deteriorating standards of service. Along with this failure of the urban transportation system to meet the needs of modern communities, the possibilities of influencing transportation demand to bring it more nearly into balance with the supply of facilities have been almost completely overlooked. As a result we find the underlying causes of congestion multiplying more rapidly than measures for the relief of congestion can be applied. It is clear that a new approach will be necessary if there is to be any real progress toward solution.

THE PRESENT DRIFT

Moving in the morning and evening rush hours has been found to be the most critical transportation problem in American communities. It has been noted that the great surge of commuter movement between city and suburb has dictated the extraordinary physical requirements of the transportation system and imposed on the urban resident some of the most exasperating conditions of urban life.

For millions of families the principal rush-hour transportation problem is transit. Antiquated equipment, overcrowded vehicles, and slow service are the common complaints of the rider. Rising costs, traffic congestion, and a continuing loss of business are the common burdens of the industry. Patronage is down to the levels of nearly a half century ago despite the tremendous growth of population and industrial employment in the urban communities of the nation.

The prospects for radical improvement in the current situation—either for the transit passenger or the transit operator—are not promising. Many transit lines have ceased operations altogether; others are on the verge of bankruptcy. Where the financial position of transit is good, it is generally because standards of service are poor. The difficulty of handling commuter peak loads makes adequate service virtually impossible. The task of providing mass transportation that is satisfactory to the user and at the same time profitable to the company poses a major conflict that present policies have tended to accentuate rather than to solve.

The key to the troubles of transit is the progressive worsening of peak-hour problems. Heavy peak loads in the morning and evening rush have remained close to the prewar level, and loss of business has been concentrated in off-peak hours. This means that the decline in transit business has not permitted parallel reductions in cost. Capacity that is idle most of the day must be retained to serve the peak. The resulting feast or famine that typifies transit operations threatens the industry with bankruptcy.

In addition to off-peak hours, public transportation must cope with off-peak days. The postwar period that brought a five-day week means that business is now bad for transit on Saturdays as well as Sundays and holidays. On these days, as in the evenings, transit is being deserted for the automobile, which provides a superior service for the social and recreational trips that, aside from the journey to work, make up the bulk of urban travel.

Along with unprofitable hours and unprofitable days, public carriers also have the problem of profitless routes. Public pressure has forced transit companies to serve the new suburbs where population is spread so thin that on many routes business is too light to pay operating costs. But public pressure demands that the service be provided. The fundamental conflict is between the interest of the carriers in economic survival and the interest of the community in the availability of service.

Rapid transit and commuter railroads have been especially vulnerable to the problems of the mass transportation industry and its patrons. Neither rail lines nor terminals are located where people live or work. While the motor vehicle can take to the road to follow the migration to the suburbs, transportation by rail has been unable to cover the vast new areas of urban growth that have filled in the spaces between the steel radials of an earlier age.

In the face of these difficulties the inclination of the urban resident has been to escape by automobile; but the attempt has met with less than complete success. The combination of transit difficulties and the shortcomings of highway and parking policies has created a serious dilemma for the American community. The urban resident who seeks relief by shifting from unsatisfactory mass transportation to the automobile is confronted by the equally unsatisfactory alternative of trying to drive on congested highways. Loss of patronage has added to the disabilities of transit, while increased auto use has compounded the frustrations of driving.

The dangerous implications of these trends for the future of the city have inspired no remedial actions commensurate with the problem. It has been shown that revisions in public policy may ease the burden on mass transportation, that transit management is in many instances making progress toward better service, and that expressway developments are providing relief in many areas. But there is little evidence of the all-out attack on the transportation system that could reverse the drift toward transport deterioration and the ultimate crippling of the urban economy.

METRO: RAPID TRANSIT
FOR SUBURBAN WASHINGTON
WILLARD W. BRITTAIN

Increasing public pressure has led many metropolitan governments to focus more attention on the improvement of public transit systems. However, although ostensibly created to benefit the less affluent members of the community, political biases in the system frequently lead to disproportionately large benefits for those whose need is least. The Washington experience provides an example of such a situation.

Reprinted from David M. Gordon, ed., *Problems in Political Economy: An Urban Perspective* (Lexington, Mass.: Lexington Books, D.C. Heath and Company, 1971), pp. 439–43, by permission of the publisher.

It has been recognized that many American cities need radically improved public transit facilities. As automobile traffic increases, downtown congestion and pollution become unbearable. As central city populations become more concentrated with the poor and the aged—those unable to afford cars—and as employment continues to move to the suburbs, many central city residents find it more and more difficult to travel to the suburban jobs.

Washington, D.C. has been suffering acutely from this syndrome of intra-urban transportation problems. Its central city population is now 70 percent black, much of it poor. Its predominantly white suburbs have been growing rapidly since the 1950s.[1] Employment has been decentralizing at an accelerating pace, and the federal government itself has been joining the exodus in recent years.[2] Increasingly, Washington's central city residents are those most in need of rapid transit. They have the fewest cars, they have to travel farthest to work, and they suffer most from rapidly increasing fares caused by the area's presently inefficient system.

The Washington metropolitan area is finally going to have a rapid transit system. Construction has started on a 98-mile system called Metro, which will extend into suburban counties in Maryland and Virginia.[3] Metro has its own authority, the Washington Metropolitan Area Transit Authority (WMATA), and by the time the system is finished, it will cost roughly $2.5 billion. Along with the new system in San Francisco, Metro has been hailed as the latest panacea for metropolitan transportation problems. It will be modern, cheap, accessible and efficient, its planners say. It has the personal blessing of President Nixon, and many consider it the most masterful plan for the city since L'Enfant's original design. Its economic planners predict that the Washington area, because of its unique characteristics, will benefit more from Metro than other cities have from their own rapid transit systems. In their own "money talks" language, they predict: "For every local dollar invested in the system, approximately $9.40 would be returned in quantifiable benefits by 2020."[4]

With all its attendant fanfare, Metro provides an interesting test of the biases of Washington's political structure.

Washington's central city residents, because they need better transportation the most, should receive a disproportionate share of the benefits from the Metro system. Its planners acknowledge this argument; indeed according to the cost assignments, they contend that the District will clearly benefit most from Metro. But contention does not create reality. In fact, the structure of power in the Washington metropolitan area, and the District's own political powerlessness, is producing a rapid transit system which will principally serve the suburbs. It will assign the District the largest share of its costs and return to District residents the smallest share of the benefits. In doing so, Metro's biases will simply complement those of Washington's other public services.

QUANTIFIABLE BENEFITS

The economic measurements for the Metro system were made by a consulting firm, Development Research Associates.[5] They quantified benefits for the entire system, including the District, the five participating jurisdictions from Virginia and the two participating jurisdictions from Maryland. With their formulae they intended to reflect the distribution of putative benefits from the system in 1990, with the implicit assumption that those who benefit should pay their fair share of the costs. WMATA, however, suggested an allocation formula based on relative populations (weighted 15 percent), relative ridership (15 percent), level of service per jurisdiction (30 percent) and the amount of construction per jurisdiction (40 percent). According to their figures, the relative shares of costs produced by this formula would closely reflect the relative ridership projected for the system and therefore, they argued, represented a reasonable basis for assigning costs. In 1990, the District was expected to have 34.2 percent of Metro riders, Maryland

37.1 percent and Virginia 28.7 percent. The WMATA finally agreed on a similar allocation of costs: the District would bear 37.73 percent of the total costs to the local areas, Maryland 34.35 percent and Virginia 27.91 percent. Although the District was expected to have a smaller population than the suburbs by 1990, its large share of the costs was justified by its projected ridership and by its heavy share of construction (on the assumption that construction provides jobs and a boost to the local economy).

At the same time, however, Development Research Associates was suggesting a very different basis on which to estimate benefits from the system. Quite correctly, they argued that the real monetary benefits would accrue from the system in categories like the following: cost savings to those who would ride the system, time savings to those who would ride the system, time savings to commuters who continued to drive but could travel more quickly as a result of less congestion, and parking cost savings to peak period commuters. In calculating their estimate of the 9.4:1 benefit-cost ratio for the entire system, they used a very sophisticated set of calculations developing these categories into an aggregate estimate of the benefits. Table 1 presents their calculations of total benefits from the system for all jurisdictions annually by 1990.

And yet, although they clearly felt that these categories most accurately reflected the potential benefits of the system, they did not try to use these categories to calculate a disaggregated set of benefit estimates *by jurisdiction,* to help in making an equitable allocation of system costs. Nowhere in the proliferation of literature commissioned by the transit authority did any disaggregation of these benefits by jurisdiction appear. Because I was interested in the real benefits District residents could expect to receive from the system, I used the categories of Table 1, the same formulae

a. Time savings to those who use public transit now and will continue to do so in the new system	$82,920,600
b. Auto drivers and passengers diverted to the Metro system	
1. Time savings to peak period commuters	11,130,000
2. Operating costs savings	11,638,700
3. Parking costs savings to peak period commuters	15,441,100
4. Insurance costs savings to commuters	2,177,700
5. Additional vehicle savings	17,908,400
c. Non-diverted peak period motorists	36,750,000
d. Business community	
1. Trucking industry (time savings and operating costs savings because of less congestion)	4,620,000
2. Suburban employers (they will no longer have to provide parking spaces for those who use the Metro system to get to work)	3,484,000

TABLE 1. Annual Benefits by 1990 (In 1968 Constant Dollars)

and methods for estimation, and developed my own estimates of benefits separately for each jurisdiction. I used separate ridership forecasts, car ownership data, and income figures for each jurisdiction. Making some reasonable assumptions about the value of time to riders in the different jurisdictions, I derived estimates of the absolute dollar and relative benefits annually by 1990 for the separate political units. In the context of cost allocation, the most important estimates were those for the District, the Maryland suburbs as a whole, and the Virginia suburbs as a whole.

Table 2 presents those estimates and compares them to the relative share of costs assigned by the transit authority, based on the much different, much less relevant formula for benefit estimates described above.

	$ Benefits	% of Annual Benefits by 1990	Assigned % of Net Project Costs
D.C.	37,214,000	20%	37.73%
Md.	87,313,840	48%	34.35%
Va.	59,542,560	32%	27.91%

TABLE 2

It becomes clear from Table 2 why the authority's literature did not present such disaggregated benefit estimates for the system; they document the substantial bias of the system against the District, in favor of the suburbs. The transit authority admitted that they picked the final categories and weights for the cost allocation formula because they were "acceptable" to all the jurisdictions involved. With the right hand they were trying to justify cost allocation on the basis of theoretical equity and objective calculation. With the left they were acknowledging that their decisions were determined by political expediency. As a result the District residents who need the system most are receiving the fewest benefits at the greatest cost.

Evidently, the District was the victim of coalition politics by the suburban jurisdictions. They had the power and the District had almost none. The District's "mayor" and the city council are appointed by the President subject to Congressional approval. Congress must also approve the District's annual budget. In five of the seven participating suburban jurisdictions referenda were necessary to approve bond issues for their share of Metro costs. In the other two suburban areas the power to issue bonds is in the hands of the city or county council who are elected directly by the residents. In both places rapid transit was an election issue. The only political process open to D.C. residents for expressing their views on Metro was testimony before Congress, since D.C. does not have the power to raise bond issues itself. The testimony could obviously not reflect public opinion with the accuracy of the referenda or mandates in the suburbs. Congressional approval was necessary in order for D.C. to borrow money at 6 percent interest to finance its share of Metro costs. Whether or not D.C. should have a rapid transit system and even how much it should pay for it were questions decided directly by the U.S. Congress —in which the District has no representatives.

The federal government has tax exempt status for property which amounts to 43.3 percent of all taxable property in D.C. The federal government does, however, make a payment to the city which for 1969 amounted to 90 million dollars—approximately 18 percent of D.C.'s total revenue. The District's payments to the transit authority and the debt service payments to the treasury will come out of revenue raised directly by the District government (except as money from the 18 percent federal share is used for this purpose). To the extent that the District's taxes are regressive, the heaviest relative burden of the city's overpayment for Metro will fall on the poor. In fact, the inherently regressive property tax is the largest source of revenue. The next largest tax is a sales and gross receipts tax, followed by an individual income tax.

NON-QUANTIFIABLE BENEFITS
In order to justify the inequitable allocation of costs among the political jurisdictions one must have much faith in the non-quantifiable benefits of Metro. In particular, poor black residents of the District must have faith in this class of benefits because their incomes and the public services provided to them will be relatively affected by most. "Many of the major, and possibly most important, benefits resulting from the implementation of the regional rail system are those which cannot be measured. Aside from the purely economic impact . . . rapid rail transit will have broad positive implications for the social environment and overall well-being of the Washington area." [6] The non-quantifiable benefits hypothesized by Development Research Associates are:

1. The reduction of air pollution.
2. Improved transportation for the young and aged.
3. The facilitation of decentralization while maintaining downtown viability.
4. The provision of accessibility to employment opportunities for disadvantaged inner-city residents.

There is much doubt about the real significance of these benefits. It is my contention that the downtown area will remain the important hub of the metropolitan area for a long time, but that Metro will not contribute significantly enough to downtown business and employment growth for District revenues to outdistance the fast expanding need for a larger tax base. Supposedly those industries with the need for much face-to-face communication will remain behind. But already insurance companies, financial institutions, and other service industries have large enclaves in the Washington suburbs, providing the attraction of location economies to new firms or those about to move. Of course the largest single employer in the city is the federal government. Within the last few years several agencies have moved into the suburbs; community protests were necessary to forestall the planned move of the largest employer of semi-skilled workers in the area (the Government Printing Office) to the suburbs.

Metro will enable many already employed central city residents to follow their jobs to the suburbs but increased accessibility alone will not help appreciably in solving the problems of unemployment and underemployment. The job market expansion exists in the suburbs, but the "type of jobs created will not match the skills of the unemployed and the underemployed in the area," according to an independent labor supply and demand study.[7] The heralded reverse commuting services of Metro will provide access for the most part to jobs to be filled by people moving into the Washington area, or by the new influx of people who commute into the SMSA. The real importance of Metro may lie in employment generated by its construction if minority hiring and training practices can be guaranteed. Experiences so far in this aspect of Metro have not been auspicious.

CONCLUSION

Theoretically, Metro could be of real significance for poor black people in the District of Columbia, those most in need of a rapid transit system. This will not be the case, however, as the largest share of the benefits from Metro has been directed to the suburbs by a political structure in which the District of Columbia has virtually no political autonomy. Fur-

thermore, the benefits to be realized by District residents do not align with the costs assigned them by a transit authority dominated by suburban members. The poor residents of the District are being asked to expect the non-quantifiable benefits of Metro to "breathe new life into the District of Columbia"—non-quantifiable benefits which are doubtful at best.

NOTES

1. Between 1950 and 1970 annual population growth averaged 11.1 percent in the Maryland suburbs, 10.9 percent in the Virginia suburbs, and 2 percent in the District.
2. Retail employment in the Maryland and Virginia suburbs is fast surpassing that in the District. (*Washington Metropolitan Area Statistics*, pp. 56–60.) Federal employment increased between 1960 and 1968 by 39 percent in D.C., 133 percent in the Virginia suburbs, and 78 percent in the Maryland suburbs.
3. The jurisdictions participating in the Metro project in Virginia are Alexandria City, Arlington County, Fairfax County, Fairfax City, and Falls Church City. In Maryland they are Montgomery County and Prince Georges County. The other participating jurisdiction is the District of Columbia.
4. This particular ratio is valid if we consider only the local cost of the project. See *Benefits to the Washington Metropolitan Area from the Adopted Regional System* (Washington, D.C.: Development Research Associates, October, 1958), p. 5.
5. Ibid.
6. Ibid., p. 3.
7. Hammer, Greene, Siler Associates, *Labor Force Supply and Demand in Metropolitan Washington*, Washington, D.C., 1968, pp. 60–61.

THE MOBILITY PROBLEMS
OF THE POOR
IN INDIANAPOLIS
CHRISTOPHER S. DAVIES
MELVIN ALBAUM

The separation of jobs and residences as a result of continuing suburbanization of business and industry has been a major problem for the urban poor in the post-war era. This paper provides an in-depth analysis of the extent of this separation and a formulation of the type of public transit system required to alleviate the problem.

Reprinted from *Antipode Monographs in Social Geography*, No. 1 (1972): 67–87, by permission of the publisher and the authors. This is an edited version of the original publication. Notes and artwork have been renumbered.

Reverse commuters are those individuals whose journey to work entails a trip from a central city residence to a job located in the suburbs. Barriers resulting from an increasing distance between low income, inner city residents and de-centralizing work place locations have created a reverse commuter problem. Interrelationships between metropolitan changes in job locations and residences, and deficiencies in public transit systems have been found to adversely affect the employment opportunities of the inner city poor.[1] Together with poor educational attainment, skill deficiencies, low motivation and discriminatory hiring practices, the reverse commuter transit problem has been offered as an additional causal factor behind the high unemployment levels of low income, inner city groups.

This paper focuses upon the reverse commuter transit problem in Indianapolis where central city unemployment is a major problem.[2] The Indianapolis Manpower Coordinating Committee found that, ". . . many of the unemployed and underemployed groups could qualify for current job openings if they had transportation available on either a personal or public basis. The locations of many major industrial plants are far removed from the target areas [poverty pockets] and many of them have no adequate public transportation facilities."[3] The major complaints recorded by the Transportation Task Force Committee of Indianapolis were inadequate service to a specific location, lack of night and early morning service, the inconvenience of downtown transfers and inadequate protection.[4]

This paper first investigates relationships among residential segregation, decentralizing job opportunities and deficiencies in public transit and the job distribution of low skilled motorized and non-motorized workers in Indianapolis. A second objective is to examine how effective the Indianapolis Public Transit System is in serving the employment needs of the disadvantaged. The third objective is to suggest how present transit services can be restructured or supplemented to provide solutions to the reverse commuter transit problem.

Ultimate solutions to the problems of central city dwellers will depend upon the effectiveness of long-range programs for education and health, residential desegregation, and elimination of discriminatory hiring practices. In the meantime, short-term programs can be designed to supplement these long-term goals. The major objective of this paper is to outline in detail one such short-run strategy. This strategy is designed to link ghetto dwellers with suburban job locations.

DATA SOURCE

Eleven poverty pockets are delineated around Monument Circle on the bases of housing quality, unemployment, income, health and welfare measures (see Figure 1).[5] The Indianapolis Employment Security Division (IESD) located an Employment Outreach Center in each of these eleven target areas for the purpose of job placement.

A complete record of personal information was taken on 4,840 job seekers who filed Employment Security 511Y (ES-511Y) job application forms in each of the Outreach Centers between August 1967 and October 1968. This is the target population used in this study. Social data registered for this population includes race,[6] age, education, marital status, sex, household size, recentness of residence, work experience and present residence. The economic data records the applicant's mode of transit for the journey to work; his labor force status; whether a school dropout in the past six months, six to twelve months, or over twelve months; the location, wage rate and period worked for each of his last three jobs; and, finally his occupational code.

The individuals who make up the sampled population can generally be considered "disadvantaged persons" as the term is used in connection with all programs under the jurisdiction of the

Manpower Administration.[7] A disadvantaged person is defined as one who is unemployed, underemployed or hindered from seeking work; and who is either (1) a school dropout, (2) a member of a minority group, (3) under 22 years of age, (4) 45 or more years old, or (5) physically handicapped.

The remaining data on the spatial distribution of low skilled basic entry jobs are obtained from the Closed Job Order files of the IESD's Commercial and Professional and Industrial Sector.

RESIDENTIAL SEGREGATION

Indianapolis exhibits two residential processes common to U.S. cities today: the exodus of middle and upper income whites to the suburbs and the influx of a poor, principally black population to areas in the central city.[8] Low income white and black inner city residents, through socioeconomic and attitudinal segregation, are residentially confined to specific areas of older housing in the city. Restrictive forms of residential zoning ordinances, house purchasing covenants and white hostility to black residential encroachment create segregated black housing patterns in Indianapolis (see Figure 2).[9] The housing market accessible to blacks has been tightened through the construction of the inner loop freeway system, Indiana University expansion and urban renewal which together dislocated 7,800 families between 1964 and 1970.[10] Black relocation into white neighborhoods distant from all-black areas has been less than one percent of all black residential moves during this period.[11] While these forces restricted the development of new black housing units, black income rose and the total population of young black adults sharply increased. As a consequence, there exists a repressed net demand for 5,000 standard housing units. Black persons per household increased from an estimated figure of 3.54 for 1960, to 3.63

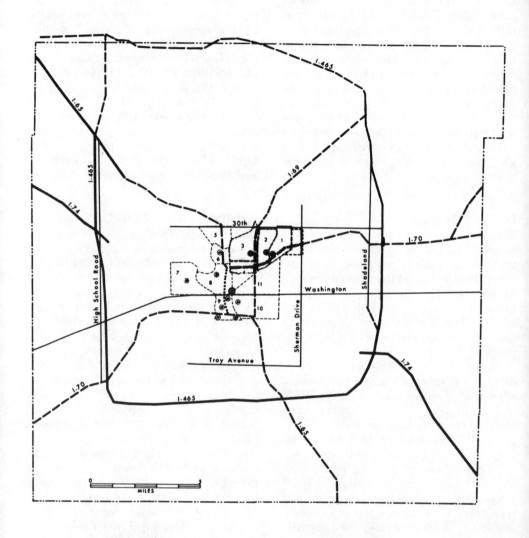

FIGURE 1. Indianapolis Target Areas and Inner Loop Freeway Plan
Base Map furnished by Metropolitan Planning Department, Marion County, Indiana

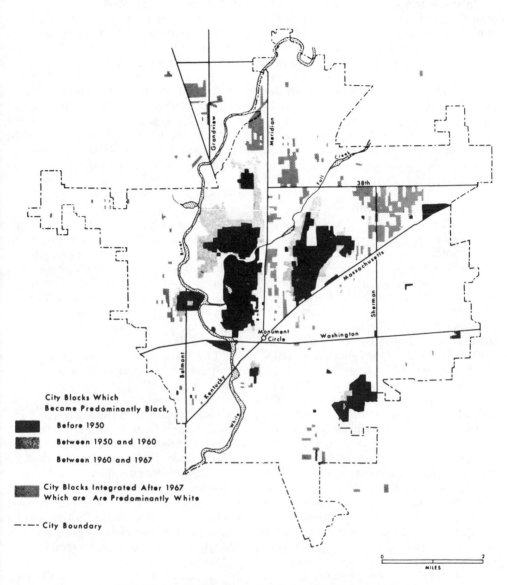

FIGURE 2. Black Residential Areas in Indianapolis
Source: Indiana Civil Rights Commission, 1967

for 1967. During the same time period white household size decreased from 3.18 to 3.00 persons per household.[12]

In these low income areas the "extended" rather than the "nuclear" family of the suburbs is found. Close-knit neighborhoods centered around local stores, church, tavern and pool hall are evident. The carless poor satisfy the majority of their social needs within the narrow confines of these poverty pockets. They generate shorter work, shopping and recreational trips than suburbanites and their limited movement has been found to reduce their motivation to seek improved positions of employment.[13]

The exodus of middle and upper income whites to the suburbs is primarily a result of the flight from the external diseconomies associated with the low wealth, higher expenditures and higher property taxes of central city jurisdictions. This movement has made inaccessible what was previously an important, if menial, source of basic entry jobs for black female domestics and male yard workers. Further, the shopping malls which are accompanying this outward movement, are finding it difficult to obtain the required low skilled help. This difficulty can be partially attributed to either the lack of transit or inadequate transit schedules. These factors contribute to the high degree of female and teenage unemployment found in the poverty pockets. It could be argued that the outward movement of whites, when correlated with the economic decentralization of jobs, would improve the black's chance of bidding more competitively for the remaining central city employment. However, since the central city is becoming more demanding in skill levels, this constitutes a negligible short-term benefit.[14]

SUBURBANIZATION OF EMPLOYMENT

The movement of jobs to suburban locations in Indianapolis has been consider-able. Forty-three percent of the metropolitan area's jobs in 1967 were located in outlying areas as compared to only 32 percent in 1961. The downtown proportion of overall employment fell from 33 percent to 25 percent, registering the only negative change. This decline occurred even though the total number of jobs increased by 61,000.[15]

A further study examined 922 affiliated members of the Chamber of Commerce between 1947 and 1968 for shifts in the location of their industrial activities. Two hundred and twenty-eight firms are found to have changed their residential location during this period. These decentralizing firms generated 11,304 job opportunities. Only 440 jobs were generated by the 17 firms which moved in toward the central city. These firms require a small and professional work force. The average outward distance moved for all firms exceeded three miles. Manufacturing firms, a main supplier of low skilled basic entry jobs, moved on the average 3.9 miles in an outward direction in this period.[16]

The hard core unemployed in this study are presently capable of filling only the lowest skilled occupations. It is therefore more important to analyze employment shifts differentiated by skill levels rather than undifferentiated job changes at the aggregate level. In rather similar investigations Hamilton, Kain and Persky utilized aggregate job statistics with no distinction by type, which raises questions as to the validity and usefulness of their results for developing transit policy for the disadvantaged.[17] Only by ascertaining the geographic distribution of basic entry jobs for the ISMSA can the spatial barrier affecting the placement of low skilled inner city residents be readily assessed. The spatial distribution of low skilled manufacturing, clerical, sales and service jobs provides an insight into those locations most suitable for the placement of the hard core unemployed.

Of the low skilled job opportunities,

clerical jobs which the inner city residents are least capable of filling are located nearest to their place of residence as well as being the most accessible by public transit. Clerical and sales jobs require far higher entry qualifications than manufacturing, and are the least accessible to the disadvantaged.[18] Clerical positions peak in the 0–10 minute zone, drop sharply, and then gradually decline outwards, whereas manufacturing demand retains a fairly constant level out to the peripheral time zones.

Two spatially opposed processes, residential nucleation and industrial dispersion, interact to increase the distance between the disadvantaged's place of residence and his prospective places of work. This contributes to the job seeker's sense of geographic isolation and job inaccessibility. The problem is further aggravated by the present national trend toward white collar employment and the movement away from skilled and semiskilled jobs. If present trends continue, the work-residence spatial separation will increase and further constrain the potential catchment area of low skilled employment opportunities for the non-motorized hard core unemployed.

This spatial barrier has two consequences for the supply side of the labor market. First, the channels of labor market information are no longer effective because of the increased physical distance. Second, those inner city unemployed who do succeed in finding employment in peripheral job locations are adversely affected by lack of transportation, inadequate routing of public transit and excessive costs in time and money.

The shift of manufacturing from the central city to peripheral areas isolated from the public transit system indicates the apparent assumption on the part of industrial employers that automobiles are generally available to their labor force. Since automobiles are becoming more important for the work trip, the non-motorized job seeker is becoming increasingly handicapped.[19] Therefore, carless job seekers are particularly dependent on the spatial distribution of the facilities of the Indianapolis Transit System (ITS). Increasing or decreasing the geographic bounds of this network increases or decreases the disadvantaged job seeker's market for basic entry jobs.

PUBLIC TRANSIT

The hard core unemployed lack automobiles for driving to work. Eighty-two percent of the 4,840 job applicants depend on public transit for the work trip (see Table 1). Moreover, 87 percent are black, of which 84.4 percent depend on the bus system. The high proportion of the hard core unemployed lacking cars suggests that automobile ownership is a variable related to the acquisition of some suitable form of employment. It is a factor necessary for obtaining job interviews and crucial to the retention of a job. These "captive riders" are forced to find employment either in the immediate vicinity of their homes or are dependent upon job opportunities along the routes of the Indianapolis Transit System.

Public transit in this study refers to bus travel; Indianapolis has no commuter rail facilities. The inner city poverty pockets are particularly well serviced by CBD oriented lines. However, the utility of these lines is considerably lessened by the lack of crosstown and outward-bound buses serving peripheral work place locations. Except for one east-west crosstown route, all 26 public transit routes are radial in character and converge on the CBD. This deficiency in crosstown transport forces the disadvantaged to journey downtown prior to any outward movement. Slow bus speeds and the necessity of downtown transfers extends the length of many peripheral journeys beyond profitable limits. The prolonged length of time between buses and the lack of late and early morning

Age of Worker and Method of Transportation	Percentage Distribution			
	White		Black	
	Male	Female	Male	Female
Workers Commuting By Auto				
All Age Groups, Sample Size	124	58	376	276
Distribution by Age				
Under 21	40%	12%	29%	18%
21–30	32	41	41	34
31–45	18	27	20	39
46–60	10	17	9	9
61 and over	0	1	1	0
Workers Commuting By Public Transportation				
All Age Groups, Sample Size	194	253	1262	2277
Distribution by Age				
Under 21	50%	29%	51%	38%
21–30	23	27	30	29
31–45	16	22	12	24
46–60	9	17	5	8
61 and over	2	5	2	1

TABLE 1. Distribution of IESD Job Applicants by Age, Race, Sex and Mode of Transit for the Journey to Work, August 1967-August 1968
Source: Indianapolis Employment Security Division ES-511Y forms, 1968

services to coincide with shift times are major complaints of industries in the ISMSA.[20]

Present trends indicate that bus travel in Indianapolis will continue to decline, and eventually offer a more restricted route distribution for its patrons. The increases in car ownership and transit operating costs do not show signs of changing direction in the foreseeable future. Inner city residents who work at downtown locations will probably continue to receive good service if the route structure of the ITS does not change from its current orientation. Those who wish to obtain access to suburban industrial parks, recreational facilities and rural areas will encounter increased difficulties.

MOBILITY CHARACTERISTICS OF THE DISADVANTAGED

No significant trip length disparities with regard to sex or race are found among reverse commuter groups commuting to work by bus; the mean trip length is 2.2 miles.[21] This implies that inner city residents of both races might proportionately benefit from improved transit facilities. Though low income whites experience less discrimination in housing and jobs, they record equally restricted work-trip distances. It might be stressed, however, that greater attention should be focused on black neighborhoods, since the data reflect a more acute unemployment problem in this social group.

No journey-to-work trip length differences are observed between disadvantaged male car users by race. The mean work trip is 3.32 miles for black males, 3.04 miles for the white males. Disparities exist between the trip lengths of car and bus users, both within and between racial groups. The work trip length of black male car owners averages 1.1 miles greater than trips of bus users. A similar relationship exists for white male car owners.

The reverse commuter work trip patterns of disadvantaged inner city residents are not very extensive regardless of the vehicular mode available, especially when these patterns are compared with trip lengths of suburban-CBD oriented commuters. Suburban commuters have longer work trips than inner city residents when their journeys are measured in miles, but shorter when measured in time.[22] The disparity is due to the difference between car and bus travel.

The shorter work trip of the disadvantaged workers reflects a more confined catchment area of job opportunities. This distorted labor shed of employment opportunities is strongly influenced by the hard core unemployed's misconception of distance and his inability to efficiently overcome the barriers to movement facing him in a complex urban environment. This restricted territorial boundary may also be the result of budgetary constraints and the lag in acquiring job information. The results of the preceding analysis suggest that while relatively few disadvantaged persons have automobiles for the work trip, improved spatial mobility exists for those who do.

JOB DURATION AND WAGE RATE CHARACTERISTICS

A series of cumulative frequency curves were constructed to test the hypothesis that variations in job duration exist between inner city groups when stratified by age, sex, education and mode of transit available for the journey to work. The overall findings indicate that inner city car users are more likely than bus users to hold jobs for a greater length of time. Comparison of the distributions show that car users are skewed toward the higher job retention periods of around 9 months as opposed to 3 months for bus users. This inequality is decidedly pronounced in the 22–29 years of age category.

It was also hypothesized that the disadvantaged, inner city residents who have a car available for the journey to work, when classified by race, age, sex and educational level, receive a higher wage rate than individuals whose mode of transit is by bus. The findings suggest that improved accessibility permits car users to obtain jobs which generally pay higher wages.[23] The mean for bus users occurs in the $1.46–1.65 wage earning category as opposed to $1.86–2.05 for auto users (see Figure 3).

The higher wage rates, longer job duration and wider employment area for motorized workers are presented as evidence to improve channels of access for carless, unemployed job seekers. Provided transit and suitable job opportunities are available to the disadvantaged, the suburban industrial job frequently offers more lucrative opportunities for the inner city resident to upgrade his standard of living.

TRANSIT DESIGN

The solution advocated for Indianapolis is the restructuring of the existing bus system by the adoption of new transit routes to link central city poverty pockets and areas of suburban employment (see Figure 4). The nature of these bus lines contrasts with the present radially oriented transit system centered on the CBD. The routes are constructed to cross both low income black and white poverty areas with frequent stops for passenger loading. Once outside the

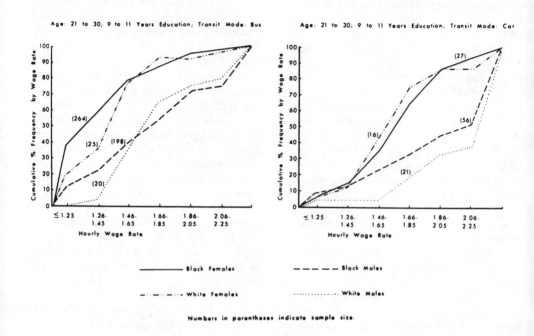

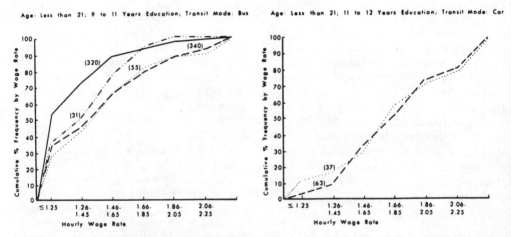

FIGURE 3. Wage Distribution for Inner City Residents of Marion County by Race, Sex, Age, Education and Transit Mode: 1968
Data furnished by Indianapolis Employment Security Division

poverty pockets, the buses show a direct path towards the areas of suburban manufacturing and commercial development.

Indianapolis Transit System provides a functional operating base and experienced administrative and managerial personnel. With the aid of federal subsidies, its equipment, maintenance facilities and work force can be adapted to the new reverse commuter transit routes. These bus lines will not directly generate new positions of employment, but they will aid in alleviating the present inner city unemployment problem by providing the opportunity for the hard core unemployed to seek and retain a position of employment in locations previously inaccessible or difficult to reach. Since a high proportion of the unemployed in the sample are below age 30, programs designed to improve workplace accessibility for the job seekers offer the potential for long-range effects and short-term alleviation for older individuals.

Several factors are important in deciding upon the spatial pattern of these new transit routes. (1) To offset expenses, there must be adequate density along the routes to generate sufficient patronage. (2) The bus routes must run as near as possible to customers oriented on a block basis. (3) The routes should be kept reasonably direct, yet provide adequate coverage of the poverty pockets and areas of industrial and commercial activity. (4) The schedules must be dependable, well-maintained and reasonably attractive to the potential rider.

The three bus lines are designed to aid inner city residents in the following order of priority. First, those hard core unemployed residing in the poverty neighborhoods will have an opportunity to obtain and then retain a position of employment in peripheral areas. Second, those temporarily unemployed will be able to resume a position of employment. Third, carless residents already employed will have the option of choosing an alternative job location. And finally, car users who are already employed along the new routes will be provided an opportunity to change to a bus mode for their journey to work.

Rather than present a definitive justification of the new transit routes, some of the major traveller and community benefits are identified. The new services offer a significant time savings in the work trip for the residents of the transit areas. Since travel costs are a function of time consumed en route plus fares paid, then a travel time reduction will result in decreased travel costs and thus provide a traveler benefit. Those presently using automobiles who resort to bus travel will find costs savings through reduced operating, parking, vehicle ownership and accident expenses. This cost reduction, however, must be balanced against the increased costs of bus travel time and the intangible cost associated with the loss of privacy.

The routes will encourage the central city job seeker to widen his range of job search by applying for what were previously inaccessible suburban jobs. The disadvantaged resident is now able to compete with the suburbanite for outlying jobs. The improved employment opportunities generated by the transit line may reduce the normal time it takes the job seeker to find employment. Few benefits would be realized, however, if jobs attained through the routes only lasted a few weeks. Likewise, no resultant overall unemployment reduction would develop if only one unemployed person merely out competed another for a scarce job. Substantial benefits would result if these routes allowed individuals previously unemployed to obtain higher paying positions for a more sustained length of time.

The improvement in the labor catchment area for firms will shorten the time span industries experience in filling job vacancies. The further possibility of a

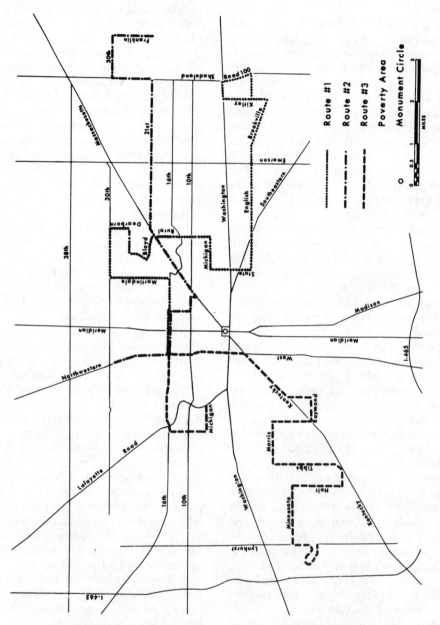

FIGURE 4. The Three Proposed Transit Routes

decrease in absenteeism and tardiness could contribute to a reduced industrial turnover rate. Employers who are presently reluctant to hire workers without the means of transport for the journey to work will be able to relax this restriction. Individuals will be able to utilize the transit routes until they join car pools or have sufficient capital to purchase their own mode of transport.

If the results of this experiment prove beneficial, the Indianapolis Transit System could bolster its declining patronage by reorienting some of its routes along the crosstown paths projected in this design. At the same time, it would provide a vital "life-line" to the hard core unemployed residents in downtown ghetto areas. Even if the routes do not prove to be self-sufficient, it may be possible to argue that they generate enough community benefits to warrant their subsidization.

The major benefits accruing to the community on the implementation of transit routes are the decline in unemployment and resultant relief to overburdened welfare services. The employment gains that accrue to welfare recipients will reduce their need and the public cost in welfare payments. Through decreasing inner city unemployment and poverty, the routes incur a reduction in the required subsidies for other social costs such as crime, health and substandard housing. Further, it will decrease unemployment compensation paid by Indianapolis employers.

After initiating the project, a benefit-cost analysis would assess whether additional public transit linking poverty pockets to peripheral areas of low skilled job demand significantly contributes to a reduction in the unemployment levels and related social ills in the city's low income neighborhoods. This analysis could determine whether total benefits from the project (traveler and community benefits) are in excess of total costs. The results will suggest a future course

of action. The alternatives facing the city will be either to retain the service, to drop it, to subsidize it by local funding or to initiate some new policy. The overall analysis will determine the relationship that exists between the transit facilities available to project area residents, and their levels of unemployment. The short-run strategy will be evaluated by the traveler and community benefits generated when balanced against the cost of the transit system.

CONCLUSIONS

The preceding research has documented that work-residence spatial disparities constrain the employment opportunities of inner city residents. The primary contributing forces to this problem, restrictive residential patterns and economic decentralization, show relatively few signs of changing.

The radial orientation of bus routes and the lack of crosstown connections reduces the effectiveness of the Indianapolis Transit System for the carless disadvantaged. These "captive riders" are forced to find employment opportunities either within walking distance of their homes or along the routes of the transit system. An increase or decrease in the spatial configuration of the transit network affects the disadvantaged residents' market for low skilled job opportunities.

The residence and work place locations of low skilled labor are not presently subject to substantial change, but it is possible to change the transportation linking them. The short-run strategy of redistributing transit routes offers potential benefits to the city and the unemployed central city resident. This short-term goal will alleviate the effects of the in-out transit problem until more comprehensive long-term goals are initiated.

It is not argued that deficient access is the most urgent problem of residents in poverty areas. Rather, it is argued that a remedy for mobility deficiencies is an important step in a series of ameliorative policies destined to upgrade the living standard of the disadvantaged. The contention is that an investment in this essential facet of urban life will contribute to the mitigation of inner city deprivation.

NOTES

1. *Conference on Poverty and Transportation, June 7, 1968: Summary and Conclusions and Papers Presented,* American Academy of Arts and Sciences, Brookline, Mass., sponsored by the Department of Housing and Urban Development and the Department of Transportation, Washington, D.C.; J. F. Kain, "Housing Segregation, Negro Employment and Metropolitan Decentralization," *The Quarterly Journal of Economics* 82 (May, 1968): 175–97. J. D. Mooney, "Housing Segregation, Negro Employment and Metropolitan Decentralization: An Alternative Perspective," *The Quarterly Journal of Economics* 83 (May, 1969): 299–311.

2. C. S. Davies, "The Reverse Commuter Transit Problem in Indianapolis" (Ph.D. diss., Department of Geography, Indiana University, 1970).

3. Indianapolis Manpower Coordinating Committee, *The Indianapolis Area Cooperative Manpower Plan, Fiscal Year 1968,* June 16, 1967, p. 9.

4. Indianapolis Transportation Task Force Committee, *Indianapolis Personnel Association Survey,* July, 1969.

5. Community Service Council of Metropolitan Indianapolis, *Social Characteristics Analysis of Eleven Selected Poverty Target Areas in Indianapolis, Indiana,* July 22, 1966.

6. "Recording Race, Color and National Origin on Local Office Records," Memorandum No. 601, Indianapolis Employment Division, July 19, 1967.

7. U.S. Department of Labor, Manpower Administration, *Definition of the Term Disadvantaged Individual,* Washington, 1968, Order No. 2–68.

8. C. S. Davies, "The Reverse Commuter Transit Problem in Indianapolis," pp. 13–30; see also K. E. and A. F. Taeuber, *Negroes in Cities* (Chicago: Aldine Press, 1965), p. 30; A. H. Pascal, *The Economics of Housing Segregation* (Santa Monica, Calif.: The Rand Corp., 1967), pp. 30–56; A. Downs, "The Future of the American Ghettos," *Daedalus* 82 (Fall, 1968): 1331–78.

9. E. L. Thornbrough, *Since Emancipation,* Indianapolis, Indiana Division American Negro Emancipation Authority, 1963.

10. Community Service Council, *Study of Relocation Problems,* Indianapolis, September 1964, pp. 1–16.

11. Metropolitan Planning Commission, *Metropolitan Indianapolis Housing Study, Summary Report,* p. 26; see also Indianapolis Regional Transportation and Development Study (IRTADS), *A Transportation and Land Development Plan for the Indianapolis Region, A Summary Report,* Barton-Aschman Associates, Supervising Consultant, Chicago, October, 1968; and Greater Indianapolis Progress Committee, "Study of Housing Conditions for Urban Renewal and of Low Income Housing," 1966 (Mimeographed).

12. Metropolitan Planning Department, Marion County, *Preliminary Projection of Housing Needs,* 67–85, Technical Work Paper No. 1, prepared by Hammer, Greene, Siler Associates, March, 1968.

13. G. Fellman and R. Rosenblatt, "The Social Costs of an Urban Highway," *Conference on Poverty and Transportation, June 7, 1968.*

14. J. F. Kain, "Housing Segregation, Negro Employment and Metropolitan Decentralization," p. 194.

15. Indianapolis Employment Security Division, *Covered Employment: Marion County, September, 1967,* Research and Statistic Department, Indianapolis, May, 1967.

16. C. S. Davies, "The Reverse Commuter Transit Problem in Indianapolis," pp. 34–38.

17. W. F. Hamilton, "Transportation Innovations and Job Accessibility," *Conference on Transportation and Poverty,* pp. 5–8; A. H. Pascal, *The Economics of Housing Segregation,* chapter VI; J. F. Kain, "Housing Segregation, Negro Employment and Metropolitan Decentralization," pp. 175–97.

18. Georgia Institute of Technology, *Methods of Job Development for the Hard Core Unemployed,* Industrial Management Center, Atlanta, Ga., January 1969. The graphs represent 3,280 Clerical, 810 Sales, 1,900 Manufacturing, 890 Miscellaneous, and 2,475 Service basic entry jobs.

19. U.S. Department of Commerce, *Special Report on Household Ownership and Purchases of Automobiles and Selected Household Durables, 1960 to 1967,* No. 18, August, 1967, p. 65.

20. Indianapolis Regional Transportation and Development Study, Transit Inventory, Job 4210, March 1966.

21. A disproportional stratified random sample is obtained from the population previously classified by race, sex and transit mode. Straight-line linear distance between the resident's exact home address and work location is measured on a map of scale 1" = 4,000'.

22. D. R. Deskins, "Residence-Work Place Interaction Vectors for the Detroit Metropolitan Area 1953 to 1965," *Interaction Patterns and the Spatial Form of the Ghetto,* Special Publication No. 3, Department of Geography, Northwestern University, Evanston, Ill., Feb., 1970.

23. D. P. Taylor, "Discrimination and Occupational Wage Differences in the Market for Unskilled Labor," *Industrial Labor Relations Review* (April, 1968), pp. 375–90.

CHICAGO'S CROSSTOWN: A CASE STUDY IN URBAN EXPRESSWAYS
ELLIOTT ARTHUR PAVLOS

The Crosstown experience illustrates two important aspects of current urban expressway planning. The first is that the structure and distribution of social costs associated with any project may be very different from the engineering costs and may lead to substantial shifts in proposed locations. The second, and perhaps more important, element is that the participation of citizen groups in the decision-making process is having the effect of preventing any decision from being made at all as the legal structure underlying the process tends to protect the rights of the minority against the broader interests of the majority.

Reprinted from David R. Miller, ed., *Urban Transportation Policy: New Perspectives* (Lexington, Mass.: Lexington Books, D. C. Heath and Company, 1972), pp. 57–65, by permission of the publisher and the author. This is an edited version of the original publication.

INTRODUCTION

In December, 1966, the Department of Transportation established a new policy with respect to highways in urban areas. In response to the difficulties that many cities were having in obtaining citizen approval of highway proposals, the Department established a policy of Multiple Development Corridors to create greater harmony between major transportation routes and the use made of the land adjacent to them. Development possibilities would include housing, shops, light industry, parking, schools, recreation areas, and mass transit systems along with the highway. Federal funding might be available from the Department of Housing and Urban Development, the Organization for Equal Opportunity, the Department of Health, Education and Welfare, and the recreation department of the Department of the Interior.

In the summer of 1967, the Department of Transportation designated the Chicago Crosstown Expressway as one of the 'pilot projects' for this multiple development concept. The project received more than 7.8 million dollars in grants, and the Crosstown Design Team was established as the interdisciplinary design consultant to the City of Chicago. The expectations were great. Milton Pikarsky, Commissioner of Public Works in Chicago, the department through which the Crosstown Design Team was funded, stated that "we want to bring all our talents together to find an almost utopian scheme, (to see) what can be accomplished with the most liberal use of land."

This was the initial directive for work on the project. But the Department of Transportation's policy was subject to differing interpretations. In the case of Chicago's Crosstown, there were two interpretations: the first that of the design team during its first eighteen months of work; the second resulted from strong community involvement at the end of that period.

STAGE ONE: EMPHASIS ON DE-SIGN ELEGANCE

During the first stage of work, between September 1967 and March 1969, the design team interpreted the multiple development policy as emphasizing aesthetic development in terms of both urban and architectural design. This interpretation, of a grand urban design concept that would restructure Chicago's future land development, and of a refined and elegant roadway that would be a thing of beauty to drivers, grew out of and was influenced by three factors:

1. A policy of studying only those highway-associated developments that clearly could be implemented under existing legislation. This was the design team's interpretation and was born of timidity coupled with a real understanding of the difficulty of putting into practice policies of the Department of Transportation.
2. The predominance, in both management and staff, of architects whose training and interests were directed towards elegance of design and whose knowledge of specific urban problems was severely limited.
3. The city's policy against contact with the local community until the team was prepared to present a formal recommendation; a policy permitting the above two factors to exist unhampered by opposition from citizens.

Each of these factors will be discussed in turn.

The Team's View of the Multiple Development Concept

From its inception, the Crosstown Design Team developed a narrow interpretation of the Department of Transportation's multiple corridor development concept.

What prompted this conservative outlook? To begin with, the "policies and procedures" of the Department of Transportation were much more narrowly defined than their public pronouncements would suggest. Two D.-O.T. regulations concern excessive appropriation of land for highway-associated developments:

1. Where the cost of paying damages to a property owner for partial taking of his property exceed 80 percent of the assessed value of that property, funds would be provided to acquire the whole parcel. Because of the small size of urban parcels, however, this would rarely provide a strip of land as much as 100 feet in width for other than highway use.
2. Authorization was given for acquisition of whole parcels to a street line or some other logical barrier or boundary line to be used for parks, play areas, or other public or quasi-public use that would assist in integrating the highway into the local environment. However, funds had never been provided for acquisition of land under this regulation. Indications given to the Design Team by Department of Transportation regional officials were that it would not be funded.

As a result, the Design Team determined rather quickly that the only highway-associated developments that seemed to have a possibility of being funded were (1) rights of way for rapid transit (but not the construction of the facility itself); and (2) park strip developments on land left over from whole parcel takings.

No funds or programs were available to build housing or to acquire land for housing, nor were there any to build schools (unless it was to replace a building cleared for the highway). A state of Illinois bill that would have authorized the City of Chicago to acquire land within a corridor one mile to either side of a highway for the provision of relocation housing was vetoed by Governor Ogilvie in August of 1969.

In addition, much of the reason for the design team's conservatism with respect to multiple development corridors must also be laid to the management of the project and the make-up of the staff: a team mostly of architects, led mostly by architects.

Design Team Background

The Crosstown Design Team began as a joint venture of three Chicago area offices: Skidmore, Owings, and Merrill (architects); C. F. Murphy, Associates (architects); and Westenhoff and Novick (engineers). Approximately nine months after the inception of the joint venture, the office of Howard Needles, Tammen and Bergendoff (engineers) joined the group, whose name then changed to Crosstown Associates. Throughout the study, most of the administrative leadership as well as most of the staff personnel came from the Skidmore, Owings, and Merrill office. The project director was Joseph R. Passonneau (architect), who for the previous ten years had been the Dean of the School of Architecture at Washington University in Saint Louis.

Funds for the study were provided by the Department of Transportation in the sum of $7,838,600. These funds were given to the City of Chicago, which passed them through its Public Works Department to the design team, who were hired as consultants to design the highway.

Also set up was the Crosstown Executive Board (CEB), an advisory group made up of transportation and highway agencies at the city, county, state, and federal level. But this group was purely advisory: the design team was contracted directly to the City of Chicago.

In June of 1968, in the midst of the design team's first stage of work, the professional staff included the following personnel:

architects	18
engineers	8
architectural draftsmen	6
engineering draftsmen	12
planners	1
traffic specialists	1
urban designers	4
economists	1

What came from this group was an architectural statement on a grand scale. It was conceived as a general design statement, on the order of the famed Burnham Plan for Chicago of 1909. Plan objectives included: linking the radials of the present Chicago Expressway system, providing a high speed bypass around the central business district, connecting Chicago's two major airports, and serving as an axis for growth and development—a new "Main Street" for Chicago's south and west sides.

At least part of the reason for these positions can be attributed to the policies for citizen participation at . Crosstown, as established by the City government. No pressure was being put on the design team to work in any direction other than the one in which they we proceeding.

Informal Citizen Contact

The city of Chicago has a general policy regarding citizen participation: that there be no contact with the community without first being armed with a formal recommendation. One reason for this may be a fear of hostile community reaction; the more advance information given out, the more ammunition for those who may be in opposition. With a firm position and recommendation, opposition would come only from those directly in a highway's path; without a recommendation, many more might oppose, all being fearful of being harmed by the roadway. This policy may have resulted from the city's inexperience with close citizen participation. Regardless, it is an unwritten policy, stated to the design team by a high ranking official of the Department of Public Works and followed religiously. As a result, corridor residents were not informed about the progress of planning (with serious misconceptions arising) and Crosstown planning could not benefit from community involvement.

Crosstown did, however, speak to the owners of major industries in the corridor. (Industries employing well over 100,000 persons exist in the general area of the expressway route.) The team learned the industries' needs and developed a working relationship with industry representatives of great significance to the planning effort, since each represented hundreds or thousands of employees. As a result, a heavy bias was built into the decision-making process, a bias favoring industries over residents in determining the location of the highway. Highway location alternatives were primarily related to industrial location, passing to one side or the other of the industrial belt or bracketing it on both sides. The effect of these alternatives upon residential communities was then studied as a secondary consideration.

One case study is useful as an illustration of these points. Lawndale, a large black ghetto in Chicago, is separated from the town of Cicero, a conservative, white, ethnic residential area, by a half-mile-wide industrial belt. Several large parcels of vacant land exist within this industrial district, and the Lawndale community has long desired to use these parcels to form a residential bridge to Cicero to relieve serious problems of overcrowding. The town of Cicero, of course, values the protection afforded by the industrial belt.

The industries interviewed indicated a desire to have the highway built between themselves and the ghetto, both as a buffer to prevent expansion of the residential area and to ward off vandalism. Their wishes ran counter to those of Lawndale, and conformed to those of Cicero. But it was the Lawndale community that was paying the price of giving up residential land to have the highway built. Because of the close and continuing contact with the industries, and the lack of any forum for Lawndale to present its views, the "buffer" was the recommended solution.

The highway was planned as a divided roadway, with northbound and southbound lanes separated by a strip ¼ to ½ mile in width. Generally, this highway would bracket a linear industrial belt. Continuous frontage roads would be located in the interior of this corridor, so that the land between expressway halves would have much greater accessibility than land on the outside. In its clearest form, this could become an effective design, providing greater (and continuous) access to high intensity industrial uses within the corridor; and lower accessibility (and therefore protection from heavy traffic) for residential areas on either side. Of course, these conditions do not exist throughout; cities are places of great variety. The grand design is far less effective where residences are located within the expressway "high accessibility" corridor, or when industries are to the outside.

It was at this point, at the end of eighteen months of work, that the city and the Crosstown Design Team were preparing to go to their first round of community meetings. The reason for going at this time was to satisfy the new Department of Transportation requirements for general corridor location meetings for a significant (eight-mile long) section of the roadway. It was to be the first test of the team's work.

Intermezzo: Behind the Facade

Chicago presents a great facade, one truly representative of its role as one of the world's great cities. Its scale is impressive: the denseness of the Loop, the downtown expansion north along Michigan Avenue, Lake Michigan and Burnham's great park system stretching north and south for a total of twenty miles, and the giant apartment buildings that follow it from city limit to city limit. Yet, in reality, this facade is but a colossal stage set. Look behind the scaffolding and you will find the real Chicago of industry, of railroads, of slums, of seemingly endless gridiron streets lined with one and two story bungalow homes; the city of great ethnic neighborhoods: Irish, Swedes, Rumanians, Germans, Hungarians, Poles, Slovaks; the city of endless black ghettos. This is the Chicago that will be traversed by the Crosstown Expressway.

The Design Team dealt with facades, with grand designs. It was necessary for citizens' meetings to bring them face to face with the people behind the facades.

STAGE TWO: EMPHASIS ON RELOCATION HOUSING

The significant change that occurred during the second stage of work on the Crosstown Expressway was the new concern for the provision of relocation housing. It became a design consideration of paramount importance as a result of Commissioner Pikarsky's announcement that no highway would be built unless adequate relocation housing was first provided. The public meetings caused this change in direction.

History of Formal Community Contact

The meetings in March and April of 1969 were the first to take place under the new regulations announced by Secretary Boyd four months earlier. They were to be general corridor hearings to give citizens a voice in determining the need for and general location of the highway. Yet the information presented to the meetings indicated that the decisions had already been made. This information included:

1. The five proposals for alternative loca-

tions of the highway, each about a half mile from the next. One of these was recommended as being more desirable than the others, although it was emphasized strongly that no decisions had been made.

2. For the recommended corridor, five alternative highway alignments were presented: one elevated highway, two conventional combined highways, and two divided highways. One of these was indicated as being the recommended highway, once again with the statement that no decisions had been made.

3. For the recommended alignment within the recommended corridor, a twenty page list, itemizing every house that would be torn down if this highway were built, was given to each person attending the meetings.

4. At the same time, a questionnaire was distributed, which was the first "social survey" made in the area. It asked residents about their homes, whether they owned or rented, how long they had lived in the area, and how they felt about their neighborhood.

This information was presented at meetings in three distinct areas along the route of the highway. The first was a community not to be affected by the expressway. The purpose of the meeting was not so much to tell the community that they were safe, as it was to go through the practice of presenting the information. It was a middle class black area, resentful of previous city activities and their effect upon residential neighborhoods. The meeting was volatile; the considerations and proposals discussed by the design team had no relevance to these people, whose concern was with their homes and the preservation of their community.

The second was also a black community, but a substantially poorer one. This was to be the area most severely affected by the highway. In a length of just over one mile, more than 600 dwellings were to be destroyed by a 400 to 600 foot wide roadway. In this community, even more than the first, housing was the overriding issue. There was indifference to the architectural design, indifference to the overall highway concept. There was a strong demand that housing displaced be replaced in kind. This issue became so heated, that Commissioner Pikarsky announced to the meeting that "if we can't produce on providing replacement housing equal or better than what the people have at the present time before the expressway requires the dislocation and removal of these people, we are not going to build the expressway. If you see that we are not producing, you will certainly see that we will not go forward." Crosstown was headed back to a policy of multiple development, with emphasis on housing.

The third community was much larger in population as well as in area. It was white, and totally ethnic: Polish and Ukranian. The residents were middle class persons living in detached single family homes in a fairly new area. They were resistant to change and feared the spread of the black community in their direction. Despite the fact that the expressway would have virtually no direct effect upon them (it passes through vacant land nearby), it was feared to an extent greater than in any other area. It represented the force of neighborhood change.

Feuding factions disrupted the meeting so that it could not take place. The result was to change the city's public meeting policies. All subsequent meetings involved only a single organization at a time, and twenty-three such meetings took place for this section of the roadway.

Results of Community Contact

During this stage of work, several studies concerned with housing were prepared: analyses of housing supply in the Chicago area, definition of relocation needs in the Crosstown corridor, investigation of available housing programs, and summaries of legislation on the national level and in other parts of the United States that might indicate a direction for the Crosstown housing programs to follow.

The result of this work was a policy report on Relocation Problems and Required Solutions indicating for each housing type and for each social and income group to be affected by the highway, the existing housing programs and the degree to which they fall short of providing equitable relocation. This report clearly indicated the specific areas in which new housing programs are needed. It was a vital document for officials, including Mayor Daley, who were lobbying in Washington for the relocation housing assistance they needed. At the time, there was no way to provide relocation housing. This was especially serious because of the severe housing shortage that already existed in Chicago, as in most other major cities. Vacancy rates, normally around five percent, had dropped to below one percent.[1]

In summary, during the second stage of work, the design team interpreted the multiple development policy with an emphasis on the provision of relocation housing for all residents whose homes would be displaced by the highway. This interpretation was influenced by these developments:

1. Alan Boyd, Secretary of the Department of Transportation, who announced in December 1968 that an early round of community meetings or hearings would thereafter be required to discuss the need for and general location of an expressway before commitment of the State Highway Department to a specific route, and before preparation of design proposals.
2. The strong expression of need for housing within the black community, coupled with their lack of interest in the

grand schemes and aesthetic concerns of the highway designs.

3. Commissioner Milton Pikarsky's response, at these meetings, that no highway would be built without prior provision of adequate relocation housing. This preceded Department of Transportation Secretary John A. Volpe's statement of that same policy on a federal level by a full nine months.

A side effect during this stage of work was the change in policy towards these community meetings. Instead of large open meetings, there were presentations to small individual organizations (upon invitation) to avoid open conflicts between competing factions.

CONCLUSIONS

Two inferences may be drawn from the Crosstown experience: one about planning process; the other about the design team concept. A bias was built into the planning process as a result of policies regarding informal citizen contact. This bias strongly favored industrial locations and the feelings of the owners of industries. It resulted from the decision to meet with owners of industries rather than individual residents or neighbor-

hood groups as a part of the plan's preparation. This bias led to the concept of highway design that evolved: concern with industrial location, involvement with detailed architectural design, and only secondary regard for community needs, of which the foremost is relocation housing.

A design team can be an effective means of planning an urban highway, if it has the proper leadership. That leadership must come from somewhere other than traditional architecture—the major issues in cities today are not those of physical design. There is a critical need in the team approach to involve citizens in planning in a more complete way, to see that their interests are served and that they provide information to the team. The primary purpose of the program must be to serve local communities and their needs.

NOTE

1. When this paper was written, the possibility of using Highway Trust funds to build relocation housing was under consideration. Pavlos suggested that the Crosstown policy report might "serve as an effective lever to push through the needed legislation." Subsequent events have borne out his prediction: the Uniform Relocation and Real Property Acquisition Policies Act of 1970 permits use of Federal project funds under appropriate circumstances to generate housing. See 42 USC at 4626.—Ed.

PLANNING FOR FUTURE SYSTEMS
WILFRED OWEN

In developing adequate strategies for future transportation systems, Owen argues that we must place this activity within a broader context of community planning since much of the current transportation problem stems from the haphazard development of our urban areas. An effective solution should integrate a wide range of transportation technologies, should encompass the entire functional urban area and not just the central city, and should be compatible with a broad range of community goals and not just the improvement of accessibility between selected nodes.

Reprinted from Wilfred Owen, *The Metropolitan Transportation Problem*, 2nd ed. (Washington, D.C.: The Brookings Institution, 1966), pp. 210–25, by permission of the publisher and the author. Copyright © 1956, 1966 by The Brookings Institution. This is an edited version of the original publication, and a new title has been added.

FUTURE REQUIREMENTS

In most urbanized areas, the task of moving people is the problem of adapting to a motorized economy. This involves streets, expressways, parking, bus lines, taxis, terminals, and traffic engineering. In some of the largest urban centers, there are additional problems of railroad commutation and rapid transit. But in general the problem is motor transportation, and increasingly automobile rather than public carrier transportation. Neither economic analysis nor transportation history suggests a return to public transportation on a scale that would be decisive. Trends in automobile ownership show no sign of being reversed to conserve the space that motor transport has made plentiful. On the contrary, increasing leisure time, the spread of the suburbs, and the new patterns of urban living made possible by the automobile will continue to increase the number of cars in operation. Planning of the urban area must recognize that car ownership has become a necessary adjunct to home ownership, a

key to widening opportunities for employment, a means of realizing recreational and other leisure time objectives, and an important factor in the loosening-up process that will gradually overcome outmoded patterns of congested living.

Public carriers, however, continue to be an essential part of the transportation system in large metropolitan areas. There is consequently a pressing need to revitalize transit and to maintain public transportation service where it can fulfill the specialized tasks it is most capable of performing. The principal task of transit will be to absorb home-to-work travel peaks. Public carriers will have to complement and supplement private transportation wherever the density of urban development and the concentration of urban travel dictate. Public transportation will continue to play an important role in the older central business districts, and along high-density, home-to-work travel routes close to the center. In these circumstances, the limited capacity of downtown highway and parking facilities in major cities will continue to make extensive use of the automobile impossible at the peak.

Improved bus transportation seems to offer the greatest potential for public transportation from both an operation and economic standpoint, assuming a system of modern highways. The bus avoids the high cost of an exclusive right-of-way, and it can serve essentially the same transportation patterns established by the automobile. The inflexibility of rail operations, on the other hand, indicates that rail rapid transit and railroad commutation services will not be greatly expanded beyond facilities now in use. Modernization will be necessary, and important additions to transit will be required in the largest and oldest cities. A satisfactory transportation system for most urban areas, however, will have only a short mileage of rail routes. But these lines may play a key role in accommodating home-to-work peaks.

Automatic trains or other rapid transit innovations now promise to provide a high standard of transport service at reasonable cost. The application of these mass carrier techniques, as in San Francisco and Washington, will help to maintain high-density routes and high-density areas. The further expansion of motorized transport and the resulting changes in urban living and traveling, however, will predominate. Transport innovations will modernize all methods of movement, but their impact is more likely to be felt in road technology rather than rail, and, for the more distant future, in the air rather than on the ground. The helicopter, convertiplane, or other direct-lift aircraft will some day furnish the transportation service necessary to spread the urban traffic load over a wider area.

Highway and terminal requirements to meet the present and foreseeable future demands of motorized traffic, however, will continue to dominate the problem. Satisfactory transportation in urban areas calls for a complete system of ex-pressways and the redesign of major surface streets to enable them to serve more effectively either for the movement of through traffic or for access to property. The attempt to serve both purposes at the same time has failed. It will be necessary to eliminate unneeded mileage and unnecessary intersections, to separate different types of traffic to minimize conflicts among incompatible street uses, and to develop new concepts of road design in conjunction with urban redevelopment and the planning of neighborhoods and commercial areas.

Only a total network of controlled-access expressways and parking facilities can provide a skeleton that will support the giant metropolis of the future. If only parts of the highway network are of satisfactory design, the skeleton is bound to collapse under the weight of the peak-hour movement attracted by expressway standards. It will also be necessary to combine the construction of main arteries of travel with adjacent land uses. Commercial enterprises serving the public, such as service stations, shopping centers, restaurants, motels, and terminals need to be located and designed as an integral part of the highway system. The acquisition of sufficient width of highway right-of-way can serve as the basis for planned commercial areas removed from the traveled way but readily accessible to it. Such an approach can combat the causes of suburban blight that have their roots in unplanned and unprotected roadsides. The need is for more effective legal and financial methods to make possible the reservation of highway rights-of-way that will be needed in the new suburbs, and the purchase of sufficient land in addition to what is needed specifically for the highway itself.

REVISION OF FINANCIAL POLICY
A program to achieve better standards of transportation for urban areas would mean very substantial increases in trans-

port facilities, including express highways, terminals, and transit systems. Yet it is clear that the accomplishment of a self-supporting urban transportation system is well within the bounds of feasibility. Three steps are necessary. First, urban areas should be granted a fair share of state-collected highway user revenues, in the form of either cash grants from the states or by more adequate state construction programs in urban areas. Second, a more scientific pricing of transportation services is called for to maximize revenues and to achieve the most effective use of facilities. Third, the pooling of transportation revenues suggests a promising means of supporting high standards of service for the transportation system as a whole, including mass transit.

The low-fare policy that has led to low standards in the transportation field must be replaced by a transportation price policy that makes high standards possible. Depressed rates have preserved obsolete roads, antiquated railroads and transit equipment, and inadequate service. General tax support has been no solution. It has generally resulted in inadequate funds, uneconomical operations, and an absence of long-range physical and financial planning.

Thus far transit fare increases have been used mainly to cover rising costs rather than to provide better service, and reduced patronage has been the result. If fares were adequate to finance improved standards of service, however, the effect might be different. Express bus service at premium fares has actually promoted transit travel, and de luxe bus service has also indicated that higher fares can lead to increased traffic. More rate experimentation is needed, and more opportunity to experiment would be provided by eliminating control by the public utility commission over transit rates and placing this responsibility in a public transportation agency or authority.

Although use of the pricing mechanism to control transportation demand has not been attempted to any important degree, its potentials are promising. Pricing policies need to be established by one agency, however, if they are to be effective from the standpoint of either revenue production or traffic control. Tolls on urban expressways might be an effective method of minimizing less essential movement in the peak hour, and parking rates downtown might further assist in regulating traffic flow. For example, low parking rates for cars arriving downtown after the morning peak or for cars departing before the evening rush hour might be effective in reducing unnecessary concentrations of traffic. Joint parking and transit rates and pricing policies for public transportation based on mileage might be more remunerative and publicly acceptable. The elimination of free parking or parking meter charges at uneconomically low levels would add considerably to the support of the transportation system. This would also eliminate an important element of subsidy now encouraging the use of the automobile, and would provide a more equitable basis of competition between auto and transit. Transit fare increases designed to furnish better service might be more feasible if at the same time the automobile user were made to pay the full cost of driving.

Financing of urban transportation might be greatly assisted by a system approach in which all revenues were pooled and all operations together made to cover their costs. The use of highway revenues to help support improved peak-hour transit service might prove acceptable to highway users in the future. Automobiles and transit already share the cost of highways they use jointly. Transit operations contribute substantial sums to highway financing through the payment of motor vehicle tax revenues to the state. In many urban centers, transit operations also reduce the volume of new highway capacity required in the peak. From a total transportation viewpoint, the improvement of motor bus operations may mean a substantial saving in road expenditures or substantial relief for motorists attempting to make use of limited highway capacity. And logic would appear to favor using motor vehicle revenues generated by urban traffic to help support a metropolitan system of transportation rather than to subsidize little used rural roads.

A further reason for pooling transport revenues is suggested by the fact that transit provides an important standby service for motorists who make occasional use of public carriers when the family car is unavailable. As automobile ownership increases, more people may be expected to use the bus occasionally rather than regularly, and thus the standby role of the transit system will become increasingly important. If transit fares were increased to cover these standby costs, the burden would fall on automobile owners and nonowners alike. This would mean that nonowners, who generally represent groups least able to pay, would be incurring a daily surcharge to help support standby capacity for the sporadic rider.

The possibility of adapting toll financing to the urban area presents a specific method of pooling that might greatly strengthen the financial position of urban transportation. Tolls could provide quickly a complete system of expressways, transit, and terminals for the metropolitan area. Such a system might consist of a bond-financed network of expressways terminating in parking areas downtown and at fringe locations. Payment for use of the highway could be included in the parking fee rather than collected at the toll gate. Private vehicles in the close-in areas could be restricted to ramps leading to parking places only, while buses might be allowed to drive off the expressways and circulate on downtown surface streets. All costs of the system would be included in charges paid either on transit vehicles or at parking lots.

MANAGING THE TRANSPORTATION SYSTEM

A major step toward planning and financing a satisfactory urban transportation system will be to establish the necessary governmental organization. Urban transportation must be removed from the administrative vacuum that has kept it from playing a full role in the development of better cities. Urban communities that divide the transportation problem into small parts cannot expect to get whole answers.

The need for organizing all available transportation facilities and for financing and operating them as a system is becoming increasingly apparent as we review the methods of supplying transport services today. The division of responsibility among political jurisdictions and among different agencies and departments within a single unit of government is the most obvious defect of current policy. The fact that roads and streets are provided by a number of jurisdictions in the metropolitan area is a frequent source of planning and financing difficulties, especially in the many instances where two or more states are involved. The large daily influx of commuters from outlying areas to the central city pose additional problems of supporting needed facilities on an equitable basis. Public transportation operations are often circumscribed by local government boundaries that impose economic burdens on both the carriers and the public. In many cases, political units have been made obsolete by the very transportation services they are attempting to furnish.

The administrative separation of different methods of transportation imposes a serious obstacle to effective community mobility. Decisions with respect to transit, for example, may have a controlling influence on the volume of automobile use, while pricing decisions governing parking may have a significant impact on transit patronage or highway requirements. The need for planning and financing all facilities with these interrelations in mind is apparent, but this is not possible with transportation responsibilities divided among separate agencies and jurisdictions.

The state highway departments have in many cases become an anachronism in the urban area. They are responsible for some of the most important travel routes in cities, and yet their limited jurisdiction precludes a broad approach to the needs of the city from the standpoint either of transportation or community planning. Urban highway work under the state is rapidly increasing in importance, but it is generally governed by the concept that city streets are merely connecting links in a state-wide system. It is little wonder that the city, confronted by the highly complex problem of accomplishing a total circulatory system properly related to over-all community goals has often found limited relief in state highway construction projects.

Transit is also the victim of partial remedies. The transit patron is not interested merely in the bus he rides but in the ride itself—which means the highway as well as the bus. Public transportation depends on both. As the transit company is not responsible for roads or their use—but only for the vehicle and its operation—the chances of getting good transit service are poor. Transportation policy needs to be aimed not simply at supplying the various elements of movement, but at improving standards of mobility.

A number of approaches toward integrating urban transportation functions can be identified. No one of them has gone far enough to achieve, in any comprehensive way, the provision of good passenger service in the urban area. In the case of public transportation, the transit system has not been made part of a total transportation system, nor has any city solved the management and financial problems that the quest for reasonable standards of public transportation service introduce. It must be concluded that the attempt to overcome urban transportation problems with privately owned transit facilities is unrealistic. The provision of tolerable standards of service in the peak hours calls for much more equipment than can be profitably provided. At the same time, it is clear that neither public ownership of transit nor the transit authority has succeeded in providing satisfactory standards of service or financial strength. Deficits persist, and patronage continues downward on private and public lines alike. Only if transit were to be made part of a total transportation system, under unified policy direction or unified management, would the possibilities of more effective operations be realized.

It is equally clear that metropolitan areas are not organized to carry out an effective attack on their highway problems. Obviously, there must be greater local autonomy with respect to the location, design, and use of highways in urban areas to permit a closer relation between highway construction and urban development. To the extent that state highway departments continue to perform road construction work in cities, they must be better equipped to deal with the specialized problems encountered in urbanized areas. The establishment of strong urban divisions in state and federal highway bureaus has become increasingly important. Administrative machinery to achieve a coordinated transportation-community planning approach at the local level is also imperative if urban areas are to adapt to the automotive age.

The transportation difficulties of metropolitan areas, then, are not likely to be overcome by anything short of a complete alteration of administration machinery. The need is for a physical plan and for investment and operating decisions designed to accomplish the plan. The solution might be a "transport authority," a "transportation district commission," or some form of metropolitan government. Some of the organizational experiments tried to date indicate what can be done. Facilities might be publicly owned and operated, publicly owned and privately operated, or privately owned and operated on a management contract basis. The essential requirement is that plans and policies should be uniform for the entire geographical area as well as for all relevant transportation facilities and services. This means uniform policies and integrated plans for major expressways and highways, related parking and terminal facilities, transit and railroad commuter services, taxi operations, and traffic engineering and control. It also means integrating the transportation function with metropolitan planning.

THE COMMUNITY PLAN

The problem of achieving satisfactory standards of mobility for urban communities is only partly a transportation problem. The difficulties of urban mobility stem from more deep-seated causes, principally the concentration and haphazard development of urban communities. There is a need to do more than organize, plan, and finance additional transport capacity. It will be necessary to exert a positive control over the demand for transportation as well.

Two approaches have been indicated that can level the peaks of travel that are placing an impossible burden on the transportation system. One, designed to furnish immediate relief, is a community-wide program of staggered hours for working, shopping, and school. A spreading of the urban traffic load might prove highly advantageous to the city, the worker, and the economy as a whole. The cost of peak-hour highway and public transit capacity and the economic losses from traffic delays and personal annoyance are heavy. Actually, it may be costing more to accommodate the peak than it would cost if the length of the work day were reduced to promote the staggering of arrivals and departures.

The peak, in addition to being spread over more time, should be spread over more space. Cities can never solve their transportation problems if they continue to crowd too many people and too much economic activity into too little space. Congestion in the rush hours is inevitable as long as we insist on living in the suburbs, working downtown, and starting off at the same time to get to the same place. In these circumstances no transportation magic can make the journey to work a joy ride. We will have to avoid unmanageable transportation demand through the dispersal of population and economic activity, the preservation of open spaces, and the planning of land-use densities and arrangements.

Both population limits and geographical limits will have to be imposed on urban development if the metropolis is to avoid strangling in its own prosperity. There is increasing evidence of the need for directing more urban growth into new towns and existing smaller towns. This would seem preferable to the overcrowding that modern transportation now makes unnecessary, or to the endless sprawl that modern transport has made possible. But there is the further need for redeveloping existing urban centers to assure a generous balancing of developed land with open space, and for planning new suburban growth to assure the preservation of surrounding low-density land. Otherwise a solid build-up will ultimately deny easy access to the open country, and communities may become so unwieldy that the task of providing transportation and other community needs may destroy the advantages of urban living.

Redevelopment of existing urban communities and plans for new urbanization can help overcome peak-hour congestion by enabling people to live and work in the same areas, either close-in or on the periphery. Traffic can in this way be reduced by the elimination of unnecessary travel, a dispersal of the total volume of movement, and a reversal of peak-hour flows. Approaching the demand side of the problem offers a real hope of halting the endless race between traffic growth and the capacity of the transportation system. The fact that major development of the urban area has already taken place frequently discourages efforts that seem too late. Yet renewal of the city is constantly taking place, and comprehensive planning is giving cities a second chance.

The seeds of better community planning that are finding fertile ground in the decay of downtown, however, need to be transplanted to the fringes. Events that have left large areas of the central city in economic ruin are being reenacted in the suburbs. Planless growth is adding to the transportation problems of the metropolitan area faster than the central city can hope to overcome its past mistakes through redevelopment. Whether in the city or in the suburbs, the isolation of urban planning from transportation planning has proved impractical. Both problems are compounded by the attempted separation. Satisfactory transportation is impossible without comprehensive planning that exploits to the fullest the relations between good transportation and good communities.

The federal government has promoted metropolitan area planning through recent housing legislation requiring urban renewal projects to be related to a comprehensive urban plan. Planning of transportation facilities has also been furthered through transportation surveys jointly supported by fed-eral, state, and local governments, with federal funds supplied through federal-aid highway legislation. A total approach is obviously desirable, and more effective federal encouragement of metropolitan area planning is badly needed, especially in connection with the accelerated program of urban highway development sponsored by the national government. Road construction can have highly damaging effects in urban areas unless there are area-wide community development plans to guide it. Approval of federal projects has now been made contingent on adherence to an over-all transportation plan. There is still need to assure a satisfactory relation to comprehensive community planning.

An effective solution to the urban transportation problem, then, should meet three tests. First, it should be functionally comprehensive by including all forms of transportation applicable to the problem. Second, it should be comprehensive geographically by including not only the city but the metropolitan area and all the affected region. Third, it should be comprehensive from a planning standpoint by assuring that transportation is used to promote community goals, and that community plans make satisfactory transportation possible.

This latter test is the most important. The basic need is to achieve satisfactory conditions of living. In the cities that made American industry the most prosperous in the world, slums and blight are an anomaly that needs to be attacked with all the resources at hand. Transportation development that merely helps to move us more expeditiously through areas of urban decay misses the mark.

The transportation industries, operating under archaic public policies, have failed to contribute their full potential to the building of better communities. Yet an attack on transportation inadequacies, broadly viewed, is not something apart from an attack on the inadequacies of the city. Transportation facilities that now provide the escape from undesirable urban conditions can help to overcome these conditions. Decisions governing transportation can exert an overriding influence on future patterns of urban development. Transportation facilities can blight the area through which they pass, or they can restore it. They can further the development of park and recreation lands and other objectives of the city, or they can simply carry traffic. And in doing so, they can support pleasant neighborhoods and prosperous communities, or they can nullify efforts to attain a higher standard of urban living.

In American communities most of the housing and commercial developments now taking place make little sense in relation to the ways that people move today or will be moving in the future. At one extreme, we are preserving the old congested way of urban living as if the technological innovations in transportation and communications did not exist. At the other extreme, we are reacting against high densities by substituting endless sprawl, with no effort to control growth, preserve open spaces, or apply our newfound mobility to the enhancement of urban life.

In a nation that is both motorized and urbanized, there will have to be a closer relation between transportation and urban development. We will have to use transportation resources to achieve better communities and community planning techniques to achieve better transportation. The combination could launch a revolutionary attack on urban congestion that is long overdue.

THE PROVISION OF PUBLIC SERVICES

Overview: The General Nature of Public Services

Residential Location and Public Facilities
David Harvey

Toward a Theory of Urban Facility Location
Michael B. Tietz

A Paradigm for Public Facility Location Theory
Michael J. Dear

Overview: Specific Problems in Health and Education

Health, Poverty, and the Medical Mainstream
Milton I. Roemer and Arnold I. Kisch

The Metropolitan Educational Dilemma: Matching Resources to Needs
Alan K. Campbell and Philip Meranto

Analysis

Locational Efficiency of Chicago Hospitals: An Experimental Model
Richard L. Morrill and Robert J. Earickson

From Asylum to Ghetto
Eileen Wolpert and Julian Wolpert

Race and Status in School Spending: Chicago 1961–66
Harold M. Baron

Strategy

Medicine for the Poor: A New Deal in Denver
Elinor Langer

Education and Metropolitanism
David L. Kirp and David K. Cohen

RESIDENTIAL LOCATION
AND PUBLIC FACILITIES
DAVID HARVEY

Extending his earlier statement regarding the "use-value" of a dwelling, Harvey underscores the contribution of access to public facilities and services. Since these benefits tend to be strongly localized, it is not surprising that there are strong spatial variations in such benefits within the metropolitan area. These variations, which greatly favor suburban environments, are reinforced by a wide range of political and institutional influences.

Reprinted from David Harvey, *Society, The City and the Space-Economy of Urbanism,* Resource Paper No. 18, Commission on College Geography (Washington, D.C.: Association of American Geographers, 1972), pp. 25–28, by permission of the Association of American Geographers and the author. This is an edited version of the original publication. Notes have been renumbered, and a new title has been added.

It is important for both members and non-members of the work force to have access to facilities and services. For non-members this accessibility may be the most important source of use-value attached to the place of residence. It is therefore important for us to consider how the facilities and services which contribute to the use value of the place of residence are distributed with respect to residences in general. Some of these facilities, such as shops, gas stations, doctors, and so on, are located by private actions, but increasingly government is taking over the provision of many services and facilities. In this regard we can look for a redistributive element in the urban economy to emerge fairly strongly.

It is useful to think of the city as a gigantic man-made resource system which contains an abundance of resources for individuals and families to exploit for their own benefit. It is, however, an areally localized resource system in the sense that most of the resources we make use of occur in fixed locations and their availability is there-

fore a function of their accessibility. Like any set of resources, the exploitation of these city resources will depend upon an individual's needs, capabilities, and preferences, which will vary from individual to individual depending upon social and economic circumstances, personality characteristics, and the like. However there can be no disputing that the location of these resources in general favors certain groups in the population while disadvantaging others. In other words, if we look at the distribution of resources within the urban system there are some resource-rich areas and some empty areas. Since the friction of distance is ever present and since the constraint imposed by that friction is a function of income, we have to look very carefully indeed at the distribution of these resources with respect to the places of residence of different income groups. Marion Clawson provides one example in his examination of the public provision of open space:

> Any use of rural open space, relatively close to the city, as a substitute or supplement to open

space within the city has unfortunate effects in terms of income class participation. Truly poor people have no chance to live in the country and commute to work, nor to play golf in the country. These uses of rural open space are limited to middle and upper income levels. Moreover, if the more articulate and politically most active parts of the total population see such use of rural open space as one major solution to the open space problem, they may neglect or oppose costly programs which would provide at least some open space in the city centers where it is most lacking and most urgently needed.[1]

We can in principle construct similar remarks concerning the provision of any facility or service in an urban system— health and education services, shopping facilities, entertainment and recreational facilities, sanitation services, and so on. Insofar as these facilities and services are accessible to people they contribute to the use value of the place of residence. Insofar as they are inaccessible they contribute nothing to the well-being of the population. Benefits from access to services and facilities thus may be unevenly distributed over places of residence. Changes in location of services and facilities have the potential to add or subtract use value to a place of residence and thereby may have progressive or regressive effects upon the real income of different individuals and groups. In short, the aspect of urban organization we are here considering—the allocation of services and facilities—provides one further (if somewhat minor) channel through which certain groups may succeed in appropriating more than their due share of the socially produced surplus. We can examine this process by way of a number of examples.

1. *Retail stores* are located by private action (subject to some public control through zoning regulations in most cities). The rationale governing the location of different types of retail stores is undoubtedly complex, although it is plain that most major forms of retail activity are highly sensitive to demand potential.[2]

It is usually assumed in location theory (such as in the Löschian theory) that demand and supply are in equilibrium, but given the rapid shifts which have occurred in the location of population and employment there is bound to be disequilibrium within the retail sector. As in the case of employment, this disequilibrium is likely to be met by a differential rate of adjustment so that areas with the greatest unfilled demand will be responded to first. Since demand is income-related, we can anticipate that adjustment generally will be quicker in high-income areas than in low-income areas. Thus if we look at the history of spread of some of the large super-market chain stores, they almost invariably colonize affluent areas first. This in itself is the source of differential benefits, for large supermarket chains can often sell goods at a lower price than can the neighborhood local store. For this and other reasons we frequently find that prices in low-income neighborhoods are higher than in the most affluent suburbs. The Kerner Commission (pp. 274–277) identified this as one source of dissatisfaction evident in the urban riots of the 1960s:

> Residents of low-income Negro neighborhoods frequently claim that they pay higher prices for food in local markets than wealthier white suburbanites and receive inferior quality meat and produce. . . . there are significant reasons to believe that poor households generally pay higher prices for the food they buy and receive lower quality food. Low-income consumers buy more food at local groceries because they are less mobile. Prices in these small stores are significantly higher than in major supermarkets because they cannot achieve economies of scale, and because real operating costs are higher in low-income Negro areas than in outlying suburbs. For instance, inventory "shrinkage" from pilfering and other causes. . . . can run twice as much in high crime areas. Managers seek to make up for these added costs by charging higher prices or substituting lower grades. . . . These practices do not necessarily involve exploitation, but they are often perceived as exploitative and unfair by those who are aware of the price and quality differences involved, but unaware of operating costs. In addition, it is probable that genu-

inely exploitative pricing practices exist in some areas.[3]

Subsequent investigations have shown that price and access variations almost invariably work to the detriment of low-income groups and that all kinds of factors can be adduced to account for these variations. For example, it is almost impossible or inordinately expensive to obtain insurance in many inner city areas and this raises the operating costs of the individual retailer quite substantially.[4] The net effect of all this is, however, that the affluent groups are serviced more cheaply than the poverty groups.[5]

2. *Medical care* is provided through the private market although many aspects of it are now being effected through public intervention. This public intervention takes a number of forms. By providing free medical care for the aged and the poor, through Medicaid and Medicare legislation, public intervention provides the finances to generate a new quantity of demand to which the private sector will presumably respond. Increasingly, also, the secondary and tertiary aspects of medical health care (e.g., hospital services) are being regulated by both state and federal intervention. Primary care (the general practitioners, the internists, the pediatricians, and the clinics) is still almost entirely located by private decision. As in the case of retail services, the location of primary care physicians is highly sensitive to demand and demand is a function of income. For this reason we invariably find very high per capita ratios of primary care physicians in rich areas and very low ratios in poor areas even though the actual need for medical care and attention may be much higher in the poverty areas.

Baltimore is typical in this regard. In the western portion of the inner city (a low-income black area) there were 53 primary care physicians caring for 142,-500 people (a ratio of approximately 2,-700 people per physician) whereas in the northern sector (an upper-income white area) there were 115 primary care physicians for 71,800 people (620 people per physician). Although the primary reason for such patterning may be regarded as the income differential, there can also be no doubt that it has in part a sociological explanation. Doctors and physicians are usually drawn from the upper-middle class strata of society and will naturally prefer to deal with people of their own sort than to face all the problems inherent in dealing with classes and groups whose mores and life style are substantially different from their own. Again, as in the case of retail trade, the causes explaining the differentials in service are complex, but there can be no doubt as to the net effect.

Similar remarks apply to the availability and accessibility of hospital care. Here we have to be very careful to look at the factors which govern access. Overcoming the friction of distance is a minor problem compared with overcoming other barriers to being admitted to hospital. Income is obviously very important, while religion, race, and ethnic type, also have an impact since both patient and hospital tend to have quite distinctive preferences. For those who can afford it, there is no serious penalty attached to seeking out a preferred hospital. Serious social problems arise for those who cannot afford it, and who are, as a consequence, relegated to a position in which they have absolutely no choice in the matter. Richard Morrill, Robert Earickson and Philip Rees have studied these access problems in detail for the city of Chicago:

The principal effects of poverty. . . . are to drive away the private physician, virtually forbid his use by patients, and thus force them to seek charity care direct from hospitals. Only a few hospitals can afford to provide more than a token amount of free care. . . . A majority of the 20 percent of all patients in Cook County who are too poor to pay for hospital care or insurance are therefore treated at one hospital—Cook County. . . . Absolutely very large numbers of patients, and probably close to fifty percent, must travel long distances, often by bus, beyond closer intervening hospitals. . . . Such callous neglect of the poor is inexcusable, especially in a city with the most superior facilities and personnel. While the physicians simply vanish from the areas, hospitals, with large fixed investments cannot so easily escape. Indeed, in the poor areas of Chicago today there are hospitals with sufficient capacity. The absurdity is that the local population cannot use them.[6]

In every American city similar patterns of provision and barriers to access exist. In some cases it is more serious than in others, but in general it is the poor and the racially distinct minority groups who receive the least benefits from medical care services.

3. *Water utilities* are provided in most cities through municipal undertakings. The municipality has to provide sufficient capacity to meet the peak demand for water (plus a suitable margin as a reserve). This water is then supplied to customers and various charges are made for its use. In some cases the charges are fixed, in others the water is metered and a charge is levied per unit used. This charge is one of the many operating costs which arise at the place of residence. The fairness of this charge depends, however, on the pricing system chosen, and on the demand generated. Much of the peak demand in American cities arises in the summer months as yard-sprinkling is added to normal residential uses. Sprinkling is almost exclusively a suburban phenomenon—the typical inner city dweller having no yard to sprinkle. In addition "customers who reside in low-density areas furthest from the water system's load center are being subsidized by those who reside in high density areas that are closer to load centers." Hanke and Davis then go on to test to see what the effect would be if a pricing system which reflected at least the seasonality of demand were introduced. They estimate that:

The typical Washington, D.C. inner-city consumer's average price per thousand would be reduced 0.8 per cent by the introduction of seasonal pricing, whereas the D.C. near-suburban consumer's average price per thousand would be increased by 10.1 per cent. Moreover, the inner city consumer would use a little more water at the reduced average price (+0.5 per cent) whereas the near-suburban consumer would use less water in the sprinkling season (−20.1 per cent) and more during the winter season (+3.4 per cent).[7]

There are, therefore, some hidden subsidies within utility pricing schemes many of which amount to an income transfer from poor inner-city areas to affluent suburban areas.

Changing the pricing system for water will affect the operating cost at the place of residence and it will also have an impact upon the exchange value. In Baltimore, Maryland, for example:

the City is in the process of installing individual water meters. . . . As a consequence, water costs have become a variable rather than a fixed charge, and in some cases are the deciding factor in the determination of whether cash-flow will be positive or negative. Today, investors who are buying at all will shy away from a house that is metered or reduce their bid if they do consider the property.[8]

In the Baltimore case prices were not seasonally adjusted and the installation of water meters has resulted in many cases in the raising of rents or to the landlord's passing on the water bill to the tenant. The latter response had led to a long-simmering dispute between tenants and landlords in many parts of the city which has recently led to court actions. This problem may arise in part because of the hidden subsidy passed on to the suburbs by a discriminatory water pricing policy.

This example of water pricing policy provides a lesson which may be applied in the analysis of the provision of all public utilities. Peak loads occur in the demand for electricity and in cities like Washington, D.C., and Baltimore, this peak load is generated in the summer through the heavy use of air conditioners. The poor groups do not have air conditioning and they contribute little or nothing to this peaking problem. Yet they are charged as if they did. Similar observations apply to the provision of sewage and sanitation services, transport facilities, and so on. There is no reason why the pricing system has to be systematically discriminatory against the poor, but in most cases it works out that way. Insofar as this result comes about, it generates an implicit transfer of income from the poor to the rich and provides one further source for disproportionate appropriation of the surplus.

4. *Noxious facilities* are defined as those things which nobody wants to be close to. This is rather too simple a definition however. Nevertheless, it is important to recognize that the use value of a place of residence can be very much affected by proximity to unpleasant facilities. The problem is that the facilities themselves are not necessarily unpleasant, but they may create side-effects or "externalities" as they are sometimes called, which spill over into the surrounding area. The obvious examples here would be air pollution, noise pollution, traffic congestion, water pollution, and the like. The reduction in use value brought about from these causes will depend upon the location of the residence with respect to the generating source, together with those factors which determine the spatial extent of the noxiousness. Thus the intensity of air pollution will vary according to the prevailing winds, the diffusion and dispersal rates from the source of emission, and the nature of the emission. The costs imposed by air pollution are difficult to total. We can get reasonable estimates of cleaning and maintenance costs, but the indirect costs to physical and mental health are virtually incalculable.

Many facilities have a curious spatial distribution of noxious effects. An airport, for example, is a noxious facility up to a certain distance away, and yet it is a facility which has positive effects upon the potential use value of the place of residence further away. This is also true of urban highways and many other facilities. Julian Wolpert, in a study of noxious facilities in Philadelphia, found that many facilities become noxious when they come too close—schools, bars, shops, and the like.[9] As a result there is often some ambiguity involved in the definition of noxiousness. The degree of noxiousness changes with distance and it will also vary according to individual variations in the definition of noxiousness (proximity to a school may be annoying to some and not to others). Other forms of noxiousness do not suffer from this kind of ambiguity, however. Proximity to major sources of air pollution, to fire hazards, and to centers of criminal activity, is presumably not welcomed by anyone. Even in situations where there is some ambiguity, as is the case with urban freeways, there is little doubt that all would regard them as a noxious facility when located close by. The distribution of these noxious facilities (or perhaps it would be better to call them noxious aspects of facilities) will clearly affect the use value of a house as well as the exchange value.

Since many of these facilities are subject to public regulation and control (and some are provided through public action), it often transpires that the distribution of political power has a very considerable impact upon the distribution of noxious facilities. Politically powerful groups (who usually have the necessary financial resources to become powerful) thus usually succeed in eliminating noxious facilities from their neighborhood and keeping proposed noxious facilities out. But noxious facilities have to be put somewhere (which is not to say that there could not be considerable advances made in reducing levels of noxiousness). Therefore it is likely that noxious facilities will be located in those communities which have the least political power. Until recently, that has meant the inner-city poverty areas or sparsely populated rural areas have only recently started to resist the implanting of facilitied, particularly highways, power stations, and other facilities which are destructive of the use value of residences. The study of highway location controversies is extremely instructive in this regard for during the 1960s most urban freeways were located through the poorest communities. Now many cities (Baltimore being an excellent example) have numerous proposed highway routes through the city but none seems to be acceptable since each proposal is destructive of use values somewhere and each community concerned is voicing strong political opposition.

The four examples we have looked at were designed to demonstrate how the use value of a residence to individuals can be affected in a number of distinctive ways, both negative and positive, through the spatial organization of the urban system. The resources made available to individuals and the burdens imposed (through noxious facilities, pricing systems, and the like) are quite significant, when taken in total, for understanding how a socially produced surplus is appropriated by different groups. Many of the resources are publicly provided on a redistributive basis. In some cases the redistribution is progressive but in others it is regressive. Much of the overt redistribution in American cities (the public provision of welfare payments through taxation, for

example) is at least designed to be progressive, but there are many covert redistributions which may well more than counteract this progressive element. It is thus quite possible, that the poverty stricken inner-cities are supporting the affluent suburbs rather than the other way round. If so, here is yet another dimension to that general process of accumulating a large proportion of the surplus in a few hands.

NOTES

1. M. Clawson, "Open (uncovered) Space as a New Urban Resource," in H. Perloff (ed.), *The Quality of the Urban Environment* (Baltimore: Johns Hopkins University Press, 1969).
2. B. J. L. Berry, *The Geography of Market Centers and Retail Distribution* (Englewood Cliffs, N.J.: Prentice Hall, 1967).
3. Kerner Commission, *Report of the National Advisory Commission on Civil Disorders* (New York: Bantam Books, 1968), pp. 274–7.
4. President's National Advisory Panel on Insurance in Riot Affected Areas, *Meeting the Insurance Crisis of our Cities* (Washington, D.C.: Government Printing Office, 1968).
5. D. Caplovitz, *The Poor Pay More* (New York: The Free Press, 1963).
6. R. L. Morrill, R. J. Earickson, and P. Rees, "Factors Influencing Distances Traveled to Hospitals," *Economic Geography* 46 (1970): 161–71. See also R. L. Morrill and R. J. Earickson, "Variations in the Character and Use of Hospital Services," *Health Services Research* 3, reprinted in L. S. Bourne (ed.), *Internal Structure of the City* (New York: Oxford University Press, 1968).
7. S. H. Hanke and R. K. Davis, "Demand Management Through Responsive Pricing," *Journal of the American Water Works Association* 63 (1971): 555–60.
8. W. G. Grigsby, L. Rosenburg, M. Stegman, and J. Taylor, *Housing and Poverty* (Institute for Environmental Studies: University of Pennsylvania, 1971), chapter 6.
9. Wolpert discusses many of the problems discussed in this section in Resource Paper No. 16.

TOWARD A THEORY OF URBAN FACILITY LOCATION
MICHAEL B. TIETZ

The location of urban public facilities is guided by somewhat different principles from those which underly conventional locational analysis. Since locational decisions are centralized within the public sector, emphasis must be placed on the efficiency of the *system* rather than on the individual facility. Furthermore, such systems typically possess hierarchical structures for both administrative and service reasons. Tietz seeks to provide a foundation for a separate theory of urban public facility location which recognizes these distinctions; however, his argument still lies within the classical mold of economic analysis with its primary emphasis on efficient solutions without regard to social or political influences.

Reprinted from *Papers of the Regional Science Association* 21 (1968): 35–52, by permission of the publisher and the author. This is an edited version of the original publication.

This research was supported in part by the Economic Development Administration, United States Department of Commerce. The author would like to thank members of the faculty and students at the Department of City and Regional Planning, University of California, Berkeley, for criticisms, suggestions, and information.

Although it is not entirely true to say that location theorists have ignored the problem of public facility location in cities, their concern has been slight.

The failure of location theorists to consider publicly determined facilities is quite surprising when one comes to consider the role of those facilities in shaping both the physical form of cities and the quality of life within them.

Modern urban man is born in a publicly financed hospital, receives his education in a publicly supported school and university, spends a good part of his life travelling on publicly built transportation facilities, communicates through the post office or the quasi-public telephone system, drinks his public water, disposes of his garbage through the public removal system, reads his public library books, picnics in his public parks, is protected by his public police, fire, and health systems; eventually he dies, again in a hospital, and may even be buried in a public cemetary. Ideological conservatives notwithstanding, his everyday life is inextricably bound up with governmental decisions on these and numerous other local public services.

Implicitly, we seem to have assumed as theorists that the character and location of public facilities simply reflect the overwhelming nonpublic decisions on residential, commercial, and industrial location. Furthermore, we have assumed that since market-based competitive models of the latter should lead to Pareto optimal location patterns under atomistic decisions, the public decisions accompanying them should likewise be optimal. It is sometimes hard to take market-based location theory seriously in the real world. Even if it does hold, one is hard put to see why the political process should respond in an optimal way. Yet, by and large, government has in the past responded sufficiently well to give rise to virtually no theoretical speculation about the nature of the response and its implications for the city.

Urban planners, for all their shortcomings, have recognized the problem in practice. But the lack of a theoretical basis for action has left their response mechanical and inadequate. Rules of thumb about size and location of facilities have been developed but, for the most part, without ways to evaluate the results or to stimulate invention of new systems. With services locked in mazes of standards and without powerful competitive pressures for innovation, only crisis has precipitated demands for reevaluation of urban services. And even then, the response tends to be a shotgun scatter of proposals—not a remarkable result, given that no framework for evaluation exists. In this context, it is interesting to note the current urban crisis in America. With it has come the usual plethora of proposals, this time including measures emanating from the federal level that could drastically change the pattern of urban public services. The schools are the first target, but no doubt others will face similar problems.

Beyond these questions lies a further uncharted territory. Although theorists may have assumed that public facilities followed private decisions, a powerful feedback of public decisions on private also seems likely. If government can use public facilities as instruments to shape urban growth and social and economic behavior, then a new level of evaluation is superimposed on the usual considerations for public services. Of course, planners have been advocating this for many years, but only now does it begin to seem a serious possibility for reasonably scientific investigation. However, even if such larger aims are not now achievable, the drive toward PPB,* systems analysis, and cost-benefit at the lo-

* Planning, Programming, Budgeting.—Editors' Note

cal level suggests a rising interest in more efficient and effective utilization of resources in urban services to achieve the direct public ends for which those services were instituted. For this alone, some theoretical structure might be invaluable.

PUBLIC AND PRIVATE LOCATION

These considerations suggest that urban public facility location is worth some theoretical exploration. They do not demonstrate that such a theory is unified, feasible, or significantly different from other components of location theory, including central place theory. In the remainder of this paper, it is scarcely possible to develop a full-blown theory of public facility location. Rather, we shall try to indicate its unique characteristics and sketch out some of its most interesting component problems.

The first question that we shall examine concerns the relation of a theory of public location to conventional location theory. There are several important qualitative differences between them. Both location and the scale of expenditure on urban public facilities are determined by some sort of public or quasi-public process. This central fact gives rise to some important characteristics. It suggests that public location theory may bear a relationship to conventional location theory similar to that between the expenditure side of public finance or welfare economics and conventional economic theory. In each case, the former focuses upon public decisions and government budgets in response to some welfare criterion in a mixed market-nonmarket setting. The latter emphasizes the role of choice, taste, and utility or profit maximization in a predominantly market context. Under assumptions of competition and many decision units, the result should be Pareto optimal allocations. Public expenditure theory constantly seeks some equivalent framework in a situation of one or few decision units and restricted personal choice.

One should not carry the analogy too far. Several writers on local public expenditures have pointed out the asymmetry between national and local public finance resulting from large numbers of governments at the local level. Tiebout (1956) used this property of local finance as a basis for a consumer behavior oriented theory of local public expenditures. We recognize the existence of many local governments but, for purposes of analysis, will begin by treating public facility location on the basis of a single government.

If a single government is responsible for provision of some service over a given area, then a second powerful contrast with conventional location theory emerges. Location theory of the firm or consumer asserts that many decentralized decisions have produced an observed pattern of locations. The pattern may be described positivistically as a system by central place theory, but its locational efficiency is not usually evaluated in system terms. For example, retail location analysts may count the number of supermarkets in an area and describe their pattern. Usually, they do not ask whether the individual markets are too small or too large. If the market is operating effectively, such questions are automatically taken care of.

For public facilities, in contrast, these are central questions. Even if we accept an incrementalist view of government budgeting, the problems of the appropriate scale and location of new facilities remain. If a more general position is adopted for theoretical investigation, the over-all scale of operation, i.e., the determination of the budget, becomes critical. Such a view has powerful implications for locational analysis. The theorist of public facility location finds himself inevitably drawn away from the problem of location of the individual facility and toward the structure and location of the entire *system* of facilities within the area over which the government exerts jurisdiction.

Location theory has not concerned itself much with multiple location systems. Operations researchers have analyzed multifacility location problems in practice; location theorists have dealt little with the theory of the multiple facility firm. Yet many interesting problems arise as soon as one begins to look at location from a system viewpoint. For example, one might ask for an appropriate retail location strategy for supermarket chains of different sizes. Or, again, what happens to the Hotelling problem under multiple unit assumptions? To my knowledge there is very little theoretical discussion of these or similar questions.

System location is not a single problem, as will be shown below. But in one form or another, it does appear crucial in most considerations of public facilities. Before we go on to examine in detail some of these manifestations, some further characteristics of public facility systems and decisions need to be identified.

Public Facility Systems

In order to talk about public facility location, it is desirable to characterize public facilities. Presumably, we mean those components of the city whose primary function is to facilitate the provision of goods and services declared to be wholly or partly within the domain of government. The range of such goods and the degree of government involvement vary greatly over time and place. Almost every function has been run at some time or place by government. For purposes of the present discussion, we will take the set of governmental urban functions in western countries, particularly the United States and Canada, as our purview. No attempt will be made here to establish a list of such functions or their associated goods and services in detail.

In the understanding of urban systems, such a list may eventually be necessary and might bear a relation to public location similar to that of the complete classification of industry to the theory of industrial location. Or perhaps a better analogy might be the relation of anatomy to human biology.

For preliminary discussion, some first approximations to classes of functions and facilities may be invaluable. We will approach this through the description of generalized ways of making such distinctions. A first cut at the problem follows the theory of public expenditures in classifying outputs and associated facility systems as public or collective use goods, zero short-run marginal cost goods, or merit goods. An air pollution monitor system is of the first kind, a noncongested street network of the second, and, so far as one can tell, a public library system of the third. This is a well-understood basis for discrimination and may have significant utility in the study of location. But, for the moment, we shall not explore it further here except to note its influence on the classifications below.

A second distinction applies to facility systems rather than to goods and services and focuses on their geometric properties. Since theorization and model building imply abstraction, we would do well to look at the most likely abstractions of facility systems. They appear to take two common forms, point patterns and networks. Point patterns characterize a variety of distributive services in which the final phase of distribution is flexible and intermittent. Medical centers, post offices, libraries, police, and fire systems are of this type. On the other hand, many services call for continuous connections in space. For these a network characterization seems more suitable. Examples might be water, sewer, electric power, gas, telephone, and highways. Let it be emphasized that these are merely suggestive distinctions.

Clearly, for any urban function the abstraction is technologically influenced and often more properly described as a mixture than a pure form of one or the other. In the present context, it is useful because we will be concerned more often with point-representable than network-representable systems.

Related to the formal geometric property is another quality which combines geometry and behavior. It often appears useful to characterize point-representable facility systems by the direction of interaction associated with each point in the system and by the abstraction of its relationship to the city, itself abstracted as a point pattern or surface. A system of facilities representable by a point pattern may take this particular form as a compromise between scale economies in operation and economies in distribution. However, there are interesting differences observable in the distribution process itself. We might distinguish on the basis of direction of flow, for example, among systems involving physical movement, between those that are distributors and those that are collectors. In a formal sense, though, these abstract to the same thing. Rather more interesting might be a distinction among distributional systems on the basis of the formal representation as mappings of their relationships with the city. If we represent the city as a point set or surface, the relations between the facility system as domain and its sphere of concern as range may be one-one, one-many, or many-many. Which of these is appropriate seems to be a function of the technical properties of the system, its status as a public good, and the role of consumer choice in consumption of its output. An example involving the first and third of these is offered by the post office. The collection and distribution facilities of the post office are asymmetric. Ideally, each letter entering the system must find a unique destination, namely its addressee, and all letters must be delivered. To achieve these ends effectively, and retain security, an obvious solution is to assign a unique one-many mapping between post office substations and addresses. Thus, at the last stage of its trip, any letter to a particular address comes from exactly one substation. Admittedly, other methods could be employed and perhaps should be examined, but this one appears to be universal. In contrast, the collection arm requires no such form. Because all letters must go into a common sorting process, there is no need for any letter to enter at a unique point. Additionally, part of the collection cost may easily and without significant loss of security be passed on to the consumer. The result is a mailbox system as the lowest order subsystem on the collection side. It exhibits a many-many relation to the set of addresses in the city and consequently is not a mapping in the strict mathematical sense.

At the risk of belaboring this point excessively, we might point out that the form of relation determines whether the city must be divided into regions for any particular function. Post office substation delivery regions exist; mail box collection regions do not. Not uncommonly, regions are established administratively with no such functional basis. Large urban public libraries offer examples of such exhaustive and disjoint region systems. They also may exhibit inconsistency in boundaries and general disregard for their existence. Given the character of the library function, this is not surprising, and, in fact, it is probably more healthy than the creation of such regions in the first place. A similar problem appears in efforts to delineate hospital market areas.

A final characteristic of public facility systems that we must mention is their hierarchical property. Almost universally, hierarchical elements appear in the technical structure of public facility systems. At least two sources contribute to the generation of hierarchies. For spatially continuous or regularly periodic distribution and collection systems, the logic of aggregation and system control calls for attenuation of capacity as the consumer is approached. Thus, electrical distribution requires a decline in voltage which is best attained in discrete steps with a transformer station at each stage. Simultaneously, the number of branches in the network increases. Water and sewer pipe capacities likewise propagate steplike attenuation and dendritic properties.

A similar effect in point-representable systems arises from variation in the functions they perform and concurrent scale variations in requirements necessary to support specific functions, either due to cost or infrequency of demand. This effect parallels the orders of stores and goods in a central place system. Every firehouse may have an engine and ladder company, but a specialized heavy rescue company will be much rarer, although located at some firehouse in the system. Whether the outcome for any system is a pure hierarchy depends on the degree to which the higher order system elements include all functions of lower order. For public services, this may not necessarily be the case, especially where specialized components reflect local peculiarities in the demand structure, such as an alcoholic treatment unit in the local medical center catering to skid road.

Empirical information on hierarchical structure in public facilities is scarce and sometimes misleading. There seems to be confusion between technical requirements and standards. In many cases, the existence of an apparent hierarchy reflects the earlier acceptance of some system of standards that may be of dubious value. Where such standards no longer reflect technology, cost, and social objectives effectively, the observed hierarchy may be quite misleading. Nevertheless, incorporation of hierarchical properties into public location models remains important.

Public Facility Decisions

Its concern with systems sets off public from conventional location theory in terms of units. The fact of being governmental similarly shifts the emphasis in the structure of optimization, that is, objective functions and constraints.

We have previously mentioned the general problems raised by governmental allocation—the need for a social welfare function, the absence of a competitive price system, and the problem of appropriate levels for allocation and optimization. The response of public expenditure economics to these problems has been cost-benefit analysis. In military systems analysis, the heavier emphasis on system design and the impossibility of attaching dollar values to some components of the cost-benefit expression, even though they are quantifiable, has led to a form of cost-benefit in which multiple effectiveness criteria are substituted for the single benefit measure. If we lump these together, calling them cost-utility analysis, they provide a technical framework for decision comparable, if theoretically inferior, to simple profit or utility maximization under competition.

Having said this much, most of the interesting problems still remain. We shall briefly comment on some broad questions first, then pursue those especially germane to public facility location. Governments and their component agencies operate under a budget allocation system. This implies at least three major levels of decision, although they may not be separable in practice. Society decides as a whole what part of its resources will be allocated to objectives whose machinery for realization is administered or heavily influenced by government. Within this over-all allocation, government allocates resources to what we will call major program areas. These

we will take to be clusters of objectives of a similar type. Within these program areas, in turn, resources must be allocated to particular programs and their associated systems of facilities. At this point, we will not consider the validity of this description in terms of behavior, nor will we speculate on the direction of determination, that is, whether the real world budget represents a sectoring of a pie or a plate of cookies. We assume that some allocation process exists whereby a quantity of resources becomes available for a program, loosely defined. This assumption is dangerous in that it tends to lead toward the specification of the system location problem in a constrained budget-effectiveness maximization form. Such a form predicates that the entire budget for the program must be used up, a view consistent with agency behavior but lacking elegance and clearly inefficient unless exactly the right amount has been allocated to ensure equality of marginal net social return in all programs. The latter, to be known, implies that the pattern of expenditures and benefits is known in each program. Thus, the problem is circular. Optimal over-all allocation presumes optimal program allocation which, in turn, requires an over-all allocation for its calculation, especially if interprogram spillovers are taken into account.

We could look at the process as a time-free iteration or a sequential response over budget cycles. In any event, it makes little difference where we enter except insofar as emphasis is placed on achieving optimality at the higher, government-wide, or lower, program-facility system, level. And, of course, it is the latter in which we are chiefly interested. For the former, it might be that a constrained effectiveness-budget minimization form proves more appropriate. On the other hand, the use of multiple nonequivalent effectiveness measures would lead to choice of this form for the system problem.

Another general problem which faces facility location, in common with local expenditure allocation, is the absence of a social welfare function. Even lacking such a function, we might be willing, if all benefits and costs could be quantified in dollar terms, to accept an aggregate net benefit outcome that appeared large enough. Without monetarily quantifiable benefits, we are inevitably forced to consider in detail the distributional consequences of an outcome both over space and over population groups. Where government policies specify "target groups" this is a desirable result. Yet, at the local level, it may lead to political complexities beyond manageability.

Given these difficulties, we may now consider relevant variables for public facility system decisions. Evidently, we need to know what it is about systems that influences their cost and effectiveness, however measured. In part, the answer depends on the form in which the public location problem is posed, a topic taken up below. In general, however, we may immediately identify the opposing forces of economies of scale and advantages of dispersion.

This is a refrain familiar to location theorists. Of particular interest here is its formulation in system terms in a context which lends itself to effective measurement. For a point-representable facility system, we might hypothesize the effectiveness of an individual component depends upon its scale and the disposition of the rest of the components in the system. The effectiveness of the system as a whole depends upon the scale of its components and their combined relationship to each other. Under an unconstrained budget, system effectiveness should increase or at least not decrease with the number of components, since new additions do not interfere with the scale of the old. The improvement might increase almost indefinitely, although with decreasing marginal gain. For example, if response time were a measure of fire system effectiveness, then any new fire house would decrease first response time up to the point where every structure in the city became a fire house. If the budget for the system is constrained, this is no longer true.

Under a constrained budget, several variables begin to interact. Let us assume that a distinction is made between capital and operating outlays but that the system structure is highly flexible. The first result of a budget constraint is that addition of a new component to a given facility system reduces the resources available to the previously existing components. Where the resources come from remains indeterminate. We could reduce the capital outlays, i.e., the scale of all or some facilities or reduce their operating expenditures, i.e., output. However, we must also take into account the interaction between these in turn.

Public facilities produce a variety of goods and services and their relationship to the consuming population varies greatly. Two important sources of variation are individual choice and pricing in the consumption of the outputs. At one extreme are those goods for which consumer choice is virtually nonexistent and direct price zero. These include most police and fire services as well as pure public goods. When a man's house is on fire he rarely pauses to consider whether or not to call the fire brigade. Nor, in our present system, is he usually presented with a bill for fire protection service that varies with the size of fire that he enjoyed during the previous year. Thus, once some communal decisions about form and quantity of expenditure on fire service have been made, the form of system will depend upon the expected scale and pattern of fires, the technology of surveillance and response, and the measures of effectiveness employed. If a measure such as response time dominates, then for a given surveillance system the result should be maximum dispersion. However, since there are some widely accepted minimum operating scales—the engine company—dispersion must be tempered by the need to retain this minimum scale of operation. This represents the present pattern of local response in fire systems. Overlaid upon this level are higher order fire suppression and rescue functions that will increase the scale of investment and operations for some system components. Additionally, the fire system incorporates many phenomena that derive from its peculiar relationship to standards established by the underwriters. Since compliance with the standards rather than empirical fire experience determines insurance rates in most cases, their influence on the configuration of facilities is immense. Other criteria also influence fire control facility location, particularly high fire risk and life risk situations such as oil refineries and hospitals, respectively. Thus, for this type of service, the existing pattern of facilities represents a series of compromises plus a certain amount of political and organizational maneuvering—the more fire houses, the higher the prestige of the chief. Consumer choice in the usual sense plays little part in determining the shape of the system.

Urban services for which consumer choice is significant but price zero present a different picture. Libraries provide a good example of such a function. In general, the larger the scale of a unit in such a system, the more consumers it attracts by virtue of providing better or more varied services, for example, by carrying a larger book stock. Since entry is free for members of the community and they commonly travel to the facility for the service, travel cost, including time and inconvenience, represents the major real cost to the consumer. Under these circumstances, we would expect to find a distance decay effect on usage. If the budget is fixed but the number of facilities variable, then a larger number of outlets implies a smaller scale at each but greater aggregate access to the population. The scale effect and the distance effect then conflict. An optimal system must solve for both scale and location.

One further complexity should be noted. We have not defined scale precisely, implicitly assuming it to involve relatively fixed cost components of total cost for any facility. But in public facility systems, as any others, variable costs depend on the volume of services rendered. Since price is zero, this volume depends on demand which, in turn, depends on the spatial structure and scale of facilities. The system is in a curious position of being able to generate demand by organizing itself appropriately, but, at the same time, its variable costs will increase and must be constrained within the budget. Demand and supply are tightly interlocked, indeed so much so that it may be impossible to talk about actual quantity supplied except in terms of the amount demanded.

In practice, many of the influences mentioned earlier temper the form of facility system that emerges. Locations of outlets for "free" services are not easily moved in the face of opposition from citizens who know well that they are not free. The influence of standards pervades system evaluation and perception by participants. Often, little or nothing is known about potential response to changes in location as against other elements that influence demand.

CONCLUSION

The chief aim of this paper has been to make a case for a field of location theory specifically devoted to urban public facilities. Such an endeavor appears to be worthwhile both for its theoretic interest and its probably utility. Theoretical problems derive chiefly from the system character of the unit of location and the public decision aspect of objective functions and constraints. Practical applications are suggested by recent attempts to improve the quality of local resource allocation through such devices as PPB.

For the most part, we have catalogued problems. Several important ones remain unconsidered. Foremost among them is the question of multiple jurisdictions providing the same services within a larger area. This can occur in two ways. Multiple governments exert jurisdiction over spatially disjoint territories within most larger urban areas. The allocation of resources under such circumstances had been examined by Tiebout (1956) and Williams (1966). Within any government, there is typically functional overlap between agencies or departments. This problem has been discussed chiefly in a nontheoretical way in the PPB litera-

ture. Both are likely to influence facility system location.

Finally, we should be well aware that public decisions are made in the political system. Political variables will enter any decision on a facility system, especially since public facilities are so often the visible symbols of delivery of public goods to particular groups in the city. We have not considered political variables here, being more concerned with an efficiency approach, but their power may be attested by any official who has ever tried to close an existing facility.

REFERENCES

Tiebout, C. M. 1956. A pure theory of local expenditures. *Journal of Political Economy* 64: 416–24.

Williams, A. 1966. The optimal provision of public goods in a system of local government. *Journal of Political Economy* 74: 18–33.

A PARADIGM FOR
PUBLIC FACILITY LOCATION THEORY
MICHAEL J. DEAR

While recognizing the importance of the contribution made by Tietz, Dear questions the methods of general equilibrium analysis that Tietz adopted with its implicit dependence on the criterion of efficiency. Dear, on the other hand, proposes that public facility location should be guided by principles of equity, leading to a redistribution of resources, a redistribution which is demanded by the failure of the private sector. In particular, Dear stresses the difference between *accessibility* to a facility which implies the ability to use it and *proximity* which merely indicates physical closeness without guaranteeing access. The weakness of many analyses of facility location is that they have only considered proximity and have ignored the role of accessibility.

Reprinted from *Antipode: A Radical Journal of Geography* 6, no. 1 (1974): 46–50, by permission of the publisher and the author.

Part of the reason for the apparent lack of concern undoubtedly derives from the classical location theorist's viewpoint of the subject as ancillary to residential location, or as a special case of retail or commercial location. Thus, public facilities are traditionally associated with service sector functions, and their location is generally regarded as being determined by the pattern of residential location. Such a viewpoint is under increasing attack from a welter of empirical evidence, testifying to the "catalytic" effect of public facility location upon land development. However, such evidence has hardly begun to penetrate the bastions of theoretical thinking. This is largely because the catalytic role of public facilities requires a radically different way of conceptualizing the locational problem. It is no longer possible to view the issue within the comfortable perspective of a public response to private market developments. Instead, one is forced to conceptualize public facilities as primary generators of land use change, including private sector responses to the public sector development. In short, new public facility paradigms would need to incorporate some sort of "planning" consciousness.

Further reason why the public facility location problem has been obscured may be found in the methodological literature. The literature on private sector location is one of the best developed in the field of location theory. The majority of these models involve a programming approach in which the total cost of transportation and facilities is minimized, subject to a number of budgetary (and other) constraints. It is unfortunately true that most scholars in the public facility field have been content simply to use this basic framework in formulating a public sector model. The easiest way of doing this is to substitute some surrogate for social utility into the objective function, and make the corresponding adjustments to the constraints. Common surrogates have included minimizing aggregate consumer transport costs, or maximizing the amount of demand created by the system of facilities. The implicit assumption behind this transformation of the private sector model into a public model is that the two models have the same underlying conceptual foundations. But nothing could be further from the truth.

The fact is that public facility location models must be judged by criteria totally different from their private sector equivalents. Although much of the rest of this paper is devoted to elaborating and supporting this contention, a few simple examples will help to illustrate the complexity of the public sector issues. It seems naive, for instance, to pursue a program for public facility location based upon the notion of maximum accessibility of service since "accessibility" means such different things to different people. Consider the "consumption" of mental health and mental retardation services (Dear, 1974). The relatives of mentally retarded children usually want to be quite close to their childrens' school, either because they wish to visit frequently, or because they do not want their child to have to travel far. For these people, "accessibility" in terms of physical proximity is obviously a major concern. For the drug addict seeking treatment however, "accessibility" means something quite different. It is often the case that the physical location of treatment centers is of little consequence to the addict. Once an addict decides that he *needs* treatment, he will travel virtually any distance to obtain it. For drug addicts, therefore, "psychological accessibility" to a sympathetic service is much more important than physical proximity.

It might be contended that the traditional model of facility location could be modified to cope with what may be regarded as only the varying perceptions of distance held by the clients for mental health care. This would have the effect of imposing distance constraints upon a "maximize demand created" model format. However, the problems with such a social welfare surrogate are even greater because the notion of "demand" for public facilities is particularly fuzzy. It is more appropriate to speak of "need,"—something quite different and thus far relatively unmeasurable.

This is meant to suggest that superficial tinkering with private sector models does not make public sector models. The public facility problem is much more subtle, requiring different criteria for modelling. An alternative approach has been suggested by Tietz (1968), who laid some very important ground rules for the theory of urban public facility location. But his analytical approach was founded in the neo-classical tradition of the theory of the firm and somehow managed to assume away the whole problem of location! In spite of the value of Tietz's contribution in conceptualizing the public facility location issue, the lack of further development of his analytical model may be interpreted as further evidence of the unsuitability of private sector analysis for public sector problems.

THE NEED FOR A NEW PARADIGM

In order to develop a more useful and realistic approach to the public facility location problem, the ties with traditional theory and practice have to be broken. Some new criteria for evaluating the public sector problem are required, and the power of public facility location to act as a catalyst for urban development needs to be explored.

Fortunately, the search for a brave new paradigm is not without any signposts. Several recent studies have pointed the way. Mumphrey and Wolpert (1973) have shown how efficiency and equity considerations may be taken into account in practical decisions on public facility locations. Seley (1973) has discussed the dimensions of conflict over public facility location, and demonstrated methods of analyzing it, while Harvey (1973) has been asking for some time for us to consider the "vast unanswered questions concerning the redistributive effects of decisions made in the public sector." We need to focus mainly on the *distinctive context* of the public facility location problem. This distinctive context categorically separates the public sector problem from its private sector counterpart. It is founded basically in the "publicness" of the public sector locational decision—the need for equity as well as efficiency in the locational outcome, the lack of competition in service delivery, and the need for public accountability and public input in the decision. In addition, whereas the private sector problem concentrates upon the structure and location of individual units, a public sector theory deals mainly with multiple location systems in a dynamic framework. Finally there is the organizational question peculiar to public facility organization: where does the responsibility for public production of a good or service stop, and public provision begin (via some contracting agency but at public expense)? And where in this hierarchy is the power of independent decision-making discretion most appropriately delegated?

Out of this distinctive context come a number of *characteristics* common to most public facility location problems. First, is their concern with public goods —either in the (almost) "pure" sense of a public park, or in the "welfare" sense of a redistribution of resources toward some target population (as with free treatment at a local health center). Another characteristic encountered is the hierarchical nature of most public facility systems. The hierarchy may manifest itself in terms of buildings (one large central library, and several smaller branch libraries) or in terms of organization (as

in a typical hospitalization sequence of intake-treatment-convalescence-release). In both cases, the hierarchical component will have spatial/locational manifestations. The problem is further characterized by the multiplicity of inputs to a locational decision: diverse groups interact, bringing differing motivations and goals to the decision-making process. Not surprisingly, conflict is inherent. Conflict can also be generated in situations where consumers lack alternatives in the private sector and cannot cease consumption of one output in favor of another (Hirschman, 1970). Among the causes of such situations are poverty, lack of information and monopoly in the provision of the public service. More frequently, the consumer group only has a "voice" option—to remain in place and sue for improvement via the political process. The process of "voicing" opinion over public facility issues is a common feature of many locational decisions as, for instance, in the construction of controversial expressway access roads.

THE FOCUS OF A NEW PARADIGM

A new paradigm for public facility location is beginning to take shape. We have argued for a distinctive context for public facility location, and have developed a set of characteristics which figure prominently in most locational decisions. However, even with these dimensions, it is possible to pursue the problem into a Tietz-like general equilibrium analysis, or into a typical programming framework. Our developing paradigm is clearly in need of a focus—some sort of organizing principle.

A focus is suggested from a simple consideration of what public facilities are all about. Public facilities (and the goods and services provided therefrom) are designed to effect some kind of redistribution of resources, or, at least patch up some failure in the private market.

Such a redistribution may be direct, as in the case of the provision of free medical care; or indirect, as in the case of a rise in property values associated with proximity to an urban park. The proper focus of a new public facility location paradigm should therefore be upon the distributive consequences of public facility location, and the manner in which those consequences are achieved.

Nevertheless, many of the present issues in public facility location theory will have continuing relevance. For example, the problem of optimal facility location is clearly still significant, although it requires some reinterpretation. However, other issues will achieve greater prominance under the suggested paradigm. Thus, the decision process and the institutional context for public facility location will be of major importance, as will the normative aspects of location.

ISSUES IN A PUBLIC FACILITY LOCATION PARADIGM

Since the above view on the public facility location problem is relatively unexplored, it would be better to concentrate initial research effort on basic issues. Attention ought to be drawn to the precise nature of the relationship between location and its distributive consequences, upon the mechanisms through which these consequences are achieved, and upon the forces behind the consequences. Let us look at these in more detail.

The location of public facilities has two major *distributive consequences*—direct and indirect. A direct impact affects only those individuals who actually consume the good or service provided by the facility, as with patients at a hospital, or borrowers from a local library. An indirect impact affects non-consumers and is usually associated with the external or spillover effect of the facility. The external effect may be quite subtle, even non-users of a local hospital might feel com-

forted that it is close at hand in case of emergency. Alternatively, the external effect may be quite obvious, as when the rate of traffic accidents increase in the vicinity of a recently-opened expressway.

It is a reasonable working hypothesis that the direct and indirect "impact fields" of a facility's location are major tangible manifestations of its distributive consequences. However, it is not always clear exactly what is being distributed at a particular location. It would be convenient if all effects could be converted to a monetary equivalent, but this is generally impossible, and the horrifying task of quantifying intangibles remains with us. In addition, care would have to be taken to insure that the *net* distributive consequences of a location were being measured, since a benefit received from a public facility may be paid for indirectly, via taxes.

Although we may feel correct in pursuing the distributive consequences of location through the notion of an impact field, a huge problem of measurement remains. In terms of direct impact, a suitable measure of the distributive consequences may simply be the number of consumers now receiving a good or service which had previously been denied to them. However, a more proper measure would involve the inclusion of the numbers of consumers who now have access to the service, whether or not they choose to use it. In short, we would prefer to measure distributive consequences in terms of access to services, or in terms of "command over society's resources" (Harvey, 1973).

Let us now consider the *mechanisms* through which the impact field achieves its effect. By far the most important factor in this respect is that location itself is an "impure" public good (Buchanan, 1968). The act of locating a facility in one neighborhood implies that its residents enjoy a greater access to the facility than residents of other neighborhoods. To understand how this factor acts to prime the distributive mechanism, we recall Harvey's distinction between accessibility and proximity. Access to a public facility is generally regarded as a positive asset: it is worth acquiring access to the output of that facility, even at the price of overcoming distance. Conversely, proximity refers to the effect of being close to a facility which is not directly utilized, which therefore imposes a cost upon those close to it.

The relevance of these concepts is immediately apparent. Accessibility or proximity to the impact field of a public facility location will have the effect of imposing benefits or costs upon households within that field. Households may want to pay either to obtain access to the impact field, or to avoid it. Theoretically, the reaction of households to the location of the impact field ought to show up in the migration patterns, or in the property market, or in land use changes. Hence when people "vote with their feet" by moving to a preferred school district, they are, in fact, responding to a particular distribution of public facilities.

These mechanisms become complicated in practice. For example, the direct impact field of a facility may be worth buying access to, but the indirect field (externality) may be worth paying to avoid—as perhaps in the case of a drug treatment center. Here the field effects counteract one another. Complexity may also derive from a coalescence of impact fields. Thus, the neighborhood impact of a single public facility may be absorbed easily by the community: however, a second facility opened nearby might be too much for the neighborhood, and a kind of "institutional tipping" may occur in the area, whereby residential land is rapidly encroached upon by institutions (Dear, 1974).

Finally, consider briefly the *forces* be-hind the facility location. The public facility locational decision is inherently a political act, in the sense that it represents a public compromise amongst a set of conflicting participants to that decision. Traditional efficiency considerations are also important (such as the minimum operating size of a fire station) but these are of secondary significance. The political nature of the public facility locational decision derives from a number of sources, each of which warrants attention. First, the almost complete lack of criteria for locating public facilities virtually guarantees that the locational decision becomes the object of unbalanced political pressures. Second, the imperfect mechanisms of information diffusion and the translation of political goals into operational objectives for location, further unbalance political decision making. The process is again complicated by the uneven distribution of power amongst the parties to the locational decision. And finally, since resources are limited, and priorities have to be established, the location of public facilities becomes a "political" issue *par excellence.*

An essential component of a new public facility location paradigm is the analysis of the political decision making behind location. It is necessary to establish how control is exercised over location, and how it may be more effectively utilized (in a normative sense) to achieve desired ends.

A LOOK AHEAD

The public facility location paradigm sketched in this essay will hopefully enliven the study of public facility location since it focusses upon the basic issue in public facility location—the nature and causes of the relationship between location and its distributive consequences. Here we are advised to turn away from the well-trodden paths of equilibrium analysis, and away from the comfortable elegance of programming models. Instead we are directed to the *human* impact of public facility location—who gets what, and how?

REFERENCES

Buchanan, J. M. 1968. *The demand and supply of public goods.* Chicago: Rand-McNally.

Dear, M. J. 1974. Locational analysis for public mental health facilities. Unpublished Ph.D. dissertation, University of Pennsylvania.

Harvey, D. 1973. *Social justice and the city.* Baltimore: Johns Hopkins Press.

Hirschman, A. D. 1970. *Exit, voice, and loyalty.* Cambridge: Harvard University Press.

Mumphrey, A. J., and Wolpert, J. 1973. Equity considerations and concessions in the siting of public facilities. *Economic Geography* 44:109–21.

Seley, J. E. 1973. Paradigms and dimensions of urban conflict. Unpublished Ph.D. dissertation, University of Pennsylvania.

Tietz, M. B. 1968. Towards a theory of public facility location. *Papers of the Regional Science Association,* XXI, pp. 38–51.

HEALTH, POVERTY, AND THE MEDICAL MAINSTREAM

MILTON I. ROEMER
ARNOLD I. KISCH

This paper provides a general review of the problems faced by the poor in obtaining adequate health services. The issue, as the authors see it, is between the provision of special services for the poor with its inevitable aura of segregation and the improvement of services within the existing medical "mainstream." While favoring the latter as the more democratic approach, they see considerable problems in guaranteeing access to services within the present system and argue for better organization of health services from economic, technological, and geographic perspectives.

Reprinted from Warner Bloomberg, Jr. and Henry J. Schmandt, eds., *Power, Poverty, and Urban Policy*, UAAR, Volume 2 (Beverly Hills: Sage Publications, Inc., 1968), pp. 181–202, by permission of the publisher and the authors. This is an edited version of the original publication.

Of the many deprivations of the poor, deficiencies in medical service to heal their ailments and promote their health can be the most distressing. Adequate health service is important not only to cope with pain and suffering, but also to permit work and maintain productivity for the individual and community. It has, moreover, come to be an expected feature of modern civilization. Inaccessibility to medical care can yield resentment toward the whole society in which deprived persons live and further alienation from its norms and values.

BASIC PROGRAMS FOR HEALTH CARE OF THE POOR

The serious handicaps of the urban poor, both in the occurrence of disease and the receipt of medical care, have long summoned corrective social actions. Were it not for numerous organized health service programs, health conditions would be far worse. One

need only look at the mortality and morbidity of the impoverished masses in underdeveloped countries to see the effects of abject poverty, unalleviated by sociomedical efforts.

Organized health protection of the urban poor has been launched along many paths. Some programs are focused especially on the poor and others, while offered theoretically to everyone, are especially useful for the poor. Some programs are directed to certain specific diseases occurring more commonly among the deprived. In all these programs, there are achievements to report and improvements that have benefited the poor; there are also weaknesses and deficiencies that persist, particularly in comparison with the health services available to the more affluent sections of the population. To record the benefits must not be interpreted as glossing over the defects and gaps.

The modern public health movement had its beginnings in nineteenth-century

Europe largely in response to the sordid conditions in big-city slums. The rich in their country manors could, in large degree, take care of themselves, but environmental sanitation to assure clean water and proper sewage disposal was a matter of life-or-death for the urban poor. Up to the present day, the task of the public health sanitarian is heavily concentrated in the tenements of the poor. Health departments throughout the United States operate clinics for prevention of disease in infants and pregnant women. While these "maternal and child health programs" are theoretically open to everyone, in practice they are used—and sometimes deliberately restricted to—families of low income. Higher income families are expected to consult private physicians for preventive as well as curative service. In these clinics, infants receive immunizations and advice is given on diet and child-rearing. Although these programs have demonstrably reduced infant and maternal mortality, they seldom succeed in reaching all the poor and rarely assure the level of service enjoyed by the well-to-do. The funds allocated from general revenues to support such public health clinics are far less than the expenditures made by comfortable families for comparable private care (Hanlon, 1960).

Public health agencies operate other services of special value to the poor. There are clinics for the treatment of venereal disease and tuberculosis. Dental clinics are held for children. Sometimes there are clinics, operated in conjunction with the schools, for treatment of heart conditions, deafness, or other disorders in children. The fact that such public clinics usually lack the gracious setting of a private doctor's office, are often overcrowded and understaffed, and may sometimes give perfunctory attention to patients, does not negate the benefits they do offer. The task is to expand the resources going into such services and to improve their effectiveness.

Public health nurses visit the homes of the poor in connection with communicable disease, advice on newborn baby care, and even bedside service to the chronically ill. The education efforts of health departments are largely directed toward influencing the hygienic behavior of the poor. Screening tests to detect chronic diseases such as diabetes, glaucoma, cancer, or hypertension, are offered by various agencies, and these have special value for lower income groups who lack regular family doctor contacts. One of the frustrating realities, however, is that the very poorest families —alienated by ignorance or apathy—often do not take advantage of such services even when they are made conveniently available (Anderson, 1963).

While public health agency services are, in practice, devoted largely to the poor, welfare department medical services are legally restricted to the poor. The historic development of these services from the Elizabethan Poor Laws, with their sanctimonious distinction between the provident and improvident poor, to the current welfare programs is a saga of evolution in social responsibility, a saga which is still in process. In relation to the past, today's urban slum-dweller is very fortunate, but in relation to the level of services that our current medical resources could provide, the deficiencies remain serious.

The medical and related services financed by welfare agencies for the poor depend on their legal "category." Since the Social Security Act of 1935 and its numerous amendments, federal grants to the states for public assistance are based on a needy person's identification in one of four classes: (1) over 65 years of age; (2) families with children and a lacking or unemployed breadwinner; (3) blind persons; and (4) persons with "total and permanent" disability. Poor persons who do not fit into one of these classes may be eligible for "general assistance," which must be financed entirely from state and local funds, typically meager. In 1962, about 7,500,000 persons received assistance under these programs, constituting about 4 percent of the national population. These persons are concentrated heavily in the urban slums.

The precise range of medical services available to the poor under public assistance programs varies with their "category," with the state or county in which they live, and with the year under discussion. Recent changes in the Social Security Act, to be discussed below ("Medicaid"), have altered these entitlements greatly. In general, however, medical and hospital services for the "indigent" and the "medically indigent" (see below) are provided under three patterns: (1) the poor person may be seen by a personally chosen physician and hospitalized in an ordinary community hospital, with the expenses being paid by the welfare department, (2) he may be seen in an out-patient clinic of a voluntary hospital and hospitalized in a special ward for the poor in such a hospital, or (3) he may be served in special governmental clinics and hospitals intended exclusively for the poor, and usually operated by special governmental authorities (U.S. Welfare Administration, 1964).

There are special human and technical qualities to each of these patterns of medical care for the urban poor. The public clinics and hospitals are typically crowded places, often badly maintained because of frugal financial support. They have little sensitivity to personal comfort and convenience (long travel time, waiting periods, etc.) although they may give a high technical quality of service—especially if the institution is affiliated with a medical school. The private doctor arrangements, on the other hand, may be more satisfactory on the human side and less on the scientific side. Some busy physicians, however, choose not to see welfare patients at all, so that the poor

tend to consult mainly general practitioners in depressed neighborhoods. Here they tend to receive a style of medical care that is deficient both technically and humanistically.

Aside from the governmental hospitals—usually municipal or county—oriented to the poor, there are also state hospitals for mental disorders and tuberculosis, whose patients are largely from the lower income groups. Generally improved living conditions in the United States and effective new drugs (especially streptomycin) have resulted in a great reduction in the census of tuberculosis sanatoria in recent years. These institutions are being converted into facilities for general chronic diseases, predominantly serving the poor. Mental hospitals, on the other hand, are still crowded with patients, mostly from the lower income groups, although there has been a recent slight decline in census due to more effective methods of psychiatric therapy. While mental hospitals have improved their quality of care in recent years, they are still far below the level of maintenance in general hospitals which are supported mainly by the private sector. The large and semi-isolated mental institution remains an unhappy last resort for many senile paupers who, if they had the money, would be cared for at home or in a comfortable local nursing home.

Other special programs of medical care help the urban poor who qualify by reason of certain diagnoses. Crippled children, as defined by various state laws, may obtain service through special clinics or private doctors at governmental expense. Disabled adults may get "vocational rehabilitation," including corrective medical care, if treatment and training would render them employable. These programs typically have a means test, so that they are concentrated in their effects among the poor. They are financed by federal and state funds and maintain high standards of quality for the participating doctors and hospitals. Their quantitative impact, however, is small, because of the restricted medical definitions for eligibility and the relatively meager level of public financial support (Roemer, 1967).

Those urban poor who happen to be dependents of military personnel (wives and children) or veterans of past military service may be the beneficiaries of special governmental medical programs. The dependents can receive care from any physician or hospital with the bill being paid by the U.S. Department of Defense. Veterans receive care in special governmental hospitals, even for non-service-connected conditions if they are persons of low income. In contrast to the local governmental administration of programs for welfare clients, the federal administration of these services is associated with higher standards of medical performance as well as with preservation of the patient's personal dignity (I. J. Cohen, 1966).

Numerous voluntary health agencies also may serve the urban poor in such fields as home nursing ("visiting nurse associations"), personal assistance to crippled children; treatment of cancer, multiple sclerosis, muscular dystrophy, or other grave diseases; and emergency care after disasters such as floods or fires (Red Cross). Alcoholics may be helped by Alcoholics Anonymous and drug addicts by other bodies. Family planning advice and provisions may be offered in clinics of the Planned Parenthood Association. All these social services help, but they tend to have an impact far below the extent of the need among the poor.

Procurement of medical care by the self-supporting population of the United States has been greatly advanced by the extension of voluntary health insurance. There are many types, under the sponsorship of hospitals (Blue Cross), medical societies (Blue Shield), commercial insurance carriers, and employers or consumer organizations. The principal benefits of this insurance relate to hospitalization and the doctor's services in hospitalized illness, although the range of benefits has been widening. Typically, these programs ease the economic access of persons to private doctors and local hospitals and indirectly they have promoted the quality of care provided. While about 80 percent of the national population is now protected, at least partially, by hospitalization insurance, the non-protected 20 percent are heavily concentrated among the unemployed, the casually employed, the migrant, and other persons who make up the urban slum population (Somers and Somers, 1961).

The foregoing provides only a sketchy review of the principal organized social programs involving certain health services for the urban poor. In a nutshell, they all help. They tend to be improvements over the past, but none of them goes far enough. In terms of our medical potentialities, and our democratic expectations, they are generally deficient. The net impact of all these social programs, as well as the effects of actions derived from their own limited private resources, on the health services received by the poor may now be reviewed.

HEALTH SERVICES RECEIVED BY THE POOR

In spite of the variety of health service programs available to help the urban poor, the net volume of health care they receive is lower than that received by the higher income groups in both quantity and quality. This situation exists in the face of the heavier burden of disease and disability which, as we observed earlier, afflicts the poor.

The basic element in medical care is the service of a physician. From an initial contact with the doctor, other services that may be necessary follow, such as prescribed drugs, nursing care, laboratory or x-ray examinations, physical therapy, and hospitalization. Using the basic measure of "physician visits," the average American receives 5.0 such services per person per year (1959 data). For persons in families earning $7,000 or more, however, the rate is 5.7 physician visits, and it declines steadily to 4.5 visits in families earning under $2,000 annually. This relationship characterizes each age group observed separately (U.S. Public Health Service, 1964).

The locales of these physician services reflect the character of medical services received by the affluent and the poor. For both groups, the bulk of services are obtained in the office of a private physician, but the proportions at different sites are revealing. As indicated in Table 1, within the lesser overall rate of doctor's services received by the poor, the rate is lower for all locales of contact, except in hospital clinics where it is much higher. In such clinics, the time allotted per patient is typically much shorter than in a private office.

In spite of conventional notions that the poor are bountifully served in public clinics, it is evident that over 60 percent of their physician's care is obtained in private offices. Those offices, however, usually belong to general practitioners rather than specialists. Among high income families, for example, a pediatrician was consulted during the year by 29.4 percent of children (under 15 years of age), compared with 9.6 percent of low income children. An obstetrician or gynecologist was consulted by 17.1 percent of women in higher income families, compared with 3.5 percent of low income women. General physical examinations are a keystone of preventive medicine, but these too are rare among the poor. In 1963, among higher income families ($10,000 and over annually) 54 percent of youth under 17 years had such check-ups, compared with only 16 percent of youth from poor families (under $2,000) (U.S. Public Health Service, 1965).

The handicaps for dental service to the poor are even greater than for physician's service. Persons in higher income families ($7,000 and over) have 2.3 dental visits per person per year, compared with 0.7 visits among the poor (under $2,000). The dental services for the higher income groups, moreover, are more likely to consist of fillings and cleanings—preventive in effect—while for the poor they are much more likely to be extractions—the end result of neglect.

Prescribed drugs are also received at lower rates by the poor. Of the total drug consumption of the lower income groups, moreover, a higher proportion consists of self-prescribed or patent medicines. The corner druggist, it has been said, is often the poor man's doctor, offering across-the-counter pills

Locale of Physician Contacts	Family Income	
	$7,000 & Over	Under $2,000
Doctor's office	3.8	2.8
Patient's home	0.6	0.5
Telephone	0.7	0.3
Hospital clinic	0.3	0.7
Other	0.3	0.2
All places	5.7	4.5

TABLE 1. Physician Contacts

which may only serve to alleviate pains and mask symptoms, thus delaying the procurement of needed diagnosis and therapy (Consumers Union, 1963).

It is only for hospitalization that the record of health services among various income groups shows a different relationship. When prevention has failed, and when early ambulatory medical care has not halted a disease process, admission to a hospital becomes necessary. The basic findings for 1959 are set out in Table 2, but more recent data show the same relationships. As the table demonstrates, the poorest families have admissions to hospitals less than middle-income families, but almost as frequently as the highest income families. Once admitted, however, the average length-of-stay of the poor is much longer, so that the aggregate days of hospital service received by the poor is significantly *higher* than among the well-to-do.

These data reflect a great deal about the disease patterns of the poor and the way in which our society has responded to the general problems of medical care. In a word, our ameliorative social measures have followed a crisis strategy. When health problems get bad enough, we move on them. Thus, the social programs for providing hospitalization are relatively well developed. As noted earlier, there are many municipal and county hospitals for the poor. The extensive Veterans Administration hospital network will serve low income veterans even for non-military disabilities, but such conditions are not eligible for ambulatory treatment. Examining the budgets of welfare departments, we find that about two-thirds of the expenditures go for hospital care of the indigent and one-third for out-of-hospital services; among self-supporting persons, the allocations are almost exactly the opposite. In New York State, the expenditures for welfare medical services in 1963 were $184 million of which nearly $160 million or 87 percent were for institutional (hospital and nursing home) services (Yerby, 1966).

Once admitted to a hospital, the low income person stays on a longer time than his more affluent counterpart. This differential is due to several reasons. His illness is more likely to be at a far advanced stage, when recovery takes longer. Having a poorer nutritional state, his rate of recovery from surgery or his response to other therapy is likely to be slower. In public hospitals, the actual management of his care is more likely to be assigned to a young resident or intern, whose skills are less than those of a fully trained physician. The non-paying patient is more likely to be "teaching material" in a medical school—kept longer for the education of medical students. On top of all this, the indigent person's home conditions are known to be meager, so that the conscientious physician cannot discharge

Family Income	Hospital Discharges per 1,000 Persons	Average Stay (Days)	Aggregate Days per 1,000 Persons
Under $2,000	92.8	11.7	1,086
$2,000–$3,999	103.5	8.5	840
$4,000–$6,999	101.3	7.2	729
$7,000 and over	97.9	7.9	773

TABLE 2. Hospital Discharges and Stay, 1959

him as rapidly as he would release the middle-class patient, with a pleasant home in which to convalesce.

All these characteristics of the health services received by the poor are ultimately consequences of their poverty, but this is not to say that lack of money is the total explanation. As we have seen, many programs of financial support have developed over the years and these have compensated to varying degrees for the inability to purchase medical service in the private market. But beyond low purchasing power, as such, the poor suffer other handicaps that obstruct their proper use of modern medical care and their maintenance of health. Having lower levels of education, they are less likely to recognize significant symptoms and seek care. The repeated physical and emotional traumas of poverty make them fatalistic and even apathetic; delays and neglect in seeking care are the result. Even when services for mothers and infants are provided by a public health clinic in a slum neighborhood, it is common for the utilization rate to be low. Initial response to a symptom of illness is more likely to be communication with a neighbor than consultation with a doctor (King, 1962).

Compounding fatalistic attitudes are many practical impediments to medical care like time and transportation. As noted earlier, the low-income worker, unlike the white-collar employee, seldom has "sick-leave" provisions in his job, and a day lost waiting at a public clinic or even seeing a private doctor often means loss of a day's wages. The slum tenement mother cannot take a sick baby to the clinic without making provision for her other small children or dragging them along. Transportation is another problem. Dependence on buses and street cars, rather than a family automobile, is time-consuming, uncomfortable, and often irritating. On top of all this are the insensitivities and long waits in public clinics and even in the private offices of doctors serving a large proportion of the poor.

In the big-city slums, the physicians and dentists located close to the poor are likely to be the least well trained. The Watts area of Los Angeles, for example, has only one-third the doctor-population ratio of the county as a whole and only a handful of specialists. Among the smaller supply of doctors in the Watts area, only 16 percent are specialists, compared with about 55 percent in the nation as a whole. Two-thirds of the 16 percent, moreover, are self-declared specialists, rather than doctors certified by the appropriate American Specialty Boards (Roemer, 1966).

Chiropractors, herbalists, and other cultist practitioners are more likely to be located in the central-city slum than in the fashionable professional sections of a city. They are used more frequently by the poor, not only because they are close at hand, but also because they are less expensive and often more reassuring than scientific physicians. They promise quick cures, about which the unsophisticated or desperate slum-dweller may be gullible. Slick patent medicine and food faddist advertising compound the fraudulence perpetrated on the poor by various profiteers (Deutsch, 1960).

NEW HEALTH PROGRAMS FOR THE POOR

The deficiencies in health services received by the poor have been recognized by socially-minded health leaders for some time. In spite of the numerous categorical programs reviewed earlier, especially the medical services of welfare departments directed to the needs of the indigent, the heavier volume of morbidity among the poor has been far from adequately served. Because of this patent deficiency, a number of new health programs have been launched in recent years by federal legislation. These programs may represent a turning point in

America's approach to health services for all the people, poor and affluent (Forgotson, 1967).

Most important of the legislative output were the Social Security Act amendments of 1965 which established the first nationwide social insurance program in the United States for medical care. Known popularly as "Medicare," Title XVIII of the Act provides a series of hospital, medical, and related benefits to virtually all persons in the country 65 years of age and over, whether or not they are entitled to a Social Security old-age pension. The significant point is that there is no means test for these benefits; every aged person receives the same hospital services and related care in an "extended care facility" (nursing home) or at home ("home health services"). For physician's care and certain ancillary services, the aged person must pay (or he may choose to forego these benefits) a small "voluntary" monthly premium ($3 in 1967), which is more than matched by federal subsidy. Moreover, Social Security cash benefits were elevated by over $3 per month to cover this added expenditure (Cohen and Ball, 1965).

Since a major share of the urban poor, especially in slum boarding houses, are over 65 years of age, Medicare will doubtless be of great value to the poor as a social class. As statistics also show, the burden of illness among the aged in all income groups is much greater than in the young, and the aged parent's children must often foot the bills. Voluntary health insurance, as noted earlier, had its least impact among the aged, especially those of low income, so that the Medicare legislation has obviously been a great step forward in social welfare.

The precise benefits of Medicare are far from comprehensive. There are limitations on the number of hospital days payable (90 days in a "spell of illness"), there are cost-sharing requirements (e.g., $40 on hospital admissions and $10 per day after the sixtieth day), and important items are not covered at all, like dental care and out-of-hospital drugs. Limitations on the "voluntary insurance" benefits for physician's care are greater, with a $50 per year deductible and 20 percent cost-sharing for all services.

In spite of these limitations, imposed in the interests of reducing the total social insurance budget and thereby gaining Congressional approval, Medicare has clearly ushered in a new era for medical care of the poor. For those poor who are aged, the law facilitates access to the same mainstream of community medical care—the private physician and the voluntary general hospital—that serves the well-to-do. In part, even the administration of the law makes use of the existing framework of private insurance plans as "fiscal intermediaries" between the central Social Security Administration and the providers of service. The mainstream entitlements, of course, apply only to those poor who are aged. If any lesson can be learned from the history of social insurance for medical care in other countries, however, it is that with time and experience both population coverage and medical benefits are expanded. There is little doubt that the same will happen to Medicare.

Although Medicare is mainly a "bill-paying" mechanism and accepts the existing framework of private medical practice, it has introduced certain modest influences on the quality of care. Hospitals, to receive payments, must be "certified," and this requires meeting various technical standards. "Utilization review" of cases is one of the most important of these requirements—a measure which should heighten the self-discipline among physicians on hospital staffs. Nursing homes, to be certified, must have a "transfer agreement" with a general hospital, a device which can reduce the previous isolation of these units from professional stimulation. Perhaps most important, the very public visibility of medical care costs—already produced by Medicare—will induce a closer examination of the whole social structure of American medicine. Soaring costs can highlight much of the extravagance and inefficiency of private, solo medical practice, and this publicity in turn can lead to corrective innovations in the patterns of organization. These innovations can have special meaning for the poor.

Along with Medicare for the aged, the Social Security amendments of 1965 also added Title XIX, which involves radical alterations in the whole pattern of medical services for the poor under age 65. "Medicaid," as it has come to be called, is a modification of the long-established public assistance medical care legislation, reviewed earlier, which rests on the principle of federal grants to the states for help to certain demographic categories. Title XIX liberalizes the basis of these federal grants—allowing substantially open-ended matching of state appropriations—and authorizes the states to include among their medical beneficiaries not only the recipients of cash assistance, but also similar persons who are "medically indigent." The latter would include a family with a missing or unemployed breadwinner and dependent children (AFDC) which was not poor enough to qualify for cash assistance but still could not afford private medical care. Theoretically, this provision could reach a substantial proportion of urban slum-dwellers who were not previously receiving medical care. Medicaid also provides that, to receive federal grants, a state must assure a minimum range of five professional and hospitalization benefits to all categorical recipients. Moreover, it must gradually expand its coverage, so that, by 1975, virtually all poor people in the state—whether or not "categorically linked"

—must be entitled to financial support for essential medical services (Greenfield, 1966).

How successful Medicaid will actually be in extending good medical care to the nation's poor is a serious question. For one thing, the state government must agree to the federal conditions and, as of this writing two years after enactment of the law, 24 states have still not done so. For another, the definition of indigency and medical indigency is still left up to each state; many of the poorest states with large numbers of impoverished people draw these lines at very low thresholds. Thirdly, the definitions of health services, even within the federal schedule of five benefits, are subject to varying interpretations; drugs and dental care, moreover, are not even among them. Fourthly, the whole Medicaid program, like Medicare, accepts the "mainstream" approach as unreservedly desirable; it incorporates no provisions that might modify organizational patterns to better suit the needs of the poor or, for that matter, the efficient application of medical science for persons of any income.

The neutrality of Medicare and Medicaid on the critical issue of patterns of health service organization in America lends special significance to two other pieces of health legislation enacted by the Eighty-ninth (1965–1966) Congress. These are the "Heart Disease, Cancer, and Stroke Amendments of 1965" (PL 89–239) and the "Comprehensive Health Planning and Public Health Service Amendments of 1966" (PL 89–749). Neither of these laws is focused specifically on the poor, but their long-term significance for those in this category may be as great as the milestone of social insurance.

The Heart-Cancer-Stroke law is based on an effort to attack the three leading causes of death in the United States by encouraging improvements in the quality of care for these diseases at the grass roots and in the average urban neighborhood. It provides federal grants for developing "regional medical programs" to improve the diagnosis and treatment of these and related diseases. The regional programs are intended to establish active professional connections between the great medical centers and peripheral hospitals around them. So far, these ties have been largely limited to the organization of postgraduate instruction for practicing physicians, but there is hope that they might be extended to include active consultation and referral services. The goal is to enable every person to receive the best scientific care for his disease, regardless of his geographic location or socioeconomic status. The regionalization concept, embodied in this law, has been applied throughout the world as a mechanism for systematizing medical care and elevating its quality. Whether the Heart-Cancer-Stroke law will evolve into such a full-dress regionalization pattern depends on other political developments in the coming years (Russell, 1966).

The Comprehensive Health Planning amendments have even a broader potential influence on medical care patterns, although the terms of the law are relatively modest. Its immediate purpose is to consolidate federal grants to the states in formerly earmarked fields, such as venereal disease control, chronic illness and aging programs, and "general public health," in order to permit each state to allocate the funds flexibly according to a "state plan" based on its own particular needs. The long-term purpose is much broader; it provides grants to the states for overall planning of health facilities, personnel, and services—in the private as well as the public sector—to best meet the total health needs of the population. If this purpose is taken seriously, the implications are great for improvement of health services to the poor. Any objective description and assessment of our current patterns of medical care, the chaotic multiplicity of agencies, the sovereignty of private, solo medical practice and small autonomous hospitals, and the irrational separation of prevention and therapy can only help to set us on the road to their correction (Stewart, 1967).

Still another federal program, with clear impacts on the health of the urban poor, is the so-called "war on poverty" administered by the Office of Economic Opportunity (OEO). Several projects of this agency, including "Operation Head Start" for preschool youngsters and the Youth Job Corps for unemployed teenagers have an indirect bearing on health. Most direct and daring of the OEO projects, from the viewpoint of health needs, are the "neighborhood health centers." These are centers for comprehensive ambulatory medical care located in the heart of the slums and open 24 hours a day. In contrast to the outpatient departments of the big municipal hospitals, the neighborhood centers emphasize a personal doctor relationship for each patient and stress participation of the local people in the management of the program and as auxiliary health workers. With such involvement, it is hoped that the poor will make fuller use of the services, instead of distrusting them as the reluctant charity of "the establishment." At this writing, only a half-dozen such centers are in operation, in the central ghettos (mainly Negro) of large cities, but some 40 are being planned. Doctors are engaged in the centers on full-time or part-time salaries, and overall direction is under medical schools, medical societies, local health departments, or other bodies. The neighborhood centers are clearly a deviation from the mainstream concept of medical care for the poor, and it remains to be seen how their character takes shape (Geiger, 1966).

Several other established governmental health programs were expanded or liberalized in 1965–1966 to improve services for the poor. The traditional "maternal and child health" grants to the states were amended to permit comprehensive maternal and child *care* in "high risk" families, meaning essentially families of the poor. The Community Mental Health Amendments of 1965 (PL 89–105) support wider funding of both construction and operation of psychiatric centers oriented mainly to the needs of the poor. The Vocational Rehabilitation Amendments of 1965 (PL 89–290) enlarge the federal share of these grants which, as we noted earlier, help principally low income persons who are disabled but employable. These and other new laws of the last few years, at both federal and state levels, mark an apparent turning point in social concern for the provision of health services to the nation's poor.

THE VIEW AHEAD

Improvement in the health of the urban poor depends, first of all, on their living conditions. Two hundred years ago Johann Peter Frank wrote that "poverty is the mother of disease." Although there are other progenitors of sickness as well, Frank's axiom is still true. Not only does an insanitary and congested environment contribute to the causation of disease, but the alienation and apathy of poverty discourage behavior that could protect health. Racial and ethnic discriminations compound the difficulties for millions of dwellers in the urban ghetto. The most basic approach to the health of the poor, therefore, must emphasize improvement of their whole standard of living. Adequate employment is obviously essential, associated with proper education, good housing, balanced nutrition, ample recreation, and above all, equal opportunity.

There are two somewhat competing philosophies at play in the current American scene with respect to health services for the indigent. One is to set up special organized facilities for the poor—municipal hospitals and clinics, specially appointed doctors, public health clinics for children, and so on. The latest implementation of this approach is the OEO "neighborhood health center" discussed above. The other philosophy has been called the "mainstream approach"—that is, arrangement for medical care of the poor through existing resources serving the general population, these being principally private physicians and voluntary hospitals. This latter philosophy is embodied in the important Medicare Law of 1965. In either case a public agency pays the costs, but the mainstream approach is thought to have a more democratic quality, because it does not segregate the poor in separate places. And as already noted, the conditions in those separate facilities—whether in massive municipal hospitals or in public health clinics located in the basement of a county courthouse—are often conducive to perfunctory and insensitive medical care (Strauss, 1967).

The issue is not so simple, however, because the quality and accessibility of medical service in the medical mainstream may also be very deficient. Free choice of private doctor, which results in assembly-line treatment in a poorly staffed office of a slum general practitioner is no blessing. Welfare department tabulations reveal shocking mediocrities and abuses of both patients and public moneys in such private practices. In the voluntary community hospital, moreover, the poor may still be segregated in second-class wards, where they do not receive the physician's care, the nursing care, and various amenities accorded to private patients (Rogatz, 1967). On the other hand, the quality and even the human sensitivity of medical care in a special facility may be excellent. The level achieved in most "segregated" Veterans Administration hospitals demonstrates this, as do the standards now being applied in several new OEO neighborhood health centers. Separate facilities for the poor, in other words, may appear to have undemocratic overtones, but they are good or bad depending on the quantity of resources put into them and the policies of management applied.

The root problem is that the mainstream of American medicine has inherent deficiencies that compromise the accessibility and quality of medical care for the affluent as well as the poor. The predominance of solo medical practice, uncoordinated hospitals, self-prescribed drugs, and similar factors represent a heritage from earlier centuries, a heritage which blocks the realization of the full potential of modern medical science. The task, therefore, is to modify the patterns and direction of "mainstream medicine," so that it becomes appropriate to the true requirements of science and the needs of people. This is a long and complex challenge to explain, but it involves essentially *organization* of both preventive and curative health services economically, technologically, and geographically.

If the character of the mainstream in American medical care is appropriately modified—with more imaginative use of comprehensive group practice, with regionalization of hospitals, and with better integration of prevention and treatment—then the care of the poor should certainly be provided within it. In a word, this would mean that certain patterns of health service organization, now applied in a faltering way in the segregated streams, would be improved in their application—through more generous financial support and competent leadership—and incorporated within the mainstream of medicine. The issue posed earlier would then disappear, and all persons, rich and poor, would receive one uniformly high quality of medical care, regardless of the source of financing.

The new legislation for "comprehensive health planning," along with several other developments reviewed above, may help to promote such a better future. If it does, one more blow may be struck against the sordid cycles of poverty and disease that now enchain the dwellers in urban slums.

REFERENCES

Anderson, O. W. 1963. The utilization of health services. In H. E. Freeman, S. Levine, and L. G. Reeder (eds.), *Handbook of medical sociology.* New York: Prentice-Hall, pp. 349–67.

Cohen, I. J. 1966. The veterans administration medical care program. In L. J. DeGroot (ed.), *Medical care: Social and organizational aspects.* Springfield, Ill.: Charles C. Thomas, pp. 425–36.

Cohen, W. J. and Ball, R. M. 1965. Social security amendments of 1965: Summary and legislative history. *Social Security Bulletin* 28, no. 9: 3–21.

Deutsch, R. M. 1960. Nutritional nonsense and food fanatics. In *Proceedings, third national congress and medical quakery.* Chicago: American Medical Association, pp. 15–24.

Editors of Consumer Reports. 1963. *The medicine show: Some plain truths about popular remedies for common ailments.* Mount Vernon, N.Y.: Consumers Union.

Forgotson, E. H. 1967. 1965: The turning point in health law—1966 reflections. *American Journal of Public Health* 57: 934–46.

Geiger, H. J. 1966. The poor and the professional: Who takes the handle off the Broad Street pump? Paper presented at the Annual Meeting of the American Public Health Association, San Francisco, California, November 1.

Greenfield, M. 1966. Title XIX and Medi-Cal. *Public Affairs Report* 7, no. 4 (Bulletin of the Institute of Governmental Studies, University of California, Berkeley).

Hanlon, J. J. 1960. Maternal and child health activities. In *Principles of public health administration.* St. Louis: C. V. Mosby Company, pp. 470–92.

King, S. H. 1962. *Perceptions of illness and medical practice.* New York: Russell Sage Foundation.

Roemer, M. I. 1966. Health resources and services in the Watts area of Los Angeles. *California's Health* 23, nos. 8–9: 123–43.

———. 1967. Governmental health programs affecting the American family. *Journal of Marriage and the Family* 29: 40–63.

Rogatz, P. 1967. Our care of the poor is a failure. *Medical Economics:* 209–17.

Russell, J. M. 1966. New federal regional medical programs. *New England Journal of Medicine* 275: 309–12.

Somers, H. M. and Somers, A. R. 1961. *Doctors, patients, and health insurance.* Washington, D.C.: The Brookings Institution.

Stewart, W. H. 1967. *New dimensions for health planning.* (The 1967 Michael M. Davis Lecture.) Chicago: University of Chicago, Center for Health Administration Studies.

Strauss, A. L. 1967. Medical ghettos. *Trans-Action* 4: 7–15, 62.

U.S. Public Health Service, National Center for Health Statistics. 1964. *Medical care, health status, and family income.* Series 10, No. 9. Washington, pp. 52–74.

———. 1965. *Physician visits—Interval of visits and children's routine checkups, United States, July 1963–June 1964.* Series 10, No. 19. Washington.

U.S. Welfare Administration. 1964. *Characteristics of state public assistance plans under the Social Security Act: Provisions for medical and remedial care.* Public Assistance Report, No. 49. Washington.

Yerby, A. S. 1966. Public medical care for the needy in the United States. In L. J. DeGroot (ed.), *Medical care: Social and organizational aspects.* Springfield, Ill.: Charles C. Thomas, pp. 382–401.

THE METROPOLITAN EDUCATIONAL DILEMMA: MATCHING RESOURCES TO NEEDS

ALAN K. CAMPBELL
PHILIP MERANTO

The continued growth of metropolitan populations and the internal redistribution between central city and suburb form the background to this discussion of educational problems. The increasing concentration of "disadvantaged" students in inner city schools means that they face more serious and complex problems than their suburban counterparts, yet the resources available to the educational process are proportionately lower. The crucial issue is therefore the redistribution of resources either through a redistribution of population or a redistribution of tax revenues.

Reprinted from Marilyn Gittell, ed., *Educating an Urban Population* (Beverly Hills: Sage Publications, Inc., 1967), pp. 15–36, by permission of the publisher and the authors.

This article is based, in part, on a Carnegie Corporation-supported larger study of *Policies and Policy-Making in Large City Education Systems* being done at the Metropolitan Studies Center, Maxwell Graduate School, Syracuse University. A description of the entire study is available.

The metropolitanization of American society has gained widespread attention in recent years from a notable variety of scholars, popular writers, and public officials. Some scholars have preoccupied themselves with tracing the historical roots of metropolitanism, while others have attempted to demonstrate empirical relationships between metropolitanism and the social, economic, and political dimensions of society. Popular writers have interpreted some of these findings for the general public, and they have usually stressed the so-called "decay" of large American cities and the multitude of problems plaguing these urban centers. While journalists and scholars have been describing and analyzing the metropolitan phenomenon, public officials have been struggling with its policy implications. For these officials, the fact of metropolitanism, however dimly perceived, complicates many of the problems with which they must deal and influences many of the decisions they make.

The extent of this concern with one of the major forces of change in postwar America has been beneficial but, on occasion, misleading. On the one hand, it has stimulated popular interest and knowledge of the changing character of American culture. Further, it has prompted a wide assortment of research efforts about the causes and consequences of metropolitanism. On the other hand, there has been a tendency to see nearly all of the changes and problems which characterize contemporary America as consequences of the metropolitan process. Too often the interrelationships between substantive problems and metropolitanism have been blurred rather than clarified by this kind of perception. Similarly, there has been a tendency to assume that the problems involved in the provision of any public service (education, welfare, health, transportation, and so forth) are all related to or result from metropolitanism. This is not the case. With every function there are problems that would exist even if the country had not become metropolitan. Further, the fact of metropolitanism is not a problem in itself, but the dynamics which underpin it and the patterns which accompany it may be perceived by individuals and groups within the society as creating problems, and in many instances the problems thus perceived can be solved only by public action.

The tendency to equate both social change and functional concerns with metropolitanism is evident in the field of education. Much of the literature which purports to discuss the implications of metropolitanism or urbanism for education is, instead, simply a catalog of the substantive issues which characterize the education function. The metropolitan component of the problems is often assumed to be self-evident, and no effort is made to demonstrate the relationship between metropolitanism and the substantive issues.

It is the primary purpose of this article to delineate those aspects of metropolitanism which produce important consequences for the performance of the education function in large urban centers. Such an analysis necessitates, first, an investigation of basic population trends and an examination of the distributional results of these trends on income, educational attainment, race, and the nature of school population. Second, the relationships between these population attributes and the provision of educational services are analyzed, as are the relationships between education needs and the quantity and quality of resources available in the various parts of the metropolis. And finally, the public policy alternatives are examined in terms of their ability to meet the demonstrated needs.

CHARACTERISTICS OF METROPOLITAN AMERICA

The most often cited statistic about metropolitanism is the growing proportion of the American population which lives in metropolitan areas.[1] By 1964 this proportion had reached 65 percent, and projections indicate that it will approach 70 percent by 1970. A simultaneous phenomenon, perhaps of even greater significance for the education function, is the redistribution of people between the central city and its suburbs. There has been a gradual but consistent decrease in the proportion of total metropolitan population which lives within central cities. In 1900 over 60 percent of the metropolitan population lived within central cities; by 1965 this share had declined to under 50 percent.

This decline in the proportion of the metropolitan population living in central cities represents for many cities, particularly those in the largest metropolitan areas, an absolute decline in the central city population. Table 1 illustrates this fact by presenting the percent of population change for both central city and outside central city between 1950 and 1960 for selected large cities. The few instances of an increase in central city population were caused, in most cases, by annexation rather than by population growth within the original boundaries of the central city. Clearly, the population within the largest metropolitan areas is decentralizing.

The significance of these shifts for the education function would be substantial even if the population redistribution between central city and suburbs was random relative to the socioeconomic characteristics of the people involved. But this is not the case. The shifting is not only a matter of numbers of people; it also involves a sorting-out process. In general, it is the poor, less educated, nonwhite Americans who are staying in the central city and the higher income, better educated, whites who are moving out, although this description

| | CENTRAL CITY | | OUTSIDE CENTRAL CITY | |
| | | Percent Change | | Percent Change |
SMSA	1960	since 1950	1960	since 1950
New York	7,781,984	— 1.4	2,912,649	75.0
Chicago	3,550,404	— 1.9	2,670,509	71.5
Los Angeles*	2,823,183	27.1	3,919,513	82.6
Philadelphia	2,002,512	— 3.3	2,340,385	46.3
Detroit	1,670,144	— 9.7	2,092,216	79.3
Baltimore	939,024	— 1.1	787,999	72.4
Houston	938,219	57.4	304,939	44.8
Cleveland	876,050	— 4.2	920,545	67.2
Washington	763,956	— 4.8	661,911	87.0
St. Louis	750,026	—12.5	1,310,077	51.9
Milwaukee	741,324	16.3	452,966	41.7
San Francisco†	1,159,932	— 4.5	1,075,495	55.0
Boston	697,197	—13.0	1,892,104	17.6
Dallas	679,684	56.4	403,997	30.7
New Orleans	627,525	10.0	240,955	109.6
United States (all SMSAs)	58,004,334	10.7	54,880,844	48.6

TABLE 1. Population Change in 15 Largest SMSAs Central City and Outside Central City: 1950–1960
* Includes Long Beach
† Includes Oakland
Source: U.S. Bureau of the Census, *U.S. Census of Population, 1960.* Volume 1, *Characteristics of the Population,* Part A. Number of inhabitants, Table 33.

must be qualified somewhat in terms of the size of the metropolitan area and region of the country in which it is located. The larger the metropolitan area, however, the more accurate is this description.[2]

This sorting-out process has resulted in a median family income for central city residents in 1959 which was 88.5 percent of outside central city income; $5,940 for central cities, compared to $6,707 for the suburbs. Although median family income for both central city and outside central city residents has grown since 1959, the gap is widening, with central city median family income in 1964 at $6,697, while for outside central city areas it was $7,772, a proportionate relationship of 86.2 percent.[3]

These nation-wide averages hide important differences between metropolitan areas which can be explained, in part, by differences in population size. Overall, the larger metropolitan areas have higher family incomes than the smaller ones. In metropolitan areas having populations of over 3 million—the largest size category—the percent of families earning over $10,000 a year is almost double the percent earning less than $3,000 a year. Further, it is only in this category that the central cities have a higher proportion of their population over $10,000 than under $3,000.

The large metropolitan areas have less poverty proportionately than the small ones. This finding, however, is not as significant for the performance of the education function as is the contrast between central cities and their suburbs. It is the large, relatively affluent areas which possess the greatest income disparity between central cities and their suburbs. In the size category of over 3 million, for every 100 families in central cities earning under $3,000, there are 127 earning over $10,000. In the suburbs, the comparable number of families with an income over $10,000 is 312 for every 100 families earning under $3,-

000. In other words, there are 185 more families with income over $10,000 in the suburbs for every 100 families under $3,000 than is true for the central cities. The magnitude of this difference in income distribution between central city and outside central city declines as the size of the area decreases and, in fact, reverses itself for the two size-categories below 250,000 population.

The differences in income characteristics between central cities and their suburbs is reflected in the educational attainment of the respective populations. Again, the contrast between central city and suburbs is substantial: 40.9 percent of central city pupils have completed four years of high school or more, while outside the central cities the comparable percentage is 50.9. Once more the differences are greatest when one examines the data for individual large metropolitan areas.

The explanation for the income and education differences between central city and suburb rests in part on differences in the distribution of nonwhite population within metropolitan areas.[4] Although the nonwhite component of the American population has now distributed itself between metropolitan and nonmetropolitan areas in approximately the same proportion as the white population, the distribution within metropolitan areas follows a quite different pattern. It is well known that the proportion of nonwhites in central cities has been increasing, while the proportion in the suburban areas has been declining. This larger proportion of Negro population in central cities helps to account in part for the differences in educational achievement and income between central cities and suburbs. Due to a history of discrimination in all aspects of life, the Negro has a lower income and less edu-

FOUR YEARS OF HIGH SCHOOL OR MORE (IN PERCENT)

Urbanized Area*	Central City	Urban Fringe*	Central City Nonwhites
New York	36.4	48.7	31.2
Chicago	35.3	53.9	27.3
Los Angeles	53.4	53.4	43.6
Philadelphia	30.7	48.0	23.6
Detroit	34.4	47.5	26.5
Baltimore	28.2	42.3	19.7
Houston	45.2	50.1	26.2
Cleveland	30.1	55.5	28.1
Washington	47.8	67.5	33.5
St. Louis	26.3	43.3	20.2
Milwaukee	39.7	54.4	26.0
San Francisco	49.4	57.9	39.1
Boston	44.6	55.8	36.2
Dallas	48.9	56.4	25.2
New Orleans	33.3	44.6	15.0
All Urbanized Areas	40.9	50.9	28.3

TABLE 2. Educational Attainment of Persons 25 Years or Older in 15 Urbanized Areas by Residence, by Color: 1960
* This table utilizes urbanized area and urban fringe as units due to the availability of data. The Census Bureau defines an urbanized area as "the thickly settled portions of the SMSA." The urban fringe constitutes the urbanized area minus the central city.
Source: Computed from U.S. Bureau of the Census, *U.S. Census of Population: 1960*, General Social and Economic Characteristics (Washington, D.C.: Government Printing Office, 1961) and *U.S. Census of Population and Housing: 1960*, Census Tracts (Washington, D.C.: Government Printing Office, 1961).

cation than does his white neighbor. In central cities, for example, the 1964 median family income for Negroes was $4,463, while for whites it was $7,212. In 1964 the percentage of all Negroes twenty-five years old and over having completed four years of high school was 17.1; the comparable percentage for whites was 31.3.

The impact of the growing proportion of nonwhite population in central cities is intensified for the schools by the even higher proportion of public school enrollment which is nonwhite. This difference in population and enrollment proportions is a result of age distribution, family composition, and the greater tendency of white parents to send their children to private and parochial schools. Table 3 shows, for 1960, the proportion of the total population of the largest cities which was nonwhite and the proportion of public school enrollment which was nonwhite. The ratio of nonwhites to whites is considerably higher in the school population than in

the total population, and indications are that this is becoming increasingly the case.

The sorting-out process which produces significant differences in socio-economic characteristics between central city and suburban populations is the chief background factor against which the educational implications of metropolitanism must be examined. To the extent that these differences in characteristics produce different kinds of educational problems, the fact of metropolitanism is important to the provision of educational services.

POPULATION COMPOSITION AND EDUCATIONAL PROBLEMS

The redistribution process described in the preceding section has left the central city school system with a disproportionate segment of pupils who are referred to as "disadvantaged," and this appears to be a trend that is continually increas-

City	Percent Nonwhite of Total Population	Percent Nonwhite of School Population	Difference in Proportions of Nonwhite School Enrollment and Nonwhite Population
New York	14.0	22.0	8.0
Chicago	22.9	39.8	16.9
Los Angeles	12.2	20.5	8.3
Philadelphia	26.4	46.7	20.3
Detroit	28.9	42.9	14.0
Baltimore	34.7	50.1	15.4
Houston	22.9	30.2	8.7
Cleveland	28.6	46.1	17.5
Washington	53.9	77.5	23.6
St. Louis	28.6	48.8	20.2
Milwaukee	8.4	16.2	7.8
San Francisco	14.3	30.5	16.2
Boston	9.1	16.4	7.3
Dallas	19.0	26.0	7.0
New Orleans	37.2	55.4	18.2

TABLE 3. Nonwhite Population Contrasted with Nonwhite School Enrollment for 15 Largest Cities: 1960
Source: U.S. Bureau of the Census, *U.S. Census of Population: 1960*, Selected Area Reports, Standard Metropolitan Statistical Areas and General Social and Economic Characteristics, 1960.

ing. These students are disadvantaged in terms of the income level and educational background of their parents, their family composition, and their general home environment. To the extent that education of the disadvantaged is a more complex phenomenon than the education of middle-income pupils, the central city school systems face a different and more serious set of problems than do suburban education systems.[5]

In the immediate postwar period, the most striking phenomenon in education related to the metropolitanization of the country was the impact on suburban areas of a rapidly increasing population. The suburbs, however, responded well to the challenge and rapidly met the new requirements in building the necessary physical facilities and the provision of a teaching staff. The significance of the suburban expansion for the central city schools, however, was only dimly, if at all, perceived. It is now clear that the suburbanization of the country, by draining the higher income families and much economic activity from the central cities, produced greater problems for education in central cities than it did for the suburbs.

As the proportion of disadvantaged students in the central cities has increased, there has been a simultaneous increase in what are known in the community as "undesirable" schools, schools to which parents would prefer not to send their children. Many of these schools are so characterized because of the large proportion (in many cases, nearly 100 percent) of the students who are Negro. Because of population trends and the residential pattern of most of our cities, it is increasingly difficult to rearrange district lines to achieve what is referred to as "racial balance" among schools. As a result, more and more central city schools are being designated as "undesirable."

The underlying cause for the undesirable label in educational terms, however, is low income, not race. Several studies have now substantiated that the single most important determinant of educational achievement is family income.[6] In the high correlation between income and test scores, income undoubtedly is a proxy, and a fairly accurate one, for a combination of factors —family characteristics, educational attainment of parents, home environment. When white parents resist sending their children to undesirable schools, this is not necessarily a racial issue, although it is often difficult to separate the racial and educational questions which currently surround controversies over central city schools.

The undesirable schools are unattractive not only to parents but also to first-rate teachers. Teachers seek to be assigned to the "better" schools within the city system, and many abandon central city districts entirely for more attractive suburban districts. Furthermore, central city systems find it increasingly difficult to attract choice graduates of the universities as new teachers.

The resource needs for central cities relate not only to teachers but to other educational needs as well. Cities have much older school plants than do suburbs, and the site costs for building new schools within central cities are substantially higher than those for the suburbs. In addition, there is greater competition within the cities for resources for such noneducation functions as police protection, street maintenance, and welfare than is true in the suburban areas. These noneducation needs compete for the same resources which the central city schools need to meet their pressing educational problems.

This set of central city education problems exists in a society which is in need of a continuous improvement in its educational output. The very fact of metropolitanization implies extended specialization in a society which is increasingly complex. The need, therefore, is for a better and better educated work force. To some extent, the suburban areas have responded to this need through the gradual improvement and sophistication of its curricula and teaching. Curriculum improvement in central cities, however, is much less discernible and is particularly lacking in the education of the disadvantaged.[7]

The answer to this problem does not rest with providing education with a different purpose for disadvantaged pupils. A suggestion by James Conant that disadvantaged pupils should be concentrated in vocational education hardly seems appropriate.[8] Improvement in the quality of vocational education is needed, but it should not be made especially for the disadvantaged. Among the disadvantaged, there are those who are capable of achieving high educational accomplishment in a great variety of fields and options, and in terms of equity the opportunities should be the same for them as for other pupils. Further, it is apparent that the greatest employment growth of the future will be in the white-collar occupations, not in vocational fields offered by most of today's vocational schools.

One of the central issues confronting large city schools, therefore, becomes the allocation of sufficiently massive resources to the field of education for the disadvantaged to help them overcome their present handicaps. To what extent are large central cities capable of providing the resources needed to meet these problems and where are these resources to come from if the central cities cannot provide them from local assets?

THE AVAILABILITY OF RESOURCES

The educational problems confronting large cities would not be nearly as critical if cities had at their disposal an ample supply of resources to deal with these difficulties. But this is not the case. The metropolitan process has not only redistributed the population in a way that presents the central cities with a population having special educational difficulties; the process has simultaneously operated to weaken the local resource base which must be used to meet their needs.

It has already been noted that the central city component of the metropolitan area population has lower income levels than the population outside the central city. This pattern is particularly significant because it has become increasingly apparent that income is the single most important variable in explaining the expenditure levels of a community for both educational and noneducational services.[9] To a large extent, it is the income available which influences the ability of a governmental unit to meet the service requirements of its population. Central cities are simply losing ground in this respect, while their functional needs are simultaneously increasing.

Metropolitanism is characterized by the decentralization of economic activities from the core city to the surrounding areas, as well as by decentralization of population. Evidence of this trend can be found by examining the distribution of economic activity within specific metropolitan areas over time. For example, an investigation of the proportion of manufacturing carried on in the central city portion of twelve large metropolitan areas demonstrates that the central city percentage has clearly declined over the past three decades, particularly in the post-World War II period. Whereas the twelve cities accounted, on the average, for 66.1 percent of manufacturing employment in 1929, this proportion decreased to 60.8 percent by 1947 and then declined to less than half (48.9 percent) by 1958.[10]

A similar decentralizing trend for retail activity can be demonstrated by examining the growth of retail store sales in the metropolitan area as a whole, in the central city, and in the central business district of the core city for the period 1948 to 1958. Such a comparison was made for a sample of twenty-two large cities. It was found that with the exception of one (Birmingham, Alabama), the entire metropolitan area had increased its retail sales more than had the central city and far more than the central business district. This evidence illustrates that the historical dominance of the central city and its business district over regional retail activity is on the decline.[11] The patterns for manufacturing employment and retail sales reflect the fact that economic activity, like population, has migrated from the central city outward. This push for dispersal is related to a number of factors, including the need for physical space, the introduction of new industrial processes, the ascendance of the automobile and truck as means of transportation and

migration for the tax base of the central city have been widely discussed. As industries continue to move outward, taxable assessed valuation, the source of local property taxes, has barely held its own in many cities and has actually declined in several large cities. For example, in a recent five-year period, the percent changes in taxable assessed valuation for seven cities were as follows: Baltimore, − 10.5 percent; Boston, − 1.2 percent; Buffalo, − 1.0 percent; Detroit, − 2.0 percent; St. Louis, + 1.1 percent; Philadelphia, + 2.8 percent; and Cleveland − 3.4 percent.[13] These changes in taxable valuation do not yield the necessary resources to deal with the problems facing these urban centers.

Translated into educational terms, the recent performance of the tax base in large cities has not kept pace with the growth or nature of the school population in these cities. Indeed, an examina-

| | Percent of Change over a Five-year Period* | |
	City	State (minus cities listed)
Baltimore	−19.3	10.2
Boston	− 5.3	not available
Buffalo	− 8.6	26.1
Chicago	− 6.0	− 0.2
Cleveland	− 9.9	4.2
Detroit	− 5.7	3.4
Houston	− 2.8	18.9
Los Angeles	5.1	5.6
Milwaukee	− 9.6	− 1.1
New York City	32.4	26.1
Philadelphia	− 0.6	13.6
Pittsburgh	2.2	13.6
St. Louis	−10.6	3.1
San Francisco	5.9	5.6

TABLE 4. Five-year Changes in Per Pupil Taxable Assessed Valuation
* Change is for the most recent five-year period for which data are available.
Source: Research Council of the Great Cities Program for School Improvement, *The Challenge of Financing Public Schools in Great Cities* (Chicago, 1964).

shipping, the building of vast highway systems, and the spreading of the population throughout the metropolis.[12]

The consequences of this economic

tion of the per pupil taxable valuation over a five-year period shows that ten large cities out of fourteen experienced a decrease in this source of revenue.

Since local property taxes are the most important source of local educational revenues, large city schools can barely meet ordinary education needs let alone resolve the problems resulting from the shifting population distribution.

There is an additional factor which weighs against the capacity of central cities to meet their pressing educational needs. The postwar intensification of urbanization and metropolitanization has resulted in a demand for a wider range and higher quality of public services than at any other time in the nation's history. These demands are particularly great in the largest cities, where the necessity for providing a wide variety of welfare, public safety, sanitation, traffic control, and street maintenance services has been most pressing. The fact that central cities have responded to these demands is reflected in the data included in Table 5. An investigation of the fiscal patterns in thirty-six Standard Metropolitan Statistical Areas revealed that for the year 1957, the central cities in these areas were spending $25.66 more per capita in total expenditures than the communities in the outlying areas. Unfortunately for education systems, this difference was not due to higher educational expenditures in the central cities. In fact, their education expenditures were $27.82 per capita less than what was spent on education in the corresponding suburban areas. It was in the noneducational category that the central city exceeded the outside central city area in expenditures. In this sample, central cities spent about $53.00 more per capita on noneducation services than their surrounding communities. Further, this difference is largely due to the "all other" classification, which includes the traditional municipal services that cities, unlike suburban communities, must provide. The cost and number of noneducational governmental services tend to increase with the size and density of a district and to consume a larger proportion of the budget in major cities where many services are provided for nonresidents as well as for residents. It is reasonable to suggest that this "municipal overburden" is supported at the expense of the education function.[14]

The figures in Table 5 also show that the central cities were supporting these expenditure levels by taxes that were $23.29 per capita higher than in areas outside the cities. In contrast, the cities received about $5.00 per capita less in total intergovernmental aid and, most importantly, $12.31 less per capita in education aid than did suburban areas, where income was higher. In other words, not only are central cities pressed to support a large array of services by a relatively shrinking tax base, but they tax themselves more heavily to do so and they receive less intergovernmental aid than the more wealthy communities in their metropolitan area. This fiscal pattern borders on the ironic when it is realized that central city education systems must compete for educational resources with suburban school districts which have higher income levels and receive a greater amount of state aid. In fact, the state aid system actually works to intensify rather than to resolve the educational crises facing large city school systems.

The multitude of fiscal difficulties faced by the central cities results in a lower per student expenditure in the cities than in surrounding suburbs. Specifically, an examination of the thirty-seven largest metropolitan areas in the country indicated that the central city school districts in 1962 were spending an average of $144.96 less per pupil than their suburban counterparts.[15] This considerable difference in expenditures per student between central city and suburb would be serious even if the educational problems were the same for the two type areas; but, as has already been demonstrated, such is not the case.

It is not known what amount of addi-

Per Capita	Central City	Outside Central City	Differences Central City —Outside Central City
Total General Expenditure	$185.49	$159.83	25.66*
Education expenditure	58.02	85.84	—27.82†
Current	49.16	61.72	—12.56†
Capital	8.86	24.12	—15.26†
Noneducation expenditure	127.48	73.95	53.53†
Total highways	16.55	14.41	2.14
Health and hospitals (current)	14.84	7.09	7.55†
Public welfare	10.22	8.34	1.88†
All other	85.70	43.80	41.90†
Taxes	109.07	85.78	23.29†
Property tax	92.06	78.58	13.48
Nonproperty tax	17.01	7.20	9.81†
Proxy Variables			
Nonaided education expenditure (education taxes)	42.24	56.43	—14.19†
Nonaided noneducation expenditure (noneducation taxes)	108.33	60.39	47.94†
Total Aid	34.65	39.72	— 5.07
Education Aid	16.12	28.43	—12.31†
Noneducation aid	18.60	11.83	6.77*
Exhibit:			
Per capita income	1,998.86	2,280.50	—281.64*

TABLE 5. Fiscal Characteristics Central City and Outside Central City Areas, 36 Sample SMSAs: 1957

* Significant at .05 level of confidence.
† Significant at .01 level of confidence.
Note: Totals do not add because of unallocated aid. All figures in per capita terms unless otherwise indicated.
Source: Alan K. Campbell and Seymour Sacks (See Note 9.)

tional resources per student would be necessary to provide an adequate education for the culturally disadvantaged. On the basis of studies yet to be published, it is clear that the present small amounts of additional resources being used in some cities for what is generally referred to as "compensatory education" are accomplishing very little.[16] The additional resources currently being allocated to these programs are simply not sufficient.

In this respect it is interesting to note the amount per student which is being expended in the urban Job Corps Center which have been established by the Federal Anit-Poverty Program to provide a meaningful education for disadvantaged pupils. Present costs for establishing and organizing the centers amount to $10,-500 per student per year.[17] It is estimated that once the camps are in full operation and their costs level off, the expenditures per student will be reduced to $7,350 per year. Even if the subsistence cost (which in the regular public school system is absorbed by parents) is subtracted from this $7,350 figure, there remains a vast gap between the resulting figure and what is currently being spent in central city public schools. Assuming that the subsistence costs are $3,000 per year, this leaves a per pupil education expenditure of approximately $4,350. This figure presents a vivid contrast to education expenditures in many cities. New York City, for example, with the highest large central city expenditures per pupil in the country, expended $603.95 per pupil in 1961–1962, while Chicago spent $409.78 per student.

Obviously the quantity of resources being put into Job Corps education exceeds what is available or likely to become available for general central city education. Nevertheless, it does point the direction which must be followed if the disadvantaged schools in our central cities are to come near accomplishing their educational purposes. Such educational services as extensive counseling of individual students, small, specialized classes, and effective job training, all of which are furnished by the Job Corps, are not provided cheaply. The Job Corps Center at Camp Kilmer, New Jersey, has a student enrollment of approximately 2,000 and a teaching and administrative staff of about 450, a student-professional ration of about 4.5 students to 1 professional. The present ratio in larger city school systems is between 25–30 students to 1 professional.

It may be argued that comparing general public schools to the Job Corps schools is not realistic, since the Job Corps concentrates on those whom the regular schools failed. The point, however, is that the regular school systems failed these students, in part because they did not have the resources to provide the kind and quality of education needed. The obvious need is for more resources and an allocation system which recognizes the areas and students with special needs.

This analysis of the resources available for central city education demonstrates the disparity between needs and resources. There is little indication that present trends will substantially alter these circumstances; in fact, there is good reason to believe that the situation is becoming more serious. If these trends are to be modified, imaginative public policy decisions must be identi-fied and pursued. What public policy alternatives exist and to what extent are they politically feasible?

PUBLIC POLICY IMPLICATIONS

A variety of means exists for attacking the lack of fit between educational needs and resources. Some of these are politically more feasible than others.

Perhaps the most obvious solution would be to redistribute the population so as to reduce the concentration of disadvantaged pupils in cities. The demand for racial integration within public education points in this direction. There are, however, both physical and political obstacles to this course of action which, at the moment, appear to be insurmountable. First, the disadvantaged are concentrated in wide geographic areas within many cities. To redistribute these pupils throughout the city and throughout the metropolitan area, which would be necessary to achieve integration in the future, would require a transportation network so extensive and costly that it is both physically and politically impractical.

Obviously, there are neighborhood school districts where the redrawing of attendance areas within cities and perhaps the redrawing of district lines between cities and suburbs would substantially alter the present student balance in the schools. Where this is the case, however, political resistance is likely to be stiff. The recently discovered attachment of many people to the neighborhood school has produced powerful political support for present district lines and attendance areas. To assume that such changes could be accomplished on a metropolitan-wide basis is unrealistic.

There is, in fact, an inverse relationship between the intensity of political opposition to accomplishing some redistribution of pupils and the size of the area and proportion of the population involved. In cities where the proportion of disadvantaged students, particularly the proportion of Negro students, is relatively low (thereby making the re-drawing of attendance area lines a mean-ingful alternative), the political resist-ance seems capable of preventing any substantial changes. Boston is a good ex-ample of this situation: On the other hand, where the political strength of the disadvantaged is great enough to initiate some change, the high proportion of student and large areas involved present a practical limitation on how much can be accomplished in this manner.

An alternative to the decentralization of disadvantaged students is the much-discussed creation of education parks or campuses which would contain many more pupils than the present single-building schools. By drawing on a larger enrollment area, school campuses would be able to concentrate services and would contain a more heterogeneous population, thereby, presumably, pro-viding a higher quality of education for all students.

The concentration of disadvantaged students also would be lessened by the return of middle-income families to cit-ies from the suburbs. It had been an-ticipated by some students of urban af-fairs that urban renewal would contribute to such a return. This reversal of the outward flow of people would have been beneficial in two ways: The mix of students in the schools would be improved and the tax base for support-ing education would be strengthened. However, the contribution of urban renewal to revitalizing the central city has not been great. Much of the current disappointment over urban renewal has resulted from the lack of recognition of the importance of low-quality education as one of the primary factors motivating the move out of the city. It seems appar-ent that physical redevelopment, unless it is accompanied and closely inter-related with a variety of social improve-ments, particularly improvements in

public education, will not attract the suburbanite back to the city.

Whatever the possibility of pupil redistribution, the central need is and will remain additional resources for the education of the disadvantaged. Whether educated where they are pres-ently located or elsewhere, the disadvan-taged have special education needs. To meet these needs, which is the only way of guaranteeing equality of educational opportunity, additional resources are re-quired.

The present allocation pattern of state aid does little to accomplish this. In fact, the aid pattern runs exactly counter to the need pattern. It is possible that as reapportionment is accomplished and as the nature of the problem becomes more evident, state aid formulas will be re-vised to correspond more closely with needs. It is important to note, however, that reapportionment will result in a much greater gain in representation for the suburbs than it will for central cit-ies.[18] It may be that the suburban repre-sentatives will recognize their stake in an improved central city education system; but if they do not, the present pattern of higher aid to the suburbs may well be accentuated rather than reversed by reapportionment.

Perhaps the single most significant policy response to the set of problems described here has been the response of the Federal government as reflected in the Elementary and Secondary Educa-tion Act of 1965.[19] This program, com-bined with the antipoverty program, has given recognition for the first time to the problem of allocating more resources to education for the disadvantaged. How-ever, although the concept underpin-ning the legislation is sound, the amount of aid provided for large cities is rela-tively small in relation to the need. In the case of New York City, for instance, the new Federal aid amounts to only 6.2 per-cent of total 1962 education expendi-tures. For Chicago, the figure is 2.9 percent, for Los Angeles 2.6 percent, with the highest figure among the fifteen largest cities being for New Orleans, where the new aid will amount to 17.5 percent of 1962 school expenditures. This program is clearly moving in the right direction; the task is to fortify it with enough money so that it can have a substantial impact.

Whatever means are used to provide the resources for the provision of adequate education services, they will have to come, in large part, from the middle- and higher-income suburbanites. If, therefore, the suburbanites resist a redistribution of population or a redrawing of school district lines to create a more equitable balance in the present pupil ability distribution, the alternative—if the problem is to be met—is greater Federal and state taxes paid by persons of middle and high income.

The fundamental issue, therefore, really revolves around the ability and willingness of Federal and state governments to raise revenue and redistribute the resources according to need. If this is not done, no major improvement in the situation confronting central city school system can be expected.

There remains, of course, the issue of the ability of school systems to make good use of additional resources. This question relates to the kinds of changes needed in both curriculum and teaching techniques if the educational disadvantages of many young people are to be overcome.

However that question is answered, the fact remains that quality education for all will not be accomplished until the resources are found to do the job.

NOTES

1. The Census Bureau definition of the metropolitan area and of its component parts is followed throughout this article. That definition is as follows: "Except in New England, a standard metropolitan statistical area (an SMSA) is a county or group of contiguous counties which contain at least one city of 50,000 inhabitants or more or 'twin cities' with a combined population of at least 50,000. In addition to the county, or counties, containing such a city or cities, contiguous counties are included in an SMSA if, according to certain criteria, they are essentially metropolitan in character and are socially and economically integrated with the central city." In New England, towns are used instead of counties.

2. For a complete discussion of these differences relative to size and region, see Advisory Commission on Intergovernmental Relations, *Metropolitan Social and Economic Disparities: Implications for Intergovernmental Relations in Central Cities and Suburbs* (Washington, D.C.: Government Printing Office, 1965).

3. U.S. Bureau of the Census, *Consumer Income*, Series P-60, No. 48, April 25, 1966.

4. The terms nonwhite and Negro are used interchangeably in this article since Negroes constitute 92 percent of the nonwhite classification as defined by the Census Bureau.

5. For a sampling of the literature which deals with this topic see F. Riessman, *The Culturally Deprived Child* (New York: Harper & Row Publishers, Inc., 1962); J.R. Kramer and S. Leventman, *Children of the Gilded Ghetto* (New Haven: Yale University Press, 1961); A. H. Passow (ed.), *Education in Depressed Areas* (New York: Teachers College, Columbia University, 1963); and C.W. Hunnicutt (ed.), *Urban Education and Cultural Deprivation* (Syracuse, N.Y.: Syracuse University Press, 1964).

6. P. Sexton, *Education and Income: Inequalities in Our Public Schools* (New York: The Viking Press, 1962); H.T. James, J.A. Thomas, and H.J. Dyck, *Wealth, Expenditures, and Decision-Making for Education* (Stanford, Calif.: Stanford University Press, 1963); Fels Institute of Local and State Government, University of Pennsylvania, *Special Education and Fiscal Requirements of Urban School Districts in Pennsylvania*, 1964; J. Burkhead, *Cost and Performance in Large City School Systems*, Forthcoming publication of Metropolitan Studies Center, Syracuse University, as part of the Carnegie supported study of Large City Education Systems, 1967.

7. W.W. Wayson, *Curriculum Development in Large City Schools*, forthcoming publication of Metropolitan Studies Center, Syracuse University, as part of the Carnegie supported study of Large City Education Systems, 1967.

8. J.B. Conant, *Slums and Suburbs* (New York: The New American Library, 1964), pp. 33–49.

9. A.K. Campbell and S. Sacks, *Metropolitan America: Fiscal Patterns and Governmental Systems*, forthcoming publication, Metropolitan Studies Center, Syracuse University, 1966.

10. See R. Vernon, *The Changing Economic Function of the Central City* (New York: Committee for Economic Development, 1960); and U.S. Bureau of the Census, *Census of Manufacturing, 1958*. The cities include: Baltimore, Boston, Chicago, Cincinnati, Cleveland, Detroit, Los Angeles-Long Beach, New York, Philadelphia, Pittsburgh, St. Louis, and San Francisco-Oakland.

11. See U.S. Bureau of the Census, *Census of Business, 1958* for the twenty-two cities which reported all three figures.

12. E.M. Hoover and R. Vernon, *Anatomy of a Metropolis* (Garden City, N.Y.: Doubleday and Company, Inc., 1962).

13. The Research Council of the Great Cities Program for School Improvement, *The Challenge of Financing Public Schools in Great Cities,* Chicago, 1964.

14. D.C. Ranney, "School Government and the Determinants of the Fiscal Support for Large City Education System" (Ph.D. diss., Syracuse University, 1966).

15. For a breakdown by individual city, see the Sacks-Ranney article in this issue.

16. J. Burkhead, *Cost and Performance in Large City School Systems.*

17. "The Job Corps," *The New Yorker,* May 21, 1966, p. 121f.

18. R.S. Friedman, "The Reapportionment Myth," *National Civic Review* (April, 1960): 184–8.

19. Title I of this law, which accounts for about $1.06 billion of the approximately $1.3 billion authorized, provides for grants to be made to local school districts on the basis of 50 percent of the average per pupil expenditures made in their state for the school year 1963–1964 multiplied by the number of five- to seventeen-year-old children in the local school district from families with an annual income below $2,000, or with a higher income resulting from aid to dependent children relief payments. Local districts receive their proportion of the funds under this formula only after plans they have submitted indicating how they will meet the special educational needs of disadvantaged students are approved by their state education department. The politics surrounding the enactment of this legislation are analyzed in P. Meranto, "The Politics of Federal Aid to Education in 1965: A Study in Political Innovation" (Ph.D. diss., Syracuse University, 1966).

LOCATIONAL EFFICIENCY
OF CHICAGO HOSPITALS:
AN EXPERIMENTAL MODEL
RICHARD L. MORRILL
ROBERT J. EARICKSON

This paper illustrates the use of modelling procedures in evaluating the characteristics of a public facility system. Using the example of a hospital system, a model is built which seeks to reproduce existing patient flows to hospitals via a simulation of the patient decision-making process. Resultant patterns of over-demand and under-demand are identified and patterns of reallocation are suggested which would lead to greater efficiency in the system.

Reprinted from *Health Services Research* 4, no. 3 (Summer, 1969): 128–41, by permission of the Hospital Research and Educational Trust and the authors. This is an edited version of the original publication. Artwork has been renumbered.

From the Chicago Regional Hospital Study, supported by National Institutes of Health Research Grant HM 00452. The Study is cosponsored by the Hospital Planning Council for Metropolitan Chicago and the Illinois Department of Public Health, with the participation of the Center for Urban Studies and the Center for Health Administration Studies of the University of Chicago.

Hospitals are costly institutions to construct and maintain, and physician and hospital care are costly items for most families. The federal government spends large sums through the Hill-Burton Act to aid in the financing of hospital construction, through Medicare and Medicaid to aid the aged and the indigent, and in other programs. It is to the advantage of all concerned therefore, that these monies be wisely spent; specifically, that the character and location of hospitals be such as to assure a viable operation while meeting the needs of the patient population.

The present study was designed to find ways for cities and regions to evaluate the adequacy of the present distribution of hospitals and to locate or relocate facilities to meet future needs. This required, first, identification of pertinent variables, that is, the variability in pa-

tients, in hospitals, and in policies that must be taken into account in any realistic appraisal; and second, derivation of a model that would adequately reproduce existing patient use of the hospital system. Only then could a normative model be created—one that could measure imbalances in the present distribution and suggest location shifts that would better meet the needs of both patients and hospitals. This article reports on the development of such a model and its application to the metropolitan Chicago hospital system.

The traditional approach to evaluation has been to take the population of given administrative units (cities, counties, etc.) and find the ratio of population to beds, comparing this to national standards. The inadequacy of this approach has long been recognized. Studies of hospital utilization and of hospital service areas have provided a more satisfactory basis for estimating needs and for measurement and planning.

Patient variables identified in earlier stages of the study as affecting the demand for hospital care were: level and type of care needed, ability to pay, race, and religion. Variables related to physicians and hospitals and therefore influencing the supply of medical care were: for physicians, location and differentiation; and for hospitals, location, level and type of care provided, and policies and type of control. Survey data on patient travel to hospitals served to distinguish the separate influences of the physician, of the pattern of hospital service areas, of distance, of level and type of care, and of economic, racial, and religious variables.

These relations and influences were summarized by a factor analysis of the characteristics of hospitals and their utilization, and regression analysis revealed that flows between communities and hospitals were about equally influenced by size of demand and opportunities and by amount of intervening demand and opportunities, with the flow modified upward when there was religious or racial similarity between hospital and community. Reduced volume was found to accompany increased hospital quality, since hospitals of high quality tended to treat smaller numbers of more difficult cases from a wide area.

APPROACHES TO MODELING THE PATIENT-PHYSICIAN-HOSPITAL INTERACTION

The first requirement of an adequate model is that it be able to replicate use of the system. This involves the recognition of a degree of irrationality or uncertainty and especially indeterminacy; that is, patients being confronted with a decision between approximately equally good choices. The model must accommodate experiment in order first to discern what modes of behavior better characterize actual decision making and then to test the effects of possible changes in behavior or outside constraints. Finally, the model must be able to evaluate the adequacy of the system and to prescribe changes that will raise the level of satisfaction of patients, physicians, and hospitals. Since patients desire easier access in space and time to physicians and hospitals with desired characteristics, physicians desire both access to hospitals and full use of their capacities, and hospitals desire a high rate of occupancy without congestion and excessive waiting, evaluation of the system should identify groups of patients and physicians who are required to travel unusually far or suffer unusually long waits and hospitals with excessive or deficient demand. The model should then be able to prescribe shifts in physician and hospital capacity that will bring all patients within maximum travel times (to be specified by society ultimately) and all hospitals to a viable level of operation.

Very simple models incorporating optimizing principles of spatial, social, and economic behavior were found able to account for much of the variation in behavior, but they fell short of satisfying the above requirements. Specifically, interactance models fairly well described use of the system and, to a degree, indicated imbalances in it. Distance-minimizing transport models failed to allow sufficient flexibility in behavior, but they proved valuable in identifying groups of patients who were poorly served and hospitals that were poorly located. In this study, therefore, a simulation approach is used that attempts to combine the descriptive advantages of the interactance model and the prescriptive values of the transport model, in order to allow the necessary experimentation, capture actual variation in behavior, and at the same time retain the ability to evaluate the efficiency of the system.

A SIMULATION MODEL OF PHYSICIAN AND HOSPITAL USE AND EVALUATION

The simulation model that has been developed is an interactance model to the extent that probabilities of patients from an area visiting various hospitals are estimated from such a construct, though modified. But this stage provides only an initial estimate of hospital use. The model has two additional useful features: a mechanism to achieve replication of the system and one to reallocate hospital capacity in order to improve on the present system.

Data on communities, physician clusters, and hospitals are presumed available. Numbers of patients with various characteristics and demands are known or can be estimated. There is obviously little or no substitution possible among obstetric, pediatric, and medical-surgical units of hospitals; similarly, the higher level hospitals have a "monopoly" on the care of many kinds of cases. Thus if data permit division of patients by types and levels of demand, the simulation model must be run separately for significant combinations of type and level of care.

The first stage allocates patients to physicians. For each community, studies of trips to services show that white patients seem to view the attractiveness of physician clusters as a simple function of the number and variety of physicians (white only). But the likelihood of patients visiting the clusters is influenced by the cost of reaching them, the existence of closer intervening physicians, and the lack of information about farther opportunities. Patient reaction to distance, determined from actual behavior, is one of indifference up to about two miles, after which attractiveness falls rapidly—that is, a physician twice as far away is viewed as something less than half as attractive. If there are large numbers of patients and not too many potential destinations, the probabilities

derived from such a modified interactance approach can become deterministic proportions; otherwise a Monte Carlo random number routine allocates the patients in accordance with the probabilities. Negro patients are similarly allocated, visiting either white or Negro physicians, with a moderate preference for the latter.

This initial allocation may be interpreted as where patients would like to go, given the present distribution of physicians. Since, however, physicians are not evenly distributed among all people, the demand for physician care at some locations will exceed their capacity and at others fall short. For example, too many patients will be allocated to a small isolated physician cluster in a heavily populated area. A large cluster of physicians with nearby competing clusters will not attract enough. Since a consistent basis for choice is applied, the differences can be interpreted as a measure of the imbalance or inefficiency of the location of capacity.

The first option shifts physician capacity until the demand on each physician cluster comes within some acceptable range of divergence. For example, assume that the initial demand on one physician cluster is twice its normal capacity and that on another cluster half. Presumably there are too few physicians in the first and too many in the second. As a guess, the model doubles the number of physicians in the first and halves the number in the second. The allocation is repeated with the altered capacities, and the divergence between normal and predicted demand is rechecked until the demand comes within an acceptable level of divergence.

The second option conversely shifts patients from overdemanded physician clusters to underdemanded ones, in order to replicate, as closely as possible, the actual pattern of travel. After the initial allocation, flows to overdemanded clusters are proportionally reduced to actual capacity. The residual demand is then reallocated to underdemanded clusters only, a procedure that also requires iterative allocation. The greater aggregate travel distance that is required will be a direct measure of the inefficiency of capacity location: that is, an estimate of the extra effort patients in fact must exert to get care. Comparison with the shifted-capacity solution measures the savings possible from such relocation.

The second stage allocates patients to hospitals. The replications of actual patient-to-physician flows are taken as inputs. Using the already identified patient variables of race, religion, and ability to pay, the patient population is divided into six subgroups: paying Negro patients (as above); charity patients (those who did not visit a physician at all but will visit hospitals directly); and four white paying subgroups—Jews, Protestants, Catholics, and religiously indifferent. Since the capacity of hospitals to care for Negro and charity patients is known, each of these allocations is done separately. All white paying patients are allocated in the same model run, but the religion of the patients is recorded. Within the white paying group, allocation to hospitals reflects a balance among the factors of distance, size, and religious character of hospital. Within the Negro group and the charity group the balance is between distance and size only.

Charity patients are allocated to hospitals in the same manner as patients were allocated to physicians above—as a simple function of distance to hospitals and their capacity to treat charity patients. For Negro patients, allocation is as before, except that the probability of visiting a particular hospital is a function of both the patient's and the physician's evaluation of size and distance. The working hypothesis here, that the choice is a function equally of distance from patient and of distance from physician,

seems more reasonable than that the desires of one or the other should be controlling (in effect, the mean of the hospital distance from physician and from patient is substituted for distance from patient).

White subgroups evaluate distance "religiously" as well as geographically—that is, a mental barrier is erected against a hospital operated under the auspices of a different religion that increases the effective distance of it. Analyses of actual flows and experimental operation of the model suggest that on the average Jews evaluate distance to non-Jewish hospitals as about three times farther; Catholics evaluate distance to non-Catholic hospitals as about twice as far; Protestants evaluate Catholic and Jewish hospitals as about twice as far but evaluate nonreligiously oriented hospitals about the same as Protestant hospitals. These factors, applied to the distances to hospitals, affect the probabilities of visiting various hospitals; otherwise the allocation method is the same as before.

Again, the first option shifts hospital capacity until the demand on each hospital comes within some acceptable range of divergence (for paying Negroes, for charity patients, and for white paying patients separately). The same iterative procedure as before shifts beds from underdemanded to overdemanded hospitals. This substage of the model has the capability, if desired, of creating new hospitals and estimating their ideal size. Plausible locations are given a "token" hospital of but one bed; if these locations are superior, beds will be shifted from poorer existing locations. Some present hospitals may in fact be eliminated by the model, although it is also possible to prevent an uneconomic reduction in size of existing hospitals.

The second option shifts patients, again for paying Negro, charity, and white paying patients separately, from initially overdemanded hospitals to underdemanded ones. Again, the greater aggregate distance traveled measures the extra effort patients must exert, given the present distribution of capacity. Comparison with the shifted-capacity solution measures the savings attributable to relocation.

Since all the disaggregated flows will have been allocated, it is then possible to summarize all flows and demands on hospitals and to make summary comparisons. Addition of initially predicted demands on hospitals by the three subgroups will yield net measures of capacity imbalance. Summing of the suggested capacity shifts will indicate net shifts as between both locations and subgroups—for example, from white paying to charity patients.

The final stage of the model is experimental. The substages of initial allocation, shifting of capacity, and shifting of patients are repeated for any desired "external" changes. For example, several new hospitals or expansions may be approved or anticipated. The effects of such planned relocations on aggregate travel of patients and on the demand for existing hospitals may be measured. Estimated populations as of some future date may provide the basis for estimates of patient demand by area. The resultant imbalances and suggested shifts become a valuable indication of where new hospitals or expansions are needed.

A particularly valuable experiment, given present demands and capacities, measures the effects of relaxation of constraints. It may not be necessary to carry out all the shifts suggested in the model in an attempt to meet the separate demands of the many subgroups. Certainly it would be so costly that only some portion of suggested relocation or new capacity would be justified. Thus it is important to discover whether it would in the end be cheaper and easier to relax some of the present restrictions on entry to hospitals. Some or much of the apparent imbalance might disappear if patients and physicians had freer access to

the system. This can be tested by appropriate aggregation of subgroups. The most feasible changes are in regard to race and ability to pay, since legal and financial arrangements can be made to permit entry to hospitals irrespective of color and income. Since preference on the basis of religion is personal, relaxation here is somewhat academic, so long as hospitals under religious control exist. Aggregations to be tested, then, are (1) all patients irrespective of race, (2) all patients irrespective of income, and (3) all patients irrespective of both race and income. These tests of relaxation of constraints may be applied to both the patient-physician and the patient-hospital stages of the model.

RESULTS

For purposes of clarity, map presentation of model results is limited to a sample set of communities across Chicago's south side, extending to the suburb of Evergreen Park. These communities are characterized by wide variations in race, income, and religion.

Allocation to Physicians

Shifts of Capacity

As expected, the initial allocation resulted in excess demand on physician clusters in newer and poorer areas and insufficient demand on older and larger clusters. Almost all demands were brought to ±10 percent of the mean demand (11 patients per physician) within five iterations. Some 1,500 physicians (about 15 percent) were shifted, mainly from the Loop (central business district) and other very large clusters to smaller clusters closer to the population (see Figure 1). Although this shift greatly reduces aggregate patient travel, it is recognized that this breakup of agglomerations may be uneconomic. Inefficient reduction of clusters can be avoided in the model, however, by disaggregation of patients and physicians by major specialty groups.

Shifts of Patients

When patients are forced to use the existing system, total travel reasonably approximates that actually observed. Aggregate travel exceeds that for the physician-capacity-shift solution by 90,000 patient-miles, or about 20 percent (see Figure 2). These model results are particularly useful in pinpointing which specific groups and areas presently incur the greatest excess travel. Not surprisingly, these are paying patients in poor communities and patients in rapidly growing newer communities.

Race and Income Barriers Removed

If patients, irrespective of race and ability to pay, are able to visit all physicians, an even greater shift of physicians is forecast by the model, mainly from the Loop and from wealthy areas specifically to Chicago's poverty areas. This physician shift is a measure of the great latent demand for physicians in low income areas—in other words, of the unmet need.

Allocation to Hospitals

For the hospital trip, patients modify the distance according to religious preference. The model worked rather well in this respect, requiring, for example, greater average travel for Jewish patients, owing to the limited number of Jewish-affiliated hospitals. The capacity-shift portion of the model also differentiated by religion. For example, in heavily Catholic southwest Chicago, bed complements of Catholic hospitals were increased and those of Protestant hospitals reduced, reflecting demand shifts in the postwar period.

Shifts of Capacity

The initial allocation resulted in excess demand on hospitals in Negro areas and in many suburban areas and insufficient demand for inner city hospitals and for charity and veterans' institutions. The model results suggest a shift of over 12,000 beds, or about 16 percent (see Figure 3). Beds for both paying and charity Negro patients are shifted to ghetto area hospitals at the expense of close-in hospitals and especially Cook County Hospital (charity), with resultant savings in patient travel (see Figure 4). Beds are added to many suburban hospitals in rapidly growing areas. Many hospitals on the Chicago north side are reduced in size, reflecting long-term population shifts.

As with trips to physicians, level of hospital care was not explicitly treated in these first runs. Thus Chicago's best and largest hospitals are slashed in size, since they are indeed too large and central with respect to general levels of care. In later model runs, a separate solution will be obtained for cases that could be handled only by larger hospitals enjoying scale and agglomerative advantages.

Shifts of Patients

If patients are again forced to use the existing system, travel exceeds that for the capacity-shift solution by 116,000 patient-miles (about 20 percent). Most of the excess travel is incurred by black and poor patients generally, since they are presently restricted to so few hospitals.

Race and Income Barriers Removed

When the barriers against unrestricted use of hospitals by paying Negro patients are removed, patients' demands are ideally met through the shifting of only 1,380 rather than 1,700 beds to ghetto area hospitals. Likewise, patients are forced to travel less far, given the present distribution of capacity. If the barriers against free entry to hospitals by charity patients are also removed, patients using the existing system enjoy great savings in travel, and a far less radical and therefore less costly shift of beds

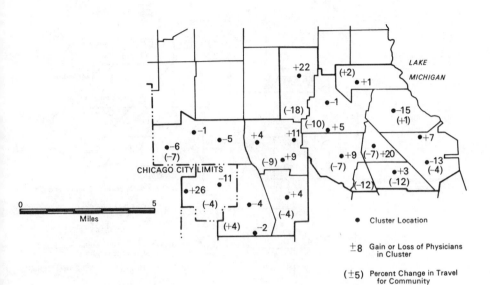

FIGURE 1. Changes in Cluster Size and Patient Travel
Resulting from Shifting Physicians

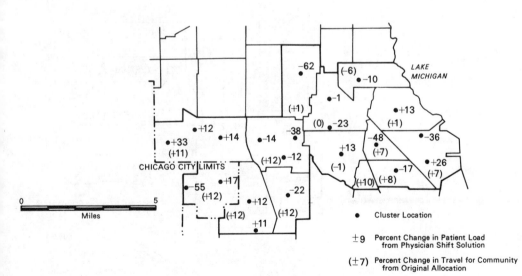

FIGURE 2. Changes in Patient Load and Patient Travel
Resulting from Shifting Demand on Physicians

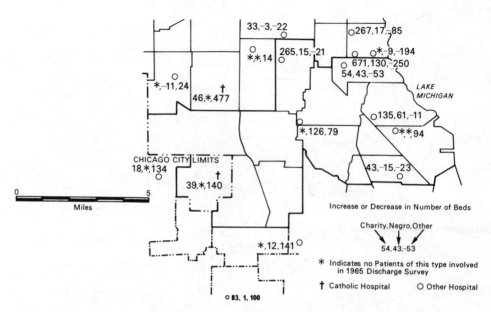

FIGURE 3. Changes in Bed Complement of Selected Chicago Area Hospitals Resulting from Shifting Capacity to Charity, Negro and Other Patients

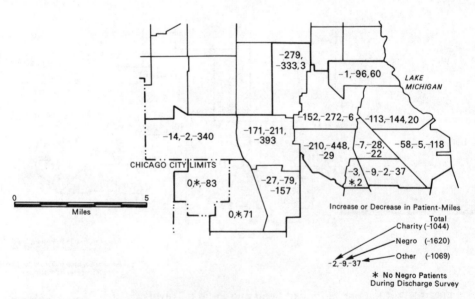

FIGURE 4. Changes in Charity, Negro, and Other Patient Travel in Selected Chicago Areas Resulting from Shifting Hospital Capacity

is required to achieve the same improvement in patient travel and hospital utilization. For example, Cook County Hospital is reduced from 2,700 only to 1,590 rather than to 800 beds, and altogether 8,650 rather than 12,167 beds are shifted, for an almost identical travel saving (see Figure 5).

CONCLUSIONS: EVALUATION OF THE MODEL

The simulation model outlined above is intended both to reproduce an actual

The model works moderately well at replicating use of the system and at evaluating locational efficiency and suggesting shifts in location and policies that would raise the general level of satisfaction with the least dislocation. On the other hand, certain problems must be noted: (1) The model results are quite sensitive to the particular parameters of the equation (patient interpretation of distance, size, and religion), hence it cannot be claimed that the results are "right" until more evidence of patient perception and behavior is obtained, in-

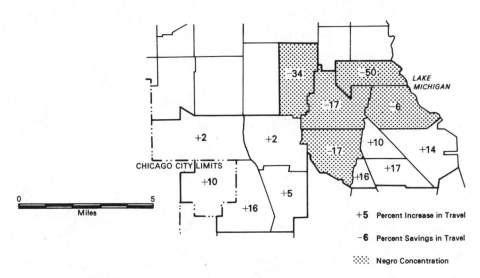

FIGURE 5. Changes in Patient Travel with Existing Distribution of Hospital Capacity when Race and Income Barriers are Removed

pattern of use satisfactorily, on the basis of properly understood and formulated decision-making criteria, and, by extension, to evaluate present imbalances of capacity and estimate the shifts necessary for desired improvement. A fair degree of complexity was required in order to depict the system realistically. A partly deterministic and partly probabilistic simulation model resulted, since the range of choice confronting the residents of an area seems too great for deterministic assignment.

cluding personal interviews; (2) the authors are not fully satisfied with the specific mathematical operations of the model; (3) the value of the present results is limited by lack of breakdown by physician specialty and by level of hospital care; and (4) the model may place too much stress on reducing patient travel and not enough on institutional viability and quality.

Anticipated experiments in the near future include some breakdown by type and level of care; prediction of the effects of estimated 1980 population distribution and of planned new hospitals and expansions; use of the model to suggest new hospitals and their optimal size; and extension to data for Seattle and Honolulu.

Although the model was developed for the hospital use context, the programming is flexible enough to permit a much broader application, at least to problems involving movements of persons, differential location of demand and supply, and evaluation of the efficiency of travel patterns and supply patterns. The authors believe the evaluative portion to be the most important contribution. If it proves useful, then further application to movements to shopping centers, schools, churches, recreation sites, and other destinations would be appropriate and necessary to demonstrate true generality.

FROM ASYLUM TO GHETTO
EILEEN WOLPERT
JULIAN WOLPERT

Wolpert and Wolpert provide an important insight into the increasing use of spatial isolation as a tool for dealing with the disadvantaged members of American society. Using released mental patients as an example, they point out that a combination of current medical policy and zoning laws hinder the return of mental patients to society after their discharge; suitable accomodation is only available in poorer parts of the inner city. As release policy changes and the rate of discharge increases, one can observe the development of well-defined ghettos; ghettos of ex-mental patients which serve to enforce their isolation from the rest of society.

From *Antipode: A Radical Journal of Geography* 6, no. 3 (1974): 63–76, by permission of the publisher and the authors.

Some communities are doing more than their share. They are salvaging ill-conceived and poorly implemented policies or those designed not to work. A number of residential communities in this country, for example, have been saturated by the placement of former patients recently released from state mental hospitals. The release of long-term patients has reached a highly significant level and placements have been concentrated in relatively few neighborhoods. Fifteen state mental hospitals have closed down in the past four years, including four in California alone. The national figures demonstrate a significant decline in resident population in those hospitals which continue to operate: from a peak of 543,000 in 1959 to a present level of 240,000. The decline in state hospital in-patients has been matched, however, by a corresponding increase in convalescent beds as well as by residential group quarters within communities. The same communities which house released mental patients are likely also to have half-way houses for ex-addicts and ex-felons, nursing homes for the elderly and other residential facilities for the disabled. The decentralization trend in public mental health care (rather than in programs for the elderly, the mentally retarded or the ex-prisoners) is singled out for discussion here because of the sheer magnitude and bias of community impaction.

THE VICTIM POPULATION

Who are the released patients? Many are the beneficiaries of recent policies designed to reduce the duration of stay in state hospitals. The predominant group had been warehoused without much pretext of intensive treatment for long periods of time or had followed a cycle of discharge and readmission. The modal group is white, indigent and late middle-aged or elderly. Long hospitalization often yielded mental hospital careerism. Over-hospitalization was the product of poor recovery prospects, professional inattention, public apathy, and family and community reluctance to receive the disabled back into the community setting.

THE PUSH FOR CLOSURE

The present decentralizing trend is the outcome of several recent developments: the rising cost of state hospital care; the chemotherapy innovations in tranquilizers; the advocacy of civil liberties for patients; and more tolerant community attitudes for non-conforming behavior. The "dumping syndrome" is caused by the accelerated rush: to close down specific hospitals; to eliminate dysfunctional over-hospitalization; and to take up the expedient option of viable placement opportunities.

A "dumping" connotation appears warranted given the haste in discharging large numbers of long hospitalized patients and their concentrated placement in residential communities unprepared for and reluctant to provide aftercare services and social integration. The dumping process operates with a low profile to forestall community resistance, but the outcome is highly conspicuous. The sensationalist press (*The New York Times, San Francisco Chronicle, Washington Post, Los Angeles Times*) has emerged as community advocates and records faithfully the bizarre and threatening behavior of the ex-patients. Discredit is reflected on the callous state officials and the exploiting operators of residential facilities. The welfare of the released patients and the merits of dehospitalization are overlooked or even worse, pressure mounts to reopen the hospitals and the wards so that released patients can be returned.

Why has the pendulum swung so far from a tendency to over-hospitalize to the present dumping trend? Why is the placement of released patients so inequitably biased? Why has the release of patients not been scheduled in a more gradual fashion that is consistent with the development of suitable residential and aftercare service facilities in a broad range of communities? What are the consequences of premature release and biased placement on the ex-patients and the impacted communities? Is there a tipping point of institutional saturation of residential communities which marks the breakdown of "normal" community functions and activities? Some of these questions can be addressed in the context of San Jose's (California) ghetto of released patients.

THE SAN JOSE GHETTO

In a growing number of communities like San Jose, the recently discharged group has become increasingly conspicuous. They are not distributed evenly but congregated in highly predictable concentrations. The primary locational factor relates to their indigent status. State hospital care is public sector care and its clients were overwhelmingly drawn from the lower socio-economic groups. Placement has occurred in the lower income areas of the inner city, in areas of deteriorating land use, where subdivided large homes and no longer fashionable hotels are prevalent, where boarding houses and rooming homes already exist and where restrictive zoning is absent.

The California accelerated release program has reduced in-patient residents in state hospitals from a peak of almost 40,000 in 1956 to fewer than 6,000 at the present time. During the same period, the average length of stay was reduced from 250 days to 71. The tranquilizing drugs, state and federal funding of county and community mental health and welfare programs for the disabled have all aided the decentralizing trend. Considerable cost savings were anticipated by the shift from centralized in-patient care to community boarding and nursing homes. Civil rights forces helped to reform the commitment procedures and to reduce the extent of over-hospitalization.

The resulting reduction in state hospital case loads led to a drive to consolidate state facilities to achieve cost savings. Fixed costs of $1.5 million could be saved, for example, by closing down Agnews State Hospital in Santa Clara County because the other nearby hospitals (Napa and Stockton) had sufficient capacity to take care of present and future treatment needs.

Accordingly, Agnews ceased admitting mentally ill patients at the end of November 1971, and was slated to close its facility entirely at the end of June 1972. Modesto State Hospital had been closed previously (mid-1970); DeWitt Hospital was closed in March 1972; and Mendocino was closed at the end of 1972. The plan for California proceeded on the basis that all the state hospitals for the mentally ill could be closed down by 1977 and those for the mentally retarded by 1982, a schedule which has since been temporarily delayed.

Mental health professionals in California appear to agree that the mental hospitals closed too abruptly, unleasing a minimally functioning population before the separate communities had time to prepare compensatory programs. In all too many cases, the released patients have ended up in prisons, in skid rows, in transient hotels and unlicensed board-and-care homes.

Strong community opposition to group quarters for discharged patients has been widely legitimized through recent passage of zoning regulations. Those communities unable or unwilling to restrict such placements found themselves quickly saturated and incapable of convincing neighboring communities to deal with the issue on an equitable basis. A local community survey demonstrated that respondents were significantly more sympathetic toward those with physical illness such as cancer or emphysema,

than they were toward the mentally ill. Released patients have a considerably lower crime rate and are much more frequently victims of violent acts than agents, but local communities over-reacted to sensational press accounts of "threatening" behavior. The legislature has now voted to retain the remaining hospitals, but this new policy will not affect those communities which have already been saturated.

A GHETTO OF RELEASED PATIENTS

The College Town neighborhood of San Jose is hardly representative of the national or even the state experience with patient release, but the primary national issues involving decentralization of care can be identified from the College Town developments. The ghettoization of 1,-100 released patients in the College Town area of downtown San Jose reveals the outcome of a locational process which is highly predictable but difficult to prevent. The steamroller of release was started by rising hospital costs with a reduced patient load at nearby Agnews State Mental Hospital and optimism about community reception and after-care program development. The outcome was a sudden upsurge in demand for community placement at the same time when group quarters were needed for nursing and half-way homes for the elderly, the former drug addicts, the ex-felons and ex-alcoholics. The supply of suitable facilities was not only limited in number but concentrated spatially in limited neighborhoods. The most immediate prerequisite for facilities was not the cost constraint imposed by the dependent care payments; a second element was access to facilities for outpatient treatment and social services; a third factor favored low risk environments both for patient safety and community acceptance.

The College Town area (with only

1.5 percent of the county's population) provided 74 percent of the bed capacity available in unlicensed board-and-care facilities within the entire county. An additional 16 percent of the county's capacity is located elsewhere within the city of San Jose. College Town is the only extensive area in Santa Clara County where zoning permits board-and-care.

At least one-third of the board-and-care residents in the College Town area are from communities outside the county and only a tiny minority lived previously in this neighborhood. Fewer than one-third of those placed in the area by the nearby veterans hospitals were Santa Clara residents. Several of the San Francisco Bay Area counties consider the College Town area as a primary resource for residential placement.

Welfare incentives to counties had been necessary to entice them to reclaim their hospitalized residents, but neighboring counties preferred to maintain their released former residents "elsewhere" despite the penalties. Some communities hesitated to establish aftercare programs because if good services were provided, released patients will saturate the catchment areas.

Released patients are not required to return to their own prior neighborhood (the California State legislation mentions only *county* of prior residence), so that the catchment areas are unevenly represented in released patient numbers. The goals of "community responsibility" and community as "therapeutic agent" are lost with the biased form of distribution represented by the College Town neighborhood.

Community reaction in College Town did not become prominent until 1971 when a retarded client died in a fire in a board-and-care home. Soon after one board-and-care resident stabbed and killed another. A developing community opposition organization (the Campus Improvement Association) al-leged that the board-and-care impaction had ruined business and lowered property values and the local media highlighted negative aspects of the affair.

In September 1972, the San Jose Council passed a moratorium, still in effect, to restrict "temporarily" the establishment of board-and-care homes anywhere in the city, thus freezing the status quo in placement and even inhibiting the relocation of clients to other parts of the city or the county.

Placement in what was to become the College Town released patient ghetto had begun more than fifteen years ago before any plans had developed for a mass release program. In 1959, a boarding home was first used to place mentally handicapped men. The landlady concerned was "interested in helping them to live in a community." Subsequent placements consisted mainly of the elderly who were moved to homes for the aged. By the middle-sixties, when the demand for placement increased, others, not merely the elderly, were brought to the same community. With the impending closure of the nearby mental hospital and the policy shift to limit hold and commitment procedures, the community placement pressure intensified and demand quickly outgrew the supply of licensed facilities. Placement staff was hired at Agnews to investigate the range of alternative options, but the deadline of the hospital's imminent closing made staff placement loads excessive. Unable to investigate the full potential range of suitable facilities and confronted by College Town operators petitioning for placements in their homes, it is easy to understand the ghetto's development.

Why was this neighborhood in San Jose suited to board-and-care facilities? The neighborhood is situated in close proximity to a downtown area, severely downgraded by suburbanization of residents, commerce and office facilities. The College Town neighborhood contains San Jose State University and a considerable bloc of large residential structures used formerly to house fraternities, sororities, and other student living arrangements. A change in student housing rules, a decline in fraternity popularity and new construction of campus housing all combined to reduce the demand for neighborhood housing, and "For Sale" signs were prominent. Many of the homeowners were elderly widows in need of supplementary income. Community placement of released patients provided some solution. The operation of a board-and-care home, not overly lucrative at best and not suited to all rooming house owners, offered some income prospects at the time to many College Town homeowners. In homes with large rooms, as many as four people could be accommodated per room, but the prevailing pattern is of lower personal density (three to six people per house). Some of the homes, however, accommodate thirty or more residents and in some cases several homes were purchased by independent businessmen to be operated by resident managers. Some operators complained to placement officials that they were not getting their share of residents and that other operators were being favored.

Licensing requirements were not enacted until August 1972, but regulations and standards have still not been fully established. Rigid enforcement of high standards and full enforcement of local and state codes would undoubtedly cause some operators to close down and inhibit others from establishing board-and-care facilities.

COMMUNITY INTEGRATION

These patients who had been confined for long periods of time were often no longer in contact with community or family. In other cases there were no families to which patients could be returned or families had made readjustments and opposed the return of their disabled member. For some of the ex-patients to return to their prior family or community setting would have been inadvisable or potentially harmful. Mental health officials may have been naive to believe that families who had surrendered relatives to the state hospital system would eagerly volunteer their return, even in sedated condition or with their illness in remission. Those, of course, who were satisfactorily returned to families have become highly dispersed but the predominant group had neither family nor community ties and have been clustered in the board-and-care facilities.

Some of the discharged patients can "pass." They bear no significant outward signs of their confinement. They can obtain employment, arrange for their own housing, build social ties and essentially merge into the general population. At the opposite end of the continuum is the larger group which has been transferred from one institutional setting to another, a group which requires more care than the board-and-care arrangement can provide.

COMMUNITY SUPPORT SYSTEMS

Seventy percent of the released patients in board-and-care facilities rarely venture into the street and are not included in any systematic after-treatment program organized by local community mental health officials. Their needs do not come to the attention of officials unless there are acts of violence or physical deterioration requiring rehospitalization. One form of confinement has been replaced by another and the former patients are as insulated from community attention and care as they were in the state hospital. The major virtue of board-and-care facilities may be their smaller scale, a characteristic frequently associated with more humane treatment.

A critical mass of released patients must exist in a community before it is economically feasible to provide ancillary services such as occupational and recreational therapy and various rehabilitation services. Release of patients from state hospitals where such services have become quite general to board-and-care facilities (where the television set is the major recreational outlet) reflects a deterioration in quality of living. The reduced patient load setting of the hospital had permitted increasing patient access to individual and group therapy and social and behavior therapy. In the community setting, the released patients are frequently overly subdued, defunctionalized and overtreated with long periods of excessive medication, or no medication at all. With the high cost of community in-patient care, pressure to seek every alternative to hospitalization has been exerted upon health care professionals, even for persons who might benefit from intensive in-patient treatment (the "hot-bed" syndrome of rapid turnover of community hospital beds).

Without coordination between state hospital authorities and community aftercare staff concerning the progress of ex-patients, there can be little systematic follow-up study of the former patient population nor an understanding of the implications of release. Since ex-patients are not required to pursue aftercare treatment nor even required legally to take tranquilizing medication, aftercare staff becomes aware of ex-patient needs for treatment or other assistance when alerted by board-and-care operators or the police.

At present, there are no minimum operator qualifications and few of the operators of board-and-care facilities have established programs of any type. The operators are untrained and frequently unaware of license regulations and recommended care procedures. No systematic follow-up of the released patients is mandated nor are the board-and-care homes monitored to insure

that care is adequate. There are no regulations which restrict dysfunctional or harmful mixing of residents within rooms or houses. Recreational and rehabilitative services are fragmented and inadequate as is the provision for general medical services. The employable residents are not adequately served in job training centers. Many of the downtown churches have chosen to withdraw from involvement rather than conduct outreach programs for the residents.

Allegations have been made that residents are frequently deprived of basic rights: to receive mail unopened; to refuse the tranquilizing medication; to keep and spend personal funds at will; to enjoy privacy, social interaction or marry. Operators appear to be over-protective and to enforce medication prescriptions but there is little indication that residents are exploited by operators for material gain.

Operators of board-and-care facilities expect fewer than 10 percent of their residents to become independent in a year's time. Initial placements in communities develop a permanency which is not easily redirected. Despite the frequent inadequacy of initial placements, board-and-care residents would not favor further dislocation or disruption, especially given the limited ability of their welfare checks to purchase adequate housing and board in better neighborhoods.

THE POLICY SALVAGE MECHANISM

Do adequate planning, expedient policies and inept implementation inevitably lead to disastrous outcomes? The College Town ghettoization represents a highly conspicuous focus for community opposition, media coverage and political campaigns. The inequity of incidence of impact is obviously grave, yet no serious local attempts have been made to disperse the released patients or return them to the state hospitals. Community opposition was aimed not at the released patients themselves but was properly directed at state officials.

Despite its ill-conceived format, the release and placement program has received an unanticipated bonus in the improved outlook achieved for many of those released. However, the salvage ingredient in College Town may be only fortuitous and placement officials should not be able to depend upon local compensation for policy shortcomings. Community responsibility and the goal of an inclusive society are pushed to improper limits with unrestrained dumping of patients by state mental health officials. The presence of some good board-and-care operators, student volunteers and indigenous leadership within the released patient community have salvaged the program in San Jose. The benefits of their efforts need, however, to be institutionalized so that these benefits can be assured.

The College Town clustering has yielded a number of unanticipated benefits which require a facilitator-gatekeeper interpretation at the community level. Two individuals have been especially instrumental in helping to transform the aggregation of the board-and-care residents into a functioning community.

John Murphy's Community of Communities

John Murphy founded the Community of Communities in the summer of 1972, after attending a meeting of the Campus Improvement Association and hearing support expressed there for returning the "insane" back to Agnews. Beginning with a small group of student volunteers from San Jose State University, Murphy built a structure for reaching out to residents of one of the board-and-care facilities. The group has now grown to 300 student volunteers and twelve paid staff

providing coverage to twenty-two homes which include 700 residents. After the one-year trial period, the expanded efforts of the Community of Communities (COC) was funded by the County's revenue sharing program. The COC's objectives are to provide recreation and companionship to the residents, to take the residents for medical care or job interviewing appointments, to perform an advocate role on behalf of the residents and to educate themselves and the outside community about both the needs and resources present in the ex-patient community. The COC is structured to avoid "casual volunteerism" by a system of house coordinators for each residence and a carefully thought-out pairing of the student volunteer with house residents. The relative stability of these arrangements allow for friendship and responsibility to emerge.

Would the COC functions have emerged without the ghettoization and Murphy's motivation and organizing ability? Student volunteers have been an important asset to the program and the clustering of board-and-care facilities in College Town has made the facilities accessible and conspicuous for volunteer efforts by the students.

Is the COC outcome fortuitous, dependent upon the simultaneous presence of a clustering of residents, John Murphy, and a large scale volunteer program? Does the clustering of released patients dependably give rise to a positive community effort to provide services? Experience in other communities would refute the undeserved optimism. Intervention is usually required to ensure local community services.

The usual problem with volunteer programs and especially those programs which rely so heavily upon student volunteers is their expected transitoriness. However eager and enthusiastic the students are, a long term commitment of friendship cannot easily be expected. Students, or other volunteers, develop other interests and commitments or they relocate. The volunteers are not peers. They provide a service for the released patient but cannot provide a community of social networks. The discharged patient community has suffered disappointments before individually and as a group when volunteers or social workers promised more in terms of friendship than they were able to give.

The volunteer effort on a one-to-one basis is a valuable learning experience for the volunteer provided that he or she has access to a resource person to whom impressions, anxieties, and successes can be related for meaningful development of insight. Fortunately, the Community of Communities does endeavor to follow through in this manner. The major virtue of this organization is its demonstration of the essential services required by the ex-patients which would normally not be provided by treatment and social agencies in even our wealthiest counties.

Organization and Leadership within the Community

Montye Rivera, the leader of the San Jose ex-patient community, would fulfill no one's stereotype of a schizophrenic, despite her many years in state hospitals. Ms. Rivera, as spokesman for the community and editor of the *Care Home News,* alerts us to the diversity of the ex-patients and their resources. The monthly newsletter, largely financed from her own maintenance check, informs the community about recreational and social events, educational programs, news about community people and the volunteers and social service people who have been active in the community. News is covered concerning hearings at the state or local level as well as new regulations for zoning and licensing board-and-care facilities. There is a liberal sprinkling of poetry, essays and letters contributed by the board-and-care residents, as well as recipes and gossip.

As unofficial spokesman for the group, Ms. Rivera serves as a liaison with local authorities and speaks out at hearings to correct outsiders' dysfunctional and incorrect stereotypes. She has opened a gift shop which serves as a social focal point in the downtown area and trains the more able residents in sales, record keeping and management. The store also provides a mechanism for community members to obtain references and have greater contact with the demands of community life.

Without John Murphy and Montye Rivera and their gate-keeper services it is difficult to imagine what positive forces would have emerged to transform the College Town ghetto into an integrated community. Their efforts have compensated for some of the disbenefits of premature and non-discriminatory release and for the absence of essential community services. The crucial issue is whether indigenous leaders and local programs will emerge upon release or clustered placement without planning, programming and funding by those responsible for aftercare services.

EVALUATION—COLLEGE TOWN

The College Town ghetto has generated, perhaps inadvertently, a number of strongly positive factors which augment the direct benefits of release. What are the advantages of a community of released patients living in close proximity to one another rather than in dispersed group homes? The "buddy" system and the other organizational structures of mutual support are more likely outcomes when the homes are themselves clustered. The clustering in San Jose has been accompanied by the development of indigenous leadership; a strong support pattern; some effective lobbying for ex-patients rights; and a monthly newsletter. The healthier and more active members of the community can call attention to the needs of the more disabled group. The leadership can claim jurisdiction over a very considerable constituency in negotiations with the providers of care and the authorities. Leaders maintain that dispersal would erode bargaining rights, invite victimization and risk stigmatization by the "up tight" suburbanites.

Exit from the ghetto is now effectively blocked through restrictive zoning ordinances against group quarters, but individuals or groups of six or fewer members can freely move out on their own. Exit from the board-and-care home implies a reduction in dependency and involves a penalty through a corresponding reduction in the monthly dependency grant. More and more of the healthier board-and-care residents have taken this alternative, however, which is to move initially, along with one or two others, to a neighborhood apartment prior to exit from the ghetto entirely. This process has been encouraged by local officials, but it is unfortunate that dependency aid declines when the individual needs help most in order to prepare for a "normal" life. The ghetto functions as a transitional community for those who are more able, physically healthy and potentially employable. The ghetto setting is valuable for those who would have no community ties in "normal" communities. The ghetto is harmful to those residents who have insufficient exposure to the conventions of the predominant society and do not take the final steps toward full community integration. The ghetto is dysfunctional in the sense that it swamps the existing aftercare services and is a barrier to interaction with outsiders.

The College Town area has benefited by having a large number of vacant residences now filled. Neighborhood land use deterioration and a depressed housing market have been forestalled, or at least postponed. Some of the local businesses have benefited from the resident clientele. Some of the neighborhood property owners have benefited, i.e., the board-and-care operators, but others have been adversely affected. The temporary board-and-care solution for the vacant rooming houses may have inhibited a progressive and general renewal of the area. San Jose State University does not have an idealized campus environment because of the close proximity of the ex-patient ghetto, but then neither was it ideal when the rooming houses were vacant. Despite the difficulties, the College Town ghetto has been as good a compromise solution as has occurred anywhere in the country. As a semi-permanent community, the ghetto would benefit from: more generous payments to the residents; more extensive aftercare programs in the form of social and recreational services; more medical attention; occupational training; and helpful, follow-up on-site visits to board-and-care facilities by social service personnel.

EVALUATION—NATIONAL TREND

The trend toward release of state hospital patients and decentralization of those discharged into residential communities has saved thousands from over-hospitalization. In states such as California, New York and Massachusetts where hospitals had been innovative, there also has been innovation in the accelerated release of patients. These early experiences provide an opportunity to consider the disbenefits of under-hospitalization and nondiscriminatory release (the "dumping syndrome"). We can learn from recent events about aftercare facilities which are both advisable and implementable. We know now, for example, that residential, general medical and social services are more crucial to patient welfare in a community setting than are aftercare psychiatric services. The released patient community is now more critically in need of attention to physical and social needs than further therapy.

The federal authorities have provided incentives to states to reduce their hospital populations through the Community Mental Health Center (CMHC) Act and welfare legislation. The states have provided incentives to the counties to reclaim their hospitalized former residents and penalties for not doing so. The counties have not intervened significantly in the zoning and licensing issues of their constituent communities. They have sought the most expedient of possible solutions, i.e., to dump those released into available housing in neighborhoods where "normals" prefer not to live. In such communities, the needs of the under-hospitalized (the more disabled of the released group) are as neglected as when they were over-hospitalized. If the release process is not managed therapeutically and humanely and if ex-patients are placed and served in a manner which fuels the anxiety of residential communities, then the penalty will be bottlenecks of the overly hospitalized awaiting their turn for release.

Remedies involve providing closer attention to differences within the mentally disabled population. Not that it is easy to predict the consequences of release, but it is reasonably easy to predict the essential social services required by the different groups among the discharged population. A separate category of the CMHC mandated services, for example, may have to be designated to enforce adherence to the aftercare plan which is supposed to accompany each released patient. Aggregate coordination of placement efforts would be highly desirable, as would be the development of standards in the development of an aftercare plan and referral network. These requirements could be built into the health or welfare systems.

Rationalization of the funding efforts at federal, state and local levels would help to eliminate incentives for dysfunctional release or transfer of patients. The development and analysis of better data on treatment and service outcome and their costs would help to dispel speculation about the economies of community care.

At the community level, neighborhoods which are highly susceptible to saturation, are readily identifiable. Few areas are zoned for group quarters and welfare allowances limit housing choices to the types of neighborhoods which violate the spirit of community-based care. Neglect of county-wide planning or failure to use an open planning mechanism to select suitable residential sites only invites the separate municipalities to pass exclusionary zoning regulations to avoid becoming saturated themselves. Rather than wait for court rulings to restore freedom of residential choice for the disabled, local responsibility could be discharged now through a non-coercive method. If many continued to be hospitalized simply because they were unwanted by communities, if those who were released faced a severe decline in the quality of their life and if community preventative services failed to reduce the need for confinement, the public mental health sector will have once again failed to fulfill its mandate.

34

RACE AND STATUS IN SCHOOL SPENDING: CHICAGO, 1961–66

HAROLD M. BARON

Even within single school board jurisdictions, strong differentials may be observed in the allocation of funds to individual schools. Baron demonstrates that such allocations within the city of Chicago exhibit marked disparities along both racial and social status dimensions. Although protests from civil rights groups and ensuing federal legislation have somewhat ameliorated the situation, such disparities still persist.

Reprinted from *The Journal of Human Resources* 6, no. 1 (1971): 3–24, by permission of the University of Wisconsin Press and the author. Copyright © by the Regents of the University of Wisconsin. This is an edited version of the original publication. Notes have been renumbered.

The author wishes to acknowledge the assistance with the statistical work of two former Chicago Urban League Research Department colleagues, Mrs. Germaine Gordon and Walter Stafford.

While the philosophic formulations and public rhetoric regarding American education have stressed the goal of creating an equalitarian school system, the actual operation of the schools largely reflects existing disparities in the distribution of power and privilege. Twenty-five years ago the authors of *Who Shall Be Educated?* wrote of the conviction that the public schools "must, and we hope that they do, provide equal opportunity for every child. This means that those at the bottom can compete through education for life's prizes with those at the top." Yet, they counterposed the dilemma that in a society with basic inequalities: "The teacher, the school administrator, the school board, as well as the students themselves, play their roles to hold people in their places in our social structure." [1]

Most of the literature that deals with the actuality of the differences in the quality, quantity, and character of the public education provided to American children has studied the variation along class or status lines. It has shown that (1) the dominant norms of the schools are supportive of the values and style of the more privileged social strata; (2) the educational system has differing goals for the education and socialization of pupils from varying racial and class groups so that status tends to be preserved from one generation to another; and (3) more resources, both monetary and professional, are spent upon training the children from better-off families for membership in the social, professional, and technical elites. Race was at best relegated to a minor position in these analyses. Only the activities generated by the black community and the civil rights movement during the last decade have occasioned extensive study of urban schools as instruments for maintaining racial subjugation.

Economic studies on educational expenditures reveal that both income and status are very important in determining the amount that is spent on each student. Reviews of this literature show that in comparisons between school systems, expenditures per pupil vary directly with median family income, the value of property in the school district, and the educational level of the adult population. The property valuation variable is not important when comparisons are made only among large city school systems. Race was negatively related to spending: the higher the proportion of nonwhite in a school district, the lower the expenditure per pupil.

Underlying racial and class advantages are manifest in the lower educational expenditures for the central cities of large metropolitan areas. In 1930 when the central cities contained the great preponderance of the total metropolitan population from all status and racial groups, their school systems spent more per student than the outstate schools. By 1960, after large proportions of the higher and middle status white families had left for the suburbs, this relationship was reversed and most of the large central cities had per pupil expenditures below the average for their respective states. One study shows that in 1962, central cities were spending an average of $376 per pupil while the surrounding suburbs were spending $439, or 17 percent more.[2]

Those economists who have considered educational expenditures as an investment in human capital have found that it has one of the highest rates of return for any type of investment. As would be expected, given the pervasiveness of racism throughout American institutions, the rates of return for blacks are markedly lower than those for whites. None of these studies has yet measured for differences according to social status.

In this study we analyze how both race and status were reflected in the allo-cation of the public educational resources in a major metropolitan region over a period of six years, 1961 through 1966. During this interim there were strong forces at work to reduce the inequalities in expenditures per pupil. The black community and the civil rights movement created a demand for the realignment of expenditures. The federal government provided a supply of funds when it gave special consideration to the education of children from poor families. While the work of these forces did narrow or reduce some differentials, the degree of greater spending on high status suburban whites remained basically untouched.

Specifically, the study examines differentials in the allotment of public funds as measured by expenditures per pupil for the public elementary schools of Chicago and Cook County. (That portion of Cook County which does not include Chicago contains two-thirds of the suburban population of the Chicago Standard Metropolitan Statistical Area.) By using this quantitative measurement, we could compare a large number of schools over time—the years 1961, 1963, and 1966.[3] However, this single measure does have the limitation that it does not provide information on the social character of the individual schools which in the long run is a more decisive factor than the magnitude of spending. Further, given the present nature of American society and education, equal expenditures in different social milieus do not give equal results.

FINDINGS AND INTERPRETATION
Over the course of 50 years, since the great World War I migration from the South, the black proportion of the total Chicago population has grown from 2 percent in 1910 to approximately one-third today. While the Chicago public educational system had always operated in some manner of differentiation and

discrimination with regard to black pupils, not until the post-World War I era did the Chicago Board of Education develop a rather stable system of racial de facto segregation. Schools that were attended primarily by black children came to be operated in a manner that systematically subordinated the pupils, both as individuals and in terms of their long-run group interests. Although there were sporadic protests against this racist system, it was only in the latter part of 1961 that a massive sustained attack was launched against it by civil rights organizations. The civil rights campaign also disturbed the mechanisms by which higher status children were given preference. The year 1961, therefore, was the last year during which the Chicago Board of Education was able to administer without challenge a system of racial and class favoritism.

Previously, major publics to which the Board of Education has had to be responsive were the business interests and their allied tax-watchdog organizations; the political interests, especially the Democratic Party; and the middle-class good-schools organizations. Local communities were recognized in proportion to their general economic and social prestige. Accordingly, the black community did not constitute a significant public for the Chicago school administration.

1961. The allocation of operating funds for the year 1961 reflected these prevailing influences (see Column A, Table 1).[4] The median appropriation for white schools was $77 more per pupil, or 29 percent greater, than for black schools. On the basis of status, the median appropriation per pupil in the high status schools was $67, or 24 percent, greater than for the low status ones.

Although the black schools also tended to be the low status schools, race and status functioned independently in the rationing of funds. Within each separate status group, race affected the allocation of funds—regardless of the comparability of socioeconomic position: the blacker the composition of the student body, the fewer funds per child. The greatest color differentiation took place among the low status schools. In white low status schools, $68, or 22 percent, more was appropriated per child than in the corresponding black schools. The range of this color differential narrowed to $50, or 18 percent, between black and white schools of medium status. In the high status range there were too few black schools to make a comparison, but the gap between the biracial and the white schools was very small.

Within each color group, status affected allocations: the higher the status, the more money per pupil. Therefore, while the per pupil allotments for low status white schools were well above those for black schools, they were still $23 below those for high status white schools. The greatest status differential in funds occurred among the biracial schools. Evidently, the prestige of the white families who had children in the middle and high status biracial schools was sufficient to have had a large influence over the allocation.

The Chicago Board of Education's conditions of operating as a unified system with one ultimate decision-making authority and a single set of basic administrative rules did somewhat inhibit the range of the status differentials. By way of contrast, the individual school districts in suburban Cook County operate as separate municipalities, each with its own taxing authority and board. Within ground rules set by Illinois statutes and the rulings of the State Superintendent of Public Instruction, the board and administration of each school district are essentially autonomous. Given this lack of uniformity and centralization, it was expected that the expenditure differentials on the basis of status would be greater among the various suburban

			Appropriations	
Color and Status	Column A 1961	Column B 1963	Column C 1966 (excluding ESEA funds)	Column D 1966 (including ESEA funds)
Black	$264 (93)	$311 (107)	$324 (159)	$371 (159)
Low	258 (77)	308 (88)	321 (130)	374 (130)
Medium	282 (14)	329 (16)	350 (24)	365 (24)
High	— (2)	— (3)	270 (5)	318 (5)
Biracial	298 (37)	333 (50)	321 (50)	352 (50)
Low	281 (22)	320 (25)	327 (23)	380 (23)
Medium	307 (10)	328 (15)	304 (15)	333 (15)
High	342 (5)	361 (10)	321 (12)	331 (12)
White	341 (248)	359 (250)	369 (257)	380 (257)
Low	326 (61)	343 (58)	356 (64)	393 (64)
Medium	332 (68)	343 (69)	356 (69)	360 (69)
High	349 (119)	372 (123)	387 (124)	389 (124)
Low	284 (160)	326 (171)	334 (217)	384 (217)
Medium	321 (92)	338 (100)	353 (108)	361 (108)
High	347 (126)	367 (136)	379 (141)	382 (141)
All	$324 (378)	$341 (407)	$355 (466)	$376 (466)

TABLE 1. Median Per Pupil Operating Appropriations for Chicago Public Elementary Schools by Color and Status—1961, 1963, 1966 (Number of Schools in Parentheses)

school districts than within the single system for the central city. The political distinctiveness of the suburban schools would act to reinforce preferred status positions. This expectation was borne out.

For the suburban schools, Column A of Table 2 shows that the spread of $155 per pupil in annual expenditures between the medians for the low and the high status districts exceeded either the status or the color differential among the Chicago schools. In fact, the variation in the amount spent per pupil on the basis of status alone in Cook County was greater than that between the black low status schools and the white high status schools in Chicago. Among the subur-

ban schools, the differences between the high status and medium status districts were more marked than those between the medium and low status schools. The Chicago school system as a whole had per pupil expenditures that fell about midway between the medians for low and for medium status schools in the suburbs. It should be noted that data in the tables for Chicago and Cook County are not directly comparable because the former cover appropriations for local school operations only, while the latter are for expenditures for total school system operation.

1963. In the two years intervening between the drawing up of its 1961 budget

			Expenditures	
Status	Column A 1961–62	Column B 1963–64	Column C 1966–67 (excluding ESEA funds)	Column D 1966–67 (including ESEA funds)
Low	$418 (26)	$407 (25)	$491 (26)	$495 (26)
Medium	488 (33)	464 (31)	539 (32)	549 (32)
High	573 (35)	570 (34)	687 (36)	690 (36)
All	$505 (94)	$482 (90)	$575 (94)	$585 (94)
Chicago[a]	$442[b]	$448[b]	n.a.	$546[b]

TABLE 2. Median Per Pupil Operating Expenditures for Cook County Elementary School Districts by Status—1961–62, 1963–64, 1966–67[a] (Number of School Districts in Parentheses)

[a] This figure is not comparable to the figures in the tables on operating appropriations within the Chicago school system. The Chicago tables do not include centralized administrative costs and are calculated on a total enrollment base as compared to average daily attendance on this table.

[b] Mean

and its 1963 budget, the Chicago Board of Education was the target of the most hard-fought and extensive protest campaign that had taken place in Chicago since the end of World War II. Civil rights organizations and black community groups relentlessly exposed the patterns of segregation, the inequalities between the white and the black schools, and the general second-class treatment of black pupils. These exposures were backed up by mass demonstrations and civil disobedience. In the wake of the civil rights campaign, there was a partial shift in the pattern for the allocation of funds. Although this reallocation was carried out basically in subsequent budgets, there were some ad hoc shifts. For example, several months after the Chicago Urban League originally presented to the Chicago Board of Education its data as to the differentials in appropriations on the basis of race, the school administration, quietly and without specific Board authorization, made a special allocation of $50 per pupil to some 100 schools in low income areas. The Chicago civil rights activities were part of the growing national movement;

therefore, concessions made in Chicago reflected not only the local pressures but also the general trend in the management of big city schools. Accordingly, in many school systems concessions were made to black schools without there having been local protest movements as extensive as in Chicago.

The major way that the Chicago schools, under the leadership of Superintendent Benjamin Willis, responded to the civil rights pressures was to increase the number of de facto segregated facilities located within black neighborhoods. By any feasible means, construction schedules were moved up, portable classrooms were placed in large numbers on ghetto schoolyards and parks, and abandoned warehouses and orphanages were made over into schools. As a result, classroom sizes fell throughout the city, with the greatest decline taking place in the black and biracial schools. In 1963, overutilization was down to 40 and 38 percent of the schools in those respective categories. Classroom overutilization in white schools also showed a decrease but of a much smaller absolute magnitude. Ten percent of the white high status schools and 24 percent of the white low status schools were overutilized. Among the white schools, clearly the low status schools benefited the most in the reduction of class size that year.

When the Chicago appropriations for 1963 are examined (see Column B, Table 1), it is clear that the basic pattern of preferment for higher status and white pupils held. However, there was a general narrowing of the differences. These changes can be explained by the aforementioned lessening of disparities in class size, by the assignment of extra teachers, and the introduction of special compensatory programs in ghetto schools. In 1963, pupils in white schools were receiving appropriations that were $48 greater than the appropriations received by pupils in black schools, a differential that was only five-eighths as large as two years previously. The range between the low status and high status medians was $41, registering about the same proportionate decline as occurred between the color groups.

Within the color groups, the status differentials narrowed for the black and the biracial schools. The white high status schools were able to increase their advantage over the other white schools, while the low status whites caught up with the middle status whites. Racial differentiation among medium and low status schools decreased. This was especially true among the medium status schools where the median appropriation for the black schools came to exceed that of the biracial schools by one dollar.

The pattern of allocation among the Cook County elementary school districts offered a contrast to the variation among the individual schools within the Chicago system. In the county there was no systematic shift in allocations by status between 1961–62 and 1963–64 (see Column B, Table 2), but notably, at all levels they tended to decline. Enrollments had increased at a pace faster than the tax base. The tax rates had remained steady so that a small but fairly uniform drop in expenditures per pupil took place in every status category. Meanwhile, Chicago, which had increased its school tax levies, was able to improve its relative standing slightly. It appears that inertia was the most characteristic feature of the fiscal procedures in the suburban school systems in the first years of the decade. The special improvements in the education of the top students that was inspired by the competition of Sputnik had already taken place. Yet, interestingly, the few suburban districts that did have a sizable number of black pupils did not show a decline in per pupil operating expenditures.

1966. In the period between 1961 and 1963, Chicago probably had the most intense and persistent controversy over its racial practices of any of the big city school systems. During the ensuing few years, as questions of racial segregation and oppression were raised in almost all of the major school systems throughout the country, Chicago lost any uniqueness that it might have had concerning this issue. Racial inequality in education was recognized as a national problem when the federal government passed the Elementary and Secondary Education Act (ESEA) of 1965.

This Act appropriated for the first time a large amount of federal money to assist local school systems with their elementary and secondary education. The money was earmarked for children from low-income families. While the funding mechanism did not have an explicit racial label, it was widely recognized that the Act would affect a disproportionately higher number of black children. The original annual appropriation under the Act was $1.33 billion, of which 80 percent was distributed under Title I to school districts to improve the education of children in families with incomes below $2,000 or those receiving Aid to Families with Dependent Children. The legislative emphasis was on special programs to meet the special needs of children in these families. Under Titles II and III of the Act, considerably smaller sums not specifically earmarked for poor children were available to school systems.

To measure the effects of the new legislation, it was necessary to analyze the patterns of allocations in the regular school budgets without the ESEA funds as well as the allocations when ESEA funds were included. From 1963 to 1966, there was no significant redistribution of the traditional state and local funds. The 1966 data on the regular operating appropriations without the special ESEA monies (see Column C, Table 1) show that among the black and white schools, the configuration was pretty much the same as in 1963, only slightly higher in all categories. The only noticeable difference was among the biracial schools where there was a decline in the appropriations for both the middle and the high status groups.

If the ESEA funds are to be considered compensatory, in Chicago they compensated only for the inequalities within the regular procedure for budgeting funds from state and local sources. They were not used, as the legislation implied, to compensate for social inequalities that were external to the school system. The infusion of federal funds provided a major new resource for meeting the continuing pressures from civil rights organizations and black community groups. After 1963 the Chicago Board of Education evidently operated on the premise that given the then potential political developments, the monies from the federal subvention would be adequate to contain the claims of the black pupils. Any further reallocation of the regular state and local funds seems to have been restricted by the inertia of a large institution and by the tremendous claims exercised through its established relationships with other groups and organizations.

A Chicago newspaper, the *Sun-Times,* conducted an analysis of the 1969 Chicago Board of Education budget on the basis of race alone. Its findings for the elementary schools show the same pattern that we found in 1966. From regular funds, the white schools received about 8 percent more per pupil than did the black schools. However, when the federal ESEA money was included in the calculations, the black schools had appropriations that were 4 percent larger. Changes in the size of enrollment over the last eight years was the factor that had the highest correlation with per pupil appropriations, including ESEA. Those school districts with stable or declining populations, regardless of racial composition, had the largest allocations. The lowest level of appropriations tended to be in those neighborhoods with growing student populations due to racial transition, new public housing projects, or new private buildings near the edge of the city. It appears that administrative inertia took an extremely long time to adjust to enrollment shifts.

CONCLUSIONS

Prior to the advent of the mass northern civil rights movement in 1961, the allocation of educational funds on a per pupil basis clearly demonstrated preferential treatment on the basis of both race and status. Those groups who had generally preferred positions in society received more public money for the education of their children than did the other groups. The pattern held true both within the central city and among the various metropolitan area school districts. In the central city, race was a more significant discriminator than status. The allocation of public educational funds in the Chicago area was so structured as to perpetuate within families from one generation to the next social advantage and privilege.

From an examination of the changes in budgeting plus a knowledge of the administrative history of the Chicago public schools, we can conclude that protest paid off—somewhat. The Chicago civil rights movement did not win desegregation of the school system which had been its primary goal during this period, but it did bring about a diminution in the monetary discrimination against black and low status pupils on the part of the Chicago Board of Education. The first move toward equalization of appropriations was carried out from the traditional state and local revenues. After 1963, when new federal funds from ESEA became available, there was no further redistribution of the traditional funds. The range of differentials in appropriation of regular funds based on race and status was still so great that the ESEA money had the effect only of compensating for the Board of Education's own discrimination.

As measured by results, these concessions won by protest might have been more symbolic than substantive. Our general information on the Chicago schools indicates that the actual processes of education and socialization continue to operate in a racially oppressive manner. The basic racial operations of the Chicago public schools have been restructured to a much lesser extent than funds have been reallocated.

Finally, the evidence strongly shows how the high status white groups are able to sustain their preferred position by securing larger investments in the education of their children. In 1961, such results were achieved both within the central city and in the suburbs. The racial crisis, nationally and locally, wrought some changes in this pattern. However, since political differentiation between the separate school districts reinforced the social and racial differentiation, the high status suburban schools were able to maintain a much greater monetary advantage than their central city counterparts. By 1966, if the ESEA funds are included, the high status white schools' advantage in allocations had become minimal in Chicago, but the high status suburban school systems had improved their relative position vis-à-vis the other status groups in the suburbs and all status groups in the city.

Regarding the protection of privilege in the allotment of funds, the medium status schools did not fare well. Those schools in the city lost any favor they had over low status schools; the medium status school districts in the suburbs lost one-third of their advantage over the Chicago schools. Therefore, for the medium status white groups, neither race nor status remained as effective in maintaining preferment for their children in the rationing out of public school expenditures. As for low status whites, race alone had once served to their advantage in this regard, but by the end of the study it was not of much effect. Therefore, only the high status suburbs remained secure in a status quo of educational privilege for their children with regard to the distributions from the public purse. In light of these conditions, the words of Charles Benson, one of the most astute students of educational economics, takes on a real meaning:

There is good reason that discussion about educational inequalities is muted. After all, the handsome couples in the suburbs who deplore de facto segregation in the large cities and who are so daring as to form local committees on fair practice in housing, are the ones who have a major stake in preserving the lifetime advantages that their privileged, though tax-supported, school offers their children.[5]

NOTES

1. W.L. Warner, R.J. Havighurst, and M.B. Loeb, *Who Shall Be Educated?: The Challenge of Unequal Opportunity* (New York and London: Harper & Bros., 1944), p. xii; see also A.B. Wilson, "Social Class and Equal Education Opportunity," *Harvard Educational Review* 38 (Winter, 1968): 77–84.
2. D.C. Ranney, "The Determinants of Fiscal Support for Large City Educational Systems," *Administrator's Notebook*, 15 (December, 1966). Some of this city-suburban differential has now been reduced by federal support for children of low-income families, or in the case of

New York State by a special increase of 17½ percent in state aid for big city schools. Nevertheless, New York City still spends less per pupil than the surrounding metropolitan counties.

3. The Chicago schools had available only information for calculating appropriations per pupil which was reported for the calendar year. The Cook County schools had information on actual expenditures which was re-ported on the basis of a school year. Accordingly, the corresponding years for Cook County in our analysis were 1961–62, 1963–64, and 1966–67.

4. The data for individual schools in Chicago are based on budget appropriations exclusive of central administrative costs.

5. C. S. Benson, *The Cheerful Prospect* ((Boston: Houghton Mifflin, 1965), p. 20.

MEDICINE FOR THE POOR:
A NEW DEAL IN DENVER
ELINOR LANGER

The Denver experience in establishing neighborhood health centers illustrates one approach to the general health problems of the poor outlined by Roemer and Kisch. While the immediate impacts on the local community seem to be highly favorable, the per capita costs are extremely high and the political pressures mounting. From a financial standpoint, many would prefer to see improvements in Denver General Hospital which would provide smaller fee increments for health services for a larger number of patients. Unfortunately, since this article was written, the pressures of both a fiscal and political nature have curtailed the OEO neighborhood health center program. Nevertheless, it has been demonstrated that such centers can be highly successful if only the price is right.

Reprinted from *Science* 153 (29 July 1966): 508–12, by permission of the American Association for the Advancement of Science and the author. Copyright 1966 by the American Association for the Advancement of Science.

One outpost of the War on Poverty that is drawing increased attention from health professionals these days is an unassuming former bakery in the heart of Denver's Negro–Spanish-American ghetto known as the Neighborhood Health Center. The Neighborhood Health Center is not the only product of the interest in medicine that is being shown by the Office of Economic Opportunity (OEO). Roughly analogous centers are operating in Boston and New York City, and the OEO has now agreed to fund five more—one in Watts, two in Chicago, one in the Bronx, and one in Bolivar County, Mississippi. So far, the amount of money spent and pledged amounts to less than $10 million, and the number of people eligible for the new services is only about 150,000. But, if the numbers are small, the aspirations of those behind the OEO projects are not. They believe not only that they may rescue medical care for the poor from

the "poor law" and charity traditions that have characterized it, but that in doing so they may develop a model that will influence the direction of the rest of American medicine as well.

OEO has gone into the health business for two reasons. The first was a recognition of the reinforcing relationship between ill health and poverty—the realization, in the words of one of OEO's physician-grantees, that "the poor get sicker and the sick get poorer." Inevitably, the agency's involvement in health has in it a measure of political calculation as well. OEO's programs have brought it into conflict with a wide range of political and social interest groups around the country, and as the uproar has increased—and the Vietnam war has been used to justify congressional budget-pruning—the OEO has looked about for activities that fulfill its mandate of liberating the poor without disrupting the Johnson consensus. It was assumed that medical centers would be like Project Headstart—the system of preschools that the OEO is funding throughout the country—and that, just as no one could be against finding places for small children to play learning games, no one could be against finding places where impoverished families already draining municipal welfare and charity resources could go to find medical treatment more convenient and congenial. That calculation was probably wrong. As long as the OEO health centers were viewed as extensions of traditional social welfare institutions for the poor, they drew nothing from existing professional organizations and institutions but a rather benign indifference. Now they are seemingly flourishing, reaching out in new ways, and opposition—chiefly from organized medicine—is clearly on the rise.

At the same time, the neighborhood health centers are finding themselves involved in a very different kind of war. To a certain extent, the doctors who have started them are reformers—even radicals—within their profession. They are fighting decades-old battles—for comprehensive, family-centered, preventive medical care; for group practice; for the development of new kinds of health manpower that cuts across lines made fast by the domination of professional associations and certification and licensing boards. But they are doing all this through the War on Poverty and—at least in Denver—have found themselves confronting radicals with a very different set of priorities, militant leaders (particularly Spanish-American) seeking to use the centers not only to improve the health of their people but to advance their political power as well.

The health center pie has a great many other fingers in it, too. There are a variety of municipal apparatchniks defending established political and bureaucratic jurisdictions, and a number of interested citizens representing local banks, charities, newspapers, real estate interests, and so forth—the group referred to in every city as the "establishment" or "power structure"—that all have an interest in preserving the status quo. In Denver the bureaucracy and the establishment were slow to grasp the significance of the health center experiment. The obstacles they created were low-grade, the product more of inertia than of opposition. But as the center develops and expands—its sponsors have just applied to OEO for money to fund a second center—the vacuum around the health center is beginning to be filled in, and not all the voices are supportive. At this stage, however, the role of old municipal alliances in the effort to create new health institutions is not yet clear.

Denver's Neighborhood Health Center is in a northeastern part of the city known as the Curtis Park–Arapahoe area (after two housing projects located there). The area includes nearly 40,000 people, at least half of whom are classified as living in poverty. Nearly 31 percent of the families have incomes under $3,000 a year. Thirty-four percent of those over 25 have completed less than 8 years of education, and 75 percent have less than 4 years of high school. Forty-six percent of the houses are judged substandard or deteriorating. In 1959 the infant mortality rate in the area was 65.1 per thousand; for Denver as a whole it was 58.5. The death rate for Curtis Park–Arapahoe was 16.8; for the city as a whole it was 9.5. About 40 percent of the residents are Negro; about 30 percent are of Spanish or Mexican origin (they are known in the record books as "Spanish surname"); the rest are white. Virtually no physicians maintain offices in the area.

Before the opening of the Neighborhood Health Center last March, Denver's poor were generally treated at Denver General Hospital or at one of a few charity clinics in the city. Denver General is probably neither much better nor much worse than most municipal hospitals. It has suffered during the past few years from the disaffiliation of its medical departments from those of the Colorado Medical Center, a unit of the state university also located in Denver. The disaffiliation, still a rankling issue, was the product of what some people refer to as a "town-gown" fight and others as a successful campaign by the right-wing elements in the local medical society. A gradual reaffiliation is now taking place, but, while the academic tie-in may improve the content of the medical services, it is unlikely to affect the style in which they are delivered.

For many of Denver's poor, Denver General is inaccessible, separated from their homes by a 60-cent bus fare on a line that is out of service on evenings and weekends. Long waits at depot-like waiting stations take patients away from their other obligations for large chunks of the day. Its clinics are specialized, and there is no one to guide the timid (or the non-English–speaking) through the basement rooms in which they are dispersed. There is little likelihood that a patient will see the same physician twice. There is a complicated fee schedule which demands intensive probings into personal resources to determine the scale of payment for the individual patients, and a kind of assumption that most of the poor must be chiselers. While leading members of Denver's medical society admit deficiencies in the city's provision for treating dental and psychiatric disorders, they claim that the quality of medicine practiced at Denver General is first-rate and that "the people get here somehow when they really need to." The poor refer to it as the "butcher shop," avoid it unless they are painfully ill, and are perhaps as concerned with the personal indignities they encounter (which they are surely capable of judg-

ing) as with the quality of the suturing (which they are not).

NEW STYLE SERVICE

The Neighborhood Health Center, although it is managed by the city's Department of Health and Hospitals (which also runs Denver General), has managed to avoid almost all these difficulties. Three Volkswagen microbuses, driven by neighborhood residents, pick up and drive home patients who are too ill or too poor to take the bus. An indoor nursery and an outdoor playground, also manned by neighborhood assistants, provide supervised care for well children while their parents or sisters are seeing the doctors. The waiting period is down to proportions more like those experienced by middle-class patients in the offices of private doctors. Every attempt is made to avoid discussing income with patients: efforts are made to check them out with the city's welfare agencies (or with Denver General), but no fee schedule has been adopted and so far all services have been offered free. Efforts are made to insure that not only individuals but whole families have their major point of contact with a single physician. Individual health records are summarized on a family record chart, reminding the alert doctor to ask a mother why she failed to bring her child back for his second shot.

The center's staff of about 130 includes 58 "neighborhood aides"—poor people living in the area served by the center and trained either there or at an earlier training program run by Denver University. These people run the switchboard, the reception area, and the transportation service and are also assigned as assistants to the various medical, dental, and other service departments. At least nine of them speak both English and Spanish and function as translators when the need arises. The center's non-medical departments include nutrition, health education, social services, and environmental health, and are meant to function as a team, with referrals flowing two ways between the medical and nonmedical areas. There is also a research department that is attempting to develop data about utilization, social attitudes, and so forth. Specialized clinics are being established, but the center emphasizes "family medicine," and most serious and surgical cases are referred to hospitals. The center uses the part-time services of about 30 Denver physicians, drawn both from private general and specialty practice and from local medical institutions, and has a handful of doctors practicing there full-time. It is open virtually around the clock, with appointments scheduled until 10 p.m. on weekdays, and it has become a kind of hub for other community services from meetings of Alcoholics Anonymous to the offering of free legal aid by the Denver Bar Association. The whole enterprise is suffused with a kind of neighborly spirit that can best be described as "easiness." People waiting to see the doctors at Denver General look like "masses"; at the health center they look like individuals.

There is absolutely no doubt that the message of the health center is getting through to the neighborhood. By 3 July, the close of the 17th week of operation, the center had seen nearly 7,000 individual patients—about 33 percent of the eligible residents. Even more surprising than the rate at which new patients are coming in is the discovery that 21 percent of the patients are individuals who have never been seen at Denver General. That figure should be interpreted with some caution: population calculations are based on the 1960 census, the population in question is fairly mobile, and it is therefore impossible to discover what proportion of that 21 percent represents newcomers. But it is clear that the health center is flooded, receiving over 1,000 patients a week—more than twice its anticipated caseload.

RHETORIC OR REALITY?

Evaluation of the medical treatment that the patients are so enthusiastically receiving is a more difficult matter. Only medically trained evaluators could perhaps arrive at a definitive assessment of how the center's rhetoric—"comprehensive, family-centered care"—squares with the reality. The heavy caseload and the shakedown period have both taken their toll. Samuel Johnson, the young director of public health and preventive medicine of Denver's Department of Health and Hospitals, and the moving force behind the Neighborhood Health Center, readily admits to certain doubts. Johnson, 39, received his medical training at the University of Colorado and a Master of Public Health degree from Harvard in 1960. He is a former professor of preventive medicine at Colorado and still maintains a part-time position there. Johnson wonders whether his doctors are referring to each other as much as they might, and how thorough their examinations are. "What gets on the charts seems too much like what goes on them at large clinics," he commented in an interview with *Science.* "We were aiming for something more. I'm not worried about errors of commission but of omission. We want to do a total job." Nonetheless, Johnson believes that the quality of care is "above average" and certainly equal to that available at Denver General. This view is corroborated by John Sbarbaro, a young physician assigned to the Denver Health Department while on temporary duty with the Public Health Service, and now acting as the center's chief medical officer. "We're sure the care here is average," Sbarbaro told *Science,* "but we want to make it better than average." There is already a weekly analytic "case conference" for the staff and visiting specialists; Johnson hopes to establish an outside visiting committee to review random patient charts as well.

Johnson and Sbarbaro, as well as the

OEO in Washington, take particular pride in the fact that the health center was mobilized around rather typical resources such as exist in nearly every American city. Unlike the Boston project, for example, which is run by Tufts University Medical School and gives Tufts appointments to its staff physicians, the Denver project has drawn only on the local medical community. Now, the fee-for-service mystique is very strong among doctors in this country, and most doctors—particularly those representing organized medicine—are prone to conclude that if the center's salaried doctors relinquish private practice it must be because the services they offer are so bad they are unable to collect the fees. (The center's part-time doctors are paid $7.50 an hour; the full-time physicians average $5.93.) Accordingly, the center has been the butt of numerous charges, mostly made off the record, that its physicians are either incompetents who could not stand the competition or are senile citizens taking it on as a pension while awaiting the pasture. In fact, the center's doctors seem to have rather different motivations. Some are frankly idealists, eager to participate in a novel social experiment. Others are physicians disenchanted with the extensive "management" activities that private practice requires. "There are two things I like about practicing medicine here," commented one center physician. "One is that I can order tests, medicines, referrals, and so forth without worrying about my patient's pocketbook. The other is that I don't have to do any bookkeeping any more. Here I can do what I really want to do. See patients and practice medicine."

The center's medical society critics often seem to be comparing it to some unreal conception of what the alternatives are for the patients involved. One prominent member of the Denver Medical Society interviewed by *Science* complained that the center was inadequate because a mother's prenatal care would not come from the same obstetrician who would deliver her baby in Denver General. In a sense he is right: the division in obstetrical (and other) services certainly reinforces the "depersonalization" in medical care that the center hopes to combat. But the past record suggests that, if it were not for the Neighborhood Health Center, the mother would probably not bother with prenatal care at all.

If all is cheery in the waiting rooms, it has been somewhat less cheery behind the scenes. The problems of the Neighborhood Health Center began early when the original proposal became bogged down in the offices of Sargent Shriver, director of the OEO. Shriver's objections to the proposal were never made thoroughly clear either to his staff in Washington or to the applicants in Denver, but they appear to have included a feeling that the plan had to be as nearly perfect as possible—both because of the OEO's vulnerability in the Republican-dominated landscape of Colorado and because of the attention-getting potential of the plan as an experiment in medical organization. Working on the other side was a desire to give the poverty program some foothold in Denver, where most of the city's other proposals had already been vetoed as inadequate. Accordingly, the OEO dispatched two medical consultants to the scene. The proposal was then revised—to include, among other things, a greater concentration of resources in a single area than initially envisaged —and, after a time, Shriver reversed himself.

Since then, the health center has functioned without any substantial supervision from either the national office of the OEO or the regional office in Kansas City, neither of which is well equipped to provide the close guidance that the health center's sponsors might have liked. The center was also left pretty much alone by its parent agency, the Department of Health and Hospitals. And it has also functioned largely independently of the metropolitan agency that handles OEO projects, formerly known as Denver's War on Poverty, Inc., recently renamed Denver Opportunity (D.O.).

DENVER'S POVERTY PROBLEMS

Nearly all the urban antipoverty agencies in the country have had their difficulties, and Denver is a first-class example. For a variety of reasons—including control by the "establishment," insufficient representation of the poor, weak leadership that is constantly changing (the entire staff has just resigned), and massive disorganization—D.O. has been in exceptionally bad shape. It has managed to sponsor only a few projects, mostly small and mostly innocuous. To all intents and purposes, the Neighborhood Health Center is the only thing Denver has to show for its War on Poverty. And, accordingly, the health center became the focus of community politics and community tensions that in other cities have been spread out among a variety of programs.

The chief factor affecting the political relations of the Neighborhood Health Center with its clientele is the rising militancy of the area's Spanish Americans. In Denver, as in much of the Southwest, Spanish Americans are at the bottom of the heap, considerably below the Negro population in status and opportunity. Negro leadership, reflecting the upward mobility of its community, tends to be relatively moderate. The Spanish-American community, until recently in a state of almost total social disorganization—and lacking in access to the instruments of political power—is increasingly radical and increasingly in a hurry. When the local war on poverty began, it offered Spanish Americans one of their first opportunities to develop and use

political power. The opening was the OEO's rhetorical commitment to "maximum feasible participation of the poor," and, because the city-wide poverty agency was virtually immobile, what the poor wanted to participate in was the Neighborhood Health Center. Their vehicle was an advisory board composed of neighborhood residents.

Among the issues raised by Spanish Americans on the advisory board are some with real relevance to the question of whether a medically innovative institution can be fused with a politically radical one. A case in point is a dispute over selection of neighborhood aides. These jobs are crucial to the success of the center both as an operating agency and as an experiment. The neighborhood aides give the center its distinctive character; they make it emotionally accessible to the area's residents; they help reduce the psychological gulf—a product of both class and function—that impedes communication between doctors and patients. As an experiment in "socialization" of the poor, the program seems already on the threshold of success. The jobs are a first step up the social ladder. Offering real responsibilities, not just make-work, they open up possibilities of better jobs in other places: a number of health center trainees are already beginning to move on to jobs with local industries or the municipal career service. The center's professional staff reports numerous instances where neighborhood aides, who entered the program with an attitude of indifference to middle-class niceties such as punctuality and neatness, have been transformed by their work experiences. In many cases the personalities and personal relationships are now such that it is difficult for an outsider to distinguish the professionals from the aides. Finally, the aide program is a test of the possibilities of creating new types of medical manpower. Success in this effort does not lie within the reach of the center alone, but the character and calibre of its trainees could play a role in the emerging national effort to soften the boundaries and redefine the scope of the separate health professions.

CAN THE POOR PARTICIPATE?

The Spanish Americans, however, are dissatisfied. They claim, accurately, that the aides have been selected not from the poorest of the residents but from among the more flourishing. (The health center was committed to taking on "graduates" of a Denver University training program that included some not-very-disadvantaged residents, including the wife of one state senator.) The Spanish Americans want jobs assigned solely on the basis of need, not on the basis of qualifications or apparent potential. They feel that, without their intervention, the aides would not have been included in the center's employee-benefit plans, and would have been generally less well treated. The center's staff feels it won a major victory in getting the local civil service to accept its graduates without preliminary testing; the Spanish Americans resent the fact that center trainees will still be placed at the bottom of the civil service scale. They are also less than enthusiastic about the part of the center's training program—the medical assistant trainees—that involves preparation for paramedical functions not yet accepted by the medical profession. In this sense, the individual trainees are admittedly being used experimentally; the Spanish Americans want the poor to be able to advance personally. At the same time, they fear that health center jobs are being used to "buy off" potential neighborhood leaders who might otherwise continue to press the city for more reforms. Each side contends that the other is seeking to use the jobs as a form of neighborhood patronage, or for professional or political advancement.

The unrest in the relations between the health center staff and its neighborhood advisory board is focused not so much on the content of particular decisions but on who makes them. It appears that the staff of the center honestly wanted advice: they wanted to know what hours would be convenient, how people felt about paying, what facilities were most needed. They wanted assistance in spreading word of the center around the neighborhood and in running a ceremonial open house. They did not want to share their authority or to include the poor in substantive policy-making decisions.

The health center is by no means the only poverty agency that has run into this difficulty. Apart from a handful of student activists organizing in the nation's ghettos, few people have been able to make the jump from benevolence to respect in dealing with the poor. The result is that institutions beginning as efforts to mobilize the poor on their own behalf are constantly threatened with slipping back into an older style of charity, where "we" are trying to "do something" for "them." At the moment, the Spanish Americans on the advisory board seem to have been somewhat neutralized by a minor revolt of Negro representatives who do not share their militance. The present advisers, chiefly Negro women, are relatively passive, seemingly content to plan dinner parties and write letters of thanks to various benefactors, to stay in a subservient place and in the good graces of the professionals. The domination of the board by these elements leaves the center less connected with an important part of its constituency than it perhaps ought to be. The situation may be changed by neighborhood elections to a new poverty board to be held in August, but, if weak representation continues, one of the major bulwarks against turning the center back into something remote and alien from the neighborhood will be gone.

The future of the neighborhood

health centers is uncertain. Their cost per patient at this stage is extremely high. (The center is being funded at over $1.5 million a year.) There is a question about OEO's priorities on a national basis. With increasingly limited funds at its disposal, how much should it spend on health? The question of priorities is also important locally, and is becoming an issue in the rising medical society opposition to the health center in Denver. The people in the Curtis Park-Arapahoe area now have access to good, convenient medical care; the rest of Denver's poor are still making the trip to Denver General. The exclusive servicing of a defined population is important for research purposes. It is also obviously inequitable and may even be inhumane. What is a sensible allocation of medical resources? Would it be more fair to use the money, as the medical society would like, to rehabilitate Denver General to provide slightly more care for all the people? Or do the experimental aspects of the health center justify the inequalities it inevitably involves? Finally, there is a question of medical politics. The health centers have passed into existence almost unnoticed. Now everyone knows they are there, and pressures— not only from organized medicine, but from Washington health agencies less than eager for the competition—are certain to increase. At this stage the most that can be said for sure is that while the pleasantness of the neighborhood health centers is now established, their practicality and permanence remain to be proved.

33

EDUCATION AND METROPOLITANISM

DAVID L. KIRP
DAVID K. COHEN

Kirp and Cohen examine the arguments for metropolitan reform of school government. They consider the traditional position that metropolitan government will help to reduce the fiscal disparities between city and suburb, promote efficiency, and encourage integration. They extend these ideas to include a discussion of the underlying delivery and decision-making arrangements which are relevant to the pursuit of equity and efficiency. Although many advantages are identified in reorganization, they take the pessimistic view that the only appropriate and relevant action is a system of direct tax subsidies to non-public schools which would transfer school decisions much closer to the individual family.

Reprinted from Lowdon Wingo, Jr., ed., *Metropolitanization and Public Services* (Washington, D.C.: Resources for the Future, Inc., 1972), pp. 29–42, by permission of the publisher and the authors.

The rationale for rearranging school government along metropolitan lines includes everything from management efficiency to racial integration. The policy of district consolidation for reasons of efficiency reaches back several decades, to the outset of the school-consolidation movement: 50 years ago the nation included more than 100,000 districts; today there are less than 25,000. Most of this consolidation has taken place in rural America, but there has been a good deal within metropolitan areas, and there are a few southern metropolitan areas that now have countywide school systems. There is, however, no sign of any major movement toward metropolitanism in education.

The reasons for this are not obscure. Metropolitan school government could spell the demise of existing local school agencies, and it would be likely to redistribute resources. But existing governments have their own vested interests, and the affluent are reluctant to surrender control of resources.

If community self-interest or myopia were the sole obstacle, however, the appropriate strategies would be fairly clear: inducements for suburbanites (the most likely objectors) to make metropolitanism fiscally attractive, legal prods for communities whose resistance was grounded largely on racial considerations, and federal support for regional planning. But this argument ignores a basic question: Is metropolitan government a sensible way to address the problems of urban public education?

Several points bear on this query.

1. Inequities in school revenues and costs within the metropolis.

2. Inefficiency in school operations caused by the proliferation of school districts.

3. School segregation.

4. Rigidity and uniformity in the quality of education and poor matching of school programs with client demand.

5. Lack of much parent involvement in, or control over, school decisions.

We shall pursue these five points in the rest of this essay.

The problems are highly visible in the metropolitan areas, but this is no guarantee that they can be alleviated by metropolitan government. Nor does the presence of problems in the metropolis mean they are absent elsewhere. Some problems may really be statewide, and if this is true, metropolitan government may be inappropriate. And even if the difficulties are uniquely metropolitan, that does not lead inevitably to a single broad and more inclusive governmental structure. Different metropolitan structures may be needed to address different educational problems in the same metropolitan area.

TRADITIONAL ARGUMENTS FOR METROPOLITANISM

The traditional arguments for metropolitism in education have turned on problems of school finance, race, and efficiency. Although none of these seems very convincing to us, the arguments have dominated discussion up to this point, and should be disposed of before turning to more recent concerns.

Fiscal Disparities

The discussion of metropolitan fiscal problems has been underway for more than a decade. Central cities are believed to have less money for schooling than their suburbs. This is attributed partly to the greater competition for tax revenues in cities, partly to the weaker city tax base, partly to higher school costs in cities, and partly to the presumption that children in the cities are more costly to educate than their suburban counterparts.

This widely accepted argument does not entirely square with the facts. Most central cities do not have less money for schooling than their suburbs: at worst, the cities are close to the average for local expenditures within their metropolitan areas. But if the poverty of city school districts is not reflected in an absolute disparity in revenues, it is evident in several other ways. The older northern city school systems have grown less affluent relative to the average suburb. It is necessary, however, to diversify our conception of the jurisdictions included in the designation "suburb." In reality, the central cities' fiscal problems represent only one manifestation of the fiscal burdens that afflict older northern urban school districts of any size or location. These districts experience higher-than-average competition for revenues, a tax base depressed by low residential valuation and industrial blight, and more poor children than most other metropolitan districts. (In Massachusetts, for example, the public schools in roughly a dozen such cities enroll more than nine out of every ten children from welfare families in the entire state.) Thus, the "crisis of the central cities" is not as neatly limited as the phrase implies; indeed, it is the crisis of all older industrial cities, whether "central" or not.

It is easy to imagine ways of correcting this situation. But, apart from creating a metropolitan tax district, none of these solutions would be uniquely metropolitan in character. One approach has been proposed by Governor Milliken of Michigan; its keystone is the establishment of both a uniform statewide tax rate and a fully equalized assessment. Districts would be taxed uniformly, and the results distributed in such a way as to take cost variations into account. Another approach, urged by John Coons, would revise state school-aid apportionment formulas so that an equal tax effort in any two districts would produce equal revenues, irrespective of local wealth.[1] The crucial difference between the Milliken plan and Coons's scheme is that under the latter full local autonomy could be retained in deciding the level of effort.

Creation of a metropolitan tax district would not be a helpful approach. It offers no fiscal advantage that a similar statewide plan would not, and it has the additional disadvantage of dealing with only part of a problem that is indisputably statewide. Even apart from such objections, a metropolitan tax district would probably be more difficult to arrange. It is inconsistent with the constitutional standard advocated by John Coons and his colleagues, and recently accepted by the California Supreme Court in *Serrano* v. *Priest,* which renders illegitimate any education revenue-raising scheme tied to local property wealth. For that reason, a court would be unlikely to take seriously a suit asserting the unconstitutionality of metropolitan—rather than statewide—taxing inequities. And if such an arrangement were proposed in the legislature of any urban state, it probably would not get far. The central cities must be able to gain enough additional support in smaller nonmetropolitan cities to make a statewide plan much more attractive as a vote-getting device.

Metropolitan government, then, seems to offer a poor approach to the alleviation of fiscal disparities among school districts. Although the metropolis will continue to be a focus for discussion of this problem, solutions will be statewide, if they are possible at all.

Efficiency

The traditional argument for school-district consolidation is that larger units permit quality educational programs at a lower cost than do smaller schools or districts. This argument has been such a standby in the struggles over school-district consolidation that it has become a part of American educational mythology.

This might not seem odd were it not for the ambiguity of research results. There have been literally scores of studies that have related the school characteristics in question to student achievement; and almost without exception they have found no consistent connection.[2] The size of schools and school districts, for example, has no regular association with student achievement: students in bigger schools or districts typically do no better than similarly situated students in small ones. Moreover, the things that larger districts are supposed to provide more of—experienced and well-trained teachers, better curricula, more differentiation among students by interest and ability, more libraries, better administrators, and more specialists—also have little relationship to achievement. Students in schools with more of these educational accoutrements seem to do no better than similarly situated students in schools with less of them. All of this was evident in hundreds of small studies carried out over the last 40 years; and it was confirmed in two massive surveys of American education completed in the last 10 years—Project TALENT, and the Equality of Educational Opportunity Survey. This research has shown rather persuasively that the things that most Americans believe distinguish good from bad schools do not transform bad students into good ones. School consolidation, apparently, will neither improve students' test performances nor the schools' efficiency in producing achievement.

Of course, students' test scores are not the sole criterion of school efficiency. Other school outcomes, such as aspirations or the ability to participate in public life, may be affected by the size of the schools that children attend or the sort of students in their classes. But the evidence on these points is also ambiguous. Students in smaller high schools, for example, seem to participate more, and to develop more self-reliance, than otherwise similar students in large schools.[3] This hardly augurs well for the advocates of large schools and districts. And the evidence on aspirations suggests that most of the differences lie among students within schools rather than between schools. That is, the variation in aspirations within American high schools is little different from the variation in aspirations among schools. Thus, redistribution of students among schools would have little effect on the distribution of aspirations.[4]

The only convincing evidence for the efficiency of consolidation is that administrative costs seem to be somewhat lower in medium-sized districts (between 30,000 and 50,000 students) than in very small ones. This is of little real importance, however, since the annual per student cost of these differences amounts to less than $3 or $4 per year, and the diseconomies of scale increase fairly steeply as district size rises beyond 50,000.[5] If the only form of consolidation that might promote greater efficiency were the creation of several medium to large districts within each metropolis, the savings would be too small to override the political resistance to this undermining of local autonomy.

These research results undercut most of the traditional justifications for creating larger schools and districts. Other arguments, of course, remain. Neither popular taste in education nor the desires of school professionals are likely to be affected much be research. Larger schools and districts are attractive to professionals because they mean newer buildings, more specialization, and more pleasing facilities: libraries, language labs, offices, etc. Since the public accepts these as valid indices of educational quality, the old arguments may still produce some support for consolidation.

Integration
This subject has been the featured item in almost every recent discussion of schools and metropolitanism. Neither the rationale nor the remedies have changed much in the last decade: The educational benefits to Negro children and the impact on black and white attitudes are the main arguments used to justify integration. The present, or prospective, black-majority character of many central-city school systems is the reason for seeking a remedy that will tie cities and suburbs together.

Perhaps the central issue here is whether the rationale is correct: Would integration have an important effect on achievement or racial attitudes? Even if the answer to this query were unambiguously affirmative, other issues would arise. What form should the new arrangements take: Unified metropolitan districts? Interdistrict cooperation? The creation of several large, but submetropolitan districts? Would a metropolitan school authority, or a state agency, be the best device to further integration?

Evidence on the effects of integration is far from unambiguous. Most research suggests that the schools' racial composition has no independent impact on students' achievement, but that their social-class composition does have some effect.[6] Disadvantaged students in middle-class schools seem to do somewhat better than similar students in uniformly working-class or poor schools. If true, this means that school integration within cities (where blacks would typically be integrated with whites from adjoining blue-collar neighborhoods) would be less desirable than city-suburban integration (where blacks would be more likely to attend school with middle-class or upper-middle-class white students).

However, it is by no means clear that this finding is true. Black students in white schools, or lower-class students in middle-class schools, might be there because of their greater talent and/or their parental motivation, which would account for their higher scores. Since information on students' earlier academic or family history is rarely gathered, it is impossible to determine whether the effect of class composition is due to such selection.

Evidence from deliberate desegregation efforts is also ambiguous. In some cases in which achievement gains appear, students have almost surely been selected by IQ; in other instances (whether there has been selection or not) there seem to have been no gains. In the only case in which students were randomly chosen (to eliminate the selection problem), small gains did appear after integration in some instances. Compared to the magnitude of the black-white achievement disparity, however, these gains were quite small. Only one study has carried out such a check (in a very small California city); it was found that if one took first-grade IQ into account this very sharply reduced, but did not entirely eliminate, the social-class-composition effect on later IQ and achievement tests.

The research results on racial attitudes are more consistent and encouraging. Blacks and whites who enjoy equal status tend to exhibit less prejudice. If they had such experiences as children, they are somewhat more likely to have interracial contact as adults, and they are a good deal more likely to hold more liberal attitudes on public issues related to race. These findings accord with common sense and general observation, and they suggest that if school integration were properly managed, it might have some effect on American racial attitudes and behavior.

But however affirmative the evidence, it does not lead directly to integrated metropolitan school districts. There is little experience with school integration within the metropolitan context, and only modest thought has been given to the issues. The experience encompasses three or four interdistrict busing programs and involves only a few thousand children. Although programs of this nature may serve to demonstrate the feasibility of interdistrict cooperation, they have serious drawbacks. One-way traffic from the inner city, after all, is hardly a promising model to apply to the entire metropolis.

Other approaches have been suggested. The U.S. Commission on Civil Rights, for example, recommended federal fiscal incentives for the construction of educational parks through metropolitan areas.[7] Presumably such an arrangement would require the creation of unified metropolitan education authorities. Although possible, this plan would almost surely be dependent on action by the state legislatures, something that legislators from many suburban districts would resist.

Another alternative would be the creation of several large districts composing both core-city and suburban neighborhoods. Although in several of the largest cities such a scheme would be unfeasible without helicopters or new rapid-transit systems, there are many more places where it would be technologically possible. In addition, such new jurisdictions, were they to enroll somewhere between 30,000 and 50,000 students, would approach administratively what seems to be the most efficient size. But again this approach would almost always require legislative action, and it is no easier to imagine Shaker Heights or Winnetka merging individually with parts of Cleveland or Chicago than it is to imagine an entire city merging with all its suburbs. Racial considerations aside, it seems politically fantastic. Would municipal administrations voluntarily relinquish the money, jobs, and power inherent in a big-city school system any more readily than would affluent suburban systems? In fact, city-suburban mergers will probably become less likely as the central cities move increasingly toward black self-government! These new administrations will badly need the money and jobs on which political organizations are based. As long as public education in the metropolitan areas retains even a tenuous fiscal viability, it is hard to conceive of the system of state or federal incentives that could produce wholesale movement in the direction of metropolitan school integration.

Other problems also exist. The most serious such problem is that pressures for other changes have recently gathered force, especially in the older and larger metropolitan areas. There has been a rapid increase in demands for greater community control in the black ghettos; it is possible to theorize that integration is consonant with community control, but it seems unlikely to be true in practice.

Is there, then, any prospect of a substantial movement toward school integration within the metropolis? If the vehicle is voluntary local action, the answer is no. If we turn to the federal government for a moment, the picture is not vastly more hopeful. In the near future, at least, executive action and new legislation will at best offer no more than support for local initiative toward integration, and it may offer some discouragement. Although both local action and federal support would be worthwhile, there is no reason to believe that the results would affect many children. Experience with the existing metropolitan busing programs—in Hartford and Boston—suggests that they do not lead to more integration. Rather, once they achieve a modest percentage of blacks in the receiving schools, the situation seems to stabilize.

Litigation is the remaining approach to metropolitan integration, and it may well prove the most promising. Courts have shown increased willingness to identify northern school segregation as *de jure*—based, that is, upon pupil and teacher assignment, school building patterns, and discriminatory housing—and to order integration *within* city boundaries. In several suits, litigants have asserted that the discrimination is not limited to school districts but is a metropolitan phenomenon; they have demonstrated areawide housing, job,

and school boundary determinations that serve to isolate black and white children. At least two federal courts, in Detroit and Indianapolis, have accepted these arguments, and ordered the submission of metropolitan integration plans; other such suits are currently before the courts. While such litigation may continue to force metropolitan governance in particular northern communities, the process is likely to be an extended one, and ultimate resolution of the underlying constitutional question by the Supreme Court seems several years away.

Thus, even the most optimistic assessment of the prospects for school integration within the metropolitan areas indicates that only modest progress can be expected in the next decade. Futhermore, the most optimistic assessment may not be warranted. Conventional approaches to integration are at cross-purposes with other forces in the Negro community; and these other forces seem likely to dissipate the thrust toward school integration.

In summary, then, the traditional arguments for metropolitanism in education are generally unconvincing. Larger schools and larger districts might satisfy educators, but there is no evidence that they will either help students or appreciably improve the effectiveness of schooling. The fiscal disparities that plague districts within the metropolis need correction, but remedies should come at the state, not the metropolitan, level. Remedies for segregation are sadly needed, but there is little impetus and less likelihood that more will soon materialize.

There is, however, a further difficulty with any discussion of metropolitanism in relation to such problems as fiscal inequity, segregation, and efficiency. To argue that these problems require metropolitan government is to assume that the existing structure for decision making about schools is basically satisfactory and that the real problems lie in the allocation of students or resources. There is growing evidence that this assumption is incorrect. One example is the persistent pressure for community control in black neighborhoods, and another is the growing use of nonpublic schools by the urban middle and upper-middle class.

Both developments are signs of a deeper problem—the public school system's inability to respond to variations in client preferences. The supply of education in urban America is relatively uniform, but the demand is for diversifying it. There has been increasing concern with the delivery and decision mechanisms in education, which must be accompanied by a decline of interest in problems of equity and efficiency. What is more, these developments are uniquely urban, for only in the metropolitan areas do diverse client preferences exist.

SOME NEWER CONCERNS ABOUT METROPOLITAN SCHOOLS

This section of the essay takes up the questions of service delivery and governance for metropolitan area schools. Although these issues lie outside the traditional discussions of metropolitanism in education, it is no longer sensible to discuss equity and efficiency in the provision of public services without also considering the underlying delivery and decision-making arrangements.

Diversity

School reform in America has not always been distinguished by a concern for educational variety. Schoolmen are fond of calling for more individualized instruction, but the development of public education during this century has been largely the story of its standardization. This has resulted partly from the growth of the educational professions, but it has also had something to do with the schools' status as a public monopoly. Effective management has been equated

with equality in the provision of resources, and sameness in the character of school offerings. This has been based both on a commitment to egalitarian values and on the view that the schools provide the principal vehicle for transmitting a common culture. The first has seemed to demand the provision of equal amounts of public education in equal quality, and the second has seemed to prohibit variations in educational taste (whether these have had an ethnic or class basis) from determining the character of school offerings.

In the last few years all this has come under increasing attack. The demand for more open, spontaneous, and creative schooling has grown (witness the hundreds of nonpublic schools now in existence), and the evidence that traditional school resources do not affect achievement has served only to reinforce this development. A number of critics argue that the main problem with public education lies in the fundamental assumption that it should yield uniform results and that it should ignore differences in educational preferences. As things now stand, families can provide a different education for their children only by changing residence or by enrolling in private schools. These possibilities are hardly adequate to ensure a match between client taste and school offering. The fiscal constraints against opting out of the public schools are severe, and the lack of direct public support for any alternatives limits sponsorship either to large-scale enterprises (like the Catholic Church) or to very wealthy small ones.

The remedies that have been advanced are tailored to this diagnosis: the cure is seen to lie in providing public support for competing institutions. It is of little practical comfort to parents that they have the right at present to send their children to whatever school they wish when they may have no money with which to exercise that option. Among the arrangements most commonly mentioned are funding for private schools (parochial schools, boarding schools, community schools, free schools, etc.), eligibility of new schools for state financial assistance; or the provision of direct financial support to parents—through tuition vouchers that could be used at any schools they chose.

The implications of such proposals are enormous. Neither direct funding of schools nor direct funding of students would remove the state from the business of public education. It would still provide financial support; it would regulate schools to ensure that they complied with constitutional requirements (for example, that they did not discriminate on the basis of race and that they provided a minimally acceptable level of education). Further, it would continue to maintain the existing public schools for those families who chose to patronize them. But the state would no longer offer single form of schooling as the only possibility for parents too poor to send their offspring to a private school.

Such schemes (a test of tuition vouchers may soon be financed by the Office of Economic Opportunity [8]) are often thought to conflict with the need to redress fiscal inequity or race and class isolation. It has been argued, however, that diversification could be structured to increase fiscal equity. Equal dollars could be provided for each child, and the state could prohibit parents from supplementing that allotment. In addition, the state could provide more money for poor children—or for schools that accepted substantial numbers of poor children—thus giving them (theoretically) a better bargaining power. (This second approach might also reduce race and class isolation by inducing schools to take more poor, and therefore black, children than they might ordinarily.) In the case of fiscal equity, then, there is no necessary conflict. Were some statewide, full equalization plan adopted, it would not necessarily interfere with either direct aid to alternative schools or direct tax subsidies to families.

The problem of segregation is less easy to dispose of. Tuition vouchers would presumably permit parents to choose whatever school they liked. Black families in mainly black districts who desired integrated schools for their children would not be restrained by geographic school attendance boundaries, any more than would suburban white parents who desired Montessori schools for their offspring. This, of course, is the great appeal of tuition vouchers; they could permit communities of limited liability to spring up around schools, thereby allowing expression of diverse tastes. But therein also lies the great difficulty of such schemes; for the individual freedom to choose schools could also be the freedom to restrict the attendance of others. Black parents might want to enroll their children in white schools, but the whites might have other ideas. An unrestricted voucher scheme could harden patterns of segregation even more than at present, and that would be a disaster.

There are devices that could avoid this problem, at least in theory. If racial discrimination in admission were prohibited, and if fiscal incentives (of the Title I, Elementary and Secondary Education Act, variety) were offered for the enrollment of poor children, many of the problems would disappear. If, in addition, a considerable proportion of applicants at every school were admitted by lottery, there would probably be more school integration than now exists.[9] The difficulty, however, is not in conceiving of schemes whereby segregation could be avoided; rather, it is in imagining how such schemes might be implemented. It is hard to see how even such relatively progressive states as New York and Michigan would approve legislation of this sort, when they have so recently been moving in the other direction.

Apart from this problem, however, our question is whether direct tax subsidies to schools or parents would be suitable at the metropolitan level.

Diversity becomes an issue only in a community large enough to include many families with quite different educational interests. It would make no sense to adopt a voucher plan in a small community in which parents shared similar perceptions of educational needs. But in the metropolitan regions such uniformity does not prevail; the differences and conflicts are all too apparent. Only in a community of that size would diversification accomplish anything new.

A metropolitan educational authority might well manage the sort of system we have described. Such an authority, unlike a metropolitan arrangement structured to promote integrated schools, should probably not operate schools in the metropolitan area. Instead it would function only as a certifying and disbursing agency: it might evaluate schools, check teacher qualifications, and assess the accuracy of schools' self-descriptions. It could either distribute checks directly to those schools that satisfied the authority's standards or it could distribute tuition vouchers to the parents who could then cash them at approved schools.[10]

Other arrangements are imaginable, such as placing the governance of such a system in the hands of existing school districts, or of the state. The first of these—district-controlled systems—would minimize the need to tinker with the structure of educational governance. But this might be a disadvantage, because it would leave the responsibility for change with the very parties who most vociferously resist the idea. It seems unlikely that the agency that already operates the public schools, and that would continue to operate those schools for the children who still elected to go to them, would effectively support educational diversity when it meant encouraging children and parents to opt out of attending those schools.

State management represents the other alternative, but it might be inappropriate. Uniformity of education offerings is not solely a metropolitan problem, but the diversity of taste in towns, small cities, and rural areas is much less than in the metropolis. Theoretically, a state-run system would permit greater educational diversity by enabling students to attend school outside of the area (city or metropolitan) in which they happened to live. The chief disadvantage is that it might be impossible for a state agency, quite removed from the actual provision of education services, to administer intelligently a voucher or direct school-funding scheme.

On balance, a metropolitan authority seems most sensible. Although its existence would require special state enabling legislation to set certain standards (and presumably to create similar authorities in nonmetropolitan counties as well), a metropolitan agency would be large enough to comprise sufficient resources for diversification, and yet not so distant as to be unable to regulate, disseminate information, experiment, and evaluate. Although the diversification of schooling is not a uniquely metropolitan matter, it is something that a metropolitan educational authority would be uniquely suited to manage.

There are, of course, quite possibly fatal political difficulties with such an arrangement. Local school districts are unlikely to surrender power willingly, and to the extent that a metropolitan authority would blur city-suburban distinctions, opposition might be swelled by suburban parents eager to preserve local autonomy. There is certainly no evidence of real movement in this direction at any level of government.

Community Control

Schemes for diversification would assuredly benefit Negro families; yet there has been little black support for tuition vouchers or direct funding for alternative schools. Rather, attention has been fixed on the public schools that serve Negro communities, and demands have centered on efforts to make those schools prove responsive.

Proposals for community control and individual choice of school proceed on inconsistent assumptions about the nature of the school community. Advocates of individual choice presume that parents may want different kinds of education for their children; that in the absence of present constraints the choice of school would not necessarily be determined by where a family lives. Thus, one ghetto family might choose to send its children to an all-black community school, but another might opt for an integrated suburban school. Tax subsidies to schools or parents would leave that choice to the family. Advocates of community control, on the other hand, regard the geographic-ethnic community as the proper focus for school attendance and decision making. They seek to give the poor and black communities the power to run neighborhood schools in a manner that they feel will more adequately address community needs.

The demand for community control is frequently couched in educational terms. Such control, it is argued, will afford the child a sense of mastery over his environment, and this will enable him to succeed; teachers in such schools will be obliged to respond to the particular needs of the children in their charge; parents will be more involved, and children will therefore perform better. Educational evidence to support these propositions is lacking, but advocates argue that communities could run their own schools no less successfully than the existing bureaucracy.

The demand for community control is, of course, in good measure political. The result would be real power: the right to determine how education dollars are spent and who gets what jobs.

But whether viewed as an educational or political effort, community-run schools address different concerns from those that motivate other reformers to call for an end to racial isolation, or for increased educational diversity, or even for more equitable distribution of educational resources. To be sure, one can imagine heterogeneous school districts. There is no intrinsic reason, for example, why Bronx-Westchester or Queens-Nassau districts could not have been created when the New York State Legislature was considering alternative ways to decentralize New York City's schools. That such arrangements were not even proposed, let alone considered, reveals the political barriers to such a notion. Moreover, the ideology of control depends on the assumption of homogeneity and likemindedness.

It is not clear, however, whether this inconsistency between direct tax subsidies to parents and demands for community control is inevitable. Public education has been the focus of attention in the ghettos for more than a decade, and it is very nearly the sole source of schooling available there. Given these circumstances, and the relative inability of blacks to afford alternatives, it is not surprising that efforts have focused on diverting public resources to community use. But a system of tax support for parents, or alternative schools, would serve most of the educational and political ends sought by advocates of community control and yet provide more choice for ghetto residents. What is more, this scheme would offer a way around some of the more obvious political problems of decentralization. Chief among these is the possibility of a fiscal crisis, which could arise if black ghettos tried to support themselves from the existing tax base. Of course, legislatures alone could correct this, but black communities would find no new allies on this point beyond those already clamoring for revision of state-aid formulas.

In any event, decentralization is not really relevant to the metropolis, at least not at this point in time. It would offer the cities much conflict, and the suburbs could gain nothing from it.

CONCLUSION

In general, then, the prospects for relieving the educational problems of the metropolis through more comprehensive government are bleak. A remedy for the underlying fiscal problems is available only at the state level; larger districts promise nothing; there is no likelihood of anything but minimal progress toward integration via metropolitanism; and city school decentralization is really irrelevant to most jurisdictions in metropolitan areas. The only governmental revision that would be both relevant to metropolitan educational problems and also appropriate at the metropolitan level is the most radical one: a system of direct tax subsidies or direct aid to nonpublic schools, which would transfer school decisions much closer to the family and to the individual school.

A system of tax subsidies whereby information, disbursement, quality control, and evaluation lie at the metropolitan level, and everything else is left with the schools or districts, would probably be an improvement on existing arrangements. Such a system could resolve many of the problems that presently plague schools and parents in metropolitan areas, such as unresponsiveness, rigidity, a poor match of demand and supply, and the burden of accumulated routine and bureaucracy. A properly implemented system would not increase segregation, and might reduce it.

Such arrangements, however, are unlikely soon to see the light of day. The demand is just beginning to become substantial, the church-state issues may not be fully settled for some time, and most of the established school authorities are opposed. The perception of educational problems within the metropolis is still too uneven for a workable consensus to be built around this particular scheme or other program for change. Things may have to become appreciably worse throughout the metropolitan regions—especially in their more affluent sectors—before public education has much chance of being put on a new footing.

NOTES

1. J. Coons, W. Clune, and S. Sugarman, *Private Wealth and Public Education* (Cambridge: Harvard University Press, 1970).
2. The best review of research in this area is found in J. M. Stephens, *The Process of Schooling* (New York: Harper & Row, 1967).
3. R. Barker and P. Bump, *Big School, Small School* (Stanford, Calif.: Stanford University Press, 1964).
4. These results arise from as yet unpublished analyses of data on high school students' aspirations, which derive from the project TALENT and Equality of Educational Opportunity surveys. The results are available from the authors.
5. The data on district size and administrative costs are contained in a forthcoming study of school decentralization, "Parents, Power, and the Schools," which is available from the authors.
6. For a summary of the evidence on this entire issue and a discussion of its implications for law and policy, see D. Cohen, "Defining Racial Equality in Education," *UCLA Law Review* 16, no. 2 (February, 1969).
7. *Racial Isolation in the Public Schools* (Washington, D.C.: U.S. Civil Rights Commission, 1967).
8. The planning has been under way at the Center for the Study of Public Policy in Cambridge, Mass.; a report on the program, *Education Vouchers,* is now available.
9. These ideas, and others, have been advanced in the study *Education Vouchers* referred to in Note 8.
10. It would, in fact, be necessary to devise ways to ensure that such a step did not increase bureaucratic control over education. The creation of a metropolitan educational authority with its own priorities and standards might represent simply another layer of bureaucracy. But such an authority could be structured to reduce government's power over the provision of educational services, by taking the authority out of the business of operating any but a small number of experimental schools, by leaving school operation to the existing public districts, and/or by limiting the kinds of regulations that the authority could impose.

4